THE SPIRIT OF THE LAW

SARAH BARRINGER GORDON

The Spirit of the Law

RELIGIOUS VOICES AND THE

CONSTITUTION IN MODERN AMERICA

THE BELKNAP PRESS OF
HARVARD UNIVERSITY PRESS
Cambridge, Massachusetts, and London, England
2010

Library of Congress Cataloging-in-Publication Data

Gordon, Sarah Barringer, 1955–
    The spirit of the law : religious voices and the Constitution in modern America /
Sarah Barringer Gordon.
        p.   cm.
    Includes bibliographical references and index.
    ISBN 978-0-674-04654-2 (alk. paper)
    1. Religion and law—United States.   2. Constitutional law—United States—
Religious aspects.   I. Title.
    KF358.G67   2010
    342.7308′52—dc22   2009049532

To T.V.A.O., kind father, wise counselor, gentle man

Contents

Preface

When American lawyers talk about "the spirit of the law," they refer to the higher goals of any legislation or legal rule—the praiseworthy motives that animate the law. They are trying to cut through technicalities to the essence. Often, they refer to the spirit in contrast to "the letter of the law." The gap between the law on the books and the achievement of loftier goals can be palpable. Usually, if the letter of the law dictates a result, then technicality rather than spirit rules. The phrase is common in the lawyer's lexicon, and this is not the first book to use the term as its title: in 1748, for instance, Charles de Secondat, baron de Montesquieu, published *De l'esprit des lois*.

Many lawyers do not know, however, that the phrase itself is biblical in origin. The tension between letter and spirit is far older and has deeper roots than any one legal system—or even any one religion. Paul's second letter to the Corinthians in the New Testament exhorted Christians to beware the letter of the law, "for the written law condemns to death, but the Spirit gives life" (2 Cor. 3:6, Revised Standard Version). The prophet Jeremiah spoke of the law written "on the heart" that forged a people of God (Jer. 31:33). This covenant is truly spirit-filled law in the eyes of God's people. It is internal, transformative.

In religious terms, the spirit is a driving force—law is the result rather than the source of its power. The spirit is prior; higher than earthbound systems. The "religious voice" reminds its hearers of considerations that lie outside the secular purview of law. For them, lawyers are the "lay" population. To those committed to secular law, by contrast, those who are motivated by spiritual rather than secular legal concerns are lay actors, drawing on nonlegal experience and sovereign loyalties that lie outside the state.

The Spirit of the Law explores the tension between the spirit-filled and the law-bound in modern American history. Often, the two have spoken essentially different languages even when they have used the same words: communication has been difficult, misunderstandings frequent. Yet in the First Amendment, the Constitution commands those who enforce the law to protect and honor those who live by the spirit. And those who speak of the spirit have invoked the Constitution as a shield and a sword. This mutual investment in the spirit of the law has inspired and bedeviled those who have tried to put the Constitution into practice. The fact that they have rarely agreed on how to embody the ideal testifies to the extraordinary difficulty of the enterprise, as well as to their commitment to live out its command.

Like the people in this book, I have wrestled with how to tell where religion ends and secular things begin, and how we should think and talk about the ways religion makes a difference not only in personal lives but also in the law and society where faith finds expression. Telling this story has taken me down many paths I had not known existed. Along the way I have witnessed how difficult it has been to construct, maintain, and inhabit commitments to belief and toleration in an era of extraordinary government power. In that sense, this book reflects a journey through faith and doubt, religious freedom and secular ideals, spirit and law.

THE SPIRIT OF THE LAW

CHAPTER 1

The New Constitutional World

An Introduction

Late in the first decade of the twenty-first century, a Massachusetts rabbi reflected on her decision to become an activist ten years earlier. "The religious voice," Devon Lerner said, "has trouble getting heard." But she had something she wanted to say. After rabbinical training at Hebrew Union College in Cincinnati and service to congregations in Atlanta and Richmond, she moved north in search of a community that would nurture her long-standing commitment to interfaith work. Eventually she became one of the first members of an ecumenical group of clergy, all of whom belonged to progressive religious denominations. For eight years, Lerner worked first as a volunteer and then as the full-time executive director of the organization, which litigated and lobbied in favor of same-sex marriage in Massachusetts. She looked back on this experience as both exhilarating and exhausting. As she described it, "I entered naively, thinking about separation of church and state, as though it would be an actual protection."[1]

Deciding where religion ends and government begins has never been easy or straightforward. Yet Americans are committed to the protection of religious freedom. After all, the First Amendment to the United States Constitution opens with the importance of religion: "Congress shall make no law respecting an establishment of religion, or prohibiting the free exercise thereof." These commands (known as the religion clauses) have inspired and infuriated Americans ever since they took effect in 1791. But for the past seventy years, religiously inspired Americans like Devon Lerner have had a new place to be heard—they could claim the protections of the religion clauses in courts.

There are many ways to describe how Rabbi Lerner came to law and what she learned there; any version of the central story traces how this new venue has drawn countless thousands to take legal stands themselves or to come together in like-minded communities. These were not "social movements," at least not in the sense that scholars generally use the term.[2] Rabbi Lerner was just one among many who have navigated between religious and legal life, for many divergent reasons and causes. Fundamentally, however, hers was a religious undertaking. She came because she spoke for interests outside the secular, she said, defending convictions that deserved to be heard but that struggled for an audience. The experience was often traumatic; it required courage and tenacity, as Lerner acknowledged, to "keep a principled stand." Her own principles were grounded in progressive Judaism, overlapping sometimes but not always with progressive political agendas. She will appear again toward the end of this book. For now it is most important to appreciate that Rabbi Lerner came to constitutional law through her religious commitments, rather than through politics or another secular motivation.

The lay constitutionalism of Lerner and those who shared her perspective was powerful, but it was a popular understanding. The more technical dimensions are the particular province of courts and legislatures. The tension between popular and technical constitutionalism reflected the difference between the spirit and the letter of the law. On both sides of the divide, friction and frustration animated encounters between popular and technical arguments and tactics. The uncertainty of the outcome—the dread of defeat and the hope for victory—meant that the journey to law was dangerous. Defeat at the hands of the technical law could be devastating. As many of the spirit-filled learned, however, even victory carried risks.

The group Rabbi Lerner worked with was successful, so much so that they disbanded in 2007, saying that their work had been done. After years of struggle and controversy (even secular supporters who shared their fundamental legal goals "were afraid of religious voices," Lerner recalled), Massachusetts law finally allowed them the freedom to practice their faiths by legalizing same-sex marriage. Religion, in this sense, was protected and nurtured through legal action that eventually provided the space for progressive groups to engage in the kinds of practice and ritual they believed their commitments demanded. Groups of clergy in other states around the country copied their model. Such groups were evidence that the appeal of advocacy to vindicate faith remained strong. Yet the backlash against same-sex marriage even within liberal denominations showed that dissension traveled alongside legal activism.

Rabbi Lerner and others who appear in this book were not sophisticated legal actors but motivated believers who came to law to defend their understanding of their own religious traditions. In other words, they emerged from a religious space with a felt mandate to right a constitutional wrong. They found a complicated legal world that required new navigational tools and strategies; and in the end for Lerner it was a mixed experience, even though her group made substantial progress in law. Like other religious actors who have come to law, she found herself battling those of other faiths who opposed her claims, as well as crafting a coherent community within her own organization. She learned, as religious litigants have learned for the past seventy years, that law and legal rights do not mirror or often even recognize religious arguments or beliefs, and vice versa. Her own understanding of the ways law and religion interact will never be the same.

A century ago, Rabbi Lerner would have encountered a very different legal regime. In that old world, religious voices were even more sharply circumscribed. That world was not always unsympathetic, but religious actors, especially those whose faith led them in less-traveled directions, were protected only by the rights that every citizen had to personal liberty and political participation. In general, religion was not a special concern of courts, certainly not the federal courts; there was no nationally recognized right to religious liberty. That vanished world stands in contrast to the constitutional landscape that Rabbi Lerner encountered. Like others in the modern era, Lerner's experience was sculpted by a constitutional world that first emerged in the mid-twentieth century.

This new world was not always friendly, either. But it was created by the desire to give national scope to religious freedom—to apply the religion clauses of the U.S. Constitution to every level of government, state and local as well as federal. In other words, the new constitutional world protected spiritual life through law, starting in the 1940s. The gift has been a complicated and partial one, honored as much in the breach as in actual practice. Yet it changed many things about religious life in America, as well as changing law and legal analysis.

This book explores the erosion of the older world and the contours of the new terrain and those who have populated it. As it has occurred over decades and in waves, rather than at one moment, the unfolding relationship between religious life and legal commands is evident to the historian in ways that elude those who study the present. The mutual involvement of religious life and legal arenas also is missing in the work of those who study the development of legal doctrine or a particular angle of legal controversy, and those who focus on denominational, social, or other aspects of religious history. Paying attention to law in the same depth as religion is crucial, because attention to only one obscures the long dance of interaction. Indeed, one or another facet of the stories told in the pages that follow may be familiar to scholars of religion or law—but the richer and more textured world described here can be appreciated only when seen from more than one vantage point.

This book's central argument also depends on appreciating small- as well as large-bore change. It begins with the big transformation; that is, with the collapse of the old world, exploring the stresses and pressures of a regime that was powered by state law, but that came under increasing scrutiny by the 1930s. The new constitutional world that was invoked through Supreme Court cases "incorporating" the Constitution's religion clauses and applying them for the first time against the states did not emerge fully formed. The process of molding and remodeling the new landscape unfolded over succeeding decades, and has never been complete or even satisfying to many of those who participated in its construction. These accretions and alterations are the subject of the chapters that follow. Always, they involved the collision of religious voices and legal doctrines; often, religious life every bit as much as law was changed by the encounter of spirit and letter.

Taking these encounters seriously means reevaluating the trajectory of American national life. Put in terms that historians use, the periodization of religion and law in American history challenges those who would argue for a "long" nineteenth century or even a narrative that is keyed fundamentally to political or social or military events. In the world I describe, tectonic forces tend to be legal and religious. This new constitutional world was influenced by other factors but generally followed the shifts of doctrine and practice in those two fields more closely than, say, presidential elections.

The hard labor of building the new world fell primarily on believers and religious practitioners, who attempted to construct an environment in which legal standards protected the mandates of their faith. The power to invoke the religion clauses is relatively new, however. Attempts were made well before the new constitutional world came into being in the mid-twentieth century. In that sense, the aspirations of those who appear in *The Spirit of the Law* are not entirely unique in American history. Yet their religious voices helped expand the idea of religious freedom, and embedded it deep in the fiber of American society. However imperfectly, the letter of the law now protects spiritual concepts in a regime dedicated to religious liberty. These basic—even sacred—national rights are available to all Americans and binding on all levels of government.

This is an important and fundamental change that involved undoing a long-standing legal framework and erecting new structures in its place. Nor was this the first such innovation—there are three distinct constitutional landscapes in this American history. The first period began roughly with the American Revolution in the mid-1770s and ended by the 1840s. This period was unstable but also foundational, and the states rather than the national government did the heavy lifting. This was a period of undoing, teasing apart links between religious and political institutions that were old and rusty. Yet disentangling old relationships was difficult and often controversial. Deep divisions over the place of religion in public life characterized this era, which began with widespread religious establishments in both northern and southern colonies and the new states.

When the Constitution was drafted in 1787, six of the original thirteen states had religious establishments. That is, these states had a variety of means for imparting religion to their inhabitants, usually through a tax-supported system of church support. Virginia had disestablished only two years earlier. By 1833, the final state (Massachusetts) disestablished, completing a process that officially separated religious institutions from political ones, but by no means separated religion from politics.[3] The process of disestablishment was different in each state, but all faced the question of the ongoing role of religion in a newly secularized political order.[4] What did this new arrangement mean? Enlightenment-era elites, especially the rationalist wing of the founding generation, played vital roles in debates over such questions. Thomas Jefferson, just to name the most outspoken of these (mostly southern) gentlemen, argued long and hard that religious authority should have no place in government.[5] But he lost.

Despite the Constitution's ban on "laws respecting an establishment of religion, or prohibiting the free exercise thereof" laid down by the Founders, there was little agreement about what that meant. Equally important, the small and distant national government rarely trod on religious toes. Instead, local conflicts were more common and weightier. For conflicts between religious and secular authority, state interpretation gradually delineated the metes and bounds of religious liberty in America. As they wrestled with such questions, state officials, especially state judges, created the second constitutional world incrementally. In state jurisprudence, religion was both acknowledged as essential to social and political stability, and subject to the constraints imposed on all citizens in the interest of order.

Leading state judges and treatise writers explained that the goal of disestablishment was not to eliminate religion from public life, but to eliminate "competition between Christian sects."[6] The "general Christianity" they saw as key to a democratic society was not terribly specific, but it was vitally important.[7] The punishment of blasphemers, swearing of oaths on the Bible, Sunday legislation, and more all survived disestablishment intact, even invigorated. In Massachusetts, formal disestablishment in 1833 was followed in 1834 by a major blasphemy opinion from the highest state court, assuring the citizens of the commonwealth that religious toleration did not mean that all manner of bad behavior must now escape punishment.[8]

By 1840, the second constitutional period was broadly in place. It was clear that more seemly manifestations of religious life were (often) protected by a regime of liberty, but that the abuse of liberty—frequently called "licentiousness"—was subject to very different treatment in the interests of order and discipline.[9] The "police power" of the states maintained social order by punishing the loudest and least orderly dissenters (blasphemers, especially, but also the many groups that experimented with new sexual practices in God's name). State discipline also frequently silenced those who clamored too loudly for recognition in public places and came to the attention of officials.[10]

This was the way it was for a long time. The states decided questions of religion and law; those who claimed that the Constitution's own protection for religious liberty should extend to the citizens of the states had another thing coming. In real life, on the ground, the national government was mostly irrelevant. In two key cases in the 1830s and '40s, the Supreme Court held what experts had long known: that the protections of the Bill of Rights (including the First Amendment) did not extend to disputes between individuals and states.[11] This was a lawyer's resolution, framed in terms of jurisdiction and custom instead of constitutional innovation.

Technical constitutionalism, therefore, was decided against widespread application of the U.S. Constitution's religion clauses. On the rare occasion that the Constitution was in play, federal courts followed rather than led. The states developed the ground rules, and when the Supreme Court issued its first opinions on religion late in the century, in polygamy cases, it integrated essential features of state doctrine into its decisions. Federal courts punished sexual deviance in ways that replicated the states' impatience with licentiousness.[12] This settlement endured for about a hundred years, into the mid-twentieth century. It was a powerful as well as a long-lasting resolution of the major questions unleashed in the early national period. Yet this resolution—however appealing as a technical matter—existed in tension with the far less stable interpretive structures of the lay public.

Popular constitutionalism was a very different animal.[13] Despite learned lessons in law from commentators and judges, religious dissenters insisted that the Constitution should protect them. Especially among those who opposed the Protestant majorities in the states, the idea that they were subject to the tender mercies of state law was an outrage. The spirit of the law—the glorious promises of the religion clauses—*must* shield them from oppression, they argued. Their understanding of religious freedom was not shackled to dry, technical limitations. Instead, they *knew* that the Constitution shielded them, no matter what the letter of the law dictated. Joseph Smith, the founder, president, and first prophet of the Church of Jesus Christ of Latter-day Saints—commonly called the Mormon Church—petitioned the national government to intervene to protect him and his followers against state officials in Ohio, Illinois, and Missouri (in an escalating war of words between Mormons and local officials, the governor of Missouri declared in 1838 that Mormons must be "exterminated, or driven from the State if necessary for the public peace").[14]

Predictably, Smith met an unresponsive wall of technical constitutionalism, which dictated that the national government had no power to interfere in disputes with the states. The rejection filled him with disgust. For the Constitution to be properly interpreted and enforced, he was convinced, he would have to become the U.S. president. Thus began one of the most remarkable presidential candidacies in American history. It was terminated by Smith's assassination in 1844, but not before he had been crowned as "King and Ruler of Israel" in the Mormon settlement of Nauvoo, Illinois.[15] The harsh lesson in the limits of national power in the old constitutional world was replicated many times. Even so, popular belief in the essential rightness of the Constitution survived.[16]

The conviction that—somehow—the Constitution could only be rightly understood as protecting them endured among religious groups throughout the nineteenth century, despite the settlement that was so widely accepted as a matter of law. Religious groups and individuals who claimed constitutional rights not recognized in law tapped into a powerful alternative interpretation of the Constitution that was not confined to legal language or the division between state and federal jurisdictions.[17] These constitutional interpreters were galvanized by the enormous potential they were convinced coursed through the magnificent phrases of the religion clauses. *They* had a constitutional right to freedom of religion that no official hierarchy could deny them.[18] And yet, they learned, they had no legal right outside the boundaries that states allowed for such freedom. It was infuriating, because the language of the Constitution itself—the religion clauses—was so clearly aimed at preventing just such injustices. These popular arguments and the religious voices that made them were not successful, but they were extraordinarily hard to kill.

Claims to constitutional protection were heard in the courts, sometimes sympathetically, but without a sense that the claims of religious folk were somehow genuinely different, deeper, sounding in the most resonant tones of constitutional law. An example from late in the nineteenth century illustrates how far this popular constitutionalism ranged from its technical variety—and it shows how rights claimed under the auspices of the popular constitutional vision could sometimes find support through other technical means. Raucous and inventive religious actors have often been interesting and courageous, even foolishly so. Yet toleration of noise and enthusiasm was a central pillar of a vibrant democracy in the nineteenth century—within limits, of course, but nonetheless with a beneficent respect for the people out of doors.[19] No voice was more creative—and few were louder—than the Salvation Army's. The Army's legal tactics and the results of its strategy illustrate the stubborn vitality of popular constitutionalism, in the chilly atmosphere of the old constitutional world. Its example also highlights the frustrating qualities of arguing constitutional rights before a technically schooled judiciary, even when it was sympathetic.

In 1885, Salvation Army lieutenant Lizzie Franks was arrested in Portland, Maine. Franks was a convert to the energetic and dedicated new group of evangelists. Their Christian fervor led them into poor neighborhoods, and often into the waiting arms of the law. Franks and twenty-one Salvation Army soldiers marched into the Portland police station, where they "spent the evening singing their songs and praying fervently."[20] Officer Franks and many other long-forgotten Salvationists populated jails around the country in the late 1880s, arrested for disturbing the peace with their loud drumming or for holding parades without proper permits. Often, they refused to pay fines rather than compromise their "principles." One obstreperous officer, known to the faithful as Jail Bird Smith for his many arrests, was praised in the Salvation Army press as a prisoner "for Jesus."[21] The Army's brand-new legal department was besieged with calls for help in defending the open-air work of Salvationists.[22]

Taking religion to the urban poor, as the Salvation Army was pledged to do, meant bringing the performance and excitement of a frontier revival meeting to city streets. Surreptitious or even open defiance of local authorities was common at such events, which combined the saving mission with techniques familiar from popular entertainment.[23] A well-known figure called Joe the Turk sported vivid red trousers, an ornately beaded fez, and a tasseled jacket, and carried a trumpet that he played "loud enough to wake up the old devil."[24] According to one source, Joe was actually an Armenian, well over six feet tall, and built like a prizefighter.[25] The fearless Joe boasted that he had been jailed "fifty-seven times for Jesus" and even "stoned and beaten by mobs."[26]

However painful, the Salvation Army's legal victories were vitally important. Arrests across the country were part of the Army's popular appeal and its legal strategy, and they were Joe the Turk's most enduring contribution to the Army's success. He is widely credited in Salvationist histories for "breaking" police persecution of Salvation Army parades and street work.[27] When a municipality enacted noise and parade ordinances, the local Salvation Army corps would rush into the breach, "determined to march to prison or anywhere Jesus would call them."[28] An arrest record created common cause between Army officers and the unchurched poor who were their targets. It also sent a message to fellow Salvationists that the accused had now become "fully fledged" at the hands of the local constabulary.[29] Defiance of the law was invigorating, but vindication was even more valuable in the long term. The Salvationist strategy included appeals from convictions for open-air workers across the country. The peripatetic Joe the Turk appeared in several cases, with various last names, always claiming that the Constitution's protection of religious freedom demanded he be released, or his conviction reversed. Often, but not always, he and other members of the faith were successful.[30]

The Michigan Supreme Court held in 1886 that the city of Grand Rapids had exceeded its authority when it passed a law designed to get the Salvation Army off the streets. For two years, conceded the court, the city had been inundated by noise and parades. The Army had invaded the working-class neighborhoods of this industrial center, bringing with it boisterous drumming and a carnival atmosphere. The seventeen-person Army band included men and women, African-American tuba and bugle players, and was the first ever to be formally commissioned as an official Salvation Corps marching band.[31] Respectable persons were horrified; eventually the city council enacted an ordinance that prohibited parading without a license. The Salvation Army held a parade the day the ordinance went into effect, of course, and—just as predictably—arrests followed. The court held that the city fathers had violated long-standing custom by singling out one group for special punishment and overturning the traditional freedoms of public places in a democracy. Parading in the city streets was a central aspect of such democratic freedom, stressed the court, and the Salvation Army may have been loud and even disreputable, but it was not violent or fraudulent.[32]

Defiance of the law and—just as important—court victories created a productive tension. A resistant legal order could be a boon. Salvationists claimed that their obedience to "God's command" had resulted in suffering like that endured by early Christians and the earliest Puritan settlers in North America. Like the Pilgrims, said the "red-hot" leaders of the American Salvation Army, they too fought for "religious liberty" and the real meaning of God's law.[33] The spirit of the Constitution, said these determined evangelists, meant that arrests and fines from local officials were invalid. The Salvationists also challenged the boundaries that respectable religious groups erected around slums and many immigrant neighborhoods. Mainstream churches fled poor neighborhoods, leaving immigrants, especially, with few options for worship or spiritual guidance. Between 1870 and 1900 seventeen churches closed on the Lower East Side of Manhattan, even though the area's population grew by more than 200,000 in the same period. Other cities showed a similar pattern. The Salvation Army rushed into this spiritual vacuum, invoking a visionary "cathedral of the open air" where all could worship for free.

They claimed the protections of the Constitution, maintaining that "a law made so plain as that of the United States constitution, with reference to the worship of God, is continually being violated and ridiculed by the governors of municipal affairs."[34] Salvationists understood themselves to be doing the Lord's work, clearly, and claimed constitutional protection explicitly in those terms. Even when they won, however, courts that upheld their right to parade in the open air ignored or dismissed such constitutional arguments. Judges often focused instead on the patently discriminatory impulses behind some ordinances (the noisome Joe the Turk was the target in more than one of these cases). Other cases, like the Grand Rapids ordinance in the Michigan Supreme Court, were decided in light of the long-standing custom of open-air parading for political purposes.[35]

The decibels and targeted audience of Salvation Army parades were new, and the systematic legal campaign was important in American law. By the end of the nineteenth century, Salvationists had achieved significant and widespread protection for open-air evangelizing. They won enough of their cases to claim important victories. But their conflicts with municipal governments have now been largely forgotten. The Army itself has become a respected and respectable organization, far less contrarian than in its early years. Success meant that cooperation worked more effectively than confrontation. By 1920, Christmas donation kettles rather than boisterous parades characterized Salvationists' public face. Other open-air performers encountered resistance despite the Salvation Army's example. They were received in law as beneficiaries of the customary treatment of the people out of doors, but not as holders of a special constitutional privilege.[36]

The vigor of this popular constitutionalism and its defiance of more technical lessons in law help explain the explosion of energy as the old order was plowed under. Those who believed in the spirit rather than the letter of the law had never quite given up. Instead, they were poised to explain the true meaning of the Constitution's religion clauses, even when no judge would listen. The second constitutional era lasted a full century, until the years of the late New Deal and the buildup to World War II. The third era, in which popular and technical constitutionalism—spirit and letter—have met on the same terrain, is the subject of this book.

This modern constitutional world has generated tremendous interest, as well as criticism. New questions, and challenges to practices long tolerated under the ancien régime, have created a jurisprudence that is at once innovative and hard-fought. Often judges and lawyers have reached back in history to draw comfort and lessons from the past, but the relationship of the past to a new landscape is complicated. Certainly, old solutions don't fit the contours of the new world without showing seams. Most important and most troublesome for courts, the rush of popular constitutional argument into the precincts of technical constitutionalism has created enormous tension.

Long-lasting resentments, resistance to legal commands, and erosion of respect have often characterized the popular side of the equation. Frequently, those who have brought their claims to law have been disappointed; the legitimacy of the courts, especially, has suffered mightily in their eyes. On the technical side, exhaustion, concern at the lack of stability in constitutional interpretation, and a growing sense of the inability of courts to manage the cacophony of religious voices claiming constitutional protection has chastened judges and lawyers. From their perspective, the shifting quality of religious arguments and the ever-changing varieties of religious life have made coherence and continuity all but impossible to achieve.

Yet this is hardly a tragic tale; at least, it's not all bad news. American religious life and law have flourished in unexpected ways. The unfolding of national religious liberty has never been a complete or an especially neat process, to be sure. But it has drawn believers to law and into the construction of a new legal world, a vastly expanded stage for contests over the meaning of religious freedom. Religious and legal actors have been knit together by their shared investment in the religion clauses. They have each struggled to create a jurisprudence that unifies technical and popular constitutionalism. The mixture has been a potent one. Most of all, it has involved real and vital questions of how to think about religion and religious liberty in a country that describes itself as committed to the rule of law, even as law must operate under the religion clauses. Religion and the Constitution—both fundamental elements in American life and history—have met in the lives of Americans over the past seven decades as never before.

Through the stories of those who were actually involved, *The Spirit of the Law* connects religious people to the constitutional landscape we now inhabit. Often, it tells the story from the ground up, following the experiences of believers and practitioners in the world of law, as well as the courts' reception of claims by these newcomers. Populating the new world with religious actors requires paying careful attention to the tremendous variety and dedication of religious folk.[37] From Black Muslims to white evangelical Protestant women, these are the people whose interactions with courts and judges have created and challenged and resisted—even defied—the law.

Equally important, the areas of life in which our believers have found themselves claiming protection reflect the diversity of their practices and commitments: sexuality, patriotism, parenthood, education, identity, and more. Their encounters have taken place with a powerful government, in spaces constructed by the state (prison, marriage, schools, and so on). All are sites where law and faith met in individual lives, all affected by the new constitutional world and, in their turn, transformed by the encounter. Often, one group was inspired (or horrified) by the legacy of an earlier legal campaign.

Note well, however, that this is not just a "winner's history," a tale of those who were victorious or even of those who were necessarily admirable. Instead, this book plumbs the ways that believers used and were used in a new legal era—how they came to law, what they found when they got there, and how their experience affected those who came later.

The interwoven stories begin, suitably enough, with a group that became infamous for aggressive open-air work, but whose most poignant claims were framed through the plight of children suffering for their faith. The revolution in law began with concern about vulnerable children as well as the noise of outdoor religion. The cracks in the old world were revealed by the inflexibility of customary legal traditions. When push came to shove, the old world did not adapt to changed circumstances, especially when local coercion hardened and expanded. The demands of faithfulness were more brilliantly backlit by an expanding capacity for oppression by government. The brittleness of the old system created the potential for rupture.

The destruction of the old world was a dramatic end, but it was also a beginning. In the years that followed, legal battles among believers probed the boundaries between religion and other forms of government endeavor: educational, political, penal, and even marital. The remarkable people whose beliefs are explored here confronted American legal systems with their own constitutional mandate. Theirs are stories that probe the interaction of religion and law in the third constitutional world. That this book could have included many thousands of others is testimony to the richness of this integrated constitutional world. Popular and technical constitutionalism—the spirit and the letter of the law—merged in a new era of extraordinary religious and legal change.

CHAPTER 2

The Worship of Idols

Patriotism and the End of Time, 1935–1955

Walter Gobitas was filled with joy in the summer of 1943, but he was not surprised. "We knew the Lord would arrange it. The victory is His," he said.[1] Gobitas spoke at the end of a long struggle that involved his family as well as many other followers of his faith. Walter and his two children, Lillian and William, were members of the Watch Tower Bible and Tract Society, commonly known as the Jehovah's Witnesses.[2] Beginning in the mid-1930s, they and many of the 40,000 American members of the faith had refused to partake in the ceremony pledging allegiance to the flag. To do so would violate the Witnesses' stricture against worshipping a graven image, according to the group's leader, Joseph Rutherford. Rutherford based his rejection of salutes more broadly, in response to Hitler's persecution of Jehovah's Witnesses in Germany beginning in 1935, after they refused to "Heil" the new German chancellor.[3]

The decision to resist mandatory pledges had profound consequences in America, and Jehovah's Witnesses suffered on this side of the Atlantic, too. They challenged their persecution in court, claiming that they should have the right to worship according to their faith. The Constitution, they said, guaranteed this right, despite the fact that the letter of the law clearly dictated otherwise. Like Joe the Turk, Walter Gobitas and other Witnesses invoked the spirit of the law, a popular constitutionalism that seemed undeniable to them; it mirrored and protected their right to be who they were. In the annals of law, the Jehovah's Witnesses are storied—their success has earned them a place of pride in constitutional law casebooks and histories.

In religion, they are less well known, and often less admired.[4] From the broader perspective of American religious history and life, the Jehovah's Witnesses are not particularly unusual. Instead, they occupy a place in one branch of a Protestant grouping known as Adventists, which today includes the much larger Seventh-day Adventists and a varied collection of smaller denominations and activists, such as the evangelist Billy Graham in his early years and even the mercurial Branch Davidians, led by David Koresh in Waco, Texas, until the disastrous confrontation with the Federal Bureau of Investigation in 1993 that left eighty-five church members dead. Koresh, who interpreted the Waco showdown as a cosmic battle that presaged the end of time, set the Davidian compound afire.[5] Like many of their fellow Adventists, the Witnesses also prophesied an imminent apocalypse. At the same time, Adventists condemned political institutions as demonic and organized religion as spiritually bankrupt.[6]

Jehovah's Witnesses are unique among Adventists in some crucial ways, however. In the mid-twentieth century the Witnesses invoked the Constitution in their fight for legal protection from widespread prosecution triggered by their open-air work, and eventually from persecution for their refusal to salute the flag. The Witnesses began in the old constitutional world; their insistence that God's law demanded that they refrain from all pledges of allegiance to earthly governments became the occasion for a dramatic reconfiguration. The new constitutional world emerged over a decade of furious work within technical constitutionalism and increasingly noisy calls for relief from popular sources. The growing reach and power of the national government in the 1930s revealed the harsh edges of the old constitutional regime. In response, courts and judges erected new legal structures that brought the spirit of the law into a closer relationship with the letter. The road to the new constitutional world was long and hard.

The Witnesses' experience in American courts in the late 1930s through the mid-1940s was dramatic, painful, and often exhilarating. They suffered for their faith, and from time to time they found themselves protected by the devilish government they refused to honor. In the process, Jehovah's Witnesses learned a great deal about the letter of the law. Their invocation of a constitutional right to freedom of religion also taught the rest of the country that religious meaning could be found in unlikely places—even in an entirely secular pledge of allegiance to the flag of a country without an official religion.

The Witnesses played out their drama understanding themselves to be unique among believers. Yet they, and those who defended them, took part in the first acceptance in technical constitutional law of a broad movement that had been under way in religious life for decades. The embrace of religious diversity as a positive value in constitutional jurisprudence, and in the broader society, blended a new and dynamic legal innovation with a religious movement toward ecumenicism. The encounter was stimulating to those in the legal world, as well as to people of faith. The dramatic changes in constitutional doctrine that ushered in the new world were in some part precipitated by developments in mainstream American religious thought and institutions. The Jehovah's Witnesses were vital players in the drama, however. Their plight made the need for a new understanding of constitutional protections both timely and pressing. Witnesses' lawsuits became the occasion for momentous changes that remade constitutional doctrine—in their turn, those changes also deeply affected religious life. A tantalizing new law, which seemed to reflect deeply held popular beliefs about the Constitution, was irresistible. The spirit and the letter of the law remained in profound tension, however. The new world has been made of such mutuality.

The Witnesses projected religious significance onto a ceremony that had been considered simply political—patriotic, to be sure, but not religious in any direct or practical way. When the Witnesses challenged the pledge, it included no reference to God: "I pledge allegiance to the flag of the United States of America, one nation, indivisible, with liberty and justice for all." The Witnesses' claim that a mandatory pledge violated their faith was, at first, simply not credible to its hearers. Through their tenacity, the Witnesses became standard-bearers for a new understanding of the place of believers in American life. The militantly intolerant Jehovah's Witnesses were—eventually—welcomed to a crowded and broadly tolerant religious America. They were supported by a commitment among many more mainstream religious actors to an expanded role for faith and religious pluralism in constitutional law and political life.

Illustrating just how wide-ranging the effect of this new constitu-

tional world could be in religious experience, the Witnesses themselves were transformed by the experience. As they succeeded in law,
they became just another religious group, losing their distinctive mili-
tancy.[7] One perceptive observer said of a Witness who fought for recognition of his people's right to resist the commands of state law,
"Winning for him was losing," because by winning he lost the call to
battle that sustained his faith and its practice.[8] Religious radicalism
and energy have frequently proved unsustainable in the face of constitutional victories, as the lesson of the Jehovah's Witnesses demonstrates.

At one level, this is a story about the flag. Over two decades, the role
of the flag in American life changed dramatically. The core of the
story, however, is broader. It involves not only the gestures of patriotism but also the ways that difference was understood and interpreted
among broad swaths of Americans. This tale of diversity in American
religious life is intimately connected to the birth of the new constitutional world. The emergence of this world had consequences that are
still reverberating in both religious life and law, but one such effect
concerned the pledge itself, which grew in importance and gradually
incorporated explicitly religious language. Beginning with the Jehovah's Witnesses' faith-driven resistance to a mandatory pledge in the
1930s and traveling through the Supreme Court and constitutional
law before reemerging in national political debate and public practice
in the 1950s, the Pledge of Allegiance and the flag it honored were
transformed. In the late 1930s, religion was officially considered "irrelevant" to the pledge; by the mid-1950s, it was so important that the language of the pledge itself was changed to include the phrase "under
God," reflecting the newfound importance of religion in an otherwise
political ritual.

In this era, constitutional law and vibrant popular belief were connected for the first time by innovative religious, legal, and political
doctrines. These innovations have influenced American constitutional
and religious history ever since. Lawyers, especially constitutional theorists and civil libertarians, have long celebrated the Witnesses' daring
confrontation with government restrictions on their faith as the beginning of a new era in civil liberties law and theory.[9] Religious historians
have puzzled over the evolution of a broad and long-standing prophetic tradition that seemed to contain the seeds of social radicalism,

into one that blended quietly into the American political fabric. The Witnesses went from bold, aggressive, and defiant to taking a far less confrontational stance in a remarkably short period. How could this have happened in a "popular religious tradition that found its first support among people of low social standing and that taught those people to view the American political order as hopelessly, irreversibly unjust," asks one critic.[10] Some commentators have stressed the Witnesses' prophetic beliefs and their acceptance by mainstream Protestants as an element of religious pluralism. Legal scholars focus on constitutional rights and political liberalism. These two stories are connected in broad and constitutive ways.

The Jehovah's Witnesses trace their history to Pittsburgh, Pennsylvania, in the 1870s, where Charles Taze Russell (a haberdasher by trade) conducted Bible study classes and predicted that the world would end in 1914. Pastor Russell, as he was known to his followers, was a premillennialist—like other Adventists, Russell believed that the Second Coming, or thousand-year reign of Christ (prophesied in the New Testament book of Revelation), would occur after human society degenerated into apostasy and heresy. Only the faithful would survive the destruction, in premillennial thought, and thereafter Christ would reign for a thousand years. The runaway success of Tim LaHaye and Jerry Jenkins's Left Behind novels (several of which topped the *New York Times* best-seller list in the late 1990s, with sales currently exceeding sixty-five million copies) illustrates that premillennialism is alive and well in contemporary America.[11] The popularity of these books follows others, including Hal Lindsey and Carole Carlson's *Late Great Planet Earth,* published in 1970. Premillennialism and the end of days have been part of the rhetoric of popular revivalists and televangelists of many stripes. The great premillennial evangelist Dwight Moody of Chicago preached to such large crowds in the early 1890s that the World's Columbian Exhibition was forced to close on Sundays because of poor attendance.[12]

Russell, his Bible Students Association, and other Adventist critics of late-nineteenth-century society condemned self-indulgence, materialism, optimism, and other trappings of a modern, industrialized world.[13] They revived the fervor of pre–Civil War religious leaders like

William Miller, who was intensely interested in the Second Coming and was convinced that humanity was close to its final days.[14] Miller actually predicted when the end of time would come, first in 1843, and then in 1844. Millerites, as they were known, prepared feverishly as the announced date approached. After the October 1844 date passed without Christ's return, their crushing disappointment was followed quickly by the establishment of a new and more durable group that never again specified a certain time for the Second Coming. Instead, this new community (known today as the Seventh-day Adventists) taught that the Millennium was just around the corner, and that the faithful must prepare.[15]

Such prophetic movements have fascinated and often horrified observers. Frequently, they have been started and led by lay visionaries preaching strong religion to poorer and less educated congregations. They also have seemed distinctively "American."[16] Those who embraced these movements believed they were stepping out of secular time and into sacred history, convinced that this was the only sensible course of action. Perhaps, as scholars have argued, late-nineteenth-century "positivistic science" and other conceits of modern life indirectly encouraged untutored men and women to accept the exhilarating conviction that the end was near.[17] If so, this was only one among many triggers. The yearning to inhabit biblical frames is old, deep, and recurrent in American history.

In the twentieth century, premillennialism spread across Protestant groups, coloring Holiness and Pentecostal congregations as well as fundamentalist-leaning Baptists, Methodists, and Presbyterians. The Jehovah's Witnesses, while a part of the expanding number of those awaiting the end of all time, were particularly difficult, even in an extraordinarily prickly and doctrinaire crowd. For one thing, Pastor Russell actually predicted the date of the end, despite the sorry example of William Miller. In fact, the Second Advent had occurred in 1874, Russell announced, but the final destruction was delayed until 1914 to allow time for Jehovah's faithful to work for the conversion of the unregenerate. "Millions now living will never die," went the famous slogan.[18]

Russell outlived this deadline, but the outbreak of war in Europe allowed him to revise his prophecy and claim that the war itself was the beginning of the end, which now would come in 1918. His death in 1916 freed Russell from accounting for the failure of this prediction.[19] His successor, Joseph Franklin Rutherford, had been Russell's lawyer for several years. Marital troubles, in particular, had occasioned extensive legal tangles for Russell. His insistence that his wife, Maria, remain subordinate to him, as well as his decision that their relationship should not be physically consummated, had evidently caused her great consternation. (He said she had agreed to celibacy; her lawyer countered that Russell had "deprived [Maria] of one of the chief pleasures of life.") For his part, Russell complained that Maria was a nag: she had ideas about "women's rights" and constantly wanted to correct his grammar.[20] Russell's estranged wife proved the more sympathetic litigant. At the trial of Maria's suit for separation and financial support, a Pennsylvania judge concluded that Russell's "continual arrogant domination . . . [would] render the life of any sensitive Christian woman a burden and make her life intolerable."[21]

Rutherford stood loyally by his client through painful episodes in court and the press that brought considerable embarrassment.[22] As a lawyer, Rutherford fought doggedly to clear Russell's name when he was accused of financial fraud (selling grain he labeled "Miracle Wheat") and perjury (for claiming under oath to "know" Greek when in fact he did not).[23] Rutherford also published defenses of Russell and debated doctrine with disaffected members. Jehovah's Witnesses claimed that Rutherford sat as a substitute judge in Missouri county courts on occasion; they referred to him by the honorific "Judge."[24]

As Russell's successor after 1916, Judge Rutherford made many changes. Law and legal thinking were also central to Rutherford's leadership of the Witnesses over the next twenty-five years. He had seen how damaging the legal attacks against Russell had been, and how a courtroom allowed litigants to harass their enemies. Adversary argument suited Rutherford's temperament. He was a pugilist by nature, gruff and bellicose, often uncontrollably angry.[25] He fought off challenges to his leadership with a ferocity that seemed out of proportion to what had been a loosely governed, even chaotic, small sect. His life-long alcoholism may have affected his temper and judgment as well as his health. On more than one occasion, Rutherford was reported to have physically attacked a fellow Witness who dared to challenge his authority.[26] He also spent the sect's resources lavishly. Rutherford maintained two sixteen-cylinder Cadillac saloon cars and lived luxuriously, especially at his San Diego mansion, Beth-Saarim, which was valued at more than $1 million during his lifetime.[27]

Yet despite his flamboyance and temper, Rutherford was an able administrator, far more effective than his predecessor at organizational governance and propaganda. He understood that keeping the Bible Students afire was key, and he trimmed the sails of the sect to suit a new generation. For one thing, he avoided specificity in predictions about the Last Days. By the early twentieth century, this had become standard operating procedure among premillennialist leaders. Dwight Moody put it this way: "I look upon this world as a wrecked vessel. . . . God has given me a lifeboat and said to me, 'Moody, save all you can.'"[28] This conundrum (the end is near, very near, but far enough to allow for the work of God's people) could be a vibrant and energizing message—it provided a powerful motivation those who were convinced they otherwise would face damnation.[29] Yet the mandate to save all who could be reached also drew separatist groups into ongoing relationships with the world around them. Ellen White, prophetic leader of the Seventh-day Adventists, brought her doomsday troops into politics—especially through backing Prohibition and opposing Sunday legislation.[30] Judge Rutherford first brought his people into line, and then he brought them to law.

Gradually Rutherford disciplined the group's formerly diffuse membership. He increased his own power within the fold as he painted all outside the faith—especially governments and other churches—as the handmaidens of Satan. Rutherford himself had proven his willingness to suffer for the faith and his martial commitment to confronting the Beast: he was jailed in 1917 for his opposition to World War I and for counseling followers to refuse to serve in the military, as well as for trading with the enemy.[31] On learning that he had been sentenced to an astonishing twenty years in prison (he actually served nine months before the conviction was reversed), Rutherford said: "This is the happiest day of my life. To serve earthly punishment for the sake of one's religious belief is one of the greatest privileges a man could have."[32] He blamed clergy of other faiths, especially "the Papacy," for his prosecution.[33]

Rutherford's willingness to seize and wield power was matched by a desire to defend the faith in innovative as well as traditional ways: in prison, as thousands of his followers were jailed for draft evasion; through door-to-door missionary work; and eventually through extensive litigation. By the early 1930s, the Judge was ruling the Witnesses autocratically and austerely—he banned Christmas and birthday parties as pagan celebrations in a series of decrees that isolated the Witnesses socially as well as religiously.[34] Exacerbating the isolation, Rutherford admired and encouraged displays of contempt for "Satan's world" as his followers marched through hostile crowds and endured derision and sometimes outright violence.[35]

Rutherford urged his small flock to turn outward and "advertise, advertise, advertise" the Good News that the end was near.[36] They were committed to the "Great Commission," the New Testament command in Matthew 24 to spread the Gospel. In this way, they believed, they could actually hasten the Second Coming, which would occur once 144,000 chosen souls had been admitted to heaven. This "expansion work" (that is, witnessing to secure conversions) meant that "millions more" could be saved.[37] By 1935 some 90,000 were already among the elect, and the great question, then as now, was when the "heavenly class" would be complete and the Millennium unleashed. Even at the end, according to Witness doctrine, as many as five million others who were converted to the one true faith could be reborn after Armageddon, to live again on earth and create a new generation of believers.[38]

This lower "earthly class" destined to live on after Armageddon is the target and motive for the door-to-door preaching that characterizes the Witnesses to this day. To be saved, a person must accept the message preached by the Witnesses, and thus it is the duty of all Witnesses to ensure that they share the message whenever possible. If a Witness fails to convert someone, then he or she could forfeit membership in the earthly class and miss out on everlasting life. This doctrine (called "blood guilt") explained in part the fervor of Witnesses' evangelism. One shocked observer explained to his readers in the liberal periodical *The Nation* in 1940 that Jehovah's Witnesses were not motivated by a beneficent desire to save the world, but instead were working to save themselves: "Their primary purpose is not to convert the listener, though that is desired, but to carry out their conception of God's commandments and thereby insure themselves a place in the kingdom of Jehovah God."[39]

Indeed, the Witnesses' message disturbed many listeners. Not only were they dedicated opponents of government of all kinds and at all levels, but they also condemned all organized religion, especially the Roman Catholic Church, as a "racket." Protestants and Jews, Judge Rutherford maintained, were "great simpletons," taken in "by the [Catholic] Hierarchy to carry on her commercial, religious traffic and increase her revenue."[40] Virtually all earthly institutions existed contrary to God's fundamental law and would be destroyed, Rutherford taught. One commentator, acknowledging that Witness eschatology was just a more extreme version of the apocalyptic beliefs of many American Christians, nonetheless claimed Jehovah's Witnesses were despicable because of "their violent hatred of what will be destroyed, which is to say: our country, our world, our common planet."[41] The Witnesses' dark message of the coming destruction was matched by their fervor in spreading the (bad) news.

By the mid-1930s, the Witnesses were every bit as infamous and noisy as the Salvation Army had been decades earlier. Unlike the Army, however, they frequently targeted those who were already "churched"— members of other faiths. They were often unwelcome proselytizers, known for blaring trucks that traveled through residential areas and virulent anti-Catholicism. They would descend "like locusts," as they boasted, arriving by the busload in small towns or city neighborhoods, particularly on Sunday mornings.[42] There they would "witness" the corruption of other churches (especially the "harlot" Roman Catholic Church) and distribute literature or play loud recordings from their trucks, calling on members of other faiths to "awake" and escape the snare of the devil and his minions.[43]

They opposed and resisted participation in much of civic life, refusing to vote or hold public office, to serve on juries or in the military in any form, combatant or otherwise. The expansion of government in the New Deal era, especially the expansion of the federal government, provoked vehement condemnation from Judge Rutherford. He concluded in 1935 that the new Social Security numbers were the "mark of the beast" foretold in Revelation.[44] Other groups, including the Seventh-day Adventists and other street preachers such as the Salvation Army, had made their peace with national and local governments in the 1910s and 1920s. The Army, in particular, earned the admiration of the broader American public during World War I, when the "Sallies," young Salvationist women, served coffee and doughnuts to homesick American troops in the trenches.[45] Adventists, who had refused all military service in the Civil War, adopted a more conciliatory noncombatant policy during the Great War and established Red Cross training facilities at the sect's colleges, so that young men liable to the draft would be eligible for service in medical units.[46] By the outbreak of the Second World War, the relationship between the military and Seventh-day Adventists was described in a church newspaper as a policy of "conscientious cooperat[ion]" rather than conscientious objection.[47] For their part, the Witnesses remained staunch and vocal opponents of American government and "organized religion," and all those who defended them.[48] They inundated their (often involuntary) hearers with extravagant and frequently impolitic denunciations of their country and their religion.

Predictably, audiences resented such condemnation. Yet for those Witnesses who worked as missionaries, open and vocal critique offered the chance to witness—to demonstrate their faith to the world (and to each other)—in meaningful ways. The path of the righteous has always been strewn with obstructions and dangers, they said; those called to work for Jehovah at the end of time were expected to show persistence, courage, and conviction, even in the face of violence, humiliation, or ridicule.[49] As Lillian Gobitas put it many years later, "Jesus said, They persecuted me, and they will persecute you also. We do expect that before the end there will be a tremendous, all-out wave of persecution."[50]

The Jehovah's Witnesses, including the Gobitas family, did indeed face persecution in the 1930s and 1940s, when the flag-salute controversy burned fiercely and they were widely suspected of treason. Thousands of violent attacks on Witnesses were reported; many went unpunished.[51] Thousands of Witnesses were prosecuted for refusing to serve in the military. They accounted for two-thirds of all draft evaders jailed during World War II. Whether as schoolchildren or adults, Jehovah's Witnesses were openly and loudly opposed to the war and the government that waged it. Opposition seemed to make them more determined.

Defenders of the flag portrayed the Witnesses as a threat to national unity and thus to the security of the nation itself in perilous times.[52] As concern about security grew in the buildup to America's entry into the war, the Pledge of Allegiance (or "salute" as it was often called) increased in importance as an affirmation of national loyalty. The imposition of such recitals on those who had no choice in the matter— most frequently, schoolchildren—became ever more freighted. As fascism spread in Europe, and nationalism at home acquired a deeper taint of fear and prejudice in addition to the more familiar pride and loyalty, the flag occupied center stage.[53] The importance of the symbol and the deference shown to it grew exponentially as anxiety mounted. By the mid-1930s, many jurisdictions—towns, cities, states—had enacted compulsory flag salute statutes for public schools.[54]

Other salutes also multiplied in other countries. In the Third Reich the infamous "Heil, Hitler" salute trumpeted support for the new chancellor.[55] In 1935 Germany outlawed Jehovah's Witnesses on Hitler's orders, after they refused to engage in the raised-arm salute when it was made mandatory in all schools and at public events.[56] In the end, more than 10,000 Witnesses were sent to concentration camps, where an estimated 2,000 died. In the United States, Judge Rutherford was outraged at the persecution of the German brethren. At the Witnesses' annual convention in 1935, Rutherford excoriated all forms of compulsory salute as a violation of the biblical command against worshiping graven images. "Do not 'Heil Hitler' nor any other creature," he commanded.[57] After one father and son were jailed in Lynn, Massachusetts, for refusing to participate in the local school's flag salute ceremony, Rutherford broadcast a radio address in which he praised them both for their "wise choice," and urged others to "do the same thing."[58]

Across America, Witnesses began to resist the increasingly popular flag salute, unleashing torrents of criticism and abuse, and isolating their children and themselves from the rest of society. In some communities Witnesses constructed their own schools, but in many others their poverty and small numbers prevented such self-imposed exile. And of course many Witnesses responded to abuse with incendiary statements of their own. They loudly proclaimed their belief that the flag was the symbol of the devil, and that all worldly governments were creatures of Satan. "Why, then, should I, or my son, pledge allegiance to the Devil's kingdom?" queried the father from Lynn.[59]

The Gobitas family determined shortly after hearing Rutherford's radio address that they, too, would give witness to their faith by refusing to participate in the Pledge of Allegiance. Thirteen-year-old Lillian and her younger brother, Billy, hesitated at first, primarily because they loved school and were worried they would become pariahs—as indeed they did. In October 1935 Billy announced to his family that he had actually refused to perform the pledge, and that when his teacher had tried to force him, he had kept his hand in his pocket. Lillian reported that when she, too, refused, her fellow students shunned her. Students even threw stones at the Gobitas children as they walked to school.[60] The school board met two weeks later and promptly expelled the Witness children, who were sent to a school hastily put together some thirty miles from home at the farmstead of a sympathetic fellow Witness. There they slept three to a bed in hallways, "and the books and everything just came out of the woodwork," said the unsinkable Lillian.[61]

Walter Gobitas filed suit in federal court in Philadelphia. By turning to the courts, Gobitas joined a stream of Witnesses who had been encouraged to challenge refusals to allow them to proselytize, the imposition of fines, and false arrest and imprisonment. Eventually, Witnesses were subjected to beatings at the hands of crowds or even the police, castration, and more. In the mid-1930s, many ordinary Witnesses underwent a crash course in law, including instructions in what to do and whom to call when arrested.[62]

Jehovah's Witnesses were not caught unawares by their opponents; instead, they drew attention and prosecution consciously and systematically. Like their missionary work carrying the message from house to house, the Jehovah's Witnesses' turn to law was rooted in faith. Taking their case to the courts was the plan of Witness leader and lawyer Joseph Rutherford, who lectured even Supreme Court justices on the true spirit of the law. The resistance the Witnesses mounted to the flag salute and to restrictions on proselytizing allowed them to testify about their faith in a new forum, and to confront the satanic government head on.[63] The Witnesses used legal proceedings as a means of spreading the Word—they witnessed in this legal arena as they did in other venues. The restrictive laws, in their view, were just encumbrances faced by the faithful in the final days—expected but not necessarily unwelcome. Resisting such laws undergirded Witnesses' convictions about the fast-approaching end of times and the tests that Jehovah sent his faithful. From this perspective, tolerance on the part of the government could be detrimental, for any meaningful legal change enacted at the behest of Witnesses might well undermine the cohesiveness of their identity as an isolated and embattled remnant. The Witnesses' engagement with law, if successful, could prove to be internally corrosive as well as productive.[64]

Despite his opposition to all earthly regimes, Judge Rutherford often professed his admiration for the Bill of Rights.[65] Whatever created space for the execution of God's will, Rutherford maintained, was sanctified. In this sense, Rutherford was a believer in the popular constitutionalism that traveled across American religious communities even though the technical work of constitutional law told them that they had no rights to defend. Rutherford and other Witnesses agreed with a wide variety of believers, that the spirit of the Constitution established a legal regime of religious tolerance. Yet within the Jehovah's Witness community, freedom to differ with Rutherford's regime was out of the question. Dissent among the Witnesses was an occasion for excoriation, not toleration.[66] Rutherford ruled the Witnesses dictatorially and absolutely, even as he counseled his followers after 1935 to appeal every case brought against them, in the name of liberty.[67]

Rutherford's foot soldier in this legal campaign was fellow lawyer and Jehovah's Witness Hayden Covington, a tireless advocate for his co-religionists. Covington's work exemplified both the strengths and the weaknesses of blending the Witnesses' premillennial faith with litigation. He represented the Witnesses in more than fifty Supreme Court arguments.[68] His demeanor was always energetic—so much so that a supercilious Supreme Court law clerk put it this way: "[Covington] may not have done more talking than anyone I've heard here, but he did more calisthenics."[69] He was also renowned for his low-rent clothing—a bright green suit paired with a red plaid tie drew comment from one observer—and for his tendency to treat judges, even Supreme Court justices, with thinly veiled contempt.[70] In one case, he "glowered" at Justice Frank Murphy, a Catholic, while explaining that Witnesses (unlike Catholics, we presume) "don't preach in a dead language."[71]

Witnesses preached the saving faith in the courts as they did on busy street corners. Even the famous Covington was no exception; his pride in the power of witnessing and the people who proclaimed the truth was evident: "Jehovah's Witnesses are plain people who derive their authority to preach the truth from Jehovah himself," he said in one Supreme Court argument, "not from organized wealthy groups."[72] Yet they were determined to challenge those who would silence them, including the three great institutions of Satan, according to Witness doctrine—business, politics, and (organized) religion. The law and the courts were avenues to reach an audience, as the streets were. Through the courts, Jehovah's Witnesses could challenge the corrupt institutions of the devil's minions, defy them, and perhaps even win converts in the process.

Despite their determination to pursue legal redress, Covington and the plainspoken Witnesses faced an uphill battle, particularly with regard to the flag salute. Traditionally, of course, the pledge was seen as a secular activity. The Supreme Judicial Court of Massachusetts held in the Lynn case that a mandatory salute imposed on schoolchildren had "nothing to do with religion. . . . It does not in any reasonable sense hurt, molest, or restrain a human being in respect to 'worshiping God.'"[73] In other states, courts reached similar conclusions. New Jersey, California, Florida, Georgia, New Hampshire, and New York all held that punishment of Witnesses for their refusal to salute the flag was not an undue interference with religion or religious freedom. Florida's supreme court put it most stridently: "To symbolize the Flag as a graven image and to ascribe to the act of saluting it a species of idolatry is too vague and far fetched to be even tinctured with the flavor of reason."[74] Seen in this light, the Witnesses had manufactured their own problem. By importing religion into a nonreligious exercise, they seemed superstitious and disloyal, as well as impolite and aggressive. They preached a dreadful apocalyptic prophecy, and they called all who opposed them devils.

Yet they also lived their beliefs with passion and courage. During the Second World War, some 4,120 Witnesses went to prison for their refusal to serve in the military.[75] Their plight did not stir widespread public sympathy, but Lillian Gobitas and other children were more appealing plaintiffs.

Their case, *Gobitis v. Minersville School District,* ignited a tinderbox.[76]

The suit was tried in 1937 before Judge Albert Maris in the Eastern District of Pennsylvania. Maris, a Roosevelt appointee, was known for his valor as a solider in World War I and (somewhat incongruously) for being a practicing Quaker, a group famous for its pacifism.[77] Maris broke with long-standing legal tradition by holding that forcing Billy and Lillian Gobitas to salute the flag violated their right to freedom of conscience. Judge Maris stressed that a mandatory flag salute "seems to me utterly alien to the genius and spirit of our nation and destructive of that personal liberty of which our flag itself is the symbol."[78] Both Lillian and Billy testified at the trial, a process Lillian remembered decades later as a chance to witness. She relied especially on 1 John 5:21, "Little children, keep yourselves from idols."[79] Maris's opinion stressed that the decision about what counts as religious should rest with the believer, not school officials.[80]

Nationalism and religious dissent were troublesome issues in the late 1930s. Europe had become a battleground of nationalist aggression, and it seemed clear to many Americans that only national pride—and perhaps national isolation—would save the United States from the coming conflagration. With Jehovah's Witnesses already banned in Germany, Judge Maris summed up the American version of the conflict between religious liberty and government with an eye toward Europe: "Our country's safety surely does not depend upon the totalitarian idea of forcing all citizens into one common mold of thinking and acting or requiring them to render a lip service of loyalty in a manner which conflicts with their sincere religious convictions."[81]

This was the quandary, one in which the dictatorial Judge Rutherford invoked the aid of liberal judges. As the Third Circuit noted sardonically on appeal, "The sect does not appear to practice the tolerance that it now asks for these young members of its flock."[82] When the school appealed to the Supreme Court, Rutherford's argument embodied his religious convictions. Instead of relying on recognized constitutional principles, Rutherford claimed that the compulsory salute violated the only true source of law, God's law as given to Moses (Exodus 20:3–5). Any state law contrary to God's commandments must be void.[83] "No human authority can control or interfere with [a true believer's] conscience," he told the Court.[84] Rutherford likened the Minersville regulation to Germany's imposition of the mandatory salute to the führer. The justices as well as Judge Rutherford understood that the contest—between those who would enforce the flag salute and the Witnesses who were resisting—was a new instance of the conflict over the particular brand of aggressive dissent that involved Witnesses on both continents. The relationship between war and worship was so poignant in the *Gobitis* case that the Supreme Court's final disposition of the suit—an opinion written by Justice Felix Frankfurter in the spring of 1940—was known among that year's law clerks as "Felix's Fall of France" decision.[85]

The opinion was carefully crafted, designed to acknowledge both the sensitivity of the questions involved and the overwhelming conviction of Justice Frankfurter that governments must be allowed to impart lessons in loyalty and patriotism, even to those whose parents did not wish their children to learn them. Frankfurter had every right to anticipate his opinion would generate unanimous consent from his brethren. Even Justice Harlan Fiske Stone, who famously dissented in the case, had joined his colleagues in April 1939 in denying an appeal from a conviction for failure to salute the flag.[86]

Frankfurter had two great objects in *Gobitis*. The first was to "reconcile the conflicting claims of liberty and authority."[87] Although both the district and appellate courts had assumed that religious belief was included in the "liberties" protected by the due process clause of the Fourteenth Amendment, the Supreme Court had not yet acted to confirm this assumption. Only two weeks before *Gobitis* was handed down in early June 1940, however, the Court did act. In *Cantwell v. Connecticut,* the justices held unanimously that "the fundamental concept of liberty embodied in [the Fourteenth Amendment] embraces the liberties guaranteed by the First Amendment," including the religion clauses.[88] Suitably enough, the Court used a lawsuit involving open-air work—by 1940, a form of religious evangelism well known to courts—and the proselytizers involved were Jehovah's Witnesses. The result received some press attention, but Justice Owen Roberts's opinion for the Court excited little comment, even though it was the first time that the justices had applied the free exercise clause to the action of a state.[89]

The momentous decision in *Minersville School District v. Gobitis* came a fortnight later, when the Court sharply limited the right that it had just proclaimed. The conflict between liberty and authority presented by the *Gobitis* case, Frankfurter stressed, imposed a "grave responsibility" on the judges deciding the question. He weighed the religious convictions of Lillian and William Gobitas (liberty) against the school district's "right to awaken in the child's mind considerations" of patriotic loyalty and national unity (authority). Frankfurter found the latter of overwhelming importance, "inferior to none in the hierarchy of legal values." "National unity is the basis of national security," Frankfurter wrote in language that resonated with the looming threat of war in Europe.[90]

Having decided that the government's interest was supreme, Frankfurter moved on to his second order of business. Any lingering doubts that might trouble the thoughtful judge about the result, he said, were assuaged by the knowledge that the decision in this case was based on the fact that the political avenues remained open to the Witnesses. "The court-room is not the arena for debating issues of educational policy," Frankfurter said. Instead, the plaintiffs were free to "fight out the wise use of legislative authority in the forum of public opinion and before legislative assemblies."[91] Legislatures, not courts, were the place to seek exemptions.

Justice Stone circulated his dissent only after other justices had agreed to sign on to the majority opinion. Frankfurter was surprised and dismayed at Stone's decision, especially because he considered himself to be following Stone's own admonition to give the greatest protection to liberties of speech and religion.[92] Stone's dissent was passionate, and he read it aloud in open court, a rare occurrence.[93] He understood, he said, that "the constitutional guaranties of personal liberty are not always absolutes. . . . But it is a long step, and one which I am unable to take, to the position that government may, as a supposed educational measure and as a means of disciplining the young, compel public affirmations which violate their religious conscience." Equally important, the prospects of political relief for "this small and helpless minority" were remote. Frankfurter had effectively "surrender[ed] . . . the liberty of small minorities to the popular will."[94] National unity, said Stone, must not be purchased at the expense of the Constitution.

Justice Frankfurter's *Gobitis* opinion was not a success. Even defenders of Frankfurter's reasoning were cautious in their support, and the dissent found many admirers. In liberal circles, the result struck many observers as a betrayal of American values.[95] Frankfurter's critics were vociferous, sometimes inconveniently so. In the debates over religious liberty and constitutional rights that followed, "national unity" came to mean something distinctly different than in Frankfurter's opinion.

Frankfurter had spent much of the decade before *Gobitis* as a member of the Roosevelt administration. He watched as the federal courts invalidated New Deal programs in the mid-1930s, frustrating the recovery efforts of FDR and his supporters. He was convinced that courts must not interfere with legislative decision making. Yet the application of this deference to the compulsory flag salute had a very different tone than its deployment in cases involving regulation of railroads or standards for the manufacture of margarine. *Washington Post* owner Katharine Graham described in her memoir how much the *Gobitis* decision affected many people, in a story of her wedding day in the summer of 1940. The ceremony was delayed for more than an hour, she said, as Frankfurter defended himself at the pre-wedding lunch in an argument with a group of young men. Frankfurter's own law clerk Edward Prichard (known as Prich), Phil Graham (the groom), and others, "were deeply disturbed—even shocked—by Felix's position. . . . Felix loved and encouraged loud and violent arguments, which everyone usually enjoyed, but this time the argument went over the edge into bitter passion. . . . The fight grew so intense that at one point great large tears rolled down Prich's reddened, rotund cheeks. . . . The argument went on and on, with Felix [saying], 'Everybody always talks about me as a liberal, but I never was one.'"[96] Indeed, in crucial ways he was not.

Frankfurter's character—his love of the flag, his insecurity as an immigrant, his deep commitment to public education as a force for assimilation—is no doubt relevant to the opinion he wrote.[97] Yet the liberalism he referred to in the argument before Kay Graham's wedding underlay the reaction against the majority opinion both on and off the Court. Respect for religious pluralism in this new liberalism was as much a New Deal project as more technocratic economic programs that Frankfurter championed.[98] Histories of the New Deal traditionally describe a secular movement in support of expanded government projects and programs, such as labor rights, social welfare, and racial justice. Religious influences were deeply felt in the FDR administration, however. Support for measures to alleviate suffering and counteract the ravages of market failure were crucially and articulately supported by religious bodies across the New Deal years, as they had been in previous decades.[99]

Religious belief and rhetoric were vital elements of President Roosevelt's mandate for rebuilding a more humanitarian form of American capitalism and government. As one perceptive critic put it, political liberalism and Christian humanitarianism were "pretty much the same thing" in FDR's view.[100] Roosevelt's constant use of biblical parallels to describe American life drew on his own close reading of the Bible, as well as his conviction that "faith in God and man" was necessary to reach "the goal which was set before the Nation at its founding."[101] Only by coming together as "believing Americans" across sectarian boundaries, said Roosevelt, would the country fulfill its own commitments to the common cause of "our religious tradition" in ways that "will do credit, also, to the best of our American tradition."[102] FDR connected the threads between interfaith cooperation and the moral grounding of the New Deal.

There was substantial precedent for such religious pluralism by the late 1930s. Decades of institutional support for interdenominational and interfaith cooperation in America set the stage for the embrace of pluralism in FDR's presidency and eventually at the Supreme Court. At roughly the same time that Pastor Russell and his Bible Students Association had withdrawn from more mainstream Protestant life, other Protestants had reached out and across boundaries. In 1893 the World's Parliament of Religions, held in Chicago, included a remarkable array of religious leaders and views: seven thousand people from all over the world, representing Buddhism, Hinduism, Islam, and more.[103] As one European observer put it at the time, "The Parliament . . . stands unique, stands unprecedented in the whole history of the world."[104]

Among the speakers, Julia Ward Howe, author of "The Battle Hymn of the Republic," argued against claiming that Christianity had exclusive access to religious truth. All true Christians, she said to a packed lecture hall, understood that Jesus' message was of "infinite and endless and joyous inclusion."[105] "Why should not Christians be glad to learn what God has wrought through Buddha and Zoroaster— through the sage of China, and the prophets of India and the prophet of Islam?" queried the conference's organizer, the Reverend John Henry Barrows of the First Presbyterian Church of Chicago.[106] Those who respected the value of other religious traditions would only grow in knowledge and, Howe and Barrows both implied, in faith. This was a theological stance as well as a socially and culturally informed one. God operated not just within Christian confines, maintained these new ecumenicists, but across history and throughout the world, wherever genuine belief was found.

The essential optimism that undergirded the meeting's organizers and many of its speakers presumed a commonality that operated at home as well as abroad. For the first time, American Protestants openly welcomed American Jews and Catholics to a conference on religion, and even invited women and black religious leaders to speak, in unprecedented numbers. The parliament became a milestone in a long process, among more liberal Protestants, of increasing acceptance of diversity for pragmatic as well as more high-minded reasons. This newly inclusive approach to religions and diverse believers in turn set the stage for political and constitutional transformations. Encouraged by anthropological, biological, linguistic, historical, and other intellectual pursuits of the nineteenth century, as well as humanitarian reform movements and immigration from southern and eastern Europe, religious liberals embraced the idea that all the world's great religions contain valuable truths about the divine. This liberalism achieved coherent form in the 1893 World's Parliament of Religions.

The new liberalism (and its corollary, religious relativism) haunted and inspired American believers from then on, with varying degrees of intensity. The acceptance of pluralism was incomplete at the time, and in many cases has remained so ever since. But even partial acceptance proved transformative. Protestant liberals used their new interfaith ethic to translate an individualist concept of salvation into a broader, collective one. The new inclusiveness generated a broad mandate for social intervention in the name of divine justice. This collective focus swept up unprecedented numbers of otherwise ignored or despised peoples, turning their suffering into an indictment of those who allowed such misery in their midst. It became the social responsibility of Christians, then, not so much to ensure individual adherence to one or another dogma or ritual, but to work for justice in the name of God.[107] The excitement caused by such a social mission reverberated across subsequent decades. Even its most ardent defenders, however, could hardly have anticipated the ways that this religious liberalism would be alternately championed and rejected, lauded and excoriated following its first tentative steps in the late nineteenth century.[108]

Once the conversation across faiths and over denominational fences started, it became extraordinarily hard to cabin. Cross-denominational bodies grew rapidly: the Young Men's (and Women's) Christian Associations, the Evangelical Alliance, and others extended the new ecumenical approach to religiously motivated social activism in many different settings.[109] Fifteen years after the World's Parliament of Religions, a convocation of American Christians gathered liberal Protestants together in a powerful cross-denominational body (and, of course, extended their influence). The Federal Council of Churches of Christ first met in Philadelphia in 1908. This body rapidly became the sun around which other liberal Protestant institutions rotated. At its founding, organizers noted contentedly that members of its twenty-three constituent denominations represented more than half the country's population.[110]

In the late nineteenth and early twentieth centuries, church voices in this broad liberal swath invested heavily in the optimism and Progressivism (to use the word most closely associated with the political aspects of this religious movement) of a new industrial age. Consider Chicago. In 1893, a stock market crash set off a devastating depression across the country. But that same year, the great Columbian Exposition and the World's Parliament of Religions drew tourists to Chicago from around the country and the world (estimates place visitors at twenty-seven million). Those enormous exhibitions also kept many thousands of workers busy and the local economy strong for most of that year. After the fair closed in October, however, whole "armies" of haggard men roamed the city's streets looking for work.[111]

Charles Sheldon's phenomenal best seller *In His Steps,* first published in 1896 and based on Sheldon's sermons, asked middle-class midwestern congregations "What would Jesus do?" if confronted by the want and hopelessness of Chicago.[112] Sheldon's own answers to the still-famous "WWJD" question included outreach to "sinful" people, abstinence from alcohol, and a deeper investment in an inclusive community. The Reverend Sheldon maintained that such sacrifice enriched life and intensified faith among the well-heeled, as well as among the impoverished.[113]

The Social Gospel movement that grew out of this spiritual impulse flourished in the late nineteenth and early twentieth centuries, producing Sabbath legislation (including the abolition of Sunday delivery of the mail in 1912), sustaining state laws and eventually a national constitutional amendment banning the consumption of alcohol, and supporting passage of child-labor and maximum-hour laws, among others.[114] The liberal faithful transformed their churches into instruments for moral reform and built institutions, especially the Federal Council of Churches, that intensified the commitment to reach every corner of society. Into factories, labor strife, immigrant slums, corporate wars, and more, liberal Protestants sent their most gallant soldiers to cleanse and rededicate American souls.[115]

Often, they failed. The limits of their success and the narrowness of their vision, the danger of investing so much in turning churches into centers of social activism, the fact that so many conservative Protestants were dismayed by the breezy adaptability of the new liberalism, the inconsistencies in many liberal thinkers' and activists' own versions of pluralism—all contributed to the sense, by 1920, that the optimism of earlier reformers had been badly overstated. Especially dispiriting, the staggering losses of World War I seemed to prove that human society had become more deadly, not more compassionate.[116] Realism threatened to undermine ecumenicism as progressive liberals' confidence evaporated after the experience of the Great War. Yet the war had also demonstrated the reach of interfaith cooperation. The Jewish Welfare Board, the National Catholic War Council, and the (Protestant) Wartime Commission of the Churches collaborated in bringing religious services to troops, and in appointing Rabbi Isaac Landman as the first Jewish chaplain to American soldiers.[117]

After the war, clerics who had participated in "goodwill" activities (that is, efforts dedicated to fostering goodwill between members of different faiths) explained that their wartime experience taught them that brotherhood was the best hope for recovery from the devastation wrought by hatred. Indeed, many postwar religious leaders focused intently on the refurbishment and expansion of the tentative pluralism they had cultivated for twenty years and more. In this sense, the 1920s was not just a decade of retrenchment among liberals. It was a period of spiritual extension and deepening as well.

The process was neither seamless nor smooth. Often, it rubbed nerves made raw by Protestant leaders' desire to "Americanize" immigrants, to file down their foreign edges (and religions, of course) into something more familiar—into Christianity, in short. "Unchurched" Jews, the Department of Christian Americanization of the Episcopal Church explained, were those "large numbers of Jews who have left the faith of their fathers, and whom the synagogues do not and cannot reach." They and other foreign-born nonbelievers "who have not grasped what real Americanism is" were the targets of a million-dollar Episcopal program designed to teach them that a "religious foundation" was essential to American citizenship.[18] According to press reports, the man in charge of the missionary work with Jews, the Reverend John L. Zacher (himself "a Hebrew"), claimed that missions to reach the Jews had been successful in the past, producing 75 percent of all Jewish converts to Christianity. He promised church leaders "tremendous possibilities in this field."[119]

Outraged protests from Jewish leaders, including the Reform rabbi Leo Franklin, president of the Central Conference of American Rabbis, objected to the implicit assumption that "the process of Christianization and Americanization are one."[120] Rabbi Franklin agreed that Americanization could and should be an essential component of outreach to immigrants, and that religion was the single most important ingredient in Americanization. He denied vehemently that Christianity should be assumed to be the end result for new citizens, however. A meeting between Franklin and Episcopal representatives produced a formal expression of contrition by the Episcopalians and a promise of future cooperation between the two groups.[121] Discomfort with the resolution lingered on both sides, nonetheless, as many Protestants clung to their missionary ideals and Jews reacted against broader reappearances of nativist prejudice and anti-Semitism in the 1920s, such as Henry Ford's publication of the notoriously anti-Semitic forgery known as *The Protocols of the Elders of Zion*.[122]

Despite the many hurdles, some progress was made. In important ways, too, progress in goodwill was tied to law and legal developments, presaging the importation of a pluralist ethic in constitutional doctrine in the late 1930s and early 1940s. In 1927, for example, the founding of the National Conference on Christians and Jews (NCCJ) by Charles Evans Hughes, Newton Baker, and S. Parkes Cadman brought together the future chief justice of the Supreme Court, Woodrow Wilson's secretary of war, and the president of the Federal Council of Churches.[123] Among the advisory board members were New York Court of Appeals judge and future Supreme Court justice Benjamin Cardozo, leading Jewish lawyer Louis Marshall, Catholic vaudeville impresario Edward F. Albee, lawyer and real estate magnate Henry Morgenthau, lawyer and industrialist Owen D. Young, Cincinnati judge Alfred M. Cohen, and Catholic monsignor John A. Ryan. The NCCJ instituted Brotherhood Day, eventually expanded to Brotherhood Week, to "promote justice, amity, and cooperation among Protestants, Catholics, and Jews."[124]

The goodwill movement, then, united lawyers, politicians, entrepreneurs, and religious thinkers, many of whom remained committed to the interfaith ideals of the Progressive Era. Early on, their successes were limited, especially due to the wariness born of long experience that often led Catholics and Jews to suspect that Protestants deployed such outreach as a disguise for assimilationist aims. Goodwill efforts bore fruit in the 1930s, however, as the Depression and FDR's presidency revived interest in the social vision of liberal religious leaders. The Federal Council of Churches, the National Catholic Welfare Conference, and other institutions, including the National Conference of Christians and Jews, all embraced religious mandates for government assistance to the poor and desperate. Equally important, religious liberals began to advocate what they called "interracial fellowship" as well as interfaith work. "Brotherhood is no idle sentiment; it means social equality," declared one Baptist commentator in 1932.[125] Methodists vowed never to meet in a city that did not "treat the representatives of every race with equality and courtesy," saying that it would be better not to meet at all "if no city would meet these conditions."[126] A reenergized Federal Council stressed that "economic justice" was paramount for all believers. "We are agreed that a renewed spiritual life for each of us as individuals must lead straight out into the great social issues of our day."[127]

This spiritual commitment to social justice inflected politics, as well. "We are coming to realize," as one scholar put it, that "the New Deal, for all its secular spirit, was firmly anchored in . . . moral-religious tradition."[128] President Roosevelt spoke to the nation in religious terms in his first inaugural address, invoking the biblical story of the "moneychangers of the temple" to explain his dedication to reforming American capitalism. He connected his political liberalism to religious thought in ways that echoed and recalibrated religious liberalism. When charged with radicalism, FDR responded that he was "as radical as the Federal Council of Churches."[129] Indeed, Roosevelt maintained that "in a crisis . . . the faith of the people was far more important than any other single element and that the fundamentally religious sense of the American people would be a great factor in seeing the nation through."[130]

Like other major reform movements in American history, the New Deal drew heavily on spiritual resources and commitments. In the 1930s, the religious tradition on which political liberals relied was explicitly inclusive, egalitarian, and ecumenical. Roosevelt's religious liberalism reflected this pluralist commitment. In a 1936 radio address to commemorate the NCCJ's National Brotherhood Day, FDR urged all Americans to join together as believers. Protestant, Catholic, Jew, he said, must move beyond sectarian prejudice and into true brotherhood, even as they remained faithful to their fundamental beliefs. The "road to understanding and fellowship is also the road to spiritual awakening," Roosevelt said, predicting that such an awakening could "melt" any problem, "social, political or economic."[131]

Religious pluralism as a positive good (and even a contributor to national unity) had migrated into political liberalism by the 1930s. Its spread into law had been prepared over decades of sustained thought and advocacy outside the halls of the Supreme Court, including by those who became members of the Court. By the late 1930s, those who argued that Protestant, Catholic, and Jew should be equal in all things thought they knew what that meant. This pluralism was the polar opposite of totalitarianism, especially Nazism and communism, they said.[132] The brotherhood and unity they sought, liberals stressed, was "not . . . the kind of uniformity of opinion that Stalin and Hitler have achieved."[133]

American liberal democracy, in contrast to the majoritarian tyranny of fascist Germany, was based on the Bill of Rights, said interfaith groups. It was opposed to bigotry and intolerance.[134] By the early 1940s, the NCCJ distributed millions of tri-faith prayer cards, pamphlets titled *American Brotherhood,* and even a film called *The World We*

Want to Live In, all stressing unity based not on uniformity but diversity.[135] National strength was nurtured through tolerance and mutual respect, said journalists, the Office of War Information, the Roosevelt administration, the newly formed Common Council for American Unity, and others. In this version of unity, compulsory flag salutes and violence against Jehovah's Witnesses had no place. In the end, national unity demanded the reversal of *Gobitis,* an opinion in which considerations of unity were assumed to undergird the imposition of uniformity.

Although it was sublimated in much of the contemporary debate, the questionable assumption that pluralism and liberalism were natural partners was clearly presented in the cases brought by Jehovah's Witnesses. The Witnesses never subscribed to political or religious liberalism. Debates about social progress, economic justice, interfaith dialogue—all occurred outside the scope of Witnesses' interests, and certainly went against the grain of the exclusive and isolationist strains of Witnesses' beliefs and rhetoric. In this sense, the Gobitas family was not engaged in the "neighborliness" that President Roosevelt promised would unify Americans across religions.[136] The tolerance that Roosevelt and goodwill supporters championed was not what Witnesses exemplified. Instead, Jehovah's Witnesses claimed tolerance for their intolerance; they had a right, they argued, to condemn all other beliefs.

Interfaith movements that thrived on mutual respect and self–restraint found their patience tested by such behavior. They condemned anti-Semitism, anti-Catholicism, the Ku Klux Klan, racism, and nativism as contrary to American ideals. And while they opposed the assimilationist impulses of prior generations, they nonetheless promoted an Americanism that was implicitly based on a regime of civilized restraint, rather than loud and aggressive proselytizing. Chief Justice Hughes even wondered aloud at one point whether the Witnesses' blatant anti-Catholicism took them outside the purview of the constitutional protections of the First Amendment.[137] He also questioned whether the Witnesses' objections to the Pledge of Allegiance were genuinely religious; the salute, he stressed, really "had nothing to do with religion."[138] Because their beliefs and tactics were unrecognizable to many, even in the Protestant-Catholic-Jew universe of Hughes and the NCCJ, the Witnesses frequently failed to win sympathy from liberals. The extreme millenarian doctrines of the sect still had the power to shock and dismay observers, because they "offend[ed] many of the justified norms of American society."[139]

The Witnesses had their defenders, however, especially among religious liberals committed to a more full-throated pluralism. Gradually, these liberals pushed their more moderate colleagues to agree that tolerance even of the intolerant was essential to American democracy and religious freedom. In the late 1930s and early 1940s, the Reverend John Haynes Holmes of New York City was especially vocal. He was backed up by *The Christian Century*, the publication arm of the Federal Council of Churches, which published pieces by Holmes on the Witnesses, as well as a string of editorials. Calling the flag salute "an arbitrary piece of ritual," the editors concluded within a few days of the first flag salute decision in June 1940 that Frankfurter's *Gobitis* opinion "was not a wise one."[140] By the late 1930s, the Witnesses' increasing unpopularity and their vulnerability to attack had also raised concerns among civil libertarians, especially the American Civil Liberties Union (ACLU) and more liberal Democrats. Solicitor General (later Attorney General) Francis Biddle warned that violent "Nazi methods" were the predictable result of decisions that seemed to endorse prejudice against those who refused to salute the flag.[141] Religious liberals welcomed the support from New Deal allies and partners, drawing together religious and legal arguments for reversing the flag salute opinion.

By 1939, the Reverend Holmes had established a long record of support for progressive social causes and interfaith work. He had also risen to the chairmanship of the ACLU.[142] As Holmes put it in his memoir, he believed that "all work for human betterment [was at bottom] religious work."[143] Holmes presided over the religious liberals' campaign to link their long-standing commitment to religious diversity with constitutional adjudication. In a long article in *The Christian Century* in July 1940, Holmes argued passionately for the intimate relationship of American democracy and religious liberty. The lack of restraint shown by the Witnesses' opponents made his case an easier one: widespread beatings, verbal abuse, even a castration, transformed the cause into the protection of victims from the thugs who beat them.[144] The treatment of Witnesses, Holmes said, was the telltale symptom of a country in danger of slipping into totalitarianism: "Under all the totalitarian governments, fascist and communist alike, religion is being denied and destroyed as alien to the best interests of the state. Jehovah's Witnesses, crude as may be their faith and naive their expectations, have been among the first in these countries, and now in our country, to meet the awful penalties of tyranny. . . . If religion is to be saved from the new persecutions and perils of our time, it must be in the persons of these Witnesses among others, and perhaps among them first of all."[145] He urged "the churches" to "spring to the defense of the Jehovah's Witnesses, their fellow Christians," or they, too, could anticipate attack. The Witnesses, Holmes stressed, were "among the few Christian groups in the world today who stand ready to die, as did the early Christians, for the faith that is within them."[146] In their "heroic sincerity," said a follow-up article, the Witnesses became the canary in the coal mine, the test case for the nation's tolerance and commitment to pluralism.[147]

In the months after the *Gobitis* decision was handed down, the value of pluralism seemed more evident to religious and political liberals with each passing outrage against Witnesses and with each new Supreme Court decision. New appointments to the Court (the retirement of Chief Justice Hughes led in 1941 to his replacement by Harlan Stone) and other retirements among the *Gobitis* majority brought two new justices, Robert Jackson (1941) and Wiley Rutledge (1943), each with a strong record of support for overruling *Gobitis*.[148] Three remaining justices who had joined Frankfurter's majority opinion declared in another case that they had changed their position.[149] Court watchers anticipated a reversal when the Supreme Court accepted another appeal, this time from a conviction in West Virginia in 1942.

The elevation of Stone to the chief justiceship after Hughes's retirement in 1941 gave the lone dissenter in *Gobitis* greater prominence and influence over the Court's calendar and likely decisions. FDR himself implicitly endorsed the fundamental goals of religious liberals in his State of the Union address in 1941, when he outlined what he called the "four essential human freedoms." The first two of Roosevelt's Four Freedoms, which he urged Americans to maintain at home and to advance around the world, were freedom of speech and expression and freedom for "every person to worship God in his own way."[150] FDR, of course, had for several years defended the "blessed right of being able to say what we please," a foundational "spiritual value" of the American people, who cherished their "freedom of religion."[151]

The spirit of the law had received an enormous boost from a popular and powerful president. The Four Freedoms catapulted the First Amendment's protections of religion and speech into a universal plan for the basic building blocks of true human freedom. They also focused attention on the ways those freedoms were protected (or not) at home.[152] Religious liberals were galvanized by the Four Freedoms and by the defense of the Witnesses against brutality. The mixture of legal, religious, and political support permeated the atmosphere around the Watch Tower headquarters and its beleaguered Witnesses.

Spurred by new hope, Hayden Covington filed suit in federal court in West Virginia on behalf of a Witness named Walter Barnett, whose children had been expelled from public school for refusing to salute the flag. In response to the state's motion to dismiss the suit, a three-judge panel boldly defied the reigning precedent. Because *Gobitis* had been so undermined by the subsequent decisions and personnel changes of the Supreme Court, the judges felt free to extend "protection to rights which we regard as among the most sacred of those protected by constitutional guaranties."[153] The Barnett children, concluded the court, could not be required by school authorities to salute the flag. An appeal to the Supreme Court set the stage for a resounding affirmation of the lower court's conclusion—satisfying, no doubt, to John Haynes Holmes and the editors of *The Christian Century*. At oral argument, Covington leapt and gesticulated as he always did. Frankfurter glowered. Chief Justice Stone assigned the opinion to Justice Jackson, whose words cut Frankfurter to the quick, and brought tears of gratitude to the eyes of Walter Gobitas.

Yet the victory sublimated many of the central issues posed for those who would protect religious diversity. For one thing, the opinion was framed in terms of freedom of speech rather than religion. Justice Jackson, who in prior cases involving the Witnesses had condemned their disruptiveness and the unprecedented "turmoil" that followed in their wake, abstracted the decision away from the Witnesses' claim that their objections to the flag salute were religious rather than political, moral, or intellectual.[154] Instead of grounding the reversal of *Gobitis* on a religious exemption, then, the opinion in *Barnette* rejected the very idea that government had the power to compel anyone to salute.[155]

Equally important, Jackson's opinion for the Court explicitly rejected the central holding of *Gobitis* that legislatures rather than courts were the proper place to address questions involving religious liberty.

Frankfurter's back-of-the-hand dismissal of the judiciary as having "no marked and certainly no controlling competence" in constitutional interpretation drew heavy fire from Jackson.[156] He climbed just as high on the Richter scale of rhetoric, countering that the "force of our commissions as judges [authenticates] . . . the function of this Court when liberty is infringed."[157] The purpose of the First Amendment, Jackson stressed, was the protection of "intellectual individualism and the rich cultural diversities" of American life and thought, which came "at the price of occasional eccentricity"—such as that, we presume, of the Witnesses' religious convictions.[158] These diversities were central to constitutional values and to judicial mandates to protect them, Jackson wrote. The alternative was evident in world affairs and history: "Those who begin in coercive elimination of dissent soon find themselves exterminating dissenters. Compulsory unification of opinion achieves only the unanimity of the graveyard."[159]

Indeed, the *Barnette* opinion reeks of self-conscious moral rectitude every bit as much as *Gobitis*. The quotability of Jackson's opinion—the beauty of its language—has made it a favorite among judges and legal scholars for decades. But the soaring prose is not matched by precision or clarity in the holding. As one recent study concluded, "Seldom has a case outcome seemed so obviously correct . . . and yet so difficult to justify."[160] In the annals of religion and law, *Barnette* looms large yet indistinct, a case that inspires but that eludes replication.

Clearly, Jackson's fellow justices also had concerns about precisely what his opinion said (or didn't say). Justices Black and Douglas wrote separately, seeking to give more precision to the magnificent generalities of the majority opinion. Freedom of religion, they said, governed the case. Requiring "little children to participate in a ceremony which ends in nothing for them but a fear of spiritual condemnation" could not be a cognizable government interest, they stressed.[161] The principle behind the pledge was valid but could not be applied to those with genuine religious objections. As they confessed, they had misunderstood the quality of the religious argument in *Gobitis* and wrote now to clarify that the believer must be the source of how to understand religion and the effects of secular law on the faithful. Justice Murphy also wrote separately, to reassure his readers (and perhaps himself) in a country fully engulfed in war, that in "preserving freedom of conscience to the full" the "real unity of America lies."[162]

Justice Frankfurter's dissent has long been considered as among the most personal and defensive in the Court's entire lexicon.[163] As a Jew, he began, "one who belongs to the most vilified and persecuted minority in history," he knew the full value of the Constitution. Indeed, Frankfurter's experience taught him that an exemption for the Witnesses would undermine the stability of constitutional interpretation and the rule of law: "The validity of secular laws cannot be measured by their conformity to religious doctrines. It is only in a theocratic state that ecclesiastical doctrines measure legal right or wrong."[164] Frankfurter forecast all manner of dire consequences from the Court's holding, and evidently had been jotting notes to himself about how to frame his dissent over the long months leading up to the reversal of *Gobitis*. Even though the majority opinion in the new case had barely mentioned religion, Frankfurter predicted that allowing litigants to circumvent legal obligations because of their religious beliefs would unleash a torrent of claims: "We are dealing with an almost numberless variety of doctrines and beliefs entertained with equal sincerity by the particular groups for which they satisfy man's needs in his relation to the mysteries of the universe."[165] No good could come of an invitation to litigation about such extralegal mysteries. Catering to the spirit, he predicted, would bring trouble to the law.

Frankfurter's prescience was remarkable. Government involvement in parochial as well as public schools, school prayer, conscientious objection, prisoners' religious rights, same-sex marriage, and more have become among the most divisive and difficult questions in all of constitutional jurisprudence (and are treated in subsequent chapters of this book).[166] Religion has bedeviled the courts, as the Witnesses bedeviled the once confident Felix Frankfurter. Visceral satisfaction with the result in *Barnette* has been followed at the Supreme Court by decades of tortured reasoning and unpopular rulings. At the time, *Barnette* was greeted with widespread praise. The editors of *The Christian Century* reflected on the victory with satisfaction: "[Jackson's opinion] should become part of the 'American Scriptures,' to be memorized and taken to heart by every patriot."[167]

The feel-good aura surrounding the opinion obscured more than Frankfurter's anguish, however. The outpouring of support for the Witnesses also sublimated many liberals' assumption that tolerance breeds more tolerance. But the Witnesses were not interested in brotherhood; they were after converts. And the culture of tolerance that embraced them, even after the Supreme Court recognized the constitutional dimensions of their witness, did not produce a complementary tolerance within the Watch Tower Society. Beginning in 1944, only one year after *Barnette,* the process of "disfellowshipping" former members for dissent or drunkenness or sexual impropriety was consigned to secret "judicial committees" where decisions could not be questioned.[168] As one observer remarked, the faith has stagnated and hardened since the days of the great legal battles. Like other millenarian groups, the inherent conservatism of the Watch Tower Society reappeared in the long run.[169]

Indeed, the Witnesses have all but disappeared from political and constitutional consciousness. Their protection in law has traveled alongside their increasing obscurity in society. In 1988, for example, presidential candidate George H. W. Bush excoriated his opponent, Massachusetts governor Michael Dukakis, for vetoing a mandatory flag salute bill. But Bush said that Dukakis was under the influence of the ACLU ("a card-carrying member," went the refrain) not the Jehovah's Witnesses.[170] And the ACLU is popularly associated today with secular, even antireligious liberalism, a far cry from the days when John Haynes Holmes equated all civil liberties with God's plan.

The flag and the Pledge of Allegiance still occupy a key (yet ambiguous) place in American religious and political life. Just a decade after the *Barnette* case, the pledge was modified. In 1954, the pledge was amended to include the words "under God," a change supported by the great majority of Americans at the time and ever since. In the eyes of supporters, the modification reflected both American religious pluralism and the central role of faith in American national identity. The bill to add the reference to God was signed into law by President Dwight Eisenhower on June 14, 1954—Flag Day.[171] In recent years, the pledge has again become the subject of debate thanks to a lawsuit brought by atheist Michael Newdow, who challenged the pledge on behalf of his five-year-old daughter as a violation of the establishment clause. To the outrage of many and the delight of some, Newdow was successful at the trial and appellate court levels.[172] Legal academics and polemicists of all stripes pored over the history of the 1954 change, primarily in an effort to determine whether the alteration was religiously motivated.[173] The Supreme Court, which heard the challenge in 2004, dismissed the case on technical grounds, holding that Newdow did not have standing to represent his daughter's interest, as she did not live with him. Newdow and his wife had been divorced and he was not the custodial parent.[174]

Scholars have not connected the travails of the Jehovah's Witnesses in the 1930s and '40s with the new pledge in the 1950s. Instead, the *Gobitis* and *Barnette* cases appear as stories of a bewildered people caught in the maw of an oppressive state. Scholars have treated the insertion of "under God" in the pledge as an example of "civil religion"—the use by government of religion to accomplish explicitly political ends.[175] From this vantage point, the calculated deployment of religion by political actors in the 1950s is fundamentally different from the unplanned and even innocent use of faith by religious actors as a legal defense against aggressive government.

Viewed through a more panoramic lens, the two stories are interwoven in religious and political history. The obstreperous Witnesses became the emblem of how difference—especially and most importantly religious diversity—was (eventually) treated with respect in America, while in the Third Reich the same Witnesses were banned and then butchered. Even though it took time to realize what was happening and to correct the problem, the story goes, believers in America were protected by the Constitution. Through this painful legal lesson, the country learned that the differences nurtured by the religion clauses were the surest guard against fascism and totalitarianism. The Witnesses first defied the mandatory pledge to protest the similarities between enforced patriotic rituals in America and Germany. In the end, the Supreme Court and the rest of the country changed their minds about the value of the mandatory pledge precisely because stubborn believers provided a means to distinguish the United States from its wartime enemies, especially those in Europe.

As the cold war took root at the end of World War II, a second, related political lesson about the value of religion was backlit, this time in contrast to atheism. In both instances, the role of religion as a guarantor of liberty received broad public support. Neither supporters of the amended pledge nor Jehovah's Witnesses achieved their goals at the hands of a judicial or political ideology that accepted or endorsed sectarian religious truths. Instead, they were enveloped by an inclusive politics of religion—and an accompanying reliance on the newly popular term "the Judeo-Christian tradition"—that viewed religious belief as the lifeblood of democratic liberty and the fundamental foe of communism.[176] President Harry Truman put it succinctly in 1948, saying that under communism "religion is persecuted because it stands for freedom under God."[177] In 1950, the newly named National (formerly Federal) Council of Churches hung a large banner at its annual meeting that proclaimed "This Nation under God."[178] As President Dwight Eisenhower said four years later, during the signing ceremony for the bill that changed the pledge, including "under God" in the flag salute "reaffirm[ed] the transcendence of religious faith in America's heritage and future; . . . strengthen[ing] those spiritual weapons which forever will be our country's most powerful resource, in peace or war."[179]

Eisenhower, interestingly enough, was a new church member. On February 1, 1953 (only twelve days after he was inaugurated as president), he was baptized, confirmed, and became a communicant in a single ceremony at the National Presbyterian Church in Washington, D.C. He is the only American president who has undertaken such ceremonies while in office.[180] Although for many years Eisenhower had maintained no particular religious affiliation, he had been raised as a Jehovah's Witness. His mother, Ida, had first been a member of an obscure Mennonite sect. She became a Bible Student in 1895, when her son was only four years old, and apparently remained a loyal Jehovah's Witness until her death in 1946. The sect met in his parents' living room for much of Eisenhower's childhood.[181] Eisenhower himself never spoke in any detail about his decision to leave the faith, and did not refer to his mother as a Witness. Instead, he commonly described his parents more generically, as "fundamentalists," believers in a "felt" and "enthusiastic" religion.[182] Surely his departure from Abilene, Kansas, in 1911 to attend West Point had been a marked break, however. Eisenhower often said that his mother was a pacifist, but as a Witness she would have been opposed not to all war but to secular, man-made wars. Armageddon was another thing altogether for Jehovah's Witnesses.[183] Her son was trained in the craft of war, and eventually also in politics, both hopelessly corrupt undertakings in Witness teaching. Yet

Eisenhower argued that soldiers and politicians as well as ministers had a common dedication to defend "the dignity of man and, therefore, the glory of God."[184]

Scholars, journalists, and Eisenhower's political opponents at the time speculated on the role of religion in his life and presidency. The evidence is plentiful but extraordinarily hard to fit into standard religious categories. Consider Eisenhower's second inauguration: he took the oath of office on a Bible given to him by his mother upon his graduation from West Point. It was the American Standard Version, which Witnesses prefer because it uses the name Jehovah for God. Eisenhower chose to take the oath in a private ceremony on Sunday January 20, with the Bible opened to Psalm 33:12, "Blessed is the Nation whose God is Jehovah."[185] Speaking aloud, however, Eisenhower changed Jehovah to "Lord." At the time, Witness leaders were sure that Eisenhower had caved in to anti-Witness prejudice.[186]

More likely, Eisenhower was a conscious performer of postwar religious pluralism and liberalism. He stressed the "spiritual foundations" of American democracy, and he was always quick to oppose religious bigotry or discrimination. His was an ecumenical faith in religion, combined with a broadly social (even political) vision of its manifestations: "The great tenets" of every religious philosophy, he said, "are all wise and good in that they condemn injustice, unfairness, and they do not allow complacency to recall unfairness or inequality of opportunity."[187] Our government "makes no sense unless it is founded on a deeply felt religious faith," Eisenhower said in one of his most quoted speeches, "and I don't care what it is. . . . [B]ut it must be a religion that [teaches] all men are created equal."[188] He appointed the first Mormon cabinet member (Ezra Taft Benson) as well as Jews and Catholics to his staff and cabinet, and he was broadly tolerant of all but what one observer called "extremist religious movements of the far right."[189]

Eisenhower, who began on the fringe of religious life in a group that rejected secular government as the province of the devil, spent his adult life in the heart of government. Instead of shunning military service, he embraced it. Instead of refusing to vote, he became president. In navigating from the periphery to the center, however, Eisenhower clearly brought lessons from his childhood with him. Many of those lessons he had rejected, like others before and since, but the conviction that a spiritual purpose and moral mission were vitally important stuck like a burr.[190] Eisenhower claimed that his faith gave him the capacity to govern: "This is what I have found out about religion: it gives you courage to make the decision you must make in a crisis, and then the confidence to leave the result to higher power. Only by trust in oneself and trust in God can a man carrying responsibility find repose."[191]

Amending the pledge was just the kind of religious expression that suited Eisenhower's moderate, inclusive, and deeply felt yet indistinct faith. The proposed amendment also provided a verbal anchor for how he believed Americans and their government should view their country. As one thoughtful observer noted at the time, Eisenhower's evident sincerity was matched by the simplicity of his beliefs: "Integrity, courage, self-confidence and unshakable belief in the Bible," Eisenhower listed as the keys to dealing with America's most difficult problems.[192] In 1953, by contrast, Professor William Lee Miller of Yale Divinity School (and future speechwriter for Adlai Stevenson's 1956 presidential campaign against Eisenhower) derided what he saw as the "intellectually debilitating relativism" of Eisenhower's "belief in believing": "President Eisenhower, like many Americans, is a very fervent believer in a very vague religion."[193] More sympathetic, others remarked on Eisenhower's youth in a religious household that saw the world "in clear and simple patterns. . . . There was never any difficulty about distinguishing between the good and the bad—people or deeds."[194] The connection between Eisenhower's conviction that "democracy cannot exist without a religious base" and his "trust in God" as a tool of government was grounded not only in his experience in war but also in his childhood among folk whose lives revolved around their faith.

Eisenhower's political instincts for the ways that religion functioned in American life were finely honed: support for the amendment to the Pledge of Allegiance was strong, including an overwhelming majority of Catholics and Protestants as well as a clear majority of Jews. According to a Gallup survey, the only group that opposed the change in the pledge was the smattering of atheists.[195] In a country locked in battle with godless communism, a spiritual weapon such as an amended pledge that was not denominationally specific made sense. Only after the intervening half century and more does the "Judeo-Christian" God invoked in the pledge seem less than broadly inclusive.[196]

At the time, Catholics and Protestants jockeyed for the right to claim that they provided the key support for amending the pledge. The Knights of Columbus, the largest Catholic fraternal organization in the United States, claimed they were first.[197] Supreme Knight Luke Hart was a dedicated anticommunist; the Knights adopted a resolution to amend the pledge in 1951.[198] A bill was introduced to Congress in 1953 by Representative Louis Rabaut of Michigan, a Catholic and a Democrat, who said that the new language would conform to the true America that was "born under God, and only under God will it live as a citadel of freedom."[199]

The resolution drew popular support but was ignored in Congress until the Reverend George Docherty preached a sermon on February 7, 1954. As the pastor of New York Avenue Presbyterian Church in Washington, his congregation often included the president and Mrs. Eisenhower, who sat in the Lincoln pew. The Scottish-born minister spoke on the "American Way of Life," which he said Lincoln himself had understood was dedicated to a new birth of freedom "under God." Like Lincoln when he faced the great war against slavery, Docherty said, Americans in 1954 were engaged in a momentous conflict. This time, however, it was a "theological war" of political democracy against communism, which had already enslaved 800 million people around the globe. "To omit the words 'Under God' in the Pledge of Allegiance," said Docherty, "is to omit the definitive character of the American Way of Life" and undermine the battle against Communist enslavement. Such an acknowledgment of God would be inclusive rather than sectarian, Docherty stressed. It would include "the great Jewish Community, and the people of the Moslem faith, and the myriad of denominations of Christians in the land."[200]

Eisenhower reportedly told Docherty that he agreed with his sermon "entirely."[201] Other Presbyterians lined up as well. Soon Episcopalians in Congress wanted in. Disagreements came not over the substance of the amendment, but over who should get the most credit. Even so, the resolution could well have languished had the public not been so galvanized that their support could not be ignored. One House member received between two thousand and three thousand pieces of mail from constituents in support of the amendment, far outnumbering his mail on any other subject.[202] After some posturing in Congress, the resolution passed overwhelmingly, and Americans had new spiritual support in their opposition to communism.

The Reverend Docherty called the great religious revival and boom in church building after World War II "the golden age."[203] Yet it was also an anxious age. As Justice Jackson put it in an opinion upholding the conviction of an American Communist, the country had embarked on a "never-ending, because never successful, quest" for a reliable means of protecting the United States against totalitarianism—first fascism, then communism.[204] This quest animated religious as well as legal and political actors, drawing them together as allies in the defense of American freedom.

Eisenhower crystallized the template for this defense: the spirit of the law would be memorialized in the pledge. Religious liberty as a lived experience as well as an aspiration led Eisenhower and many others like him to equate American democracy first with belief, and then with religious diversity. "The things that make us proud to be American are of the soul and of the spirit," Eisenhower said. He and other Americans embraced religious pluralism to explain the resilience of American democracy and to provide a bulwark against future erosion. The lessons of the value of pluralism were written in the *Barnette* opinion, the amended Pledge of Allegiance, and the flourishing of religious commitments (and organizations) in the postwar era. Yet the limits of this pluralism were apparent almost immediately.

For one thing, the equation between belief and human freedom grew in political resonance as its foundation in specific religious tenets became more tenuous. By midcentury, Americans broadly believed that religious commitments were good things, and that a (relatively) wide swath of religious witness and belief was the lifeblood of a healthy democracy. But this rough consensus did not entail a fully fledged commitment to respect for religious difference. Instead, it reflected the conviction that respect for the three great religious traditions of American history and contemporary life—which included Protestants, Catholics, and Jews—was essential to successfully resisting and combating totalitarian incursions.[205] Provided that no one religion was singled out for special approval, went the argument, the deployment of religion by government (and the dependence of government on religion for validity) was fully consistent with democratic freedoms. The new language in the pledge, for example, was widely viewed as descriptive of the character of the country, rather than an affirmation of a particular belief. As one congressman put it, "The phrase 'under God' is inclusive for all religions" and thus offensive to none.[206]

By the 1950s, the "American Way" was anchored firmly to the three great religious groups in America.[207] Jehovah's Witnesses, the Federal Council of Churches, FDR, and the Reverend John Haynes Holmes had taught the country how to cherish religious commitments by exempting those with conscientious scruples from saluting the flag. The Knights of Columbus, the National Council of Churches, President Eisenhower, and the Reverend George Docherty applied the lesson back to the pledge itself by inserting the words "under God," believing that it reflected how religion was cherished *here* (in America) in contrast to *there* (in Russia), where obliteration of precious liberties was the rule.

It was a nice theory. It validated at least some kinds of constitutional protection for believers and gave religious freedom a central role in legitimating the modern American state, a new powerhouse but one that rested on tried-and-true faith. The theory also unified and updated the liberalism that motivated the Federal Council of Churches during the Depression. Now, after World War II, religious beliefs became the guardian of the national conscience in prosperous times. Eisenhower's own complex and changeable religious life imbued him with a sense that many other Americans shared; he was humble, simple, patriotic, and devout. He was also genuinely welcoming to all in the "Judeo-Christian tradition."[208] This combination remade the American identity in the postwar years, creating a powerful alloy that brought individual faith into a new relationship with national unity. Building on and deepening the unity-through-diversity formula that underlay the flag salute decisions, the amended pledge (so said its supporters) was designed to express the religious convictions of all Americans.

But the theory also created yawning problems and vulnerabilities, as the next half century demonstrated. Religious life in the early 1950s was less predictable, and certainly less stable, than such a theory presumed. In part this was because American religion was much less knowable than the Reverend Docherty or FDR or many other investors in the theory understood. In part it was because believers' own claims for protection would generate enormous legal change—and additional controversy. Tolerance and respect between and for believers had been assumed but were never realized. Courts became "the arena for debating" issues of religion, government, and pluralism, much to the chagrin of Justice Frankfurter.[209] Law, religion, and tolerance may have been reconfigured in the high-toned rhetoric of consensus and unity through diversity, but older and still vigorous notions of difference and sectarian strife also coursed through the new channels of constitutional law. Catholics and Protestants, in particular, rushed in to test the new world.

CHAPTER 3

The Almighty and the Dollar

Protestants, Catholics, and Sectarianism, 1940–1965

The invocation of a new constitutional world stirred up old enmities. Would the new landscape revolutionize the relationships that had existed between governments and religious folk before? Perhaps. Certainly, liberal jurisprudes and their counterparts in liberal religious organizations hoped so. Themes of tolerance and goodwill, and inclusion rather than exclusion, dominated constitutional and religious language among the liberal elites in the wake of the flag salute cases.[1] On the ground, however, older conflicts among believers acquired added importance as their constitutional dimensions became apparent. The presence or absence of religion could now make an enormous difference, as Jehovah's Witness schoolchildren and their parents had learned. But how to figure out what counts as religion, and what to do about it, have been difficult and persistent questions in constitutional law. The extraordinary complexity of these questions was apparent early on, when long-standing disputes between religious traditions were translated into competing constitutional claims.

As Americans adjusted to the new constitutional terrain they had built during World War II, they fought often about money: for the first time, government support at the national level for schools seemed inevitable. The new regime in law meant that debates over school funding at every level now acquired a constitutional aura. Many Catholics and Protestants lined up on opposing sides. Old grievances acquired sharp new edges in these battles over money and constitutional meaning. Catholics and Protestants vied to claim the mantle of patriotism and liberty, and painted those on the other side as traitors. The prospect of funding raised the temperature of the doctrinaire on each side of the divide. In the end Catholics and Protestants both lost big, but while the battle was hot, goodwill flew out the window. In its place, constitutional litigation and vituperation stirred mutual mistrust.

Catholic leaders promised they wanted "just enough money" from the state and federal governments "to make the Catholic school an integral part of American education." Only then, they said, would a "truly democratic state" respect the choices of Catholic parents. Protestant opponents countered that aid to Catholic schools was "a departure from the American principles of the separation of church and state."[2] The result, they claimed, would be a "serious threat to our public educational system which is the bulwark of democracy."[3] Catholic leaders replied that this talk exemplified "anti-democratic notions" and denied Catholic schoolchildren the best education possible.[4] And so the issue was framed initially as a question of democratic principle and constitutional values by both sides of a religious divide. The Constitution and its interpretation took center stage as political debates shifted to legal conflict.

Debates over religious and secular education in the postwar years reveal that public schools were challenged for inculcating religion long before school prayer became a hot-button issue in the early 1960s. There were significant ties in many areas between public schools and Catholic educators. These relationships generally were based on mutual interest and local decision making. Many local officials and educators relied on Catholic priests and women religious to staff public schools. Often, they used church buildings as public elementary and secondary schools in the 1940s and 1950s. At the same time, Supreme Court decisions in those decades assumed that there were sharp distinctions between religious and secular education.

Given the ways that local educators cooperated with Catholic thinkers and Catholic schools, these distinctions were more theoretical than real in many jurisdictions. Especially between 1925 and 1950, cooperative arrangements proliferated. By 1948, according to a National Catholic Welfare Conference survey, there were at least 324 "Catholic-public" schools and most likely 340 or more.[5] The new constitutional world drew attention to such cooperative arrangements. Thanks to heightened interest and scrutiny across the country, the establishment clause dominated debates about religion and publicly funded education.

The first Supreme Court case to address the relationship between public funding and religious education was so controversial that it sparked the formation of a group dedicated to overturning the result. The case and the enduring controversy that followed pitted Catholics against Protestants as they wrestled over the shape of the new constitutional world. Given the importance of Jews and Jewish organizations to the law of religion in the 1960s and beyond, these first conflicts are remarkable for their relative lack of Jewish voices. Instead, the legal battles of the late 1940s through the early 1960s were a precursor to—even an incubator for—the development of new ecumenical communities of interested legal actors in the late 1960s and beyond. In the beginning, however, the combatants in the wars over school funding were divided Christians, particularly conservative Catholics and Protestants, each convinced that their own vision of education was the only valid and sustainable one for American schoolchildren. Their battles were fought out in courts and through threats of litigation as the power of the Constitution drew opposing religious actors to the law. In the early years, Catholics won significant victories. But Protestants soon turned to the cooperative arrangements between public officials and parochial education.

By the late 1940s, Protestant opponents had discovered and begun to publicize the quiet, often informal practice of having schools that were Catholic and also public. The line between religious and secular education became a crucial one: public funding flowed without restriction to secular schools, but religious training was a different matter. Disentangling religious from secular education required courts to decide what belonged in which category, a process that was contested in courtrooms and around negotiating tables across the country. Although today we think that we know the difference between public and parochial schools, sixty years ago the lines were more permeable. In classrooms nationwide, religious practice came under new constitutional scrutiny. As one former student reports, he remembers vividly the day in the 1950s when his school, St. Elmo's School in Travis County, Texas, announced that all crosses and religious statuary were to be removed immediately.[6]

Like many thousands of schoolchildren across the country, this student and his schoolmates were now inhabitants of new legal terrain. The key battles were conducted in lower courts and have been all but forgotten, even though they were vitally important to establishment-clause theory and practice on the ground. In this formative era, "captive schools" like St. Elmo's became central to both sides in conflicts over parochial-school funding.

Skirmishes between Catholics and Protestants were nothing new in the late 1940s, but this one took place in a changed constitutional climate. Now, the financial power of the national government combined with the Supreme Court's power to interpret the Constitution, drew litigants like moths to a flame. The conflict over funding did not involve all Catholics or all Protestants. In some ways, those who took the lead harkened back to a more traditional Catholic-Protestant divide. Similar battles had been fought by Americans from the earliest days of the settlement of the United States and in earlier constitutional landscapes, and had even grown violent in patches, especially in the nineteenth century.[7] From one perspective, the mid-twentieth-century conflict was the last big gasp of a long-standing mistrust and suspicion between the most doctrinaire on both sides. More important to twentieth-century religion and law, however, this conflict produced new inquiries into how and where "sectarianism" had invaded public schools.

At the same time, the cold war and Soviet atheism meant that both Catholics and Protestants had a stake not only in education but also in claiming that their strategy was the surest defense against communism. The Constitution provided the connective link between education and anticommunism. Religious liberty in the new era meant that constitutional law would decide the outcome of conflicts between Protestants and Catholics. Law was everywhere in the powerful postwar state; to navigate this behemoth required new tactics and knowledge. The new field of conflict also required new weapons; the language tended to be legal and constitutional as well as theological and cultural, and strategies were set by litigants and their lawyers. The story is not one of secularists versus sectarians but rather one of dedicated believers on both sides.[8]

In 1947, the Supreme Court decided a landmark case involving state support for religious education. *Everson v. Board of Education* applied the federal establishment clause to the states for the first time, once again requiring all jurisdictions to conform to national standards, even though the standards themselves had not yet been fleshed out.[9] Now every state would be bound by the injunction that had originally been directed to Congress, requiring all governments "to enact no law respecting an establishment of religion." Such is the way of constitutional worlds, which are built not by planners and engineers but from the ground up by litigants and by judges reacting to the conflicts that come before them. The Supreme Court has considerable discretion in deciding whether to take a given appeal, but for most courts, most of the time, litigants control the docket.

The new constitutional regime, of course, raised more questions than it answered. What would the establishment clause mean for an environment where states traditionally had policed the boundaries between religion and government? The Supreme Court's opinion in the *Everson* case is known for its extensive discussion of the history of church and state, an (unsuccessful) attempt to ground the new landscape in early national language and law.[10]

Like many other Americans, the local participants in *Everson* cared more about the result than the niceties of "incorporation" or the Court's history lesson. Their story begins with a lawsuit that challenged state funding for parochial school transportation in New Jersey. Plaintiff Arch Everson was the vice president of the New Jersey Taxpayers Association. He and his circle were among the "Clean Republican" opponents of Democratic Jersey City mayor Frank Hague's political machine.[11] There were other political machines in the twentieth century, but Hague's was especially brazen. In 1940, when the New Jersey legislature debated funding for parochial schools, Hague controlled much of the state through party patronage. There were Hague cops, Hague judges, and Hague governors.[12] His vast network included schools, churches, police departments, and more. Biographers, like his contemporaries, referred to him as "the Boss."[13] Hague himself famously remarked, "I am the law."[14]

Everyone in Jersey City, which was 75 percent Roman Catholic in 1940, also knew that Frank Hague was a loyal son of the church. He donated an altar to St. Aedan's Church that cost a staggering $50,000. He raised many times that amount for Catholic charities, which were supported not only by Hague's Catholic followers but also by Jewish and Protestant members of the Hague machine, who were ordered to sign contribution pledges: the mayor himself collected overdue payments.[15] Hague frequently accused opponents of parochial-school funding of being anti-Catholic, stoking ethnic-religious loyalties and prejudices.[16]

In the late 1930s, Hague and his opponents sparred over public funding for busing to Catholic schools. Eventually their battle drew national attention to the relationship between local government and religious organizations, especially the Catholic Church. The beginning of the fight was colored by the currents that guided New Jersey's brass-knuckle politics. The Knights of Columbus, the Catholic Daughters of America, Monsignor Ralph Glover of Newark, the Newark and Jersey City newspapers, the "Hague Republicans," and others supported Hague's Parochial School Bus Bill.[17] The bill directed school districts to provide transportation to all New Jersey schoolchildren "living remote from the schoolhouse."[18] Because almost all private schoolchildren in the state attended Catholic parochial schools, the bill meant that parochial schools would have state-funded transportation for their students. The legislation passed easily, no surprise to Hague watchers.

The opposition, in addition to organizations such as the New Jersey Taxpayers Association, the League of Women Voters, the Seventh-day Adventists, the American Association of University Women, and others, included two obscure fraternal groups that formed a counterweight to the Knights of Columbus: the Junior Order United American Mechanics (JOUAM) and the Patriotic Order of Sons of America. The former had connections to the Ku Klux Klan as late as the 1920s. The latter was active in the (often violent) movement for enforced rituals of patriotism that saw the Jehovah's Witnesses as dangerous enemies in the 1930s and early 1940s.[19] In debates over the Parochial School Bus Bill, the Knights of Columbus and these "patriotic" supporters of public schools clashed repeatedly, each accusing the other of betraying American ideals.[20]

Battles over funding for parochial schools occurred around the country in the late 1930s and early 1940s. By 1938, free transportation was provided to Catholic students in thirteen states.[21] Although most state constitutions contained provisions prohibiting state funding for "sectarian religious organizations," language that clearly targeted Catholic parochial education, growing pressure for support resulted in new forms of aid.[22] Increased tax burdens to support public schools in the 1930s fell on Catholics and non-Catholics alike. Even opponents of aid for parochial schools acknowledged that "the Catholic[s] must pay an enormous bounty to protect [their] children from the secular influence of the public school," because they paid school taxes like other residents but generally did not use public education.[23] Lawsuits challenging state-supplied benefits to Catholic schools—including textbooks, teachers' salaries, and health care for students and teachers—appeared in state courts with increasing regularity. Courts divided over the constitutionality of the various aid programs, but most held that free public busing for parochial-school students violated state establishment clauses or other constitutional provisions.[24]

By 1941, when New Jersey's Parochial School Bus Bill became law, the U.S. Supreme Court had twice dodged the question of whether such assistance violated the Establishment Clause.[25] One of those decisions denied a challenge to a Louisiana statute that gave nonsectarian textbooks to all school students.[26] The Court relied on the theory that such a policy benefited individual schoolchildren rather than any particular institution, even though private-school students in Louisiana overwhelmingly attended Catholic schools.[27] This approach became known as the "child-benefit theory." If the direct beneficiary of state aid was a schoolchild, the theory went, then the sectarian institutions, such as parochial schools, were being helped only indirectly, which was allowed.

Into this maelstrom fell Arch Everson's lawsuit. It began peacefully enough, which suggests that the Ewing Township School Board welcomed the opportunity to fight back against state-imposed tax burdens. The desire to expand educational opportunities for public school students beyond the traditional cut-off point at eighth grade had prompted town leaders to send students to high schools in nearby Trenton.[28] Beginning in 1941, the cost of transportation for students attending parochial schools was added to the responsibilities of Ewing's taxpayers.[29] All of the students involved attended Catholic schools.

The lawyer who represented Everson had appeared before the New Jersey legislature for both the Junior Order United American Mechanics and the Patriotic Order of Sons of America to oppose the school busing bill.[30] Indeed, the Junior Order sponsored and paid for Everson's suit, and Everson himself was reputed to be a member of the organization.[31] On the other side, the Catholic Church "assisted" the school board in its legal defense of the busing statute.[32]

The case was decided without trial; none of the essential facts was in dispute. A divided three-judge state supreme court (then a trial court) held that the Parochial School Bus Bill violated New Jersey's constitutional mandate that no funds set aside for public education could be used "for any other purpose, under any pretense whatever."[33] Justices Charles Parker and Joseph Perskie wrote that the provision was "designed as an insurmountable barrier to giving free state aid, and to donations to private or *sectarian* schools, and should be rigidly enforced."[34] In dissent, Justice Harry Helier relied on the Supreme Court's child-benefit theory, which had guided a few majority opinions (and several dissents) in other state courts.[35]

After some hesitation, the school board authorized an appeal.[36] In the Court of Errors and Appeals (as New Jersey's highest court was then called), a six-to-three majority held that it could not presume that the state's funds had been spent unconstitutionally. The state was obligated to pay only 75 percent of the costs of transportation. The funds for the transportation of the Catholic school students, the majority reasoned, may have come from the 25 percent raised by local taxation.[37]

The three dissenters dismissed this line of reasoning with understandable contempt. The dissenters instead tackled the serious argument that had been debated in the parties' briefs and in other state courts, but elided by the majority. The child-benefit theory, contended the dissenters, suffered from "vagueness and the impossibility of satisfactorily distinguishing one item of expense from another in the long process of child education." As a result, they said, "There is no logical stopping point."[38] Anything from cafeterias to health care to sports fell within the bounds of a "benefit" to the child. The theory was just "an ingenious effort to escape constitutional limitations rather than a sound construction of their content and purpose."[39]

The weak majority opinion and the corrupt New Jersey political and judicial system that colored the result might have tempted the U.S. Supreme Court to reverse outright. Yet the Court reached beyond the case's tawdry history and engaged the debate between state courts on the child-benefit theory. At the hands of Justice Hugo Black, the theory roared back to life.[40]

Justice Black commanded a bare majority of the Court, and his opinion in *Everson* has long been an object of criticism, even derision. In key respects, he focused on children: "It is much too late," Black declared, "to argue that legislation intended to facilitate the opportunity of children to get a secular education serves no public purpose."[41] Education must be available to all children, Justice Black cautioned, and the Supreme Court should "be careful, in protecting the citizens of New Jersey against state-established churches, to be sure that we do not inadvertently prohibit New Jersey from extending its general state law benefits to all its citizens without regard to their religious belief." To exclude some children *"because of their faith, or lack of it"* would breach the command to separate church and state just as surely as would the financial "support of an institution which teaches the tenets and faith of any church." The reimbursement of transportation costs, he said, extended a general and purely secular benefit to all schoolchildren.[42] In this opinion, as in the flag salute case decided only a few years earlier, the justices showed a keen interest in the flourishing of children, regardless of their parents' religion.[43]

The emphasis on secular education in parochial schools, rather than on their inculcation of religious belief, was central to the briefs that supported the township's position, especially the one written by the National Catholic Welfare Conference and submitted jointly by the National Council of Catholic Men and the National Council of Catholic Women. In their brief they labored to distinguish between secular education and religious worship, arguing that "[a] school does not lose the character of a school by virtue of [also] teaching moral principle and religious truth."[44] They embraced the metaphor drawn from Thomas Jefferson, that the First Amendment created a "wall of separation" between religion and government. In their reading, a holding that the Parochial School Bus Bill violated the Constitution would "wall off some citizens from participation in ordinary educational benefits decreed by the State."[45]

The *Everson* Court accepted this distinction between a valid benefit directed to pupils of all schools and an unconstitutional benefit that would "aid one religion, aid all religions, or prefer one religion over another."[46] Such aid would cross the "high and impregnable" wall between church and state, which must not be subject to "the slightest breach."[47] Justice Black also claimed to have found a limiting principle for the child-benefit theory. Constitutional history, Justice Black emphasized, clearly indicated what the Framers intended. Invoking Thomas Jefferson as a source for understanding the constitutional text, Justice Black drew on the legacy of Virginia as the template for a nationally applied establishment clause.[48] Thomas Jefferson occupied a foundational place in the history of disestablishment in Virginia and in the movement that supported the addition of the Bill of Rights to the Constitution.[49] By 1947, when *Everson* was decided, admiration of Jefferson had been cultivated anew with the opening of the Jefferson Memorial in 1943. Just as important, Black connected Old World ways and ideas with the spread of totalitarianism. In America, he stressed, religious liberty and democracy were dependent on the separation of church and state.[50] Catholics as well as Protestants were entitled to the benefits of religious liberty.

Catholicism of the European sort, to be sure, Justice Black did not embrace. His opinion dripped with disdain for a Europe in which "Catholics had persecuted Protestants, Protestants had persecuted Catholics, Protestant sects had persecuted other Protestant sects, Catholics of one shade of belief had persecuted Catholics of another shade of belief, and all of these had from time to time persecuted Jews."[51] Indeed, Justice Black distrusted the church and its power, and promised privately that *Everson* would not open the floodgates for aid to parochial schools.[52] In recent years, scholars in favor of greater government support for Catholic institutions have argued that "the main thrust" of the opinion actually limited aid to parochial schools, or even that "Black . . . understood what he was doing" and deceived Catholics into thinking that they had won a lasting victory.[53]

At the time, however, the criticism flowed from the other direction. The amicus brief submitted by the American Civil Liberties Union

(ACLU) argued that the "better-reasoned" view was that there was no coherence or stability to the child-benefit theory.[54] The dissenters in *Everson* agreed, and hammered away at an opinion that stressed the separation of church and state and then sustained a tax to aid parochial school students. Justice Robert Jackson was the most explicit: "Catholic education is the rock on which the whole structure rests, and to render tax aid to its Church school is indistinguishable to me from rendering the same aid to the Church itself."[55] Justice Wiley Rutledge predicted that *Everson* would be "corrosive."[56] James Madison, he maintained, "opposed every form and degree of official relation between religion and civil authority," not just those that granted a direct benefit.[57] Even "three pence" was too much for a people dedicated to the perfect insulation of religion from government, and vice versa.[58]

Newspaper coverage of the decision was extensive, and scholars quickly weighed in.[59] Columbia University professor John Childs accused the Court of "weakening" American democracy.[60] As others joined in, *Everson* became the most controversial Supreme Court decision in years. Within weeks, many had memorialized their contempt for Justice Black and his analysis. A piece in the *Harvard Law Review* called the majority opinion "a failure."[61] Justice Black himself received telegrams and even hate mail decrying the decision.[62] The first major establishment clause case, like *Gobitis,* the first major free exercise decision, was broadly unpopular.

Everson is important not only because it completed the incorporation of the religion clauses, however. It also deepened and reshaped the battle over sectarianism, education, and money. The idea that the Constitution protected even schoolchildren in the places where they learned about their government and its power opened new avenues for arguments. New combatants as well as veterans of old conflicts charged to the fresh field of combat. After *Everson,* litigants in lower courts fought with each other over how to distinguish religious from secular education. Captive-school cases reveal a little-known history of confusion at the local level about what means could be deployed to ensure all children received an education.[63] Much of the real work of disestablishment in the first fifteen years after *Everson* was in disentangling these existing relationships. Captive schools blurred lines between public and parochial schools; the process of forcibly redrawing the boundaries across the 1950s suggests that we have misunderstood how quickly and dynamically the new constitutional world affected education around the country. The landscape was recrafted locally and interstitially rather than by Supreme Court fiat. Captive-school lawsuits (and threats of litigation) produced rapid and widespread change on the ground.

These conflicts drew support not from the interfaith organizations and ecumenical spirit that animated arguments for exemptions for Jehovah's Witness schoolchildren. Instead, the divisions were sectarian. Protestants used the new national vocabulary of disestablishment to sharpen and target the attack. They claimed that Catholic schools (and by extension all Catholics) did not believe in separation of church and state; thus they were "un-American." Catholics in their turn charged their Protestant opponents were agents of secularism and intolerance—equally devastating "un-American" vices.

The *Everson* decision disturbed an influential group of Protestants. In the late 1930s and across the 1940s, many Protestant leaders tailored their traditional critique of the Catholic Church to suit what they believed to be a new era in church strategy. There were many sources of friction, especially as Protestant leaders sensed that Catholics had gained confidence and popular support during World War II. They condemned the Catholic Church for supporting General Francisco Franco in the Spanish Civil War. They also spotlighted fascist tendencies among Catholics at home, especially Father Charles Coughlin, whose thinly veiled anti-Semitism led him to embrace the infamous *Protocols of the Elders of Zion* and to encourage the thugs known as the "Christian Front" during the 1930s.[64] Protestants also criticized President Franklin Roosevelt's unprecedented decision to send a "personal representative" to the Vatican.[65] They implied that the Catholic Church's virulent anticommunism was a shield for church officials such as Archbishop Aloysius Stepinac, who was accused of collaborating with Nazis in Croatia and forcibly converting thousands of Serb Muslims.[66] They bitterly opposed the aggressive Cardinal Francis Spellman of New York, and they sparred with church spokesmen and defenders about the real motives of the Catholic Church and its designs on American government.[67]

Most of all, these Protestants obsessed about sectarianism and the possibility that Catholic schools might benefit from new funding. The obsession became urgent in late 1946 and early 1947, as Congress debated a bill to provide grants to the states for education. Federal support had been proposed before but had never passed.[68] This time, Protestant leaders and educators, including Harvard University president James Bryant Conant, openly declared their opposition to the parochial-school system as a "threat to our democratic unity."[69] In 1947, Professor Childs of Columbia accused the Catholic Church of blocking federal aid because church leaders knew that many state constitutions (including New Jersey's) would prevent the diversion of federal dollars to parochial schools.[70] Only the exclusive support of public schools, argued Professor Childs, would prevent "serious religious cleavages [that would] divide and embitter the American people."[71] Two years after the end of a war that featured the horrific slaughter of religious minorities, such allusions resonated along jangled nerves.

The *Everson* decision fell plumb into these squabbles between Protestant and Catholic leaders. The case and its constitutional grounding emboldened Catholic spokesmen. Protestants, they now charged, created a "smoke screen for secularism" and "bigotry" when they argued that the Constitution was an obstacle to "school buses or emergency school subsidies or any other democratic aids to education."[72] Catholic educators explained that they wanted funding only to maintain religious liberty and constitutional balance, and to prevent "discrimination" against Catholic parents.[73] Thanks to *Everson*, Catholic leaders could invoke the Supreme Court to support their position. Cardinal Spellman charged that even raising the question of funding for parochial schools after *Everson* was evidence that "our nation which prides itself before the whole world as an exemplar of fair play and tolerance" still shielded "bigotry . . . [that eats] into the [country's] vital organs."[74]

Alarm bells sounded in Protestant quarters. An influential group of Protestant theorists and educators, including John Dewey and Louie Newton, wrote to the *New York Times*. They declared that the country was "troubled" by the threat to "our historic American doctrine of the separation of church and state." The Court's decision in *Everson*, they lamented, "feeds fuel to the flame."[75] In Washington, New York, and Chicago, Protestant leaders met to discuss how to revive their separationist vision. For a century, American Protestants had congratulated themselves on having "solved" the vexing problem of religion and government. Nineteenth-century treatises on religion and government had stressed that "uncoerced liberty" of belief married personal freedom of religion to other American virtues like democracy, patriotism, and equality.[76] By consigning conscience to a private space, argued the Reverend Jesse Peck, the United States embodied a "living justice" that emancipated Americans "from the fetters of priest-craft."[77] For much of American history, "priestcraft" meant Roman Catholicism, tout court. By the mid-twentieth century, many Protestant scholars identified Protestantism with religious tolerance and American freedom; Catholicism, in contrast, was sectarian and authoritarian.[78] They protested that they were by no means anti-Catholic, but that the recent attempts of church minions to undermine sacred American principles simply could not go unanswered.

These newly politicized Protestants, many of whom were ordained and active within their own denominations and in pan-Protestant groups, met several times in 1947. The original group included Episcopalians, Presbyterians, Methodists, Quakers, Baptists, Seventh-day Adventists, Lutherans, and Christian Scientists. There was also a sprinkling of concerned politicians, educators, and lawyers, as well as a delegation from the Scottish Rite Masons.[79] Charles Clayton Morrison, editor of the Protestant magazine *The Christian Century*, drafted a "Manifesto" for a national "action agency"; the group chose the unwieldy name Protestants and Other Americans United for Separation of Church and State (POAU).[80] POAU's first president was Edwin McNeill Poteat, dean of the Colgate-Rochester Divinity School. John Mackay, president of the Princeton Theological Seminary, served as the first vice president. The board included Morrison, Methodist bishop Bromley Oxnam, the head of the National Education Association, and other prominent Protestant ministers and businessmen. At long last, they congratulated themselves, they had begun to fight back against sectarianism.[81]

However separatist, POAU was still a religious organization. It was formed and maintained with what POAU believed was a genuinely Protestant goal: the separation of church and state. Although its members rigorously opposed sectarianism, which they associated primarily with Catholicism, POAU's view should not be confused with the secularism of the ACLU of the same era. As the founders of POAU put it, their mission was to protect and defend "religious liberty as this monumental principle of democracy has been embodied and implemented in the Constitution by the separation of church and state."[82]

"Free" religion, in this sense, was carved out by Protestants who opposed what they considered to be a monolithic Catholic hierarchy, but they did not consider themselves to be engaging in sectarianism. Theirs was a mission of goodwill, they claimed. It was based in a pan-Protestant ideal that avoided the rituals or dogmas of a particular "sect." Thus, it is vital to distinguish the advocacy of separation that animated POAU in its first decades from true secularism. The group's publications carefully explained that separationism and godlessness were entirely distinct. The organization's newsletter stressed that separation of church and state ensured "goodwill among the sects" but by no means undermined "public recognition of God, our dependence on His bounty, or our duty to follow His will."[83] In this view, the goal of separation was not antireligious; it was antisectarian.

Early in 1948, newspapers across the country published POAU's Manifesto, which declared a great political awakening among Protestants. They argued that religious liberty was imperiled not just by a "powerful church, unaccustomed in its own history and tradition to the American ideal of separation of church and state," but also by national and state governments, including the Supreme Court.[84] Sectarianism was the real enemy, in this view. POAU and its followers drew on deeply ingrained notions from the old constitutional world, in which admiration for religious liberty coexisted comfortably with Protestant disdain for Catholic institutions and practices.

Yet the Manifesto and the founding of POAU were also conditioned by changes in law that had destabilized the Protestants' sense of their place in America. For the first time, government itself had become a problem, and at the highest as well as local levels. Public officials were all too likely to succumb "weakly" to "political pressure" to fund parochial schools, claimed the Manifesto. State legislatures had already buckled. Worst of all, the Supreme Court had betrayed fundamental constitutional principles. The Manifesto quoted the four dissenters in the *Everson* case, predicting ominously that each breach in the wall of separation would bring on "still others . . . we may be sure."[85]

The authors of the Manifesto conceded that "the free churches of America have been slow in recognizing the gravity of the situation that was developing before their eyes."[86] Now, however, they saw clearly that "the effect of the first amendment is to invest the makers and administrators of our laws with the ultimate guardianship of religious liberty and religious tolerance."[87] In their eyes, the new constitutional world was a dangerous place, where "free" religion needed powerful champions. They promised to make officials in Washington feel their presence, as well as "to invoke the aid of the courts in maintaining the integrity of the Constitution." If they were not successful in purging the government of "entanglement [with] a particular church," they promised, "shameful religious resentment and conflict . . . will inevitably ensue."[88]

The Catholic Church fought back. The *New York Times* printed a statement issued from Cardinal Spellman's office, charging that POAU was tainted by "bigotry."[89] Far better to battle the "godlessness which is tearing away the very roots of our American political and social institutions," and to combat the Communist influence that such secularism implied, than to quibble over lunch money for "undernourished parochial school children."[90] Other Catholic leaders called the organization procommunist.[91] Some Protestants joined them, cautioning that secularism might hide behind the group's ostensibly religious veneer.[92]

POAU founder Bromley Oxnam countered that Catholics were ruled by "authoritarian and autocratic" leaders. Protestants, he said, were "organized around democratic principles." These differing "cultural traditions" meant that Catholics could not understand "our insistence that power corrupts, and that it will corrupt a church as well as a state, that it will corrupt a bishop as well as a business man."[93] Baptists, Methodists, public school educators, and others rallied to POAU's call. Letters to newspaper editors poured in; speeches and sermons at church meetings and school boards were inflected with a new constitutional language of religious liberty and disestablishment. But vitriolic confrontations with Catholic leaders in the press, however stimulating, were not a positive program for the new organization. Nor did POAU have any real home, or even a permanent staff. Instead it had one room, on temporary loan in the Baptist Joint Committee headquarters in Washington, and a fundraising goal of $100,000. POAU members burned with conviction, but they were rudderless.[94]

They were sustained temporarily by an apparent victory. Just one year after *Everson,* the Court spoke again.[95] This time an eight-to-one majority, again in an opinion written by Justice Black, held that religious instruction in public school classrooms violated the establishment clause. *McCollum v. Board of Education* distinguished *Everson* on the ground that "the State's compulsory public school machinery" and its property were being used "for the dissemination of religious doctrines."[96] Parents could send their children to parochial schools, Justice Black stressed, but they could not bring parochial education into public schools.

Although *McCollum* built on the groundwork laid by *Everson,* it involved a fundamentally different equation. This time, the question was the importation of religious training into public education. The blending of religious instruction and public schools, however, was far more common than even POAU leaders had guessed. And while the Supreme Court had spoken twice, POAU had many more questions and concerns about sectarianism and education.

Protestants and Other Americans United needed a leader. Dr. Charl Williams of the National Education Association, a founding member of POAU, suggested that Glenn Archer of Kansas might be available. Indeed he was. Archer was a recent graduate of the Washburn Municipal University Law College, a small institution in Topeka. Before law school Archer had been a school administrator, Republican Party loyalist, and aide to Alf Landon in several campaigns, including Landon's 1936 run for president. He had also served briefly as a Washington lobbyist for the National Education Association.[97] There he caught Williams's eye and cultivated a taste for the corridors of power: "I was able to go up on the hill and talk to almost any Congressman or any Senator because my name was familiar," he wrote, "I had been to the White House, my name was in the *Post.*"[98]

POAU founder J. M. Dawson, a Baptist, assured Archer that God had called him to POAU and would bless him for accepting the vocation. Archer, who had once considered becoming a Protestant missionary, decided that running POAU would satisfy his religious leanings as well as his professional ambition. The Catholic priest in Archer's hometown canceled the church's contract with the family lumber business when he learned of Archer's new job. Still seething with anger thirty years later, Archer wrote in his memoir that Father Keogan preached against him "before [his] employees, tenants, and relatives, as a stooge of Joe Stalin, working against God and country."[99] Archer was now a true believer. As the director of POAU, he combined his own deep religious commitments and public relations skills with his new legal training. Over time, he developed techniques that drew attention to POAU's campaign against sectarianism. He gave speeches around the country, urging his audiences to form POAU chapters, and to contact his Washington office with stories of Catholic influence in their public schools.[100]

In the pre–Vatican II era, POAU exploited well-worn charges of Catholic authoritarianism and priestcraft to good effect among the intelligentsia as well as in rural church halls. Paul Blanshard joined the cause. Blanshard, a union activist, editor, lawyer, ordained Congregationalist minister, and author of the best-selling book *American Freedom and Catholic Power* (1949), went with Archer on marathon lecture tours in Florida and the Midwest.[101] He too was a bitter foe of the Catholic Church. Blanshard advised Archer on legal strategy and continually stirred the pot by writing new books and touring the country.[102] He lent credibility to the organization; John Dewey, Bertrand Russell, and even Albert Einstein publicly admired Blanshard and his work.[103] A second book, *Communism, Democracy, and Catholic Power* (1951), argued that the Catholic Church was a natural vector for authoritarianism and thus incommensurate with democracy.[104] The book drew a review from the renowned Harvard historian Perry Miller. Although he conceded that Blanshard's style was "shrill, not to say strident," Miller agreed with Blanshard's central point: "[The Catholic Church pursues] a basic, a centuries-old and a calculated policy, which at heart is utterly and irreconcilably antagonistic to the democratic way of life."[105]

In Blanshard, Archer had found a mind that worked like his own; both men integrated their Christian faith and legal training with a flair for the dramatic.[106] They delighted in opposition from Catholic apologists. Scholars and prelates protested in vain that the church was not the inquisitorial behemoth described by Blanshard and Archer. POAU tactics were supported by *The Christian Century,* which denounced "timid Protestants who fear to have this issue brought into the open."[107]

Among other charges, Catholics called POAU "a reorganized Klan with a 'new look.'"[108] The white supremacist KKK embraced a virulent anti-Catholicism, along with separation of church and state and support for public schools. POAU supporters, however, distanced themselves from what they called "the Ku Klux and nativist level."[109] Indeed, Dawson of the Baptist Joint Committee had been an outspoken critic of racism and the Klan as early as 1916.[110] There is no record of Klan activity involving Archer, Blanshard, or any POAU founders. POAU defenders dismissed Catholics' invocation of "Ku-Kluxism" as a desperate attempt by the conspirators to tar their critics with their own tyrannical brush.[111]

Archer and other POAU officials were Masons, however.[112] Representatives of the Southern Jurisdiction of the Scottish Rite Masons were active in POAU's founding, and the Masons provided essential support in the organization's first year and beyond.[113] Well into the 1950s, Archer advised struggling local chapters to turn first to the Masons for financial assistance.[114] The group's affiliation with the Scottish Rite Masons might well have roused Catholic suspicion. Earlier in the century, the Masons had been instrumental in supporting Oregon legislation that required all children to attend public school. The Scottish Rite Masons, who were already committed to a campaign to limit Catholic attempts to "sap the strength of the common school," had been used by the Klan as a front in Oregon in the 1920s.[115] But the KKK was ultimately unsuccessful, despite the fact that the compulsory school referendum persuaded a majority of Oregon voters. In 1925, the Supreme Court held that the Oregon statute was unconstitutional, in *Pierce v. Society of Sisters,* a suit brought by the Society of the Sisters of the Holy Names of Jesus and Mary, which maintained Catholic schools as well as junior colleges and orphanages in the state. The Court held that "the child is not the mere creature of the State," and may not be forcibly "standardize[d]" by government.[116] This defeat was followed by others, yet the appeal of POAU demonstrated that distrust of the Catholic Church and its educational system remained widespread. Opponents of parochial schools had lost again—publicly and infuriatingly—in the *Everson* case.

Inevitably, POAU attracted those whose sympathies lay further out on the spectrum of anti-Catholicism. Two decades after *Pierce,* suspicion of "the Roman Monopoly" found new resonance as Blanshard and Archer argued that sectarianism should have no place in the new constitutional world.[117] None of POAU's leaders could honestly be charged with representing the KKK. Yet POAU's campaign against parochial-school funding appealed to sympathizers who might hesitate to utter aloud Klan-like sentiments, and POAU stepped neatly into the same legal space that Arch Everson and the Junior Order had filled in the *Everson* litigation.[118] Despite POAU's disclaimers, a whiff of bigotry hung in the air.

Individual POAU members and local chapters clustered in the South, with pockets of the organization spread across the Midwest and along the Pacific Coast.[119] Despite persistent efforts to build membership in New England, local Protestant groups resisted, telling POAU that its support would get in the way of negotiations to limit funding for parochial schools. POAU officials soon understood that the same sentiments that attracted political and religiously conservative Protestants also alienated many of the liberal leaders whose support had been crucial at its founding.[120] Some mainline Protestants quietly avoided POAU. Large ecumenical organizations that had been instrumental in the goodwill movement, such as the National Conference of Christians and Jews and the Federal Council of Churches, also kept their distance. They were concerned that POAU activities were often "an excuse to attack the Catholic Church," rather than a genuine effort to grapple with issues of church and state.[121]

Such charges eroded the credibility of POAU with some audiences, especially in areas where Protestants worked in goodwill organizations alongside Catholics. By the early 1950s, the Catholic Church itself had become more effective at outreach, and better at explaining how parochial education fit comfortably into American life and democratic values. Leading Jesuit theorist John Courtney Murray supported a liberal interpretation of Catholics' approach to the distinction between church and state.[122] Sociologist Will Herberg's influential 1955 book *Protestant-Catholic-Jew* announced to readers that "Protestant and Catholic and Jew stand united through their common anchorage in, and common allegiance to, the American Way of Life."[123] Herberg recognized Catholics as increasingly confident and reasonable. Jews, according to Herberg, were preoccupied with "public relations and appearances." Only Protestants, he said, were caught in a truly divisive and "paralyzing negativism" that could be traced to the "anti-Romanism" of Paul Blanshard and his allies at POAU.[124]

Herberg had good reason to celebrate such unity within diversity. For one thing, he was applying lessons that he had learned from his own interfaith experience. In 1935 the influential theologian Reinhold Niebuhr famously advised an intense young Will Herberg to search for spiritual meaning in his own Jewish tradition before converting to Christianity. Twenty years later, Herberg (then a well-known sociologist) translated the success of this formula into a landmark analysis of American society.[125] Herberg's *Protestant-Catholic-Jew* was a huge hit, and is quoted and relied upon to this day to explain how faith could flourish amid the change and mobility of the post–World War II era. It turned out, Herberg taught us, faith was portable in ways that national identity and even language were not. Religion survived in the new American climate, growing by leaps and bounds in a consumer age characterized by growth and mobility. Religious identity provided an anchor in the turbulence, peace of mind in a world of anxiety.

Herberg focused on how and why Americans had escaped the tribulations that tore Europe apart and then raised the Iron Curtain. He also provided a formula for future success: respect for belief would insulate Americans from the deadly forms of national pride that infected Hitler, Mussolini, and Stalin. But POAU and its allies were not convinced. They tapped into an older strain of antisectarianism to explain American liberty and strength.

Archer, Dawson, *The Christian Century,* and the southern Baptist and Methodist constituencies of POAU painted the world in unsophisticated black and white, charged liberal easterners. POAU's relentlessness galled those who found that the constant invocation of a repressive Catholic past got in the way of progressive interfaith strategies. A study conducted in the early 1960s concluded that POAU was an "organizational pariah," viewed with distaste by the organizations that had learned to get along with the Catholic Church.[126] Old divisions along religious lines, liberals suggested, were not appropriate boundary markers in the new constitutional world.

Despite this disdain, Archer and POAU congratulated themselves on many victories. Their appeal was significant, revealing that interfaith goodwill had formidable opponents. POAU in its first decades built on and even deepened such divisions. The group hammered home their claim that sectarianism crept into public schools under the tutelage of Catholics—especially priests and women religious—who exploited local officials and duped gullible parents. The effectiveness of this tactic was undeniable. Not only was POAU the best-funded and largest of all groups dedicated to the issue of church and state, but it also achieved notable success in its primary form of advocacy—captive-schools litigation. The bread and butter of the organization's legal strategy was distinctively its own.

Archer became a highly visible presence by the early 1950s, leading POAU brilliantly, if controversially. Captive-school cases were his calling card. In case after case, POAU charged that public schools had been "captured," and public coffers raided, by the Catholic Church. After two years on the job, Archer reported that POAU had already undertaken "significant litigation . . . to curb violations so flagrant that they cry out for our intervention."[127] He also stressed that "negotiation" and "conferences" had produced favorable results in other "important cases." He told the story of POAU's intervention in St. Bernard, Ohio. A "brazen raid on the public treasury" was halted after a POAU member visited the local Catholic bishop to object to the estimated $55,000 in public funds paid annually to the diocese, an amount that included not only the rent for church property used as a "public" school but also the salaries of teachers (all nuns and priests). During the meeting, "the Bishop was informed that counsel had been employed, that POAU representatives were in Cincinnati, and that a suit would be brought if the contract favoring the Church were not canceled." POAU refused to accept the bishop's promise that he would abandon the lucrative contract. Instead, the group stayed in St. Bernard until the school board met and the bishop made good on his promise. Archer declared that "the real problem in St. Bernard now is to determine whether the Bishop will permit his people to vote for the construction of a new public school building."[128]

POAU was onto something. In the 1930s and 1940s, municipalities around the country had indeed deployed parochial schools as sites of "public" education. Catholic and POAU records as well as newspaper reports from the Midwest and Southwest make it clear that many school districts had responded to new state and federal mandates for education by relying on local parochial schools.[129] In some areas, there had never been a distinction between Catholic schools and public education.[130] If *Everson* and *McCollum* established any clear division in the new constitutional world, moreover, it was that parochial schools must be differentiated from state-run schools. POAU built on this requirement of differentiation.

Publicizing and litigating instances of "capture" was an extraordinarily successful tactic for POAU. Archer understood that allegiance to public education was a central premise for many conservative Protestants. The notion that public schools had been infiltrated by Catholic priests, women religious, or even dedicated laypeople operating under ecclesiastical supervision was a red flag to POAU members. In St. Bernard the controversy did not produce a lawsuit, but even informal campaigns to dismantle the relationship between Catholic leaders and public schools promoted POAU's separationist cause.

Archer capitalized on the ways that local officials had cooperated with church leaders in an earlier constitutional era. Although neither he nor POAU founders anticipated that they would find such a gold mine, captive-school controversies proved to be POAU's most valuable target for more than a decade.[131] By the early 1950s, captive-school cases were a distinct form of litigation, more common than lawsuits over busing, released time for public school students attending religious classes, or other funding issues. They were also the special purview of POAU.[132]

Archer matched hard-hitting legal tactics with publicity campaigns in the captive-school cases. In many situations, the results were not the outright victory of St. Bernard, Ohio. Instead, Archer used law and legal strategy opportunistically; he saw litigation and the threat of litigation as the means of getting what POAU wanted. Often, what it wanted was publicity and new members; legal victory was a bonus not strictly required for success, from Archer's perspective.[133] This combination of publicity and litigation was a winning formula. Within its first year, POAU had drawn support from 600 churches and was prominently featured in Protestant denominational newsletters and magazines.[134]

The organization encouraged interested people to contact POAU with complaints about excessive Catholic influence in local schools. Indeed, POAU leaders emphasized that they never went "into a community unless we were invited in by responsible citizens."[135] By the early 1950s, the group had received hundreds of complaints; in almost all cases, they came to naught. Yet POAU impressed upon its members (and Catholic leaders) that it stood ready to litigate at a moment's notice. Many cases that POAU supported were brought in state court, deploying state constitutional provisions that prohibited aid to sectarian education. Despite the POAU founders' pledge to overturn *Everson*, state courts and state constitutions were frequently Archer's first choice of venue.

The captive-school cases were popular with Protestant audiences. Everyone, it seemed, could still be drawn in by a dustup over Catholic infiltration of public schools and local government coffers. Archer and Blanshard played on lingering doubts about Catholic bona fides, and fears that schoolchildren were especially vulnerable to inculcation with religious beliefs required by Catholic teachings. Such children were, in fact, a "captive" audience. POAU briefs and oral arguments drew heavily on provisions of the canon law mandating religious education for the children of the faithful and rejecting the concept of separation of church and state.[136] The Catholic Church painted by POAU rhetoric was rigidly hierarchical and monolithic. By contrast, and often through innuendo rather than direct argument, Protestants were portrayed as open, free, and public-spirited.[137]

One early case set the stage for POAU strategy. In northern New Mexico, a Protestant minority became increasingly vocal during the 1940s, as public support for education increased but flowed into Catholic coffers in many towns. Lydia Zellers, a resident of Dixon, New Mexico, was already determined to sue by the time she heard about POAU. Once involved in the case, Archer directed the litigation from Washington and chose Harry L. Bigbee, a Santa Fe lawyer and fellow Mason, as local counsel. The trial court found that in many public schools, especially those in the Archdiocese of Santa Fe, "there is no separation between the Roman Catholic Church and the State of New Mexico."[138] In Dixon the elementary school was simultaneously listed on state records as a public school and on diocesan records as a parochial school. The teachers were all Sisters of the Order of St. Francis. One outraged Baptist observer reported that several of them were

"German refugees who could not even speak intelligible English—and they were teaching in a high school!"[139] Students attended Mass each week under the supervision of their teachers. The teachers were chosen by their superiors in the order, rather than the school board, taught Catholic morals, and wore traditional habits and insignia; the school had crosses and religious statuary throughout the building.[140] Although the situation in Dixon was particularly egregious, many other jurisdictions also mixed secular and sectarian influences in their schools. In Kentucky, Ohio, Illinois, Indiana, Michigan, Missouri, Iowa, Texas, and other states, captive schools blended parochial and public education, often with nuns teaching in full habit, in church-owned buildings.

The *Zellers* case announced to the legal community that POAU had arrived. The trial court in *Zellers* permanently enjoined 139 nuns from teaching in the New Mexico public schools, held that busing and textbooks for parochial-school students violated both the New Mexico and U.S. constitutions, and shut down public schools located on church property.[141] The well-known lawyer Leo Pfeffer, legal counsel for the American Jewish Congress (AJC), wrote Archer to congratulate him, but also to urge caution. Pfeffer advised POAU that it was "exceedingly doubtful" that the New Mexico Supreme Court would hold that religious status determined the legitimacy of a teacher's employment.[142] Archer, however, wanted to push for a total ban on teaching by the religious in public schools, even without religious garb and in secular subjects. Archer appealed, arguing to the New Mexico Supreme Court that "the Religious [were] bound by their oaths of obedience" to place the orders of the Church above those of the school board.[143] In an amicus brief, the ACLU argued that only teachers in traditional religious habits could validly be prohibited from teaching in public schools. The ACLU's position persuaded the New Mexico Supreme Court and most courts around the country.[144]

Archer often ignored advice that a particular strategy would not produce a legal victory. He had little patience for the fine parsing of doctrine. POAU members and legal strategists such as Blanshard were generally comfortable with this approach. It served them well for years, highlighting POAU's opposition to religious influence in government and education. Archer learned early that filing a lawsuit, or even threatening to file, brought otherwise reluctant officials to the table. The tactics used in St. Bernard, Ohio, and Dixon, New Mexico, were quick, efficient, and relatively cheap. The *Zellers* litigation cost POAU approximately $5,000—money well spent.[145] Newspapers around the country carried stories about the litigation, often accompanied by photographs showing a smiling class of children arrayed before women religious in full habit.[146] In the new world of the religion clauses, a nationwide strategy such as POAU's made sense as never before.

The translation of POAU's agenda into one dominated by legal thinking happened almost painlessly.[147] Blanshard added his powerful voice: the "Catholic hierarchy," he charged in *American Freedom and Catholic Power,* had gone to great lengths to "capture public schools."[148] Another victory in Missouri settled a dispute that began in 1950 and confirmed the success of captive-school litigation. In the fall of 1950, Archer flew to St. Louis, where he found a situation almost as widespread and complex as in the *Zellers* case. The resulting lawsuit, *Berghorn v. Reorganized School District No. 8,* was constructed of ingredients similar to those that had been so important in *Zellers.* Women religious teaching in full habit, school closings on Catholic holidays, "sectarian instruction in the classroom," and more, POAU argued, "painted the composite picture of school systems under the total domination of a church."[149]

In 1953 the court held in *Berghorn* that the public schools installed in church-owned buildings that were leased to the Franklin County Consolidated School District were not "free" from pervasive sectarian influence.[150] For twenty years, three former Catholic primary schools had been "rented" without a lease by the school district for a small fee. Title to all the school buildings was retained by the archbishop of St. Louis, and the local priest's house shared the grounds of one school; nuns who taught at another lived in that school building. A cross adorned the roof of another school, and all three schools closed in observance of the Feasts of All Saints and the Immaculate Conception. All the teachers were nuns, and were assigned by the mothers superior of two religious orders; all wore religious habits while teaching. They did not give religious instruction in the school buildings, but students attended Mass every morning in nearby churches, and were escorted there by the same nuns who taught secular subjects throughout the school day. According to one source, the eighteen counties involved in the suit paid "an annual flow of tax funds via teaching nuns to the Roman Catholic Church of at least $350,000."[151]

The Missouri case followed the pattern that had begun in New Mexico and that was deployed in subsequent cases in Kansas, Texas, Illinois, Kentucky, and beyond.[152] Archer always worked with local lawyers, and gave them substantial latitude to prosecute the cases. This guaranteed personal involvement and encouraged the formation of new POAU chapters by local counsel. Frequently, lawyers on the scene better understood how to appeal to potential plaintiffs, politicians, and the press. Archer kept a tight financial rein on cases, however, establishing himself as the decision maker of last resort. He often traveled to localities that POAU had targeted in order to raise the profile of the dispute and discuss legal tactics.[153] By the early 1950s, Archer had created a system as centralized as the Catholic Church he so bitterly opposed, said one critic.[154]

This system also made potential allies uneasy. Archer and Blanshard, although both trained as lawyers, never developed a particular regard for legal craftsmanship. Instead, theirs was a more sensational legalism, a blend of religious commitment and popular constitutional ideas. Their effectiveness and energy drew on constitutional ethics that were grounded not in high theory but in a deeply Protestant dedication to separation of church and state. Their evident anti-Catholicism flew in the face of the focus on goodwill among more liberal commentators, including the established groups in the field.

The AJC and the ACLU, both older and more scholarly in their outlook, often disagreed with POAU's tactics and arguments.[155] To them, Archer was a loose cannon. The "reckless litigation and sub-standard legal work" of POAU strained relations with the other two organizations.[156] One study conducted in the mid-1960s reported, for example, that "the other groups . . . have more than once kept [POAU] out of 'their' sponsored litigation," primarily by delays in responding to requests for information, rather than outright confrontation.[157] Especially at the appellate level, both the AJC and ACLU aimed to set sustainable constitutional precedents. In contrast, POAU members and local counsel were prone to filing "improvident appeals," as in the *Zellers* case.[158] POAU's success rate was also lower than that of the other organizations.[159]

The discomfort with POAU's tactics was exacerbated by its anti-

Catholic agenda. The AJC and the ACLU opposed public funding for parochial schools as a matter of general policy, but they were keen to purge all religious influences from public schools, not just the Catholic ones. As Pfeffer saw it, POAU appealed in a populist vocabulary to audiences that were passionate about removing Catholic influence from their children's schools, but less interested in thoroughgoing separation of church and state.[160] POAU's popular appeal was purchased at the price of an anti-Catholic image and a lack of attention to the potential consequences of these court decisions.[161] Yet POAU generally dismissed such concerns. Charges of anti-Catholicism nurtured Archer, Blanshard, and other POAU stalwarts, who were conditioned to welcome attacks and draw strength from them, even as they claimed that they had no bias against any religion or its members.

Pfeffer's concern with promoting secularism in public education was one that POAU leaders should have heeded.[162] Instead, they plowed on, rooting out and publicizing tax support for parochial schools, especially captive schools that masqueraded as public institutions.[163] Pfeffer remained a warm, if distant, supporter of POAU's attempts to weed out captive schools, but he studiously avoided cases that he thought could raise charges of bias.[164] Pfeffer detached himself and the organizations with which he worked from POAU's attacks on publicly supported busing, textbooks, and lunches for parochial-school students. Both Pfeffer's AJC and the ACLU were more likely to be staffed by secularists and Democrats—products of the New Deal and supporters of the tolerance and diversity that had ushered in protection for Jehovah's Witness schoolchildren. They also dismissed POAU's one-issue focus, arguing that separation of church and state could not sustain a true "mass politics" or influence policymakers.[165] Although they generally disagreed with the result in *Everson*, they were not willing to trade in a generally secular agenda to cater to conservative Protestants, even though POAU had demonstrated the appeal of its tactics.

Yet POAU had a broader reach and (in most years) a bigger budget than the more liberal groups. Until the mid-1960s, it reigned over a large and dedicated constituency. In its heyday, POAU had more than 100,000 individual members, and over 1,000 churches contributed funds and distributed its monthly publication, *Church and State*, to parishioners.[166] In 1959, POAU conducted a "survey" that revealed hundreds of captive schools were active in twenty-two states, with an estimated 2,000 priests and nuns on public payrolls.[167] The group followed up the survey with a film entitled *Captured,* which featured Archer and POAU rescuing Protestant schoolchildren from Catholic oppressors.[168] The thirty-five-minute film was described by POAU as a "semi-documentary" based on actual cases.[169] Like those cases, *Captured* explored fears about Catholics' secret plans to impose their sectarian agenda on unwitting Americans. It was shown in churches and town halls, and POAU members used the screenings to collect donations, recruit new members, and answer questions about the organization.[170]

A decade after its founding POAU looked strong, and poised to grow even stronger. Its active policies of litigation and publicity guaranteed substantial attention and sustained a loyal following among more traditional Protestant groups. The new constitutional world was inhabited by a restyled version of an old Protestant-versus-Catholic playbook. Will Herberg notwithstanding, POAU translated long-standing enmities into new constitutional weapons. It also exposed and routed the pattern of local, often quietly cooperative arrangements between Catholic teachers and administrators and public school districts. By exposing such arrangements in a landscape that had been created to respect religious rights, to be sure, but also to draw lines between religion and other things, POAU was able to blend an older, antisectarian (read, anti-Catholic) ethic with the new national mandate for disestablishment. While the going was good—across the 1950s and into the early 1960s—the formula delivered publicity, donations, and members for Archer and POAU.

The constitutional world, however, changed in ways that POAU and its allies did not anticipate. Separation of church and state, POAU said again and again, meant that religious influences in public schools violated the establishment clause. Their own work contributed to the erosion of legal standards that had silently yet effectively screened the kind of religious education that most POAU members thought *should* be supported by public funds. Prayer in the schools catapulted into the headlines when the Supreme Court held in 1962 that ecumenical invocations of divine blessing were unconstitutional. *Engel v. Vitale,* once again in an opinion by Justice Hugo Black, held that even a nondenominational prayer composed by a specially chosen, interfaith committee violated the mandate to separate church and state.[171] No matter how much the committee had struggled to ensure that the prayer was "inoffensive," its undeniably religious character meant that the government had an unconstitutional position. The King James Bible and the Lord's Prayer fell the following year, in *School District of Abington Township v. Schempp.*[172] The boundary between even nonsectarian religious and secular education was a central focus of the new constitutional jurisprudence.

The Supreme Court began to carve fault lines in the new constitutional landscape, the most fundamental of which divided the practice of religion from other sorts of endeavor. Religion, not just sectarianism, became the key element in the analysis. In this sense, POAU and its supporters had invested in an older approach to constitutional analysis that emphasized the absence of sectarian influence as the key to church-state separation. Yet in the new constitutional world, religion itself became the operative category. In this approach, secularism replaced antisectarianism as the central focus for the establishment clause. The result was devastating for POAU.

By the early 1960s, prayer (and Bible reading) in schools had long been controversial—opposed for more than a century by Catholics who saw them as attempts by Protestants to impose their faith on Catholic children.[173] Such exercises were also openly opposed by some traditionally separatist Protestants (including many Baptists) and quietly dreaded by most Jews. The reluctance of Jewish organizations to litigate school prayer cases was driven by fear of anti-Semitic reprisals as well as concern that the federal courts would endorse the prayer.[174]

POAU had helped create the atmosphere that made such longstanding practices a constitutional problem, however. Archer and other activists were caught in a position that weakened the Protestant coalition when the Supreme Court applied the standards it had developed in parochial-school and released-time cases to public education, purging openly religious activities from public schools altogether. The organization swallowed hard and declared that it was willing to live by the decisions, even though many of its members opposed them.[175] One reporter said that Archer confided privately that POAU mail from supporters had shown strong grass-roots opposition to the decisions. As Archer complained, "We're damned if we do and damned if we don't support the decision."[176] There was grumbling even within POAU about the decision to support the ban on prayer and Bible reading—an unusual circumstance because Archer was so widely admired.

The allegiance of conservative Protestants to school prayer ran deep. In one captive-school case from the mid-1950s, the local POAU lawyer, a United States congressman, initially argued that the nuns employed in a public school should be fired because they refused to read the required chapters from the King James Bible.[177] The national office altered the complaint, but many POAU supporters assumed that Protestant practice and convictions were fully consistent with a "secular" (that is, not sectarian) public education. Catholics, in a shift from long-standing opposition, attacked the prayer decision. For the first time, they openly welcomed the attempt to battle secularism and materialism in the schools by "affirm[ing] our founding fathers' wishes that all actions of mankind must be referred to the Creator."[178] Methodists split over support for the prayer. But most Protestants endorsed the New York State Board of Regents' ecumenical prayer, at the center of *Engel v. Vitale.* In other words, the school prayer and Bible decisions caught Protestants and POAU in a double bind.

It is difficult to overestimate the importance of *Engel* and *Schempp* to many believers. *Engel* alone produced more hate mail than the Court had ever received.[179] However predictable the holdings may seem decades later, they fell like a meteor into American society. The decisions shocked POAU supporters and many others, most of whom had never conceived of ecumenical school prayer or Bible reading as establishment clause concerns. The acknowledgment of God, after all, had been added to the central patriotic creed of the country only a few years earlier: the pledge to the flag included the words "under God," widely seen as a nonsectarian means of honoring the multiple faiths of Americans. In *Engel,* the New York State Regents' prayer had been composed by a delegation of rabbis, ministers, and priests, all of whom agreed that the prayer was nonsectarian.[180] People of "goodwill," including the Board of Regents, which included five lawyers, had certified the tolerant heritage of the prayer, which was only twenty-two words long and omitted any explicitly Christian language: "Almighty God, we acknowledge our dependence upon Thee, and we beg Thy blessings upon us, our parents, our teachers, and our country." New York's governor also supported the prayer, saying it defended freedom against the "slave world of godless communism."[181] Even Leo Pfeffer, who opposed prayer in public schools, thought this case was an unwise attack, given that the prayer at issue was as "nonsectarian as a prayer can be." He was convinced that the litigation would provide the Supreme Court and the country "another opportunity . . . to become religious and patriotic."[182]

The new constitutional world, Americans learned in the prayer cases, was unstable. It contained contradictory impulses of such power that when they rumbled across the new territory, those who followed only one side of the issue were stunned to meet the opposing force. Goodwill advocates and ecumenicists who defended religious diversity and simultaneously celebrated the integrity and creativity of American religious life worked hard to create a truly "nonsectarian prayer." But the Supreme Court held that they could not possibly succeed.

Any prayer in public school, no matter how carefully nonsectarian, violated the establishment clause, the Supreme Court said. For those whose ecumenical convictions sustained religious cooperation and goodwill, the decision was a shock. For many of the traditional interfaith coalitions, such as the National Conference of Christians and Jews, which prepared guidelines for how to conduct respectful interfaith observances and ceremonies, the banishment of even ecumenical prayer was a violation of the painstakingly crafted bargain that welcomed religious diversity as essential to American survival. To the contrary, this new regime smacked of the enforced secularism that many Americans associated with communism. Former presidents Herbert Hoover and Dwight Eisenhower condemned the opinion; polls suggested that 80 percent of Americans agreed.[183]

For conservative Protestants, whose involvement with law had primarily been a staunch defense of public education against a perceived Catholic onslaught, the decisions were unexpected and disastrous. Charles Wesley Lowry's *To Pray or Not to Pray!* published in 1963, was just one of thousands of outraged responses from Protestants who argued that prayer and Bible reading were cornerstones of public education.[184] Methodist bishop Fred Pierce Corson said the ruling "makes secularism the national religion."[185] Some southern Protestants complained that the Court had "put the Negroes in the schools, and now they've driven God out."[186] Barry Goldwater made much of the "moral . . . rot" of the Supreme Court's decisions.[187] Overnight, it seemed, the

Court had gone from a sometime friend to an incomprehensible, unpredictable, and seemingly immutable enemy of American religious life. To many, secularism was most decidedly not a welcome presence in the classroom, however uncomfortable they had been with explicitly Catholic practices or captive schools.

Secularism, and particularly the ban on school prayer, was resisted throughout the country.[188] Often critics claimed that secularism would sap the moral foundations of the country, reducing it to the level of the Soviet Union. One congressman from Mississippi called the decision a "carefully planned conspiracy to . . . communize America." "God pity our country when we can no longer appeal to God for help," lamented the influential evangelist Billy Graham.[189] School prayer amendments were introduced annually for many years in Congress.[190] Equally important, resistance occurred at all levels of government.[191] Many battles were local, but they were nonetheless widespread and powerful. Especially in the South, *Engel* was decried from countless pulpits.[192] The growing migration from the South to California carried resistance westward.[193] From those churches, supporters of Goldwater's 1964 presidential bid and Ronald Reagan's 1966 California gubernatorial campaign painted the ban on prayer as forcible imposition of moral relativism, the erosion of patriotism, and the sexual revolution. The new threat emanated from Washington, not Rome, and it wore judicial rather than clerical garb.

The Catholic Church quickly and forcefully condemned the prayer decision.[194] Cardinal Spellman, long the sparring partner of POAU and its supporters, said that "America ha[d] surely traveled far from the ideals of her founding fathers" when the Supreme Court held that "the prayerful mention of God's holy name" violated the Constitution.[195] Bishop Fulton Sheen, famous for his popular television show *Life Is Worth Living* in the 1950s and 1960s, made the comparison between banning prayer and the atheism of the Soviet bloc: "Our schools are now officially put on the same level as the Communist schools. In neither may one pray; in neither may one acknowledge a Source whence came the liberties of the people."[196]

Leo Pfeffer and most Jewish organizations enthusiastically supported the result. Although he had initially opposed the *Engel* litigation as too dangerous, Pfeffer was exuberant that it had been successful. Even among Jewish groups, however, division grew after *Engel*. The Union of Orthodox Jewish Congregations of America condemned the exclusion of religion from public life; increasing dissension over support for public aid to religious schools separated Orthodox Jews from other Jewish activists.[197] The prospect of Orthodox Jews making common cause with Catholics irked Pfeffer and the AJC. As Pfeffer noted bitterly, Catholics traditionally had objected to religious exercises of all kinds in public schools.[198] In the nineteenth century, Catholics opposed prayer and Bible reading because they objected to the Protestant character of the underlying texts. In 1859, a young Catholic student at the Eliot School in Boston was whipped until he fainted for refusing to recite the Ten Commandments from the King James Bible.[199] By the mid-twentieth century, however, concern over secularism, as well as the favorable light the ban shed on parochial schools, outweighed Catholics' lingering memories of prejudice and conflict.[200]

Liberal Protestants were divided, with the Court's opinions drawing more support from the elite, but the response was overwhelmingly negative among the people generally.[201] Even Congregationalists, such as Union Theological Seminary professor Roger Shinn, "question[ed] the wisdom of this absolute prohibition."[202] Longtime POAU supporters—including the National Association of Evangelicals and the Episcopal bishop of San Francisco—also condemned the Court.[203] POAU, the AJC, the ACLU, and the Unitarian Universalists stood against the tide of condemnation, but they were in a minority nationwide. Of them all, POAU was the most unexpected supporter of the ban: it was torn apart by its determination to support the Supreme Court decisions.

The prayer and Bible-reading decisions affected religious life as much as legal history. Most important was the disintegration of a unified Protestant approach to the Constitution, caused in part by POAU's own agenda. Archer and his followers were extraordinarily successful in purging "sectarianism," yet they had turned a blind eye to generically Protestant practices in public schools. The organization had worked long and hard, stressing the differences between public and parochial schools and harping on the sectarian nature of the latter. Such an emphasis inevitably drew attention to the religious dimensions of public education itself. Widespread practices in public schools, such as Bible reading and prayers, were backlit by court decisions that prohibited government funding for openly religious education. In this light, the Supreme Court's decisions made POAU look like a traitor to much of its own constituency. The erosion of the Protestant coalition was gradual, so it is easy to overlook how damaging it was to POAU to have prayer excised from public schools.[204]

In the South, POAU's traditional stronghold, the story of religious change emerges most starkly. From World War II to the early 1970s, the South went from being a separate, self-identified, and even isolated region to a more politically, culturally, and religiously integrated part of the nation.[205] As Southerners confronted the broader society, especially as they absorbed the painful lessons in secularism at the hands of the Supreme Court, many southern Protestants understood their religious identity was under siege. To preserve it, they forced themselves to enter a newly charged atmosphere in which separation of church and state had become the enemy. They had long understood separation of church and state as an antisectarian mandate. In its new jurisprudentially sculpted incarnation, separation was something distinctly different. The divide between sacred and secular became the central focus of separatist constitutionalism by the mid-1960s and was written into law by the Supreme Court. The funding of programs for parochial schools was now evaluated based on the programs' *religious* content, rather than on their sectarian nature. In public schools, nonsectarian religious exercises were subjected to the same scrutiny.

The results horrified many more traditionally minded separatists, highlighting the differences between those who embraced the school prayer decisions and all they stood for, and those who opposed secularism as the greatest danger. As this latter group grasped the potential for political organizing along religious principles and connected the battle for the schools to broader questions of family and sexuality by the 1970s, they met Catholics on the battlefield once again, but this time not as antagonists. In this sense, the new religious right was a coalition born in resistance to a blasphemous national government, exemplified by the nine old men in Washington who imposed godlessness on the entire country.

The story of the Southern Baptist Convention (SBC) illustrates the bitterness of the debate, and the ways that the school prayer decision was a catalyst for Protestant fission. Baptists, particularly Southern Baptists, had long been key members of POAU. They were there at the founding of the organization, had sustained it through its uncertain early days, and remained supporters throughout the 1960s.[206] Initially the SBC supported the result in *Engel,* based primarily on a misunderstanding, thinking that the Court had prohibited only those prayers composed by the state. This interpretation was soon undermined by subsequent decisions, such as the *Schempp* case that prohibited the Lord's Prayer, and the Southern Baptists came to believe that the federal judiciary had betrayed the long-standing tradition that provided time for voluntary prayer within the school day.[207] The SBC's position on separation of church and state was revolutionized as this painful lesson sank in, and the SBC eventually transformed into an opponent of POAU. The process was long and drawn out, yet in the life of the Baptist churches in America, the change was precipitous.[208]

In 1979, the SBC underwent what is known as the "conservative takeover" by those who favored a strict doctrine of biblical inerrancy and patriarchal authority. A key supporter of the takeover, Tim La-Haye, pastor of the enormous Scott Memorial Baptist Church in San Diego, also cofounded the Moral Majority, and popularized the idea that secular humanists were plotting to subvert American culture and promote communism. His wife, Beverly LaHaye, became a prominent legal activist in her own right in the 1980s. Her organization, Concerned Women for America, conducted a legal campaign to carry the battle against secularism back into courtrooms.[209]

The opposition to secularism that so galvanized conservative Protestants in the 1960s owed much of its fire to the Supreme Court's prayer decisions. One perceptive critic has speculated that the SBC's new emphasis on traditional authority and even inerrancy was in part a reaction "to the disturbing, revolutionary decisions of the Supreme Court under Chief Justice Earl Warren."[210] Racial desegregation and social welfare, of course, also figured large in the decisions of the Warren Court, but religion was an equally vital issue among many conservative Protestants. The cultural revolution that so disturbed them in the 1960s and early 1970s was enabled by Supreme Court decisions that supported secularism and its challenges to parental authority and traditional sexuality. The SBC formally endorsed a school prayer amendment to the Constitution in 1982, becoming the first denomination to do so.[211] As one delegate put it, "The atheists, humanists and secularists are against prayer in schools, and that's not the company we need to be keeping." Another called the ban on prayer a vital "step in the demoralizing of America."[212] Charges that secularism and communism went hand in hand were a constant refrain.

The Supreme Court's prayer and Bible reading decisions had other unanticipated effects: they brought many Catholics and conservative Protestants closer together in their outrage. *Engel* and *Schempp* created a new dividing line when Catholics, who had long complained that reading the King James Bible was hardly an ecumenical approach to religion, rallied around prayer as key to education in a democracy.[213] Like the Orthodox Jews who so dismayed the AJC, Protestants who began to see Catholics as potential allies in the battle against secularism reacted to the new constitutional world by abandoning traditional sectarian allegiances. To the chagrin of POAU, the wedge between Protestants created a deep and long-lasting split, eventually becoming a division between liberals and conservatives (in its latest incarnation, the controversy in 2002 over the words "under God" in the Pledge of Allegiance only widened the rift). Those who opposed prayer in schools found themselves allied with liberals politically as well as religiously, embracing a new coalition forged by the most controversial religion cases since *Everson*.[214]

The turn to law thus had dire and unintended consequences. Over time, it propelled many traditional Protestants away from their long-standing belief in separation of church and state, a doctrine that for Baptists had ancient roots. The new divide galvanized a fresh phalanx of believers, as committed to the proposition that school prayer was vital to the nation's flourishing as POAU had been convinced fifteen years earlier that aid to Catholic schools was the death knell for democracy. Protestants were no longer "united" by a common vision; POAU's very name hearkened back to a more univocal (but undeniably dated) past.

The 1960s became a nightmare decade for POAU. The prayer cases were the watershed, but other events added to the pain. Anti-Catholicism no longer played to sympathetic audiences in many parts of the country. The election of President John F. Kennedy undermined claims that one could not be a good American and a Catholic. Vatican II and the acceptance of the principle of religious liberty by the Catholic Church, as well as the church's role in the civil rights movement in the late 1950s and early 1960s, showed that it was not the reactionary monolith painted by Blanshard.[215] In the late 1960s, when one in three parochial schools closed in a three-year period, it became increasingly difficult to argue that church leaders stalked the halls of government with the goal of taking over, when they were desperately seeking the help they obviously needed just to survive.[216] In October 1964, *Newsweek* ran a story headlined "POAU in Crisis." The story detailed the recent "defection" of long-time supporter Dr. Ellis Dana, who charged the group with anti-Catholic prejudice. The ACLU began to appeal to other, more liberal separationists who wanted to "wage the fight for their principles without overtones of anti-Catholicism." A Methodist professor of church history in Chicago explained that "POAU is an illustration of Protestant culture lag." Critics said that the group increasingly depended on "small-town, latter-day fundamentalism," despite Archer's disclaimer that POAU had always been controversial. He did admit that some of the group's pamphlets "seemed a little acidy."[217]

POAU became Americans United for Separation of Church and State (AU) in 1972, formally dropping the Protestant label. In practice, the group had used the Americans United name for several years and had labored to shed its anti-Catholic skin. AU has embraced separation of church and state in a different religious climate, yet in ways that reflect the divisive atmosphere surrounding the law of religion.[218] Through the 1970s and beyond, AU deployed the language of "pervasive sectarianism" to denote the presence of religion, rather than speaking of Catholic domination.[219] By the late 1970s, AU was actively monitoring the new religious right, including many evangelical Protestant groups that would formerly have been among POAU's supporters.[220] Today, AU is liberal politically, ecumenical in the broadest sense, deeply involved in lobbying and outreach, and it cooperates consistently with the AJC and ACLU in lawsuits and amicus briefs. Separation of church and state, once so central to conservative Protestant thought and legal activism, has become the special province of liberals who have embraced secularism.

The legacy of the prayer decisions has been division, despite the Court's emphasis on divisiveness as a dangerous consequence of the *failure* to separate church and state. The new constitutional landscape exposed and widened latent rifts in Protestant communities. Ironically, these divisions prompted new forms of interfaith cooperation in a distinctly different register. When Orthodox rabbi Moses Feuerstein joined Cardinal Spellman and Billy Graham in condemning the prayer decisions, they discovered unexpected commonalities across conservative religious traditions.

In some ways the major issues in the constitutional world of religion and education remain familiar today. They have been reconfigured to suit the new religious times, however. The child-benefit theory has reappeared, sustaining new ways to give schoolchildren access to religious as well as secular education.[221] Coalitions first seen after the school prayer decisions have grown, and their membership is far more likely to be ecumenical. Consider Citizens for Educational Freedom, founded in 1959 to combat the "virtual monopoly" of public schools, and supported now by the Heritage Foundation, the Heartland Institute, and the National Catholic Education Association. In the early 1960s, the group's members were "estimated by its leaders to be 90 per cent Roman Catholic."[222] They claimed then that aid for parochial schools was the only way to counterbalance the government's discrimination against the constitutionally protected right to "turn to a parochial school."[223] Like AU, this group has sloughed off its original one-religion identity. Today it frames its argument differently, primarily in terms of tuition vouchers, which promote "school reform through competition," as well as constitutional freedom: "Parents defend religious liberty for all when they work to make it possible for all parents to have the choice of placing their children in God-centered schools rather than being assigned to a secular public school."[224]

AU counters stalwartly that aid to religious schools disguised as voucher programs is unconstitutional, still battling against sectarianism and aid to religious schools in any form.[225] But however constant the rhetoric, the world in which POAU fought against captive schools in the name of democracy has disappeared. And while POAU and its allies did not achieve the separation of church and state they sought, they were an integral part of another division—the separation of conservative from liberal Protestants. The "united" group that POAU championed splintered into far more complex and contentious groupings, making a focus on sectarianism seem outmoded. In this new constitutional world, allies (and enemies) were created by legal categories rather than traditional religious boundaries.

The interfaith coalitions that helped usher in the new constitutional world in the 1930s and '40s welcomed the idea of religious pluralism. Like POAU, their vision was overtaken by those who claimed a place in the new world. Sociologist Will Herberg's Protestant-Catholic-Jew formula, it turned out, was inadequate and underinclusive, even when he coined the phrase in the mid-1950s. In a footnote, Herberg acknowledged that his three-part religious identity story did not address the history or present circumstances of "the Negroes" or their patterns of worship. He conceded that the "future of the Negroes . . . constitutes a much more difficult problem [than that of other groups], about which very little may be said with any assurance today."[226] Indeed. The explosion of religiously motivated and articulated civil rights activism by African Americans was just around the corner, however. Desegregation, voting rights, marches, sit-ins, and more all testified to the capacity of prophetic religion to work broad change in American society.[227] The story of the Nation of Islam is less well known yet vitally important for its capacity to challenge the most unyielding of all state structures, prison. Race, liberation, and faith created a potent and stubborn mix behind prison walls. Even in a space of confinement and despair, inmates embraced both constitutionalism and the right to believe.

CHAPTER 4

Faith as Liberation

The Nation of Islam and Religion in Prison,
1940–1975

In the 1930s, a small group of believers claimed that to salute the American flag was to worship a false god. The flag was the national symbol of a corrupted race that had oppressed true believers for centuries, they said. In the 1930s and 1940s, the Jehovah's Witnesses were prosecuted for their refusal to salute the flag.[1] Yet the Witnesses were not alone; other groups had similar scruples. The Nation of Islam, like the Witnesses, condemned all secular governments as satanic. Like the Witnesses, it was a homegrown faith, a religion begun and celebrated primarily in America. And like the Witnesses, the Nation of Islam opposed mainstream religious and political life, yet became central to the development of religious freedom in the twentieth century.[2] The new constitutional world expanded to include prisons and prisoners through the work of the controversial and uncompromising members of the Nation of Islam.

The Nation of Islam conducted an extraordinary legal campaign to bring the faith to prison inmates in the 1950s and 1960s. The Nation took key lessons from the Witnesses, even though on the surface the two faiths appear very different. Ideas, legal strategies, and even religious doctrines traveled between the two groups of believers, who understood themselves as beset by a hostile and diabolical state. To confront the devil was exhilarating, a confirmation of the suffering of the faithful and a vindication of the power of the faith. The Nation's own story, while acknowledging the role of Jehovah's Witness belief and tactics in Black Muslim history, illustrates how a new group of outsiders spoke truth to power, combining religious innovation with legal action to carve out a distinct space for believers. Litigants emerged even from the darkest places. And they brought with them unyielding and often unwelcome new beliefs.

Followers of the Nation of Islam faced two formidable challenges as they argued for the right to practice their faith. First, their claims were brought against the single most authoritarian arm of government—prisons. Until Black Muslims won constitutional protection, federal courts had maintained a "hands-off" approach to state prisoners' lawsuits. In this sense, the Nation succeeded where Witnesses had failed. Jehovah's Witnesses imprisoned for draft evasion in World War II had been tenacious but unsuccessful litigants. In case after case, they had sought freedom to practice their faith while incarcerated, but had been turned away. In suits brought by Muslims in the 1960s, however, federal courts for the first time held that claims of religious discrimination by prison officials invoked the special constitutional expertise of the federal judiciary. This alone was a significant victory. Equally daunting, however, was the second challenge: refuting the argument—made repeatedly in lawsuits, public speeches, editorials, and elsewhere—that the Nation of Islam was not really a religion. Instead, said opponents, Black Muslims were hiding a racist political movement behind a veneer of religion.

The origins and growth of the Black Muslim faith, and its campaign for recognition and protection even—or especially—behind prison walls, are landmarks in American religious and legal history. In key respects, the Nation of Islam grew in importance and breadth through its role in prison life. From the 1950s through the 1970s, as rates of incarceration for black men ballooned in the United States, the Nation offered prisoners meaning and direction through faith. It also offered a path to resistance and self-expression that could not be matched by other beliefs. The Nation made sense of the black prisoners' world, and in turn Black Muslim litigants taught the courts and the country that religious life had transformative power even in the most confined and apparently hopeless places. This lesson has reverberated throughout American law and culture. The Nation's victories in court destabilized comfortable theories of the role of religion in American society, rekindling awareness of the raw edges of faith, the separatism of dissenting religious groups, and the capacity of believers to challenge the mainstream. Like the Witnesses, members of the Nation were often aggressive, arrogant, intolerant, and above all courageous. They were also motivated deeply by their faith. In this sense, they had much in common with other believers who sought protection from the courts.

The claims of Black Muslims were related closely to earlier arguments made by the Witnesses, focusing on the right to practice—to live separate and religiously focused lives, even behind prison walls or in public institutions (that is, schools). The Witnesses fought for their claim that what others viewed as political (the Pledge of Allegiance), they saw as religious (idolatry). The Nation fought for a related yet distinctive position: others viewed them and their beliefs as fundamentally political, yet they claimed they were religious. Even in a country that had seen the outpouring of disdain and hatred for Jehovah's Witnesses in the World War II era, however, Black Muslims were uniquely polarizing; they challenged the presumed boundaries of faith in an American constitutional landscape that had been designed only a decade before. Unlike the sociologist Will Herberg, who confined his list of "American" faiths to a far less threatening Protestant-Catholic-Jew triumvirate, this group defied the religious mainstream and eventually redrew the map of the constitutional world.[3]

Virtually as soon as it was created, the new national law of religion revealed (and helped sustain) unprecedented and often unwelcome religious diversity. The convergence of religious and constitutional lives in the prison setting drew attention and often condemnation. Having called a new constitutional landscape into being, its judicial designers found that the inhabitants moved quickly beyond their control. The reality of American life was far more interesting, more varied, more chaotic than legal experts and liberal ecumenicists had anticipated. Popular constitutional life defied categories and predictions. Gradually, the vigor as well as the variety of the religious beliefs and practices in America were revealed by the new constitutional world.

The Nation of Islam was distinctly and vocally non-Christian; it was also racially separatist. The combination tested Americans' commitment to pluralism. If the Jehovah's Witnesses established that believers could have valid religious objections to otherwise secular practices, the Nation of Islam proved that religion could not be confined in a genuinely pluralist society to "Judeo-Christian" traditions. American religious life was impossible to control; the faithful refused to live within bounds. For the Nation, the road to prominence (and controversy) started among the urban poor in the upper Midwest.

In 1930, a peddler sold his wares in African American neighborhoods in Detroit. Reportedly, he sold raincoats first, and then silks. He had more to offer than exotic goods, however. He came bearing a new and mesmerizing truth for his customers. His origins were mysterious and are still hotly disputed; at the time, he was widely believed to be an Arab and he called himself Mr. Farrad Mohammad, or Mr. F. Mohammad Ali, or W. D. Fard.[4] He was also known as Professor Ford, and Mr. Wali Farrad. One early convert reported that he introduced himself as "W. D. Fard, and I come from the Holy City of Mecca. More about myself I will not tell you yet, for the time has not yet come. I am your brother. You have not yet seen me in my royal robes."[5] Whatever his origins or true name, Fard plied his wares in a city familiar with Muslims: Turks, Syrians, Albanians, and Lebanese immigrants had come to Detroit in the early twentieth century to work in the city's factories.[6]

Fard told his African American customers that his silks were from their true country, where people ate the healthiest foods and were "free from rheumatism, aches and pains."[7] He also told them that their true sacred text was not the Christian Bible. The Black Nation in America, he said, was actually a wrongfully oppressed branch of the black peoples of Asia and Africa. Their scripture was the Holy Qur'an, which had been wrested from their ancestors amid the horrors of the Middle Passage, after they had been kidnapped and sold into slavery. Fard had been sent, he said, to wake the slumbering blacks of North America, where they had been "surrounded and robbed completely by the Cave Man."[8]

Fard's bitter denunciation of the white race ("blue-eyed devils") and his tale of a wronged Black Nation found a ready audience among the increasingly desperate population in the black slums of Detroit. In the early 1930s when Fard began teaching new converts, the Depression cut deep into poor African Americans' hopes of a better life in the North. Especially among new migrants from the South, the promise of advancement evaporated as they suffered from dislocation, alienation, and even the aches and pains from living in a new, far colder climate.

Hunger, discrimination, and violence drove home the unwelcome conclusion that the North was plagued by a racism every bit as ingrained as that of the South, although northerners spoke a deceptive language of equality.[9] As Fard put it to members of his fledgling Black Muslim movement, they owed no allegiance to a flag that shielded "the depravities of the white devils [who] by their tricknollogy keep our people illiterate to use as tools and slaves."[10]

Religious historians speak of "preparation" to accept religious innovation.[11] Preparation essentially creates an opening for a message to be heard in a culture or segment of society. In this sense, the message itself is of course vital, but timing and environment also help explain its cultural and social power. In the early 1930s, transplanted Southerners who aspired to self-improvement and higher status could embrace Fard's message. At the same time, they could reject the condescension of Detroit's black middle class and its (Christian) religious leaders.[12] If Fard's audience in Detroit was prepared economically, politically, and even socially to receive a harsh, anti-American message, they had also been prepared religiously for the new vision that Fard unfolded to his startled and entranced followers.

African American religious leaders before Fard had posited that Christianity in all its guises was a fundamentally European (that is, white or "palefaced") faith. Noble Drew Ali, born Timothy Drew in 1886 in North Carolina, taught that those of darker skin, or "Moors," were naturally Muslim, not Christian. In the early twentieth century, Ali founded the Moorish Science Temple of America, which united the inclusiveness of Eastern philosophy with a strong concept of nationhood for all African Americans. Noble Drew Ali gave his people that nationality: they were Moroccans. Thenceforth, they would be knows as "Moors," "Moorish Americans," or the more general "Asiatics," rather than as blacks or Negroes.[13]

The first Moorish Science Temple was established in Newark, New Jersey, in 1913, according to Ali, and followed by others in Pittsburgh and Detroit. Drew Ali exerted his greatest influence in Chicago, however, where one historian of the movement credited Ali's "magnetic charm, sincerity of purpose, and . . . real determination to lead his people out of the difficulties of racial prejudice and discrimination" with making his South Side temple a magnet for hundreds who longed for a dignified way to claim a heritage that distinguished them from the "Negro."[14] Ali's teachings, including his explanations of the historical roles of Jesus, Buddha, Confucius, John the Baptist, and more, were contained in his *Holy Koran,* a secret sixty-page scripture that does not resemble the Qur'an of Islam. Ali's *Holy Koran* connected Moorish thought to all of human history, as well as specifically to North America.[15]

The Moorish symbol for Islam, a star over an inverted crescent, had appeared in the heavens, said Ali. This sign marked the arrival of a new era, when Asiatics would be ascendant and, correspondingly, the Europeans would be vanquished. Temple members, who wore distinctive fezzes and carried cards identifying them as Moorish nationals, became infamous for confronting white Chicagoans and praising the Prophet Noble Drew Ali for freeing them from white domination. Ali, however, counseled all followers: "Stop flashing your cards before Europeans as this only causes confusion. We did not come to cause confusion; our work is to uplift the nation."[16] Distrust of the Moors was widespread among officials, however. According to one white police officer in Detroit, the entire movement was a pretense: "Those Moors never saw anything before they came to Detroit except Florida and Alabama!"[17]

Ali died in 1929 under mysterious circumstances, after substantial conflict had arisen between his leadership and subordinates who apparently began to exploit members by selling them potions and charms.[18] According to one source, Fard then assumed the leadership of the Moorish movement, claiming that he was the reincarnation of Ali.[19] Whether or not there was an actual connection between the Moors and Fard, it is clear that Black Nationalism, religious innovation, and non-Christian or even "extra-Christian" cosmology had been yoked together before Fard began teaching in 1930. Muslim ideas, symbols, and rhetoric were familiar to African Americans across the urban North.[20]

Fard's teachings quickly moved beyond those of the Moorish Science Temple, answering the burning question of where African Americans really came from, and what their suffering meant in history and theology. He taught that black people in North America were members of a lost tribe of Shabazz, stolen from Mecca by slave traders. He, the prophet sent by Allah to redeem his people, had come to restore their lost nation and religion, Islam (thus, the Nation of Islam, sometimes called the Lost-Found Nation). The tribe of Shabazz was the "original" and "noblest" of all the earth's peoples, Fard said, and members must relearn their language (Arabic), their culture (especially astronomy and mathematics), and avoid all unclean food, including hogs, ducks, geese, opossums, and catfish, and all stimulants, especially liquor. If they obeyed His law, Allah would return them to Paradise—the holy city of Mecca.[21]

Like other powerful religious innovators, Fard connected the longings of his audience to divine history and the end of times. Fard appropriated Islam to his own ends, sculpting a narrative and a set of beliefs that were heterodox from the perspective of traditional Islam. At the same time, he spoke to the core of "Black Religion" in America; that is, to a deep yearning for and belief in divine justice, combined with a profound awareness of displacement in a racist society.[22] The Nation grew out of those who resisted and defied evil, he said, and would be rewarded by Allah after the final battle.[23] They had endured much, and had seen through the falsehood of Christianity, rejecting the social and religious tools of the oppressor. They had cleansed themselves of the taint of the devil, and would be rewarded in paradise.

Fard's message found willing listeners. Especially among disillusioned African American migrants to the urban North, there were many who welcomed an alternative religion tied to an ancient civilization outside European domination, complete with its own moral codes, language, culture, and history of armed resistance. The brotherhood of all Muslims and the promise of justice resonated with the central concerns of black men.[24] The discipline of dietary restrictions, rigid moral codes, and worship also lent legitimacy to the new faith. The differentiation of those in the Nation from those outside divided the world neatly into "us" and "them," providing a sense of group identity that affirmed the experience of those who already knew they existed outside the broader culture.[25]

Fard drew on a variety of sources to augment his own oral teachings. He relied, of course, on those who had come before him in black and Muslim circles. But he also ranged wider, clearly influenced by Black Nationalist Marcus Garvey and his United Negro Improvement Association, and even by the Baptist preacher Frank Norris.[26] Most important, Fard advised his followers to study the writings and radio addresses of Jehovah's Witness leader Judge Joseph Rutherford, which he interpreted for followers at temple services.[27] Like the Jehovah of the Witnesses' faith, Allah in Black Muslim belief was exacting, un-yielding, even vengeful. The approaching Armageddon, both groups proclaimed with satisfaction, would reverse their current powerless-ness.[28] The dire prophecy in both sects celebrated the coming destruc-tion of despicable millions and their governments, and the elevation of those who suffered in the dark times. This shared vision depended on an approaching end of all time, and anticipation of the most mo-mentous of all battles, which would upend injustice, especially the domination of governments, (other) religions, markets, and universi-ties.[29]

Indeed, the tenets of the Nation of Islam mirrored those of the Wit-nesses in key ways. Both sects marked the beginning of the Apocalypse in 1914, and also claimed that God delayed the final battle to allow true believers to bring the Word to potential recruits.[30] God's final punishment for the earth would come in the form of natural disasters, from which an elect 144,000 would be preserved and transported to heaven, in Witness versions; in Muslim eschatology the elect would re-main to rule on earth.[31] Both sets of the elect would live in a Paradise of "perfect food" and perfect health, while others not among the elect could nonetheless achieve a lesser form of salvation through good works and faith. Like the Witnesses, early members of the Nation of Is-lam were virulently anti-Catholic and anti-Semitic, condemning the pope as the head of a conspiracy to corrupt innocents and attack the righteous, and Jewish rabbis as priests of Baal. Especially important from the perspective of constitutional law and religious freedom, both groups also eschewed the flag salute and military service.[32]

By the time Fard disappeared in mid-1934, between 5,000 and 8,000 members had joined his Temple Number One in Detroit.[33] Some scholars believe that Fard simply went underground; others have charged that Elijah Muhammad or a rival leader killed him. Some ac-counts paint Fard as a lifelong petty criminal who in the end preached human sacrifice as a cleansing ritual.[34] FBI files on Fard report that one of his followers ritually slaughtered a white victim and claimed that Fard, God of Islam, had commanded him to do this work. Accord-ing to the FBI, Fard agreed to leave Detroit in return for dropping charges of accessory to murder.[35]

Whatever the actual story behind Fard's disappearance, his succes-sor, Elijah Muhammad, known to his followers as the Messenger of Allah or Messenger Muhammad, ensured the survival of the young

movement, and developed a more precise and sustainable set of beliefs and practices. Muhammad, born Elijah Poole in Georgia in 1897,
came to Detroit in 1922. He was among Fard's earliest converts in
1931, and became Fard's constant companion and student.[36] Muhammad taught that Fard was actually an incarnation of Allah, and that he
had been designated Fard's messenger. Muhammad was the son of a
Baptist preacher, and the ideas of his youth permeated his teaching to
the Nation. He imported a dispensational ethic typical of early twentieth-century Baptists into the faith, dividing all of history into distinct
"dispensations" or eras that were governed by cosmic direction. He
maintained, for example, that the separatism advocated by the Nation
was grounded in scripture. Integration was fundamentally misguided,
in his view, because the Nation taught that "the world has been under
the rule of Satan (the devil) for 6,000 years, and now separation must
come between God's people and the devil so that the righteous can
survive."[37] In this way, Muhammad imported Christian interpretive
structures into the Nation's own critique of Christianity and, especially, black Christian advocates for integration.

Muhammad's adaptation of prior doctrine to suit a new religious
movement was a successful strategy. The Nation of Islam tapped accepted ways of thinking for converts and also took them into radically
new religious territory. In Muhammad's teaching, the religious language of the outsider deployed long-standing, even conventional con-
ceptions in ways that spoke to his audience. As leader, Muhammad
gave voice to Fard's doctrines but connected them more intimately to
the lives and religious habits of his followers, drawing them into a community of believers. This capacity to draw new connections and com-
parisons became a hallmark of Muhammad's leadership, and a testament to his brilliance as a religious thinker. For the first decade and
more of his leadership, however, Muhammad's life was turbulent and
unstable. He moved from city to city in an effort to avoid challenges to
his leadership from within the Nation, as well as harassment by police.
The movement was marked by internal dissension until Muhammad
was convicted of draft evasion in 1943 and then served three years at
the Federal Correctional Institution in Milan, Michigan.[38]

Muhammad and other Muslims had been suspected by the FBI of
working with anti-American Japanese conspirators even before the

bombing of Pearl Harbor. Initially, Muhammad was charged with sedition—that is, advocating the violent overthrow of the government.[39] The Nation was accused of working with Japanese radical Satohata Takahashi, who was deported in 1934, then arrested in 1939 after returning illegally to the United States, and interned with other Japanese Americans in 1942. Takahashi had given money to Black Nationalists, especially leaders of the Nation of Islam, said the FBI. He had promised them that after America's defeat they would enjoy liberty and wealth formerly denied to them.[40] The appeal of such propaganda in the 1930s was widely felt among poor urban blacks. In a speech in 1933, Elijah Muhammad is reported to have said, undoubtedly in reference to Takahashi, "The Japanese had sent a teacher to the black people[; they are] brothers and friends of the American Negroes."[41] Elijah Muhammad's son Emmanuel declared at his arraignment for draft evasion: "I hope the Japs win the war. Then all the Negroes will be free!"[42] Like other religious dissenters before them, Nation members interpreted cataclysmic events in their own lives and around the world in religious terms. One Black Muslim defendant challenged the court: "Sentence me to fifty years if you want. The white man is reaching the end of his rope after six thousand years and I won't do anything to stop him."[43]

However offensive government officials found the delight showed by members of the Nation of Islam at the prospect of a victory by "Asiatics" over "the Devil and his host," there was no evidence to sustain the charge of sedition against Muhammad.[44] Instead, prosecutors reportedly told Muhammad that they wanted to keep him out of the public eye in wartime. According to one biographer, Muhammad viewed his imprisonment and that of many of the group's other leaders as further proof of "the white man's innate adverseness to truth and fairness."[45] The conviction and imprisonment of so many of the group's leaders took a heavy toll on the members, despite their bravado. With much of the Nation's leadership incarcerated, attendance at temple services plummeted. When Gunnar Myrdal published *An American Dilemma* in 1944, he reported that Muslims were widely believed to be "abnormally weak" or "totally lacking" in all identification with the American nation.[46]

Muhammad's prison experience was transformative, however. His imprisonment became a form of martyrdom, an immersion in the belly of the beast, where he was a witness to the Truth. Like the persecuted prophets of the Bible and Jehovah's Witness leader Judge Rutherford, Muhammad understood his incarceration as the price of leadership, confirming the divinity of his mission. Upon his release from prison in 1946, Muhammad's claim to leadership of the sect had been cemented by his sacrifice.[47] Like followers who were jailed with him, and those who came later to the faith while incarcerated, Muhammad learned that his beliefs survived even the total deprivation of liberty. He was released after three years' imprisonment as a hero to his people, ready to oversee the movement. Equally important, Muhammad's newfound confidence and sense of command earned him deep and abiding loyalty.[48] He emerged a more practical man—full of plans and ready to direct his anger outward.

Muhammad served his entire sentence in the federal prison in Milan. There he met other conscientious objectors, including many Jehovah's Witnesses (more than 4,000 of the approximately 6,000 convicted draft evaders who claimed conscientious scruples against service during World War II were Witnesses) and a sprinkling of Quakers, and Italian Americans who refused to fight their former countrymen.[49] The Milan prison was a center of antiwar thought in the early 1940s, with its mixture of radical pacifists and those like Muhammad and the Witnesses who believed only in the war to end all time. The possibilities for open resistance were limited, but this mixed population challenged prison officials constantly. Milan became fertile ground for cultivating disobedience. The notorious "absolutist" pacifist Corbett Bishop attacked the Quaker-run American Friends Service Committee as a tool of the Selective Service Commission, rejecting alternative service as "blasphemy." After going on a four-month hunger strike Bishop was sent in 1943 to Milan. There he was force fed, but he refused to cooperate in any way for a remarkable 426 days. He was finally discharged in 1946, never having compromised his position.[50]

Like the Jehovah's Witnesses, but unlike Corbett Bishop, the Quakers, and other radical antiwar conscientious objectors, Muhammad and his followers were not pacifists.[51] What they objected to, they said, was fighting a war on behalf of their own oppressors. The Witnesses blamed the Catholic Church for the war; the Nation of Islam blamed "white devils," among whom the Catholic Church figured large.[52] Within prison walls, the Witnesses created a disciplined and separate group, under the direction of a leader chosen by the Witnesses in each prison.[53] Besides their evangelization of fellow prisoners, Witnesses were generally isolationist, unlike Quakers and most other socially conscious reformers. They challenged prison authorities only when they felt that their faith called on them to do so. Witness literature was a constant trouble spot; Witnesses were commanded to "sell" copies of *Watchtower* publications to potential converts, and most prisons would allow them to have only one or two magazines at a time. The resulting protest by Witness prisoners took various forms, including work "slow-downs" that made them a constant disciplinary problem for prison officials.[54]

The Witnesses also filed lawsuits, claiming that they should be allowed to practice their faith in prison. Hayden Covington valiantly argued on behalf of imprisoned Witnesses, but the courts rejected their suits. Federal judges held that state prisoners must pursue their claims through state courts, and state judges were unsympathetic. In *Kelly v. Dowd*, a leading case in this line of claims, the Seventh Circuit Court of Appeals decided against the plaintiff. Jehovah's Witness Garfield Kelly had sued the warden of Indiana State Prison, claiming that the warden had denied Kelly "Bible study helps [published by the Watch Tower Bible and Tract Society] . . . so that petitioner can study and determine the will of Jehovah God." The court followed the hands-off doctrine in such cases, holding that interference with "the prosecution and punishment of offenders" was "exceedingly delicate" and should be considered only in cases of dire "emergency," a standard that Kelly and other Witnesses did not meet.[55] The Witnesses lost these prison cases, but their example eventually inspired Black Muslims with similar grievances.

Elijah Muhammad had long believed that he shared much in common with the Witnesses. According to one source, Muhammad relied surreptitiously on Judge Rutherford for interpretations of contemporary events as well as techniques to inspire his followers. In 1935 Muhammad called the new Social Security numbers assigned to citizens by the Roosevelt administration "the mark of the beast," and claimed the end of the world was near. At the same time, he strictly prohibited all radio listening for Muslims, making it unlikely that his followers would learn that Rutherford had made the same claim only a few weeks earlier.[56]

One unsympathetic treatment portrayed Muhammad in the late 1930s as "increasingly dependent upon Rutherford's broadcasts and writings for his own interpretations of scripture and for ways to lure underclass African Americans to his temples."[57]

Muhammad himself thought the influence flowed in the other direction. Rutherford was among the very few white men whom Muhammad admired. On several occasions he claimed that Judge Rutherford believed that Fard was God, and that the Nation had a great deal to teach the Witnesses.[58] The repackaging of Witness doctrines and practices in Muslim thought illustrates the relationship between these two isolated and vilified groups. Many Muslims apparently were aware of the connection, even if most Witnesses were not.[59] In recent decades, however, African American Witnesses, who have always been part of the movement but now make up an increasingly large proportion of the faithful, have recognized the long-standing congruence between the two groups, even claiming that the Nation of Islam and the Witnesses should be natural allies.[60] Muslims generally denied that there was any causal connection between Witness beliefs and their own, however. Certainly, similar ideas and concepts were put within the Nation to new and distinct uses.[61]

For the most part, however, the Witnesses seem to have led rather than followed. Their example and influence extended beyond particular doctrines, as Muslims also adapted Witness techniques for survival in a hostile culture. The millenarian prophecy and scriptural interpretation that so impressed Fard and then Muhammad were matched by the Witnesses' strategies for the cultivation and defense of the faithful. The strong group identity among Witnesses and their cohesion in prison life became a template for Black Muslims.[62] Like the Witnesses, Muslims used their time in prison to recruit and communicate with those who were held fast like them. Both groups united a sense of deep alienation and degradation with a powerful new way of looking at the world.

Muslims' sense of group identity and access to a hidden truth offered converts an inversion of the imprisonment, discrimination, and rootlessness that characterized life for black men in northern cities and especially in northern prisons. Equally important, Muslims used the law and legal thinking to challenge the state that held them fast. Muhammad and his followers developed their own ways of seeking new converts, using the end-of-times cosmology and personal outreach deployed so effectively by Jehovah's Witnesses. At the same time, they tailored their message to suit a racially specific and distinctly legalized vision of the Nation's place in prison culture and the broader society. The use of legal tools by the movement was among the most important means of confronting the devil—a vitally energizing form of witnessing for the faith and speaking truth to power, as it had been for Jehovah's Witnesses before them.

Muhammad saw that even though he had suffered imprisonment for his faith, he and other members of the Nation of Islam, unlike prisoners from more mainstream Protestant, Catholic, and Jewish groups, were not allowed the means of celebrating worship or observing dietary and other laws.[63] According to one study conducted by pacifists of various faiths at the end of the war, only 3 percent of imprisoned conscientious objectors were black. These prisoners were categorized by the researchers as "Moslems," and were clearly understood to trace their resistance to a religious tradition outside the scope of most pacifist groups. By organizing a small temple within Milan federal prison, however, Muhammad began to carve out a space behind prison walls for his established followers, as well as new converts. He also internalized the enormous pain that imprisonment inflicted on inmates. Their suffering gave them a thirst for knowledge, a keen sense of what and who held them captive, and—most important of all—a capacity for growth and change in the midst of deprivation and loneliness.[64]

Upon his release, Muhammad demonstrated how much he had grown through suffering. He developed new programs for the movement, focusing less on open confrontation and more on enterprise, including not only business but finance, education, self-help programs, and more. Especially important, Muhammad reached out to prisoners, corresponding with those who were interested, and bringing many into the fold. The basic tenets of the faith, including concepts of racial separatism, the blue-eyed devil, and the approaching retribution, remained unchanged. In Muhammad's new, less rhetorically violent and confrontational view, the fundamental message of the Nation was one of self-contained dignity and enterprise, a model for separatism and innate self-worth.[65]

Muhammad had also learned—from the success of his friends, the Jehovah's Witnesses, and from his own experience in prison—that through law, believers could wrest some breathing room even from a hostile government. He combined the lessons he had learned in prison with the insight that legal recognition of the Nation of Islam as a religion would bring a measure of safety to followers and leaders alike. Jehovah's Witnesses often spoke of "using the Devil's weapons against the children of darkness"—law, especially constitutional law, being their primary example.[66] As Witness lawyer Hayden Covington put it, he and his fellow Witnesses had secured victory by being "wily as serpents and harmless as doves."[67] The Nation followed a similar path. With a model for recruitment and economic growth, and a rough understanding of what law could do, Muhammad was poised to become the undisputed leader of the most important of the Black Islamic movements in postwar America.

Malcolm X, as he became known to posterity, was galvanized when he first began to correspond with Muhammad from a Massachusetts prison in 1949. He had been convicted of burglary, weapons violations, and larceny. As Malcolm put it in his famous *Autobiography of Malcolm X,* "I had sunk to the very bottom of the American white man's society when—soon now, in prison—I found Allah and the religion of Islam and it completely transformed my life."[68] From Muhammad, he said, he learned that history's "greatest crime was the traffic in black flesh when the devil white man went into Africa and murdered and kidnapped . . . millions of black men, women, and children, who were worked and beaten and tortured as slaves."[69] The sympathy, education, and even the odd five-dollar bill he received from Muhammad were balm to his wounded psyche. The religious message awoke his soul.

Through prayer and study, Malcolm converted, becoming one of Muhammad's most devoted followers and defenders for a dozen years. Muhammad also taught Malcolm about the role of prison in the faith: "The black prisoner, he said, symbolized white society's crime of keeping black men oppressed and deprived and ignorant, and unable to get decent jobs, turning them into criminals." Malcolm's new faith gave him so much to read, think about, and do, that months passed without his even remembering he was in jail. "Up to then, I had never been so truly free in my life." He understood that other prisoners, too, were prepared for Muhammad's message: "Among all Negroes the black convict is the most perfectly conditioned to hear the words, 'the white man is the devil.'"[70]

Although he later understood how profoundly different the teachings of Muhammad were from more orthodox Islam, at the time, Malcolm was mesmerized by Muhammad's story of Yacub. Malcolm learned that the evil scientist, Mr. Yacub, was banished by Allah to an island, where he "decided, as revenge, to create upon the earth a devil race—a bleached-out, white race of people." It took centuries for the program to be completed, but the resulting white humans, as Yacub knew they would, became "lighter, and weaker, progressively also more susceptible to wickedness and evil." Eventually this wicked race overran the superior black races, especially the tribe of Shabazz, and ruled the world through wickedness and cruel oppression. The savior and redeemer was to appear after 6,000 years of this domination. He came in the person of W. D. Fard, "the greatest and mightiest God who appeared on the earth . . . , appearing in North America at a time when the history and the prophecy that is written was coming to realization, as the non-white people all over the world began to rise, and as the devil white civilization, condemned by Allah, was, through its devilish nature, destroying itself."[71]

Inverting the relationship between dominant and subjected races in twentieth-century America was key to Fard's and then Muhammad's thinking, transmitted to Malcolm and to thousands of other prisoners and new converts. But the Nation of Islam's concept of racial identity and color was more complex than a simple black-white dichotomy. In Black Muslim cosmology, whiteness was not created by God, and was inherently more susceptible to evil than the noble black race.[72] Within that construction, however, Muhammad said that degrees of evil characterized various white races. "Some are better than others," he said. "White Americans and Germans [who had oppressed the Jehovah's Witnesses]—Allah has taught me—are the most wicked of the white race."[73] The Nation itself included many who were of mixed racial heritage, among whom Fard (whose mother was widely acknowledged to have been Caucasian) is just the best known.[74] Malcolm himself once said that the mixed racial heritage—and thus the racial indeterminacy—of many Black Muslims was just a "little technicality," given that in the larger society "one drop of black blood makes you black."[75] This "one-drop" cure for whiteness formula upended the antiblack racism of Jim Crow. Muhammad transformed what had been considered a form of racial pollution into an inclusive vision of blackness, in which a redemptive single drop salvaged an otherwise hopeless heritage.[76]

For Malcolm and many other prisoners, the Nation and its beliefs gave structure and meaning to their desperate and demoralizing confinement. Equally important, both Muhammad and Malcolm, after his release in 1952, continued to pay attention to prisoners and their plight. Muhammad wrote personally to many prisoners, as he had to Malcolm. Temple resources supported communications between members on the outside and prisoners within, and included financial assistance as well as religious training. While more mainstream civil rights organizations overlooked prisoners, the Nation paid for lawsuits and organizing activities for Muslim inmates, especially when they sought to secure freedom of worship and practice.[77]

Inside the prison walls, members worked diligently, and usually secretly, to educate new converts and build their organization. Although whether the Nation was a religious organization was hotly contested by prison officials, theirs was not primarily a political movement. For the most part their battles were religious, undertaken in deference to a higher authority and on behalf of a separatist community of the enlightened that existed within and yet apart from the larger prison society.[78] Like the Witnesses before them, they kept to themselves, rarely engaging in idle chatter or making friends outside the group, but always seeking converts.[79] They could readily resort to more militant, even violent action and rhetoric, but on religious grounds and only on provocation, when resisting what they saw as prison authorities' transgression into the realm of the spirit. As one student of the movement put it, in the 1950s the interest of the Nation was in recruiting disciples who would join the larger community outside and be active in building the organization. Apart from protecting their spiritual observance and belief, anything that prevented a convert's transition to the outside got in the way of the work.[80]

Building a protective structure around the transmission and practice of the faith was crucial, however. With an eye to the many successes that Witnesses secured through litigation (including by the mid-1950s the recognition of Witness adult men as "ministers" who qualified for exemption from military service), Black Muslims developed coherent legal strategies.[81] They brought something new to the world of law, however—they argued that theirs was a religious movement, even though prison officials, politicians, and others claimed that the Nation was political. The role of race in the movement's theology and cosmology, as well as the argument for black separatism and moral superiority in its social thought, provoked outrage in the mainstream press. For decades, scholars and religious leaders debated whether or not the Nation was primarily religious; in law, the debate was over relatively early. It was clear by the mid-1960s that the Nation of Islam had succeeded in establishing its bona fides as a religious movement, and in securing unprecedented protections for its members.[82]

In the late 1950s, Muslim prisoners turned to the courts, claiming that they were members of a faith and had been discriminated against because of their religious commitments and beliefs. New York state prison officials reported in late 1959 that Muslim prisoners were active in at least three state facilities, and had filed suit from Clinton state prison in Dannemora, a remote facility in the far north of the state. "They attempt to express everything on a religious basis. But it is our opinion that they are not religiously sincere—that they have ulterior motives," said a corrections department spokesman.[83] By early 1961, mainstream newspapers reported a "widespread legal attack" on the part of the Nation, with more than a hundred separate lawsuits filed around the country. Rising levels of strife in prisons where Black Muslims were active demonstrated that a genuine movement was under way that showed signs of coordination and discipline.[84]

When Muslim prisoners first complained of their treatment, they inhabited a legal universe that has now vanished. The classic description of prisoners, drawn from a nineteenth-century Virginia case, labeled them "slaves of the state."[85] Until the 1960s, prison administrators and most prisoners invoked the master-subject relationship as the single best description of the status imposed by incarceration.[86] Even prison riots, such as two uprisings in New Jersey and California in the early 1950s, were couched as challenges to the brutality of control rather than as objections to the master-subject theory of imprisonment itself.[87] Within the authoritarian structure of the prison, inmates were subject to strict discipline and allowed few opportunities to socialize or share information.[88]

Even in this rigid and largely unquestioned penal universe, however, Jehovah's Witnesses had posed a distinct challenge. During World War II their apparently ineradicable group identity and internal discipline defied the logic of midcentury punishment. As prominent criminologist Donald Cressey put it in the late 1950s, prison administrators strove "to keep inmate society as unorganized as possible, to prevent individuals from joining forces."[89] Jehovah's Witnesses' collective resistance to even the harshest penal regimes made them such difficult prisoners that in U.S. prisons their presence deeply troubled prison administrators.[90] Even in the notorious concentration camps of the Third Reich, one scholar maintained that "psychologically speaking, the SS was never quite equal to the challenge offered them by the Jehovah's Witnesses."[91]

Like Elijah Muhammad, the Witnesses convicted of draft evasion were released from American prisons shortly after the end of the war; yet their example left an imprint. They proved that prisons could be vulnerable to believers whose allegiance to a higher power emboldened them to resist the authority of the state. Theirs had been a challenge framed in terms entirely outside the dominant vocabulary of master and servant. The Witnesses deployed law and legal thinking—the defense of the faith and the faithful against a satanic state. Their successors, the Black Muslims, inherited and built upon this foundation.

The new constitutional world penetrated even prison walls, thanks to the Muslim prisoners whose faith emboldened them. In their claims, religious freedom became a transformative, liberating force. Their legal battles established that even prisoners had religious rights, sparking prison activism as well as inspiring (and intimidating) those on the outside.[92] Their burgeoning numbers alone made members of the Nation a force to be reckoned with, but it was their use of the devil's own law against a punitive state that profoundly disturbed prison officials and transformed their own and the country's understanding of the relation of law to faith.

The numbers of Black Muslims had indeed grown in the late 1950s—estimates place membership between 65,000 and 100,000 by

1960.[93] Many of the new members were themselves prisoners, as incarceration rates for black men and many black inmates' allegiance to the Nation both rose precipitously.[94] Traditionally, observers assumed that Muslims were inspired by *Brown v. Board of Education,* the Supreme Court's 1954 decision that held that "separate but equal" public school facilities divided by race violated the equal protection clause of the Constitution, setting the stage for integration of schools and eventually the nationwide dismantling of Jim Crow.[95] Many also assumed that the Nation was the first organized group within prison to have a coherent legal strategy.[96] Yet Black Muslims were dedicated separatists, not integrationists, and they were not the first to organize by faith in prison. Instead, the Jehovah's Witnesses provided a model for Elijah Muhammad that fit both theologically and legally. Black Muslim prisoners' claims confirm this interpretation. Muslims repeatedly claimed discrimination, but not on the basis of race. They focused instead on religious discrimination—with racial difference among the core beliefs they sought to protect. In 1959 the National Association for the Advancement of Colored People (NAACP) legal counsel Thurgood Marshall derisively described the Nation of Islam as "run by a bunch of thugs organized from jails."[97] Muhammad shot back, "Mr. Thurgood Marshall is the most *unfit,* and worse enemy of all to the real cause of freedom, justice, and equality for the so-called Negro thugs. . . . He is in love with the white race. He hates the preaching of the uplifting of the Black Nation, unless it is approved by the white race, and is totally against his brother Negro ever thinking of being the supreme."[98] Muhammad, Malcolm, and other Muslim leaders had a different legal agenda than the NAACP.

There were several centers of Muslim activism, including state prisons in California and Illinois, the Virginia prisons that housed those convicted in the District of Columbia, and more.[99] The infamous prisons of New York State, however—Attica, Green Haven, Dannemora, Auburn—were particularly fertile sites for legal and political activism among Black Muslim inmates. The first major breakthrough for the prisoners came in late 1961, when Judge Charles Clark of the Second Circuit held in *Pierce v. LaVallee* that the traditional "hands-off" approach to intervention by the federal courts in state prisons no longer applied in cases involving religious persecution.[100] Three Muslim inmates at Dannemora claimed that they had been denied permission to buy the Qur'an or to correspond with spiritual advisors, and—most egregious—that they had been put in solitary confinement because of their religious beliefs. A charge of religious persecution, Judge Clark stressed, invoked the "preferred" freedom approach developed by the Supreme Court in cases involving Jehovah's Witnesses in the late 1930s and early 1940s.[101] A long list of contrary opinions involving other prison issues, such as physical abuse and personal liberty, were not directly relevant, Clark held. The only true precedent involved the same issue as that raised by the Muslims. The Seventh Circuit's opinion in the 1944 Witness case, *Kelly v. Dowd,* was precisely on point.[102] Despite this case, Clark stressed, the importance of religious liberty meant that federal courts should no longer turn away complaints brought by state prisoners when questions of faith were involved.[103] Although this New York case was not appealed to the Supreme Court, in 1964 the justices did take a case from the Seventh Circuit that dismissed a suit brought by a Muslim inmate in Illinois who complained that he was denied the right to buy religious publications solely because of his Muslim faith. The Supreme Court reversed the decision below, which had relied on the earlier Witness case, *Kelly v. Dowd.* Citing Judge Clark's opinion in the New York case, the Court held unanimously that a claim of religious discrimination was valid grounds for legal action.[104]

The federal court breakthrough was followed by an equally heady victory in *Brown v. McGinnis,* decided by New York's highest court in January 1962.[105] Clarence Brown, a Black Muslim, and other inmates from Green Haven filed a petition claiming that they were not allowed "religious services and spiritual advice and ministration from [a] recognized clergyman of [their] profession and choice." Brown also claimed that he and other Muslims were "forced to hold religious services in the prison yard."[106] Both the trial and intermediate appellate courts had disposed of these petitions swiftly and without written opinions. Under prior state decisions, *Brown v. McGinnis* looked like an easy case.

Prison rules were crystal clear. Commissioner Paul McGinnis reported that the closest temple, on West 116th Street, known to Muslims as Temple Number Seven, was ministered by "one Malcolm X. Little, who, according to the records of the New York State Department of Correction, has a previous criminal record."[107] No minister with a criminal record was allowed in the prison, according to the rules of

Green Haven and other state prisons. The commissioner also argued that the "dangers inherent in permitting the dissemination of [the Muslims'] belief among the prison population" justified "the curtailment or withdrawal" of even the admittedly limited privilege of religious worship enjoyed by prisoners of other faiths.[108] The Court of Appeals held that the commissioner's speculative invocation of danger was not enough to foreclose all consideration of Brown's and others' ability to practice their faith, however. The case was sent back to the trial court for a hearing to decide how best to maintain appropriate prison discipline while also respecting Muslims' rights under the religious liberty clauses of the New York and the U.S. constitutions.[109] This pattern—of litigation at both the state and federal levels, and of more or less constant judicial review of the treatment of Muslim prisoners in correctional facilities—continued throughout the 1960s, changing prison culture and the ways prisoners understood the scope of their own rights.

Thus commenced the odyssey of litigants Martin Sostre, William SaMarion, and James Pierce, whose tenacity placed them in the center of Muslim "agitators" at Dannemora (and eventually Attica, where two of the three were transferred during the long course of their litigation).[110] Their story, as it emerged in Chief Judge Steven Brennan's federal district courtroom in western New York State in 1962, was a remarkable one in the annals of prison activism. In early 1959, some thirty Muslim prisoners were assigned a court in the recreation yard, where they regularly congregated, heard addresses by one of their number, wore black fez-style caps (like Elijah Muhammad), and spoke only among themselves. When a guard approached, they would stop talking immediately, which raised the suspicions of prison officials.

Guards broke into a homemade locker on the Muslim court in August, and found something totally unexpected—a constitution. Instead of treating the court as a place to play sports like other prisoners did, these followers of Elijah Muhammad had held meetings and created an alternative form of governance for themselves within the prison. The constitution established and governed a group called the Muslim Brotherhood (which expanded to many prisons during the 1960s, although this was the only full-fledged constitution ever found by officials). The "aims and objects" of the Brotherhood were listed as "complete unity among our brothers by employing the unifying force of Islam," promotion of "unity of action and organization through the study of: Islam," and the training of "leaders for the future struggle." The organization was broadly democratic and deeply secret, and membership was based on acceptance of Islam and the "Rules of Court" of the Brotherhood (all "homosexuals" were explicitly prohibited; violence was to be deployed only as a last resort; all actions were to be taken as a group and based on majority decision).[111] The Brotherhood established, in effect, a separate religious community—a monastic order within the walls of Dannemora, with allegiance to a divine sovereign more powerful than anything the warden could conjure.

As Judge Brennan noted, the drafting of such a constitution is vanishingly rare in prison history.[112] Everything about prison culture at midcentury meant that this democratically structured and religiously based order would be viewed as a threat to security. Prison officials responded swiftly and with predictable severity. Sostre, SaMarion, and Pierce, the three plaintiffs, who were identified as leaders of the group, were deprived of "good time" and sentenced to an isolated confinement known as "segregation." Two were transferred to Attica directly from segregation a year later. The third plaintiff was transferred to Auburn after eighteen months of segregation. They argued that they were punished for their religion alone, a defiant and resistant faith, to be sure, but nonetheless a collection of ideas and commitments that, they claimed, should have been immune from state oversight, even for prisoners.

The Muslim Brotherhood's constitution deserves further exploration, as it drew plainly on the "constitution-mindedness" of this distinctively American faith.[113] With this document, popular constitutionalism acquired tangible form inside the prison, providing structure and legitimacy to a new way of thinking about faith. The Muslim Brotherhood's constitution also demonstrates how profoundly lawbound Black Muslim inmates understood themselves to be. Through the drafting of this document, the organizers of the Brotherhood declared they were more completely bound to each other and their aspirational vision for redemption through faith than subject to the controls of the prison warden and his guards. They knew, of course, that at some level they were individually vulnerable, but in concert they found strength to resist. Their reliance on the rightfulness of their Brotherhood was sustained through the study and practice of Islam. In some ways, this constitution tapped into a very traditional (and time-tested) mode of American rights talk: the liberating potential of a constitutional text has long held immense power in popular thought and theory.[114]

So it was here. That they turned to an explicitly legal understanding of their place in society, and then deployed a constitution (and then a lawsuit challenging punishment imposed on them for having drafted such a document), illustrates how the Nation of Islam and its followers participated in a venerable lay constitutionalism among African Americans. Like other black activists in the mid-twentieth century, they deployed the descendant of constitutional claims that were first developed in the great nineteenth-century struggles over slavery. Such arguments also helped develop a viable American constitutional tradition of liberation. The location of an emancipatory potential in the U.S. Constitution fueled a vigorous tradition of rights talk among freedmen and women, especially during the Civil War and Reconstruction.[115] One legacy of this tradition surfaced in Dannemora. These were not the parsings of lawyers dealing with the official pronouncements of courts, but grander, more utopian—yet also more experientially grounded—claims of constitutional meaning, drawn from deep wells of faith in justice for those who have suffered. This was a religiously *and* racially infused version of popular constitutionalism. Yet there can be no doubt that the political act of constitution making was undertaken in the service of an overarching religious ideal. The spirit of the law was reinscribed in a homemade document that defied the state's prison discipline.

In this sense, the Muslim Brotherhood in a remote New York state prison drafted the constitution for a legitimate organization, to stand in contrast to their understanding of an illegitimate hierarchy—the prison system, the racist society that created it, and those who abused the "rights" of Black Muslims everywhere in America. The Brotherhood's constitution attempted to create a law-filled society, separate and uncorrupted by that racist society even within its most powerful and oppressive space, the penitentiary. Like other religious actors before them, they sought a sacred place within the profane world. The sacralization of their lives was memorialized in the constitution. This marriage of religion and constitutionalism illustrates once again how thoroughly popular notions of sacred and secular justice were combined in the lives of believers in America.

This combination also deepens the conclusion that the Nation of Islam in this period was a distinctly and indelibly American phenomenon. From this perspective, the experience of almost half a millennium in the cauldron of North America had transformed "Blackamericans" into a new people.[116] In religious-studies terminology, "peoplehood" is a productive term, signaling a group's investment in a particular religious history that has the power to explain the course of events and spark faith across generations.[117] The experience of peoplehood in the Nation was a matter of both religious and constitutional history, understood clearly and expressed in both arenas in terms of justice over time and through faith.

The construction of peoplehood in religious thought often includes a profound sense of outsider status, reflecting instability and also opportunity in the broader society. As one historian put it, a cosmic story of rejection can "exude self-confidence rather than fear, a sense of growing influence rather than a feeling of social isolation."[118] Among the Muslim Brotherhood in upstate New York prisons, a sense of growing influence underlay their self-awareness as well as their religious self-identification. The Nation of Islam, like the Witnesses before them, deployed their suffering as a badge of inclusion marking those who were saved.[119]

The Nation also gained momentum in prison, as well as in the society outside the walls, through its challenge to black Christianity, especially the integrationist model of civil rights leaders.[120] Dismissing integration as a "cunning Christian strategy of the white man," Black Muslims did not rely on the assimilationist equal protection clause of the Fourteenth Amendment.[121] Instead, they used the explicitly separatist free exercise clause. This strategy allowed them to attack the illegitimate hierarchy that kept them from their faith, and also to vindicate their own distinct identity in law as well as in religion.

In 1962, three years after the guards at Dannemora discovered the Muslims' extraordinary constitution, the prisoners' case was finally heard on the merits. The warden now claimed that the Brotherhood "is not a religion." Instead, he said it was a separatist, subversive organization that "sets itself up as an adjunct to the Islamic faith."[122] Judge Brennan agreed, emphasizing that Black Muslims were troublemakers, not believers—certainly not when they uttered such vengeful statements as: "[God] hates his enemies. In fact, He tells us in the Bible and the Holy Qu-ran that He will destroy them with hellfire."[123] Or insurrectionary sentiments such as: "When the box [that is, segregation] ceases to work, the entire disciplinary and security system breaks down. This is what happened in Dannemora. . . . Eventually the warden had to ship us out of the box to different prisons."[124] Brennan upheld the punishment inflicted on the three plaintiffs, drawing a line between religion and politics that ultimately proved untenable.

Attica was also ripe for a challenge, however, as Sostre and SaMarion found after they arrived there straight from "the box" in late 1960. Within a few years they had filed another claim of religious discrimination in federal court, which yielded mixed results at the trial level. Federal district court judge John Henderson held that the Nation of Islam was a religion rather than a political movement, but decided against Sostre and SaMarion on their claim of religious persecution. He dismissed their request that prison officials be required to refrain from all interference with religious activities of Muslims, including congregational worship, communication with ministers, and possession and distribution of literature. On appeal in 1964, the Second Circuit again addressed the arguments of this prolific and confrontational group. Writing for the court, Judge Paul Hays, known, as the *New York Times* put it in his obituary in 1980, "for his strong views on judicial restraint,"[125] stressed that "no romantic or sentimental view of constitutional rights or of religion should induce a court to interfere with the necessary disciplinary regime established by prison officials." This group, Hays said, was not religious "in the same way as are Catholics, Protestants and Jews." Instead, religious values were "only of secondary importance" to Black Nationalism and the cultivation of black supremacy and solidarity. In other words, the Nation and these prisoners were political rather than truly religious.[126]

Most commentators agreed with this assessment. By the mid-1960s, the presence of prisoners like Sostre and SaMarion in both state and federal courts drew the attention of legal scholars, as well as journalists and pundits. Legal journals, including the Harvard and Columbia law reviews, published student notes on the growing jurisprudence of Black Muslim rights in prison. Scholar Eric Lincoln, journalist Louis

Lomax, and others researched the Nation of Islam and Elijah Muhammad.[127] Malcolm X spoke at Columbia and Harvard; everyone was talking about the new Black Nationalism and the Nation of Islam. In California, the state Supreme Court held that Muslim prisoners did not have the right to practice their faith because of the "potentially serious dangers to the established prison society presented by the Muslim beliefs and actions."[128] The *Columbia Law Review* argued that Muslim prisoners were so unruly that they satisfied the "clear and present danger" test for prohibiting activity otherwise protected by the First Amendment.[129]

Judge Hays's opinion recited many of these concerns about Muslim prisoners and their claims to religious freedom, noting that "at Attica Prison the authorities were fortunately able to nip in the bud a sit-down strike of Muslim inmates in protest against punishment of Sostre."[130] Riots, threats against non-Muslim prisoners, jubilant speeches at the crash of an airplane that killed 120 white people—all these actions and more disturbed the court.[131] Nonetheless, the trial court's decision was reversed in part, with a direction to the court to retain jurisdiction over the case for one year (that is, until late 1965), during which time state officials were to draw up regulations to govern Muslim inmates' rights to practice their faith. If no progress had been made in that time, Sostre and SaMarion could apply to the federal courts once again for action.[132]

Back in state court in 1965, the trial court held unconstitutional the draconian regulations proposed by the commissioner, including the stipulation that all ministers qualified to visit and counsel inmates must hold degrees from four-year, accredited colleges or universities and have served a minimum of five years in full-time parish ministry.[133] On appeal, state officials conceded that it would be "difficult, if not impossible, [for Muslims] to practice their religion" under such regulations. At the same time, they also said that "practice of this particular religion in a State prison is incompatible with the preservation of prison security and discipline."[134] A special hearing was to be scheduled in the trial court, but by March 1966 there was no real progress and more than a year had elapsed since the Second Circuit had directed the federal trial court to retain jurisdiction. In April, Judge Henderson of the district court, clearly exasperated by the delay, entered an order directing the commissioner to issue regulations within thirty days. Henderson stressed that the current regulations were unconstitutionally overbroad, and could not reasonably be relied on to address the problems raised by Muslim claims to religious freedom.[135]

On May 2, 1966, the commissioner submitted a revised proposal, which Judge Henderson held represented a good faith attempt to comply with the mandate from the Second Circuit. Although clumsily drafted, these rules provided that Muslims had rights like those extended to inmates of other faiths. In addition, their dietary needs would be taken into consideration, ministers would be allowed to visit, and Muslim prisoners could receive religious publications.[136] Over the next several years, the regulations were refined in state court proceedings as Muslims battled for administration of the rules that actually achieved the same religious liberty granted to more mainstream religious groups. At the same time, of course, their activism increased access and rights to practice for all religious groups in prison. To prison officials in the 1960s, the Nation of Islam represented the outer boundary of danger. And yet because Muslims had the right to practice, other minority faiths were swept into the same protective constitutional embrace.

By the early 1970s, when the pace of confrontation and litigation cooled in state courts, Muslim inmates had achieved the right to hold weekly services, to wear religious insignia, to have their clergy accorded the same treatment as the ministers of other faiths, and to recruit new members.[137] In 1978, Sostre and SaMarion's suit, initially brought by a handwritten, pro se complaint from Attica prison, was finally resolved. Under the case name *Bryant v. McGinnis,* Chief Judge John Curtin of the Western District of New York held that the three Muslim prisoners, all of whom had been incarcerated in Attica, had been denied their constitutionally protected right to practice their religion for the period between October 1964 and May 1966. Each of the three now middle-aged plaintiffs received $3,000 in damages.[138]

As Muslims achieved significant victories in state and federal courts beginning in the mid 1960s, however, the Nation of Islam outside prison walls was imploding. Malcolm X was disciplined by Elijah Muhammad in late 1963 and finally broke from the Nation in 1964; he outlined a new, politically active Black Nationalism within days of the final split.[139]

Malcolm's subsequent trip to Mecca and Africa changed his outlook on race and racial difference forever, leading him to a new sense of political involvement distinct from religion. Less than a year later, Malcolm was assassinated. Black Muslims who were widely believed to have been acting for Elijah Muhammad opened fire as he spoke in Harlem.[140]

The death of Malcolm X, formerly the Nation's most popular and articulate spokesman and publicist, undermined confidence in the movement for many. The phenomenal growth of the Nation slowed significantly as Muhammad's health suffered and his long-standing pattern of adultery became undeniable after two former secretaries filed paternity suits against him in the early 1960s.[141] Some converts had followed Malcolm out of the Nation, and many more who never had been Muslims admired him greatly.[142] Muhammad's own son Wallace embraced Sunni Islam, and began to criticize openly his father's distinctly racialized, unorthodox form of Muslim faith, further reducing sympathy for the Nation's dire beliefs.[143]

The fracturing of the movement became a constant as it spun off many much smaller groups. In 1975, after his father's death, Wallace declared that a new "Universal Nation of Islam" had taken the place of black essentialism and supremacy. He reached out to Christian civil rights leaders, and adopted orthodox Islamic practices and beliefs.[144] A breakaway group organized by Louis Farrakhan in 1977 married some of Elijah Muhammad's black dispensationalism with universalist Islamic rhetoric. Farrakhan became the standard-bearer of fiery Muslim separatism, with controversy following close behind. For all his sound and fury, however, Farrakhan presided over a much smaller and more diffuse group, based in Chicago still but with scattered clusters of members in the Caribbean, Africa, and London.[145]

Yet for incarcerated African Americans, the Nation remained a key for identity, respect, and a life of faith in a place of despair, long after the movement outside had begun to stumble. Other prisoners, having witnessed the success of Black Muslims, reconsidered their own agency and dignity, sparking a broader prisoners' rights movement.[146]

For some, conversion to the Nation's Muslim beliefs provided life-long benefits. Others turned eventually to legal and political activism in more traditional Christian or secular ways. Repeat litigant Martin Sostre, for example, initially found both purpose and a means to resist constant humiliation and harassment through his faith. Sostre, who often represented himself in legal proceedings, was released from Attica in 1964 after serving his entire twelve-year sentence for a drug conviction. In 1965, he opened the Afro-Asian Bookstore in Buffalo. The store became a center for radical activism of all sorts, including anti–Vietnam War protests and Black Nationalism. Officials immediately suspected Sostre when race riots broke out in Buffalo in 1967, and charged him with incitement to riot and arson. Both charges were dropped, but he was eventually convicted for possession with intent to sell of a small amount of heroin (reputed to be worth only fifteen dollars), after a half-day trial at which he was not represented, on the testimony of a witness who later recanted.[147] He was sentenced to thirty to forty years, with an additional sentence of thirty days for contempt of court.[148]

Sostre was imprisoned overnight once again at Attica, then was transferred to Green Haven. After he attempted to mail his attorney a letter containing legal papers he had drafted for use by a codefendant from Buffalo, Sostre was placed in "punitive segregation," where he remained for more than a year. Sostre was the only prisoner at Green Haven to spend such an extended time in isolation, which meant he remained in his six-by-eight-foot, windowless cell for twenty-four hours a day. He was permitted a shower once a week and was kept on reduced rations. He was not allowed to read newspapers, see movies, or attend school or training programs. Federal judge Constance Baker Motley of the Southern District of New York granted his habeas corpus petition in 1969, ordering his release into the general prison population.[149]

The court found that Sostre was subjected to cruel and degrading punishment because of his active litigation strategy and because of his allegiance to the Nation of Islam, especially during his imprisonment from 1952 through 1964. Judge Motley awarded Sostre $13,000 in actual and punitive damages. She also granted injunctive relief, prohibiting the warden and other Green Haven officials from placing inmates in punitive isolation for more than fifteen days at a time, and prohibiting such segregation altogether as punishment for political or religious views.[150] The attorney general of New York wrote to Motley soon after the opinion was handed down, complaining that discipline in the prison had been undermined. He also reported that Sostre had "been doing exactly what he pleases, including walking off his job and holding meetings with other inmates in the galleries, corridors and lavatories." He added, "The administration has been virtually powerless to restrain him" because of the judge's order.[151]

On appeal, the entire Second Circuit heard the case en banc, a process reserved for the most important and divisive cases. The court held that while punitive segregation of Sostre because of his political beliefs and legal activities was unlawful, it was not "cruel and unusual"—that is, not a violation of the Eighth Amendment to the Constitution. Sostre was not entitled to recover damages, therefore.[152] By 1971, when the Second Circuit considered Martin Sostre's remarkable career as a litigant and self-proclaimed "jail house lawyer" for the last time, Sostre was represented by elite legal talent.[153] Victor Rabinowitz of the left-leaning New York law firm Rabinowitz, Boudin was supported by Jack Greenberg of the NAACP Legal Defense Fund and Haywood Burns of the National Conference of Black Lawyers. References to his membership in the Nation of Islam were all in the past tense. What mattered to Sostre in 1971 was not religion but politics.[154]

Sostre, who since his first trial in Judge Brennan's courtroom had been widely recognized as an articulate and effective advocate, became a cause célèbre. By 1975, his case was known nationally and internationally. Prominent left-wing groups and activists took up his cause, including Andrei Sakharov, Philip and Daniel Berrigan, and the Reverend Ralph Abernathy, as well as Amnesty International and PEN American Center. He was the subject of a book that claimed he had been framed by Buffalo police, and a documentary called *Frame Up.*[155] The Buffalo police officer in Sostre's case was dismissed from the force after the disappearance of $10,000 worth of heroin from a police evidence locker.[156] On Christmas Day 1975, the former Black Muslim and now self-described "revolutionary anarchist" was granted clemency by New York governor Hugh Carey.[157]

The exception to the waning influence of the Nation after Malcolm's departure in 1964 was the famous and enormously popular heavyweight boxer known at the time as Cassius Clay, but soon to become instantly recognizable as Muhammad Ali. To the Nation and particularly for Elijah Muhammad, the newest recruit brought attention, vast sums of cash in the form of tithes, and a fresh face that was attractive to young potential recruits.[158] Although Muhammad traditionally had discouraged sports of all kinds for followers, and called boxing "wicked," the pliant Ali became the poster boy for the movement, temporarily filling the hole left by the mercurial Malcolm X.[159]

Ali's allegiance to the Nation brought him legal trouble as well as spiritual peace. By the late 1960s, as the Vietnam War grew larger, more complex, and controversial, members of the Nation were counseled by Elijah Muhammad to refuse to bear arms. If necessary, said Muhammad, Muslims must endure imprisonment, as he had, rather than serve in the oppressor's army.[160] When Ali learned in 1966 that his draft board in Louisville, Kentucky, had classified him 1A, eligible for military service, he retorted that he had "no personal quarrel with those Vietcongs" and refused to serve.[161] His Muslim faith taught him "not to take part in any way with infidels or any nonreligious group."[162] An independent investigator, retired Kentucky judge Leonard Graumann, concluded that Ali was sincere and entitled to conscientious objector status, but the Department of Justice was determined to prosecute.[163]

Ali hired veteran Hayden Covington to represent him. As the chief legal counsel for the Jehovah's Witnesses from the late 1930s through the early 1960s, Covington had represented schoolchildren in the landmark Supreme Court cases that challenged the mandatory Pledge of Allegiance during the 1930s and 1940s. Covington had also supervised the legal defense of thousands of Witnesses who refused to serve in the military. By 1966, however, when Ali needed a lawyer, Covington was far less active. He had been disfellowshipped as a drunkard by the central office at the Watch Tower in Brooklyn, only to find that he could not hold down a job in a more traditional law firm.[164]

One NAACP Legal Defense Fund lawyer, a member of Ali's legal team at the Supreme Court, commented that "Covington was hardly a sophisticated constitutional advocate."[165] Nonetheless, Covington had long and distinguished experience in selective-service cases, especially on behalf of an isolated and deeply unpopular group of believers. Elijah Muhammad admired his impressive record of victories; the longstanding affinity between Witnesses and Muslims—especially their shared legal activism—also made Covington an attractive choice.[166] Covington knew all about defending draft resisters against the devil and his government. As he explained to Ali, this case involved more than anything a conflict between the government—the arm of the devil in both Ali's and Covington's cosmology—and a faithful resister: "They want to make an example out of you," Covington told his beleaguered client.[167] Ali also understood the fight in racial as well as religious terms. As he told *Black Scholar* magazine, "I was determined to be one nigger that the white man didn't get. . . . You understand? One nigger you ain't going to get."[168]

Covington added a defense he had used for hundreds of Jehovah's Witnesses: he claimed that Ali was a minister and therefore should be exempted from service. The argument that every Witness was a minister had not saved the thousands of Witness men sent to prison for draft evasion in the 1940s; in Ali's case, the strategy backfired even more dramatically. The public reacted with outrage when the world heavyweight boxing champion, who had listed his profession on the Selective Service's questionnaire in February 1966 as "boxer," claimed a ministerial exemption only a few months later.[169] The claim was rejected by every judge who heard it. As federal district judge Joe Ingraham of Texas noted in oral findings in 1967, Ali had asked for permission to travel to England, Germany, and Mexico for prize fights both before and after he claimed a ministerial exemption. Ali had also complained that if drafted he would not be allowed to pursue his "occupation [a]s a professional boxer."[170] Although Ali had explained in letters to the draft board that he had scruples as a Muslim against killing or bearing arms, he had never claimed that he was a minister of the faith.[171] Whatever the ultimate reason for the change, a new team of lawyers replaced Covington by 1968. Ali never paid the old litigator, although in his autobiography he generously credited Covington with contributing to "the biggest victory of my life."[172]

Ali became a far more popular man in the late 1960s, when his Legal Defense Fund lawyers successfully challenged New York's revocation of his boxing license and public support for the Vietnam War began to melt, especially among African Americans.[173] His draft resistance made Ali a hero among many young black Americans, who saw his defiance as a watershed moment in the capacity of African Americans to claim respect from government and society.[174] Most important, the long, hard road to recognition of Muslim prisoners' beliefs as genuinely religious (rather than political) bore fruit unexpectedly. In his brief and at the oral argument in the United States Supreme Court for Ali's appeal from his conviction, Solicitor General Erwin Griswold conceded that "the petitioner's beliefs are based upon 'religious training and belief.'"[175] The Department of Justice, however, had written to the Selective Service Appeal Board at the outset of the case, declaring that Ali was insincere and that his "claimed objections to participation in war insofar as they are based upon the teachings of the Nation of Islam, rest on grounds which primarily are political and racial."[176] Federal law, by the time Ali's case was heard, had clearly established that the Nation of Islam was a religion. The Justice Department's letter, held the Supreme Court, was a fatal error: because it was impossible to tell precisely what grounds the Appeal Board had relied upon in convicting Ali, the flawed advice about the political nature of Ali's beliefs required a reversal of the conviction.[177]

The new constitutional world of religious liberty, thanks to the dogged, decade-long campaign of Muslim prisoners, now indisputably included Ali and other followers of Elijah Muhammad. Commentators at the time and since have wondered why the government made such key concessions late in the game—at the last moment, virtually.[178] The change in political support for the war and the draft may have been relevant, to be sure. Solicitor General Griswold must also have understood, however, that the nation's prison system, which had only recently digested the mandate to respect the religious practice and beliefs of Black Muslims, would be thrown into massive disarray (even chaos) by a decision that rested on construing the Nation of Islam as "political and racial," rather than religious. That issue had been resolved in their favor, thanks to Martin Sostre, William SaMarion, and thousands of other Muslim prisoners who fought to make it so.

Only three months after the *Clay* decision, in September 1971, Attica erupted in a four-day uprising that left forty-three men dead (all but one from state bullets) after the state regained control of the prison.[179] The radical Black Panther leader, author, and inmate George Jackson famously argued that "the ultimate expression of law isn't order, it's prison."[180] Two weeks before the uprising, 700 Attica inmates fasted and wore black armbands to protest Jackson's death after he was shot by a prison guard in San Quentin Prison in California.[181] During the Attica riot, according to eyewitnesses and participants, Muslim prisoners ensured the safety of noninmate hostages, kept order and arranged for food and sanitation, and imposed a rudimentary rule of discipline. As one participant put it, "The reason why the Muslims took control is because of our discipline and our unity. This frightens the authorities. . . . We treated the hostages the way we had always wanted to be treated. It wouldn't have taken anything away from their manhood to treat a prisoner like a human being, and it didn't take anything away from ours to treat them like men."[182]

But the entire time, the Muslim inmates knew well that they were protecting the devil; according to one Muslim leader, they only did so because to do otherwise would expose them even more to state retribution.[183] In the end, the central fear of prison officials—that Black Muslim prisoners would be ungovernable and vengeful—was not realized, at least not in any direct or easy way. Yet their loyalty to a sovereign entirely outside the state, opposed to the state, and above the state rendered members of the Nation, as it had the Jehovah's Witnesses, a disciplinary puzzle, a challenge. Equally important, the Black Muslims' sense of their own constitutional right to believe and practice, especially to be faithful in a place where despair was the norm, exposed the vulnerability of the prison system to precisely such liberating faiths.

The popular constitutionalism that spread initially through the Nation developed in unexpected ways. However controversial Elijah Muhammad and his followers were, their example has been replicated by other faiths. In the decades after the Attica uprising and its bloody suppression, religion and prison ministries have spread across the American penal system, thanks in large part to the preparatory work of Black Muslims. The Attica riot made things worse in the short run, said one observer, but marginally better in the long run.[184] Prison ministries today run the gamut from Baptist to Wiccan to Roman Catholic to atheist, and provide significant support for prisoners, generally without official prison roles.[185] Instead, they function the way the Nation's ministers did in the 1960s and 1970s, working outside official structures and within communities of faith. This often informal yet widespread network of religious actors grew steadily as prisons themselves expanded in a second great wave of incarceration in the United States in the late twentieth century.[186]

Three years after the tragedy of Attica, a very different prisoner found God behind bars. In his best-selling memoir *Born Again,* Charles "Chuck" Colson, former special counsel to President Richard Nixon, described his journey from the White House to faith, through his trial and conviction for activities involved in the Watergate scandal that had finally brought down the Nixon administration in 1974.[187] Colson became a member of the prison population just as Americans invested heavily in expanded prison systems and lengthier sentences after the upheavals of the 1960s and early 1970s.[188] His experience—of his trial, his conviction, and especially of serving time—brought him to a new faith. Colson was "born again" through his suffering and eventual total surrender to God, he said, in ways only an inmate could understand. In prison he experienced true brotherhood, devastating isolation, and, finally, salvation. "Prison is friendly terrain for Satan's warriors," Colson explained, as he (like Malcolm X) learned to combat the devil, and to "prais[e] God for putting me in this prison."[189]

Colson did not conceive this religious breakthrough as a mandate for resistance, however. His evangelical faith led him instead to a new interpretation, a doctrine of submission and obedience to authority.[190] Within limits defined by a theological doctrine of just punishment, Colson embraced personal responsibility for suffering as the cornerstone of redemption.[191] In this sense, Colson traveled through faith to an acceptance of the extraordinary deprivation of freedom that prison imposes on its inhabitants as key to personal growth. He gloried in his incarceration, which he finally accepted as just.

Over the more than three decades since his release, Colson has built the Prison Fellowship ministry, a well-funded network of organizations dedicated to bringing this message of contrition to prisoners across the country and around the world.[192] He has also become a public speaker and an icon among conservative Christians as an advocate for the work of "faith-based" organizations in a society gone badly awry.[193] Colson's entrepreneurial approach, he says, is simply a response to the commands of his faith and a testament to the work of God in his life.[194]

Colson's approach to punishment and its role in the life of the inmate, of course, was a far cry from the Nation's cosmology. Muhammad and Malcolm described a racially constructed society, with prison as the ultimate expression of the oppression imposed on black men in America. After Muhammad's death in 1975 and his son Wallace's embrace of orthodox Sunni Islam, the separatism that had provided such powerful glue for Black Muslims gave way for all but a small remnant.[195] Chuck Colson showed that the legal rights first exercised by the Nation of Islam could be turned to multiple directions. Colson inverted the Nation's explanation for criminal behavior in a decadent society, placing the blame squarely on the convicted transgressor. Yet like the Nation of Islam, Colson's Prison Fellowship ministry hopes to transform the lives and commitments of inmates when few outside the walls are paying attention to their numbers or their suffering.[196]

The religious awakening that sustained Chuck Colson brought him to acceptance of a traditionally Christian view of sin, redemption, and rebirth. His was only one of a wave of such awakenings in the 1970s and beyond. Like Colson, the conservative Christian activist Beverly LaHaye described her lifework as the result of such an epiphany. And like him, LaHaye built a powerful organization on her grounding in evangelical religion. Concerned Women for America, LaHaye's unique and powerful women's group, led the legal battle against secularism in American public education, much as the Nation of Islam had led the fight for religious freedom in American prisons.

The Salvation Army made lots of noise in the nineteenth century parading through the streets in interracial and mixed-sex bands, as shown in this early photograph of the Grand Rapids, Michigan, corps. They marched and played even when prohibited by laws enacted specially to target the Army. In Grand Rapids, one such law was struck down by the Michigan Supreme Court in 1886. Courtesy of the Salvation Army Central Territory Museum.

Salvation Army officer Joseph Garabed, also known as Joe the Turk, was arrested dozens of times in the 1880s and 1890s for playing loud enough to "wake the devil." His name appears on several cases in different states where he challenged his arrests. Courtesy of the Salvation Army National Archives.

Jehovah's Witnesses William, Walter, and Lillian Gobitas after the Gobitas children were expelled from school for refusing to salute the flag in 1935. Courtesy of Watch Tower Bible and Tract Society of Pennsylvania.

Jehovah's Witness lawyer Hayden Covington, famous for loud ties and big lapels, found battling in court his way of promoting and protecting the faith. Courtesy of Watchtower Bible and Tract Society of Pennsylvania.

A public school class in 1943, saluting the flag with the raised-arm Pledge of Allegiance that was held unconstitutional in the Supreme Court's second flag salute opinion. Courtesy of Library of Congress.

In 1957, President Dwight Eisenhower took the oath of office for his second term on a Bible given to him upon his graduation from West Point by his mother, a Jehovah's Witness. Courtesy of Dwight D. Eisenhower Library.

The cover of the *Christian Herald* in 1948 depicted a shadowy but pervasive domination of public schools by the Catholic Church. Protestants and Other Americans United for Separation of Church and State, a new organization, vowed to fight the perceived threat. Courtesy of Princeton University Library.

This photograph of students at a New Mexico public school involved in the *Zellers v. Huff* litigation was reprinted in newspapers around the country in the early 1950s to illustrate the problem of "captive schools," which used Catholic nuns as teachers, displayed crucifixes and religious statuary, and often included attendance at Catholic Mass. Courtesy of Princeton University Library.

School prayer, pictured here as practiced by first-graders in South Carolina, was said to be essential to morality, which proponents said would be undermined by the Supreme Court's bans on school prayer and Bible reading in two cases in the early 1960s. Courtesy of Corbis Images.

Opposition to the Warren Court's establishment clause opinions was so
high in the early 1960s that this 1964 *New Yorker* cartoon showed
Whistler's mother embroidering the slogan "Impeach Earl Warren," a sentiment that also appeared on signs around the country. Courtesy of the
New Yorker Collection, Lee Lorenz, cartoonbank.com.

Islamic influences among African Americans predated the Nation of Islam. Pictured here are members of the Moorish Science Temple in Chicago in 1928. Founder Noble Drew Ali counseled followers that they were not "Negroes" but Moors, descendants of a venerable Asiatic race. Courtesy of the Moorish Science Temple.

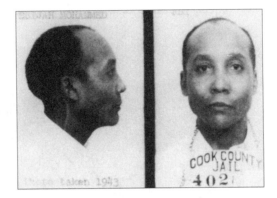

This 1943 mug shot of Elijah Muhammad was taken after his arrest on draft evasion charges during World War II. Muhammad served three years in federal prison in Milan, Michigan, where he met other conscientious objectors, including Jehovah's Witnesses, and developed an abiding interest in prisoners' right to practice religion. Courtesy of the Federal Bureau of Investigation.

Malcolm X, then minister of the Nation of Islam's Temple Number Seven in New York City, addressed an outdoor crowd in Harlem in 1960. He galvanized audiences in the 1950s and early 1960s as he carried the Muslim message around the country. Photo, Robert L. Haggins. Printed with permission of the Estate of Malcolm X. All rights reserved. Courtesy of Schomburg Library.

After the departure of Malcolm X, championship boxer Muhammad Ali became a public face of the Nation of Islam. Like Elijah Muhammad, Ali was prosecuted for draft evasion. Here, he is pictured delivering a speech in 1968 in Chicago, with Elijah Muhammad in the background. Courtesy of AP / Wide World Photos.

Jean Peffer participated in a local Concerned Women for America "prayer chapter" outside Pittsburgh, Pennsylvania. Courtesy of the *Pittsburgh Post-Gazette.*

HUMANIST ORGANIZATIONS	NEWS NETWORKS	FEDERAL GOVERNMENT
A.C.L.U.	T.V.	SUPREME COURT
A.H.A.	RADIO	STATE GOVERNMENT
E.C.S.	NEWSPAPER	GOVERNMENT BUREAUCRATS
N.E.A.	HOLLYWOOD MOVIES	PUBLIC EDUCATION (K-12)
SIECUS	MAGAZINES	COLLEGES UNIVERSITIES
N.O.W.	PORNO MAGAZINES	TEXTBOOKS
UNIONS	FOUNDATIONS FORD ROCKEFELLER CARNEGIE	

Tim LaHaye's book *The Battle for the Mind* (1980) claimed that humanists had taken over vital government institutions, including the United States Supreme Court and television news networks, as well as organizations such as the National Organization for Women, the prime opponent of Beverly LaHaye's Concerned Women for America. Courtesy of Tim LaHaye Ministries.

President Ronald Reagan, pictured here with Beverly LaHaye, addressed CWA's annual convention in 1987. "It is as if the reinforcements have arrived," he told the cheering audience, praising LaHaye and her work on behalf of conservative causes. Courtesy of Scott Stewart, AP Photos.

A gathering of the Religious Coalition for the Freedom to Marry in early 2004, in an Episcopal church, illustrates the interfaith nature of the group. The coalition's executive director, Rabbi Devon Lerner, addressed the gathering from the podium. Courtesy of Marilyn Humphries.

Jack Baker and Mike McConnell applied for a marriage license in Minnesota in 1970, in the office of the Hennepin County Clerk of Court. When the application was denied, they sued, claiming that the marriage statute did not specify that a couple had to be a man and a woman. Courtesy of the Minnesota Historical Society.

Baker and McConnell were featured in *Look* magazine's January 1971
"American Family" issue, which included this picture of them at their local
Catholic Church, where, they reported, they attended services regularly
and were made to feel welcome. Courtesy of Charlotte Brooks.

The Reverend William Sinkford, the first African American president of the Unitarian Universalist Association, officiated at the wedding of Hillary and Julie Goodridge in 2004. Long among the most liberal of Christian denominations, the UUA was the first organized religious group to ordain an openly gay minister (in 1969), and was active in the ecumenical group the Religious Coalition for the Freedom to Marry. Courtesy of Thomas Reuters.

CHAPTER 5

Holy War

Evangelical Women and the Battle against
Secularism, 1975–2000

Like Chuck Colson, Beverly LaHaye experienced a painful awakening
in the mid-1970s. She awoke to a lurking danger. As she put it a decade
later in her autobiography, it was as if "the churchwomen had been
asleep."[1] The quiet lives of conservative Christian women were threatened from outside, by a new society in which women had lost their
bearings. "Lesbianism, Marxism, and extreme social change" were on
the horizon, LaHaye said, espoused by feminists and their fellow trav-
elers.[2] Secularism was the vector for these threats; it spread like gan-
grene.[3] But churchwomen were oblivious, as she tells it. LaHaye understood that unless she and those like her did something, her opponents
—and thus the opponents of believing women across America—would
undermine morals and the traditional family entirely and forever.

LaHaye's holy war had both familiar and new elements. She drew on
long-standing patterns in anticommunist thought to explain the threat
she saw building in modern America. She also built on the Protestant
tradition that animated the work of Protestant and Other Americans
United for Separation of Church and State (POAU) in its first two
decades. POAU members, too, had worried that secularism would sap
American strength and faith. LaHaye connected these older anti-
secular ideas to newer political and social movements, especially feminism and the "humanist" texts used in public education. LaHaye used
new tools and strategies as well: in 1979 she established Concerned
Women for America (CWA), a formidable organization dedicated to
defending conservative Christian women's values. She mobilized a new
constituency that could "lobby from their kitchen tables," as she put

it.[4] Most important, and perhaps least expected for an organization of evangelical women dedicated to preserving biblical and family values, LaHaye hired lawyers; law and legal action became central to CWA's mission.

Unlike her predecessors and the few other women leaders of what was known by the late 1970s as the religious right, LaHaye and CWA were widely known for their commitment to legal charge. They challenged the legal structures of secularism in an effort to bring America back to a religiously defined social order. Only then, they maintained, would the country return to the path that God and the Founding Fathers had designed for America. Only then would women once again be secure in their homes. As one of LaHaye's local CWA leaders put it, they were the vanguard of a spiritual army of women, whose "warfare [took] many forms."[5] They carried their martial commitment into battle, knowing well that they were involved in a holy war. Those who disagreed with them, they said, were defying the will of God and undermining the best interests of their own country. In their turn, LaHaye and CWA were demonized by their enemies. In part because they were so effective, and in part because they exposed weaknesses in American law, education, and respect for the rights of believers, LaHaye and her followers were deeply controversial.

The beliefs and work of LaHaye and CWA, as well as the legal strategies that were the hallmark of CWA's early years, were remarkably successful. The organization grew quickly in the late 1970s and through the 1980s, garnering the admiration of President Ronald Reagan and catapulting LaHaye into the national limelight. LaHaye and her "concerned women" were not alone on the evangelical right, of course, but CWA and its president became uniquely powerful.[6] By the mid-1980s, CWA claimed to have 500,000 members, which was over eight times the size, just to give one example, of conservative Catholic Phyllis Schlafly's Eagle Forum.[7] LaHaye's group was also richer; she commanded an impressive six-million-dollar annual budget.[8] LaHaye was so respected that feminist author Susan Faludi claimed that other New Right leaders were envious of her power to command hundreds of thousands of women. Paul Weyrich reflected on her remarkable control: "[LaHaye] has the kind of loyalty from her people where literally she can call them up and say, 'Don't do that,' and they'll drop it."[9]

LaHaye and CWA brought a new legal consciousness to conservative women; their litigation strategy linked religious conviction to innovative legal claims that had the potential to reintegrate conservative Christians into public schools. Through CWA, popular constitutional theories found new life. As an opponent of secularism, LaHaye picked up threads for Protestants that had been dropped by POAU. She worked on issues that conservative Catholic women also cared about, maintaining a separate non-Catholic organization but without the anti-Catholic aura of Archer and Blanshard's POAU. For all these reasons, CWA and its long-time president deserve a place in legal and religious histories, especially those that hope to describe the vibrant, intensely conflicted world of religion and constitutional law in the late twentieth and early twenty-first centuries.[10]

Long before she founded CWA, LaHaye was active in religious circles. She and her husband, Tim LaHaye (best known today as the coauthor of the apocalyptic Left Behind novels), met as students at Bob Jones University in 1946. They became part of the wave of Southerners who by the late 1950s had migrated to California; there, Tim became the pastor of an early megachurch in San Diego. Beverly LaHaye described herself as shy and retiring throughout the 1960s, although she was a frequent public speaker. She was also the costar of a Christian television show called *The LaHayes on Family Life* that ran for four years.[11]

In the mid-1970s, the LaHayes became well known in conservative Christian circles as the authors of a how-to book about sex titled *The Act of Marriage*.[12] In the book they described sex in unapologetic, even graphic terms, including recommendations for lovemaking positions, foreplay, and more—it was joyful and also blessed sex within marriage. They were frequent guests on talk shows and at church programs.

Clearly, the LaHayes were beneficiaries of and participants in the revolutions of the 1960s and beyond. Like the wildly successful *Joy of Sex*, published only four years before the LaHayes' manual, *The Act of Marriage* built on a new openness about sexuality that allowed even respectable Christian husbands and wives to learn about the pleasures of the flesh.[13] The '60s, in the LaHayes' view, did not provide critical justifications for abandoning traditional social structures. Instead, they demonstrated how timeless biblical truths could be expressed in new ways. One might well believe, for example, that new knowledge about sex was valuable, and at the same time believe that truly joyful sex could occur only within marriage. The "other side" of the '60s was

deeply grounded in innovative religious thought among conservatives.[14]

The LaHayes' broad comfort zone in matters sexual was matched by
a profound commitment to other, older evangelical values. The first
book that Beverly LaHaye authored on her own, *The Spirit-Controlled
Woman*, advised Christian women to take themselves seriously as individuals. At the same time, she warned them to remember that in the
marital hierarchy, God comes first, husbands second, and Christian
wives owe a duty to "die to oneself" and submit to their husbands.[15]
The book sold more than half a million copies.[16]

Scholars might once have dismissed such mixed messages as irrec-
oncilable; now it is clear that many modern American conservatives
have built on just such combinations of innovation and preservation.[17]
We live in a world, as LaHaye herself might have put it, in which we
know well that it is possible to believe that, according to God's commands, a married woman has an inherent right to practice birth control, but not to obtain an abortion.[18] A woman might choose to plan
her family, but once God blessed her marriage with a pregnancy, she
was bound by God's law to dedicate herself to the new life she carried.
Feminism was not the *only* logical consequence of the changes LaHaye
and other activist women of her generation witnessed and helped unleash. LaHaye's commitments led her in a very different direction.
And the fact that her activism fit so seamlessly into her husband's life
and work just proved to LaHaye how vital it was to have engaged Christian women defending marriage and the traditional family.[19]

LaHaye emerged from the safety of family life, she said, only because her world was in grave danger. Like other conservative Christians in the 1970s, she felt at once empowered and victimized. The
growth of evangelical churches, and the complementary sense that
more liberal Protestants and their churches were anemic and unwill-
ing to meet the challenges of a deeply threatening world, drew conservatives into the fray. Most painful for LaHaye, however, was the conviction that the country had been led astray by those who should have
known better. Political leaders, judges, and especially women in liberal
groups such as the National Organization for Women and Planned
Parenthood had deceived American women and perverted the innate
morality of the American people.[20]

It was up to faithful women, LaHaye believed, to engage these forces
of evil, protect the sanctity of marriage and freedom of religion, and

preserve the family as the center of American society. "Never underestimate the power of a woman," LaHaye said. Women in America "have found themselves threatened by a permissive society, by humanistic thinking, and by a legal system that often protects the guilty and punishes the innocent."[21] In response, they—like their mothers and grandmothers before them—were called upon to organize powerful movements to strengthen family stability. LaHaye understood CWA and her own leadership as a counterweight to recent decay and corruption, and as part of a tradition of women's activism and religious organizing that had saved America in the past and could do so again, if only given free rein. LaHaye claimed an impeccable lineage among women for her activism, especially the Woman's Christian Temperance Union.[22] She also explained how it could be that so much of what she worried about came from women in the opposing camp: 'twas ever thus— women across American history divided into corrupt and incorruptible, radical and reliable. Out of this confidence in the strength of good women, and her compelling sense of danger from the likes of well-known feminists "Bella Abzug, Gloria Steinem and Betty Friedan," as LaHaye tells it, she founded CWA in early 1979.[23]

LaHaye's followers embraced the message of inherent power and imminent threat. "[A woman] has the power within her hands to either make or break a nation," wrote one CWA member. "As we submit to God and become all we can be under God's authority, we find fulfillment. There's no limit to what women can do today."[24] It was time, said CWA leaders, to assert the spiritual authority of women as mothers. "I'm a grandmother and I'm a mother and I'm a woman, and I've had enough," one activist declared. "It's time now to pick up my skillet and my rolling pin and charge. It's time to say, 'I'm a homemaker, and I'm proud of it, and I carry that title with dignity.'"[25]

Spiritual combat was a mode evangelicals knew well. The Salvation Army, whose legal campaign presaged modern legal activism, used martial imagery and language to describe its work for the Lord.[26] Yoking together nostalgia, recrimination, and hope for the future in a single message had been a favorite preacher's tactic for many generations, moreover. Sermons known as jeremiads excoriated but also uplifted—strong medicine for a wayward people.[27] In the late 1970s and early 1980s, LaHaye brought these time-tested formulas to a new audience. The women she motivated to concern themselves with the legal and political life of the country responded with lawsuits against secularism in the schools and protests against Communist influences in government. To LaHaye and her followers, both corruptions were cut from the same cloth; both were incarnations of the atheistic central core of liberalism. LaHaye sent her troops into courts, where, like the Jehovah's Witnesses, they confronted the source of the contagion and testified to the Truth.[28]

In the prosperous "insta-communities" of the postwar Sunbelt and also across the South, Midwest, and mid-Atlantic, religious life tied a transient people to eternal verities and a metageographical sense of morality.[29] Transplanted Southerners (and many who stayed in the South) recalibrated their religious conservatism to suit new surroundings and a new age. They gained credibility as religious critics of what they saw as coordinated assaults on traditional womanhood and familial morality.[30] The emergence of conservative Protestants as a powerful religious voice by the late 1970s was wedded to their defense of what formerly had seemed like unchallengeable social structures, especially those tied to gender and sexual difference.[31] Marriage and family life, once intensely private, became a public battleground. Personal morality provided the backdrop for the growth of vigorous new conservative religious organizations in the late twentieth century.[32]

The union of deep religious commitment with legal consciousness allowed newly motivated believers to deploy legal tools as deftly as they did television appearances and mass mailings. The development of this legal campaign drew religious activists into new arenas, and gave them fresh strategies for the defense of their core beliefs. Beverly LaHaye may seem at first to be the least likely of the Christian right to enter the once all-male world of conservative lawyering. Yet her story illustrates how, in the late twentieth century, traditional women belied easy stereotypes. Their legal mobilization was tethered firmly to arguments that law (especially government oversight) must not invade the private precincts of marital or parental prerogative. The new legalism was tied to claims (in some tension with the privacy argument) that religious life and expression had been unfairly—and unconstitutionally—severed from the public domain. LaHaye was at the forefront of an energized union of conservative religious and legal activism; she drew strength from law in her very modern crusade to salvage the traditional world of Christian women.[33]

LaHaye projected a deeply personal faith, impatience with those who sought to invade this private space, and a call for volunteers of like mind. Her organization was avowedly "Christian" and Protestant, but also nondenominational. This capacious identity became a hallmark of evangelical organizing in the 1970s: it reflected a commitment to offering authentic religious experience and accompanying political drive to all who felt the call.[34] Yet it would be a mistake to assume that all conservative or evangelical Christian women were attracted to CWA. LaHaye's audience (and CWA's membership) was overwhelmingly Protestant and white.[35] LaHaye claimed that she reached a bigger audience than the Catholic activist Phyllis Schlafly. "Phyllis has a wonderful ability to attract those who are already activists," LaHaye said. "I develop women into activists, who have never done it before."[36]

CWA's mission was based on using prayer to combat "the spiritual forces of darkness," and political, eventually legal, advocacy to fight back against secularism and its handmaiden, women's rights activism. LaHaye called her nationwide system of two thousand "prayer chapters" the "quiet strength of CWA," and she kept them updated with monthly Prayer/Action Alerts. Legal action, of course, is less quiet, and needed more explaining to the membership. Here, too, LaHaye tied CWA firmly to the deployment of new strategies to preserve the family. CWA was compelled to take up the sword, she declared, because the "humanists" had taken over public schools, propagating their corrupt "religion" to innocent children.[37]

LaHaye's success was built on the support of believing Protestant women, who felt that LaHaye captured their frustration with feminism as well as their commitment to their faith. As CWA member Laura Krocka of Pomona, California, put it: "Like Mrs. LaHaye says, the difference between us and NOW is, we're the group that likes men."[38] Marriage, family, religious liberty, education, sanctity of life, and national sovereignty—all keyed to "biblical principles"—formed the core concerns of the organization. One study reported that religion was so important in CWA members' lives that they would not have joined but for the biblical mission of the organization.[39] Early battles centered on coordinating members' prayers in opposition to the Equal Rights Amendment. As LaHaye put it, after she urged all CWA members to pray for the defeat of the ERA every Wednesday, "We began to see miracle after miracle occur on Wednesdays!"[40] In Idaho, Oklahoma, Illinois, Georgia, and Missouri, ERA defeats proved, she claimed, that "feminists may have access to the media, tax dollars, and the influence of notable personalities, but we have access to the Creator through fervent prayer!"[41]

Lawsuits became central to CWA's holy war early on. Michael Farris, a young graduate of Gonzaga Law School, urged LaHaye to "wag[e] legal battles against humanism." She recognized that constitutional litigation in defense of believers—especially mothers and their children—would inject the fight against secularism into a new arena. The association with Farris was "providential," according to LaHaye. Farris brought a lawyer's vocabulary to CWA and the means to connect long-festering complaints with targeted claims for redress. Within months, Farris became a full-time CWA employee; he began to file high-profile lawsuits on behalf of aggrieved CWA members and sympathizers.[42]

CWA became active in multiple cases in behalf of Larry Witters, a seminary student whose application for vocational rehabilitation services was denied by the Washington Commission for the Blind, even though his degenerative eye disease qualified him for educational funding. The case produced a significant victory for Witters and CWA. The Washington Supreme Court held that the federal establishment clause would bar supporting Witters's education at the Inland Empire School of the Bible, because that would be state support for "religious instruction."[43] The United States Supreme Court reversed, however, stressing that the aid would go to Witters personally, and would then be directed by him to purposes that suited his goals and educational needs. The State of Washington, emphasized Justice Thurgood Marshall, had construed the establishment clause too broadly, turning it into a means of interfering with private choices of qualified students like Witters.[44]

CWA also initiated precedent-setting access cases for religious speakers and groups. In one Pennsylvania case, Student Venture, an evangelical Christian organization dedicated to youth outreach, wished to sponsor a performance by a well-known magician, André Kole. Kole combined entertainment with evangelization, explaining to his audiences that his investigation of the miracles of Jesus Christ had changed his life. When Student Venture approached a Bucks County high school, it was told that Pennsylvania law prohibited all religious instruction and events on school property. The school had allowed dance groups, the YMCA, the County Board of Elections, Bloodmobile, meditation classes, tarot card reading exhibitions, and other groups and performers to rent school property. The Third Circuit Court of Appeals held that the school had discriminated against religion when it expressly excluded all religious (and only religious) activity.[45] Beverly LaHaye and CWA helped clarify the ways that religion may validly appear or be supported in public life. In this sense, they were agents of a more pluralist public sphere, where religious as well as other voices have a right to speak. Religious freedom (and, some studies conclude, significant support as well for tolerance of the rights of other believers) remains a central value among many fundamentalist and evangelical Protestants.[46]

Yet LaHaye had an even more ambitious agenda—she supported a series of cases that tapped into a core concern of evangelicals across the country. According to one survey from the early 1990s, more than 90 percent of those who described themselves as evangelicals agreed with the statement that "Christian values are under serious attack in the United States today." Most often, survey respondents blamed "secularists" and "liberals" for the attack.[47] Nowhere was the contagion more evident than in public education, they said, where the Supreme Court had banned religion and the National Education Association had quickly substituted sex education.[48] "I am convinced," LaHaye wrote, "that the humanists are going to do everything they can to preserve the grim stranglehold they have on our children. They are the priests of religious humanism and are evangelizing our children for Satan."[49]

Beverly LaHaye and CWA members were not ready to give up entirely on public education, however. Their "Christian values" were worth fighting for, they believed. The federal courts, they charged, had imposed a rigidly secular agenda on the public schools by the mid-1970s (prohibiting school prayer and Bible reading in the early 1960s, to be sure, but also overturning statutes that prevented the teaching of evolution, and so on). But energized Christian conservatives felt new power to reclaim the fabric of faith and morality. The rescue of schoolchildren from the humanists was something gallant Christians like LaHaye saw as a worthy mission indeed. Like others before her, she turned to popular constitutional ideals to support her mission.

LaHaye was not alone in her commitment to exposing and routing humanism. In the 1970s, many conservative Protestants became convinced that humanists were secretly perverting government, media (including newspapers, television, and film), and especially education. The theologian Francis Schaeffer drew admirers through his passionate rejection of what he considered a degenerate modern world. Eternal verities, he argued, had been compromised by those who elevated man to godhood at the same time that they attacked the moral commandments that God had revealed in the Bible.[50]

Schaeffer's influence was spread across American evangelical religion through his seminars, and even more through his books and videos attacking secularism as itself a religion. He maintained that secularism was the product of humanistic philosophy, which inverted true religion by making man the center of all things. Humanism, Schaeffer explained, began with Aristotle and might well have ceased to plague civilization had not Thomas Aquinas "re-enthroned" the ancient "non-Christian philosophy" and set the stage for the Renaissance, Voltaire, Thomas Paine, Bertrand Russell, and their corrupted progeny.[51] The result was rampaging abortion, rape, pornography, infidelity, and the degradation of parents' rights across the Western world.[52]

Schaeffer's message found a prepared audience among conservative Protestants. They had long condemned secularism in public life, especially after the Supreme Court in the early 1960s banned prayer and Bible reading from the public schools.[53] Once Schaeffer connected secularism to humanism, and drew a straight line through all of history between those who stood with God and those who played for the other side, religious conservatives understood why they felt so pushed out of schools, government, and the media. As one outraged CWA member put it, "I don't have the freedom to express my views as a Bible-believing Christian in the schools, yet at the same time humanists can instruct my children."[54]

Tim LaHaye popularized Schaeffer's analysis. LaHaye's 1980 book *The Battle for the Mind* was endorsed by fellow evangelicals, including the Reverends Jerry Falwell, president of the new Moral Majority (Tim was a founding member), and Adrian Rogers, the new leader of the Southern Baptist Convention, which had undergone a conservative "coup" in 1979 that cemented Southern Baptist support for school prayer (Tim was a key supporter).[55] The Protestants' world had been shaken by the courts' growing record of targeting religion itself (rather than sectarianism, the more traditional concept) with the constitutional mandate for separation of church and state. They began to fight back in the late 1970s.[56] Drawing the boundary between religious and secular was a very different enterprise; it represented a new understanding of disestablishment that outraged Protestants like Beverly and Tim LaHaye. As they internalized the new separatist threat, these former supporters of antisectarianism were transformed into dedicated opponents of the new secularism in law and the liberals who embraced it. In their world, there was no such thing as neutrality in religious life. Being "secular" was just a fancy name for being antireligious. Tim LaHaye's book "took the fundamentalist world by storm," according to the evangelical magazine *Christianity Today*.[57]

Tim argued that secular humanists were actually (anti)religious zealots. Equally important, he said, they had designs on American freedoms and traditional values. The common enemy of true religion, then, was a wolf in sheep's clothing—the humanist religion disguised as "secularism." Tim LaHaye claimed that the secularist tenets of atheism, evolution, amorality, human autonomy, and one-world socialism combined to produce an ominous (yet largely unperceived) threat.[58] Neither Schaeffer nor LaHaye limited dedicated secularists to the small number who actually belonged to humanist associations, although LaHaye, especially, quoted extensively from the first Humanist Manifesto, which was drafted in 1933 with the support of thirty-four signatories, including the philosopher and educator John Dewey.[59] Secular humanism, LaHaye charged, had produced the moral relativism that had allowed Mussolini, Hitler, and Stalin to rise to power.[60] The danger had spread across the Atlantic and now threatened American society.

The signs were everywhere. Many of the danger signals flowed from the new law of religion; others were more political or social. All pointed to a society in which healthy religious commitments had been undermined by highly placed yet covert conspirators who worked to subvert American principles. Sex education instead of prayer in the schools, abortion on demand, gay rights, children's rights, the "giveaway of the Panama Canal," the size of government and deficit spending, gambling, increased taxes, women in combat, unnecessary busing, attacks on patriotism, disarmament, and subsidies to the United Nations—all added up to "degeneracy by design," said LaHaye.[61] The secular humanists' endgame, he claimed in *The Battle for the Mind,* was one-world government: the dissolution of the United States and its merger "with the Soviet Union and all other countries," under the control of elite humanists.[62]

LaHaye, Schaeffer, and the religious right drew on a venerable

American legacy of anxiety about secularism, of course.[63] POAU, for example, fought doggedly to distinguish advocacy of antisectarianism from secularism, only to have the school prayer decisions decimate the carefully crafted distinction. The trajectory played out over decades, argued conservatives, as did the conflict between the superpowers. When Beverly LaHaye labeled the threats of the 1970s as "Lesbianism, Marxism and extreme social change,"[64] she recalibrated cold war standards. LaHaye's triptych was a descendant of earlier anticommunist theory, but also very much a creature of a new, reconfigured Christian right.

The arc of opposition to communism in Protestant thought illustrates how American anticommunism adapted to new challenges. In the late 1940s, when the LaHayes were newlyweds, and through the 1950s, secularism loomed large in national consciousness and rhetoric. So large that politicians and religious leaders maintained almost without dissent that America was locked in a fight to the death against the forces of secularism. Communism, liberal politicians as well as conservative clergy also agreed, was an enemy of religious dimension. "The anti-Christ stalks our world," declared presidential candidate Adlai Stevenson in 1952. "Organized communism seeks even to dethrone God from his central place in the Universe. It attempts to uproot everywhere it goes the gentle and restraining influences of the religion of love and peace. One by one the lamps of civilization go out."[65] Christianity and communism were so innately and indelibly opposed, American leaders said, that one simply could not be both a Christian and a member of the Communist Party.[66]

With words of apocalyptic magnitude, anticommunists described the "creed of world-wide import . . . [that] Party members are spreading with missionary zeal throughout the world."[67] The atheism of Communists, said their opponents, was held with a dedication that mirrored (and undermined) truly religious commitments. In *Christianity, Communism and History,* Lutheran theologian William Hordern claimed in 1954 that "these two religious systems face each other in the world. . . . [I]f we lose the struggle with Communism, it will not be because we have been outproduced: it will be because we have been less dedicated and less inspired by our [Christian] religious faith than the Communist world [by its beliefs]."[68] Former Communists added fuel to the flames, among them the writer Richard Wright, who argued that even though he had escaped the thrall of the Communist faith, the religion still had hold of countless others.[69]

The mercurial *Time* journalist Whittaker Chambers became the poster boy for recovering Communists. After turning from the party to the Episcopal Church and later the Quakers, Chambers turned on Alger Hiss, a former State Department official and by the late 1940s head of the influential Carnegie Endowment for International Peace. Chambers accused Hiss of being a Soviet spy; the resulting congressional hearings and criminal trials rocked the nation. The rotund and rumpled Chambers unleashed a storm of controversy that reverberated for decades. Betrayal, fear, accusation, treason, and, above all, lies made for riveting and unsettling times.[70] The decades-old debate over Hiss's espionage trial was rekindled in the late 1970s.

A revived cold war coincided with the publication of Allen Weinstein's *Perjury: The Hiss-Chambers Case.*[71] In devastating detail, Weinstein painted a portrait of Hiss's guilt.[72] Conservatives crowed with victory. George Will quipped: "The myth of Hiss's innocence suffers the death of a thousand cuts."[73] At the same time, conservatives lamented that years of détente ("a fancy French word for 'appeasement'") and inaction had paved the way for the Soviet military buildup and debacles such as the Panama Canal Treaty of 1977.[74] They called the treaty a "give away," "degenerate"—even evidence of President Jimmy Carter's "impotence."[75] The new constitutional world, which the Christian right claimed protected the secular at the expense of religion, had actually turned against national interests. In their view, secularism and communism traveled hand in glove, while religion and American democracy provided the only reliable safeguards against the Communist conspiracy.

Labeling secularism as a religion, Beverly and Tim LaHaye deployed their own legal and political logic. They inverted the bright-line distinction between what counts as "secular" and what is "religious," forcing their opponents onto the defensive. And by connecting secularism to other liberal causes (feminism, sex education, and even détente), the LaHayes brought otherwise abstract and distant developments in law into sharp focus. Families, they said, were in danger when secularists took control.[76]

Women were especially at risk in a secular world, according to Beverly LaHaye. The reinvigorated, manly cold war of the late 1970s and

1980s was matched by an updated and pointed assertion of wifely submission in religion. God created men and women to fulfill distinct roles, LaHaye said.[77] "The woman who is truly Spirit-filled will want to be totally submissive to her husband. Regardless of what the current trend towards 'Women's Lib' advocates. . . . God's design is that the husband be in charge." As LaHaye explained, wifely submission was the first step on a Christian voyage that would bring fulfillment and peace of mind. "Submission is not a status of inferiority. The husband is the head of the wife in the same way the Father is the head of Christ. . . . Oh, that [women] could just grasp the attitude in the heart of Jesus—the willingness to be humbled, to be obedient unto death, and to be submissive." The other path, she said, led straight to communism.[78]

The controversy over the Panama Canal Treaty became a national referendum on President Carter's manhood, as the *New York Times* put it, complete with claims that he was "soft," and had been duped into trading away American strength by agreeing to turn the canal over to Panamanian control.[79] Defeating the Equal Rights Amendment became the means by which evangelical women could assert their womanhood—protecting their own submission to God through their husbands. Support for the ERA, LaHaye said, had "been fomented by conscious agents of Marxism."[80] Defending America against communism by defeating the ERA reinforced conservative women's commitment to the hierarchical nuclear family as the best shelter from a cold war in a cold world.[81] As LaHaye saw it, the new cold war became a battle for the survival of the divine order, steeped in vital issues of manhood, womanhood, patriotism, education, and more. The 1950s version of the religious defense against communism had reflected deep anxiety about the staying power of democracy in a consumer-driven society that was fragmented spatially and materially. The late-twentieth-century version played on subtly different themes, especially those of femininity and the family. In this version, a newly sexualized politics infused the reincarnated attack on secularism as the servant of communism.[82]

Tim LaHaye explained that this "battle for the mind" was caused by the erosion of the true faith that made America strong: only in the '70s had the scope of secular ambition become so monumental that the conspiracy was visible to the Christians who were its primary targets. Especially insidious was the plot to use sex education and pornography "to create such an obsession with sex among our young people that they have no time or interest in spiritual pursuits."[83] As one CWA member put it, "Where were the Americans when they allowed the minds of their children, the next generation of leaders, to be polluted by the filth that was coming through the television set?"[84] Tim LaHaye called on his readers to vote humanists out of office while there was still time. A secularist takeover was "neither predestined nor necessary," he said. "[O]n the contrary, Christians are commanded to resist the devil and to put on the whole armor of God" in the battle against godlessness.[85] To many readers, LaHaye's call to arms was an exhilarating battle cry. Beverly LaHaye proved his most capable battlefield commander, translating their shared outrage into action.[86]

Tim LaHaye spent the early 1980s in Washington, working with televangelists and pastors of megachurches in two groups he founded, the Coalition for Religious Freedom and its successor, the American Coalition for Traditional Values. LaHaye and his organizations eventually were scarred by the revelation that LaHaye had accepted funds from a controversial religious organization, the Korean minister Sun Myung Moon's Unification Church. Moon's support for conservative causes and yearning for religious respectability among Americans had made funding LaHaye's groups particularly attractive.[87] LaHaye was not engulfed by sex scandals such as those that destroyed the popular televangelists Jim Bakker and Jimmy Swaggart in the late 1980s. His decision to leave Washington in 1986 and join the enormous Prestonwood Baptist Church north of Dallas, however, may well have been a reaction to the pummeling that Washington politics routinely doles out.[88]

The heady atmosphere of the early 1980s gave way to a more chastened climate. The Moral Majority, once heralded as the primary organization of the religious right, also dissolved around the same time, in 1985. As one observer reflected, "Jerry Falwell's Moral Majority was supported [almost exclusively by] white fundamentalists, and active support for Pat Robertson . . . was limited almost entirely to [charismatics]. . . . Neither ended up having much political impact."[89] By the late 1980s, scholars (rashly, it turned out) declared the religious right was in its death throes.[90] The LaHayes remained influential despite the turmoil, even if Tim's Washington experience had ended unpleasantly. By the end of the 1980s, some twenty million of Tim LaHaye's books had been sold, and critics credited both LaHayes with identifying secular humanism as the central enemy of conservative Protestantism.[91]

Beverly LaHaye clearly was more than just a follower, however. She was the only leader of the Christian right to found and build an organization that grew more rather than less effective across the 1980s and well into the 1990s. She appealed beyond her original fundamentalist base, eventually attracting conservatives across the Christian spectrum, including evangelicals, mainline Protestants, and Catholics.[92] She emerged unscathed from her years in Washington. Whatever the leaders of the Moral Majority had expected when women began flocking to Beverly LaHaye's new organization in 1979, by the early 1980s CWA had emerged as a force to be reckoned with.[93]

LaHaye's legal strategy exemplifies her determination to map out her own agenda within an energized religious conservatism. While one contemporary critic dismissed secular humanism as "less a national conspiracy than a heuristic device," in law the term had a rich and interesting life.[94] CWA demonstrated the depth of its members' outrage at public education through several defining legal encounters, the most important of which charged that secular humanism pervaded the public schools. CWA's legal campaign drew attention and amicus briefs from many organizations identified by both Beverly and Tim LaHaye as bastions of secular humanism, including the American Civil Liberties Union, the National Education Association, and even the National Council of Churches. The newly established liberal group People for the American Way (PAW) paid the expenses of the defendants.

The legal ground took time to prepare. Conservative Christians had limited but powerful material to work with as they argued that secular humanism had invaded constitutional law and, through constitutional jurisprudence, public education. Most important was the fact that the Supreme Court had never defined religion. Across the decades, courts had struggled to decide how to deploy the religion clauses, wrestling with the constitutional mandate to protect religious exercise without violating the establishment clause. This work had yielded a rich body of case law but no reliable test for determining the presence of religion versus, say, political or moral commitments. By the 1980s, the law had welcomed a growing list of beliefs and practices as religious.[95]

The pressure to say precisely what counted as religion for legal purposes had grown with each new expansion of the category. Two attempted resolutions in the late 1970s, one by a law professor and the second by a judge, revealed the difficulty of the task, and the perils of making the attempt. Liberal legal scholars had pressed the courts to embrace a "progressive, modern understanding of religion," especially for the free exercise clause, including "any concern deemed ultimate . . . regardless of how 'secular' that concern might seem to be."[96] Such deference to individual beliefs could make all sorts of government actions subject to crippling objections by eccentric believers, some commentators responded.[97] Equally important, if all ultimate beliefs counted as religion, then governments could be charged with violating the establishment clause's prohibition against promoting particular religious beliefs, as it was spelled out in the school prayer cases. Any important commitment could be vulnerable to an establishment clause challenge, if religion was found wherever ultimate concerns were present. The implicit tension between the two clauses, said one Supreme Court justice, created a "double barreled dilemma."[98]

In response to these concerns, some scholars advocated a dual definition, treating religion one way for establishment purposes and another for free exercise analysis.[99] Harvard law professor Laurence Tribe proposed a simple formula: when an activity or belief was "arguably religious," it should be protected under the free exercise clause; when such activity or belief was "arguably not religious," government support or encouragement would not violate the establishment clause. By using different standards for each clause, Tribe maintained, courts would be able to balance the protection of practices that were not widely regarded as religious (such as the flag salute that was so bitterly contested by Jehovah's Witnesses in the late 1930s and 1940s) with programs in public schools such as the practice of transcendental meditation, widely viewed as entirely secular even though it was religious for some devoted practitioners.[100]

This bifurcated approach to religion was strenuously countered by Judge Arlin Adams in a long concurring opinion in a case involving just this problem—was transcendental meditation a religion for purposes of the establishment clause? Conservative religious groups argued that it was, and objected to the teaching of transcendental meditation in New Jersey schools. When the Third Circuit Court of Appeals upheld the trial court's conclusion that transcendental meditation could not validly be taught, Judge Adams laid out trenchant objections to the scholarly trend exemplified by Laurence Tribe. First, Adams pointed out, the word religion in the First Amendment refers to both what is prohibited by the establishment clause and what is protected by the free exercise clause. Equally important, he said that dual definitions would skew results in favor of less-traditional religions like Transcendental Meditation (allowing them to sneak in under the establishment clause because they were "arguably not religious") while punishing more familiar religious traditions. As Adams put it: "If a Roman Catholic is barred from receiving aid from the government, so too should be a Transcendental Meditator."[101]

As Judge Adams stressed, the word "religion" is used only once in the First Amendment. Clearly the Founders had a single meaning in mind. Working within the constitutional framework, then, meant finding a unified approach. Adams went on to outline what should count as religious: first, the ideas and questions that underlie the faith must be the most important in human life; second, these ideas must be comprehensive; third, and useful but not a prerequisite, an organizational structure that includes ritual, clergy, services, and so on would be evidence of religion. In other words, if a belief had the scope and shape of a religion, then it should be credited as such for all constitutional purposes. Adams's opinion effectively discredited the dual-definition approach. His analysis was influential but controversial. For one thing, it invested extraordinary power in the judiciary to decide where religion begins and secular life ends. Judge Adams himself held that transcendental meditation was religious, over the objection of those who taught it. In a subsequent case, he held that a naturalist sect was not religious, despite the claims of a prisoner who practiced the faith.[102]

Most judges—including the Supreme Court—dodged the definitional question; religious life in America moved so quickly and unpredictably that avoiding a definition may have been the better part of valor. Yet the lack of a clear definition meant that the entire category was unstable. If courts could not say with any precision what religion was, they were vulnerable to claims that they misunderstood what was truly religious. This vulnerability was especially evident in the late 1970s and early 1980s, when debates about how to decide what counted as religion were most heated.[103] Capitalizing on the fuzziness of the legal category, and at the same time describing the true nature of the conspiracy they believed was at work across America, Beverly

LaHaye and CWA became the most adroit proponents for including "secular humanism" in the law of religion.

Certainly, secular humanism had explosive potential in law. In Beverly LaHaye's view, the federal courts had wrenched prayer out of public education and imposed an equally religious alternative. Secular humanism should be as constitutionally suspect as any other faith in public schools, she reasoned. Given that the courts' own decisions had "established" secular humanism, taking such claims to federal court confronted the beast in its lair, making legal activism an especially appropriate method of vindicating the rights of aggrieved Christians.[104] Tantalizingly close yet frustratingly inconclusive, the Supreme Court itself had mentioned secular humanism in a footnote in 1961: "Among the religions in this country which do not teach what would generally be considered a belief in the existence of God are Buddhism, Taoism, Ethical Culture, Secular Humanism and others."[105] However, the two cases cited by the Court both involved groups that had regular Sunday worship services and formally trained clergy (predominantly Unitarian Universalists, many of whom were theists), property dedicated solely to worship services, celebration of marriages, funerals, and so on.[106] Admittedly, these cases did not provide the full-blooded affirmation of secular humanism sought by LaHaye and her supporters.

Instead, conservative lawyers tackled secular humanism first in law reviews. In 1979 John Whitehead (who would go on to found the conservative Rutherford Institute) and John Conlan (a former press secretary to evangelist Billy Graham and Republican congressman from Arizona) argued that American courts had abandoned the "theistic" understanding of religion that had prevailed at the founding.[107] In this way, they charged, courts and judges betrayed the central meaning of the religion clauses. Reducing religion to "belief" or "conscience," they said, meant that psychology instead of law governed constitutional analysis.[108] By equating religion with individual convictions, courts had elevated all beliefs to the status of religion. Thus humanism, which places humans at the center of ethics and morality, became just as much a religion as the convictions that support school prayer, in Whitehead and Conlan's reading. Given that courts could not reliably distinguish between religion and other profound moral and ethical convictions, for legal purposes secular humanism fit the bill as a "belief system."[109]

Equally important, Whitehead and Conlan claimed that this new religion was intolerant. Secularism they described as a "religious ideology opposed to any other religious system," especially the notion of a deity and any nonnaturalist explanation for life or human nature.[110] Together, secularism and humanism elevated science and human autonomy to the status of dogma, they argued, setting the stage worldwide for totalitarianism and genocide.[111] Traditional theism, said the authors, acknowledged the Creator and His human creation, was central to the Declaration of Independence and early national thought, and must be returned as "the basic cornerstone of law and jurisprudence."[112] Francis Schaeffer and Tim LaHaye both relied on Whitehead and Conlan in their work; Beverly LaHaye and CWA developed a strategy for deploying this reinvigorated traditionalism in test cases.[113]

By late 1982, when CWA member Suzanne Clark, "a Tennessee mother and school teacher," called the organization's office and spoke with Michael Farris, CWA already claimed 120,000 members and was growing fast.[114] Clark had been sued for writing an article that the National Education Association (NEA) claimed was defamatory. She charged that the NEA favored one-world government, the use of drugs on school children, "brain washing," and hiring homosexual teachers. Beverly LaHaye summarized Clark's article as a well-documented exposé that "quoted extensively from humanistic educators and from the NEA's own materials to show how morally subversive public school education is today."[115]

Clark's was just one in a long series of religious challenges to public education, which had become almost routine since the early days of the cold war.[116] The Clark case, however, pitted the NEA directly against parents for the first time. An earlier conflict in the mid-1970s in Kanawha County, West Virginia, was notable for its political and social violence, but also for the conciliatory role of the NEA, which issued a report recommending "reasonable alternatives" and perhaps even alternative schools using "traditional" methods of instruction.[117] By the early 1980s, however, the NEA had become identified with unyielding humanism in the work of Tim LaHaye and the publications of CWA.[118]

Farris worked on Clark's defense, probing the NEA's opposition to "prayer in schools and the teaching of scientific creationism [as opposed to evolution]," as well as its support for the Equal Rights Amendment and abortion. The defense stressed especially one NEA official's concession that she felt herself caught in a "war" with the "New Right."[119] Two weeks before trial, LaHaye reported, the NEA dropped the suit. LaHaye announced proudly that CWA had taught the NEA a lesson, adding: "and our CWA Education and Legal Defense Foundation is just as prepared today to defend the constitutional rights of those whose free speech is stifled."[120]

Suzanne Clark's case raised hopes at CWA. A second suit, more difficult and yet more promising, had come with Farris when he joined LaHaye but came to trial a year after Clark's confrontation with the NEA. In that case, Carolyn Grove of Spokane, Washington, claimed that the reading assigned in her daughter's class "denigrated Jesus Christ and Christian moral values."[121] After she objected to the book (*The Learning Tree,* by Gordon Parks), Grove's daughter Cassie was tormented in school, even though her teacher agreed to allow Cassie to read Mark Twain's *Pudd'nhead Wilson* instead. Grove became convinced that assigning *The Learning Tree* was anti-Christian, and attempted to persuade school administrators that they should remove the book from the required reading list. As LaHaye put it in her memoir, *The Learning Tree* "was a direct attack on Christianity and promoted the religion of humanism."[122] At a school board meeting attended by more than 300 parents, teachers, and students, Michael Farris "warned the school officials about the possible legal dangers of keeping the book in the class."[123] The board voted unanimously to retain the book, however, and CWA filed suit.

The trial court judge granted the school board's motion for summary judgment without an opinion; the Ninth Circuit sustained the trial court's ruling in *Grove v. Mead School District No. 354* with a concise majority opinion, supplemented by a lengthy concurrence.[124] In his concurring opinion, Judge William Canby rejected the claim in CWA's brief for Carolyn Grove, that "secular humanism . . . is a religion dedicated to affirmatively opposing or showing hostility toward Christianity. It has declared its pulpit to be the public school classroom and its 'bible' is adolescent literature like *The Learning Tree.*"[125] Canby stressed that CWA's approach divided the universe into two categories, "the religious and the anti-religious," which left no room for either secularism or humanism, both of which could be compatible with various religious beliefs.[126] *The Learning Tree,* for example, did not fit into a particular religious category, Canby said. Instead, "it remains an autobiographical novel only tangentially concerned with religion."[127]

Especially pointedly, Canby dismissed CWA's argument that the school inculcated the religion of secular humanism. Farris had claimed that "this is not a case where we must show that the State has been too intertwined with religious agencies. In this case, the State *is* the agency of (anti)religion. It is hard to become more entangled than that."[128] Unlike cases involving "orchestrated prayer, Bible reading, [the] Decalogue or creationism," Canby responded, the selection of *The Learning Tree* was not based on loyalty to any "secularist credo" or hostility to Christianity or religion in general. Reading the book and discussing it did not promote religion or antireligion. Instead, the novel informed students about "the crucible of black rural life."[129] Judge Canby's rejection of the central theory of CWA's (and the LaHayes') analysis of public education in the mid-1980s was discouraging, but defeat in the *Grove* case did not deter them.

In some senses, CWA's reaction to the *Grove* litigation was an example of a classic "paranoid style."[130] Beleaguered Protestants, who lamented the erosion of morality in the broader society and the decline of Christianity in public life, explained their sense of loss in ways that sustained a communal identity among the faithful.[131] This narrative of declension thrived on opposition; secularism, in this story, became an active strategy—Satan's design for an unsuspecting America. When push came to shove, many conservative Protestants did not actually want to sacrifice tolerance and respect across religions forcibly to "reclaim" America for Christ. But studies have shown that they did want religion taken seriously, even if they supported a voluntaristic and personal understanding of religious faith.[132] In Beverly LaHaye's 1980s, discrimination against Christians in public life was a deep and abiding concern among evangelicals. They traced the desire to excise religion entirely from the public square to misguided and even conspiratorial liberal judges and the secular organizations that prevailed in their courts.

Opposition to secularism formed part of a new racially inflected debate about law, as well. Secularism imposed by bureaucratic elites acting on the orders of the Supreme Court created new incentives for conservative believers to withdraw from a hostile society. The school prayer decisions that so divided the membership of POAU were at first misunderstood by many traditionally conservative proponents of separation of church and state. Once it became clear, however, that the Supreme Court meant all forms of prayer, and Bible reading to boot, these traditionalists resisted—massively. Studies of prayer in public schools across the 1960s and well into the 1970s show that the forces of secularism were met by resilient local practice.[133] When sex education was added to the mix in the late 1960s, the moral fiber of public education was seen as entirely degenerate. One popular television special in the mid-1970s featured a delighted Phyllis Schlafly accusing a beleaguered school superintendent of encouraging students to have premarital sex, while the superintendent protested weakly that sex education just explained the process.[134]

With powerful religious incentives for withdrawing from a corrupt school system that did not respond to their needs, conservative Christians invested heavily in new religious schools throughout the 1970s. At the same time, they built on older but still powerful resistance to racial integration, merging separatism between the godly and the secular with separatism among the races.[135] The new schools were deeply imbued with religion and also overwhelmingly enrolled white students. The complex politics of race in America swirled into these new Christian schools, as opponents accused them of being little more than reconstituted "segregation academies."[136] Outraged defenders pointed to the deep religiosity of their schools, arguing that they fought secularism rather than encouraged racism. Many liberal observers conceded the former point, but argued that the latter was the crucial problem.[137] Failure to enroll minority students, they maintained, meant that while segregation may not have been the goal, it would be the inevitable outcome of the new Christian schools. The Internal Revenue Service (IRS) focused its scrutiny in the 1970s on schools without a "significant" proportion of minority students, promising to revoke the tax-exempt status of any school that could not prove its bona fides. Conservative Protestants were outraged, especially when the IRS exempted Jewish, Muslim, and Catholic schools from this new standard.[138]

The stage was set for a direct confrontation between religious freedom and racial equality. Arguing that conservative Christians also had "civil rights," the LaHayes and their allies mobilized to defend religion. Ironically, they framed their defense in the language of discrimination, accusing the IRS of exempting everyone except conservatives.[139] The case that finally resolved the dilemma involved the LaHayes' alma mater, Bob Jones University. In some ways, Bob Jones was an ideal defendant for those who wanted to make the strongest statement in favor of integration. Based on its interpretation of Scripture, Bob Jones had long denied entrance to African Americans entirely, then had admitted only married black students. By the time the case was filed in 1976, the university admitted unmarried black students but prohibited interracial dating.[140] During his 1980 presidential campaign, Ronald Reagan spoke at Bob Jones, calling it a "great institution" and challenging government interference in private religious decisions as the introduction of "racial quotas." The *New York Times* called the speech one of the most pivotal of Reagan's campaign: a cheering crowd of 6,000 basked in the implicit support for religion over integrationist policy.[141] Tim LaHaye predicted that the 1980s would witness a resurgence in religious rights, as brave Christians reversed "the moral decline in our country."[142]

Their jubilation was short-lived, however, as once again secular interests triumphed. In early 1983 the Supreme Court rejected the religious defense in *Bob Jones University v. United States*.[143] Writing for an eight-to-one majority, Chief Justice Warren Burger held that the government's "compelling" interest in eradicating racial discrimination overrode the free exercise rights of the university.[144] The bitterness of this defeat reinforced the intolerance and aggressiveness of secularism, in the LaHayes' view. They have remained loyal alumni of the school and other fundamentalist educational institutions, donating the LaHaye Student Center at Jerry Falwell's Liberty University in Virginia, sponsoring lectures and events at Bob Jones, and generating donations through the powerful yet little-known Council for National Policy, cofounded by Tim in 1981.[145] As Beverly LaHaye put it, the IRS was part of a ruse by liberals to "suppress religious freedom." "We may disagree with [Bob Jones's racial] policy," LaHaye continued, "but that's not the issue. . . . This cleverly concocted case [produced a ruling that] can now be used as a blanket indictment of *any* religious practice which may be held to violate 'public policy.'"[146] The rights of believers, she maintained, were endangered by just such open-ended state power over education.

The *Bob Jones* and *Grove* decisions of 1983 were setbacks, but hardly the end of the story. Beverly LaHaye learned early on in the *Grove* litigation that legal battles could focus valuable public and media attention on the problem of secular humanism in public education. Local lawsuits built on the grassroots membership of CWA and connected their struggles to the larger picture. Intuitively, many conservative Christians linked the rejection they felt to the work of the federal judiciary, which had rejected religious practices while welcoming new and often unfamiliar ways of learning. Using the language of discrimination and the concept of separation of church and state, Beverly LaHaye and her concerned women explained their profound sense of loss as a violation of the Constitution. Like the Jehovah's Witnesses who argued in the 1930s that the Pledge of Allegiance (which others saw as a purely secular ritual) was inherently religious, CWA claimed in the 1980s that many secular school textbooks in fact were harbingers of a dangerous humanism.

LaHaye retooled quickly, working on a new and more promising dispute. In December 1983 she held a press conference in Greeneville, Tennessee, to announce that CWA was filing a complaint against the local Church Hill schools on behalf of Vicki Frost, her husband, children, and other Christian families. The new case offered CWA a fresh opportunity to argue that secular humanism had been enthroned and that Christianity had been denigrated and then excised from the school curriculum. As Michael Farris put it in a *New York Times* interview about the case, "There's a widespread feeling . . . that secular humanism has permeated public education."[147] Frost's case fit the formula that characterized CWA's membership and central areas of concern: Vicki Frost was a devout Christian and a mother concerned for the spiritual welfare of her children, and her Bible-centered beliefs had been utterly rejected by those in charge of her children's education.

LaHaye welcomed the prospect of litigating another secular humanism suit, especially when Frost complained that she had been arrested and imprisoned for several hours.[148] Frost's relationship with school authorities had deteriorated over the autumn of 1983 as she became convinced that her children were being inculcated with anti-Christian messages. After the school board of Hawkins County, which governed the Church Hill schools, voted unanimously to compel all students to read from the same school textbook (in this case, the 1983 edition of the Holt, Rinehart and Winston basic reading series), Frost became confrontational. She asked the local chief of police to accompany her to Church Hill Elementary School, where she upbraided the principal, charging him with assigning books that not only "taught about occult practice, but . . . also about reincarnation, gun control, situation ethics, one-world government, socialism, evolution and pacifism."[149]

Instead of protecting her, Frost claimed, the police chief complied with the principal's request that Frost be arrested for trespass. Frost sued partly for false arrest (eventually she won a judgment of $70,000 on that count, but the award of damages was reversed on appeal). Primarily, however, she was determined to protect her children by establishing that they could not constitutionally be compelled to read materials that violated their religious beliefs. CWA argued on her behalf that the basic aim of the Holt books was to convince the children who read them that all religions are the same, to lull them into accepting a "new world order."[150]

Vicki Frost's case is known as *Mozert v. Hawkins County Public Schools*. Frost had felt that a man should represent her and the other protesting parents in court. Bob Mozert, the named plaintiff, had more formal education than the others; he was more at home in secular surroundings. But everyone in Hawkins County knew it was Frost who had unearthed the moral contamination in her children's schoolbooks. Frost became the central figure in the case; she was the target of opponents as well as the primary representative for the plaintiffs. In consultation with her spiritual mentor, Jennie Wilson, Frost spent hundreds of hours reading the Holt, Rinehart series, documenting the ways that the occult, moral relativism, and one-world government were insinuated into stories masquerading as "critical reading." Wilson had read Tim LaHaye's work, and she helped Frost connect her fears for her children's spiritual welfare to a broader claim about humanism in public education.[151]

This new lawsuit addressed a question left open in the *Grove* case. Judge Canby had said in his concurrence in *Grove* that if school authorities *required* children to read material that their parents viewed as violating their religious beliefs, a free exercise question would "probably" be presented. Because it was clear that Cassie Grove had not been compelled to read *The Learning Tree* or to be present when it was discussed, her case had rested on exposure to the attitudes and beliefs of others rather than on coercion—too slender a reed to support a constitutional claim.[152] But Vicki Frost's children, in contrast, were expressly required to read the Holt, Rinehart series. Frost and the other parents who objected to the book series had instructed their children not to participate in assignments involving the books. Several students (including two of Frost's children) had been suspended in late 1983 for refusing to read the textbooks or to attend classes that used them.[153]

Frost and her fellow plaintiffs argued that their faith should be respected, and that their children should be allowed to read alternative texts. Carolyn Grove had attempted to impose her views on others; when the *Mozert* suit was filed, Vicki Frost said all she wanted was to protect her own children from spiritual harm. Yet the case was a complicated one, with charges of censorship flying throughout the litigation. Local religious groups and many townspeople felt exploited by outsiders who seemed to have no understanding of their confidence in their local schools.[154] School superintendent Bill Snodgrass complained to a community meeting of nearly 1,000 local residents that the controversy was manufactured and then funded by "outside agitators and their fat wallets."[155]

The *Mozert* case began with another defeat when the trial judge, Thomas G. Hull of the Eastern District of Tennessee, a recent Reagan appointee, dismissed CWA's complaint.[156] On appeal, however, the Sixth Circuit held that the school district had challenged the plaintiffs' sincerity and their claim of a burden on their religious beliefs, so that material facts were disputed in the case and deserved to be heard and decided in open court.[157] On remand, Judge Hull presided over a nonjury trial that was dubbed "Scopes II" in the press.[158] Frost was the star witness for the plaintiffs; she spent hours explaining that situation ethics, feminism, pacifism, disobedience to parents, occultism, evolution, and telepathy were larded throughout the Holt books. She also said in every possible way that "the word of God is the totality of my beliefs," and that secular humanism as it was revealed in the Holt series "denies God as the Creator." One exercise, for example, asked seventh graders to imagine themselves as part of nature. "Our children's imaginations have to be bounded," Frost maintained.[159]

Opposition to Frost ranged from concern to contempt: "Lift the petticoat and look underneath, and it's just censorship," one defense lawyer quipped to a *Time* reporter attending the trial.[160] Neighbors in Greeneville and, according to some press reports, many members of Frost's own community resented her campaign and CWA's intrusion. "I find very little support for what they're espousing," commented the Reverend Gary Gerhardt, pastor of the First Baptist Church of Church Hill. Gerhardt and other conservative ministers in the area reportedly read the textbooks in question and found nothing wrong with them. "'If you want to,' Gerhardt said, 'you can read just about anything into anything you read.'"[161] Another minister, after explaining that he was the head of the Parent-Teachers' Association at his daughter's school, declared that he "cared about education" and would have complained "loudly" if he saw anything amiss with the reading series. Local attorney Nat Coleman charged that Frost and CWA had put teachers and school administrators through "hell." He also accused Michael Farris of sensationalism, especially when he called local media outfits before filing his complaint.[162]

Concerned Women for America's legal strategy was sophisticated and effective, and it was met by an equally formidable opponent. People for the American Way (PAW) provided the defense for the school district and brought in a top-flight litigator with a golden résumé, Timothy Dyk of the prestigious Washington, D.C., law firm Wilmer, Cutler and Pickering, educated at Harvard and a former law clerk to Chief Justice Earl Warren.[163] Anthony Podesta, then president of PAW, conceded that Beverly LaHaye was "shrewd and subtle." Instead of arguing that the school should ban offensive books outright, CWA "filed suit asking for alternative readers," Podesta explained; "[LaHaye's] position seems more sympathetic, so it makes those of us on the other side carry a heavier burden."[164] PAW claimed that the plaintiffs *really* wanted to "censor" the reading materials made available to all schoolchildren. Podesta boasted that it was his idea to call the case "Scopes II" and say that history was repeating itself in Tennessee, a charge that predictably attracted intensive coverage in *Time, Newsweek,* and other popular news media.[165]

By the time *Mozert* was tried in 1986, CWA's legal staff had grown to five full-time and three part-time lawyers, and there were plans for further expansion. CWA claimed a membership of more than 500,000.[166] The *Mozert* case had the highest profile of the fourteen lawsuits CWA had become involved in. The result at trial justified the resources CWA poured into the lawsuit. Judge Hull held that the school board "[had] effectively required that the student-plaintiffs either read the offensive texts or give up their free public education."[167] Equally important, Hull found that the school board did not have a compelling interest in using the Holt series exclusively, as opposed to other readers that had already been approved by the state of Tennessee for use in public schools.[168] Hull held that the plaintiffs must be allowed to opt out of the reading program, study at home, and be required thereafter to take standardized tests for reading skills.[169] Although the plaintiffs initially had asked that they be allowed to use alternate readers in school, they (and especially their lawyers) considered the result a win.

An exuberant Michael Farris called the opinion "a major victory for fundamentalist Christians everywhere. Except for a sentence or two, we couldn't have written it better ourselves."[170] The trial, the result, and the outpouring of criticism and praise from points along the spectrum fed both the growing prestige and the attention-grabbing status of CWA. The *Boston Globe* called Hull's opinion "far-fetched," and the *Baltimore Sun* labeled it "preposterous."[171] One expert in education predicted that *Mozert* would lead to "anarchy."[172] As the *New York Times* put it, CWA's greatest "impact, and where it provokes the most worry among its opponents" was in law.[173] One young CWA attorney, Jordan Lorence, explained that the organization had now made its name as the defender of the faithful in cases where "the rights of conservative Christians are abused."[174]

Mozert also brought substantial press attention to CWA members around the country. Beverly LaHaye, mindful that her organization drew otherwise private women into public life, presided over conventions where members were coached on how to apply rouge, how to cultivate a "more melodic" voice, and then how to answer hard-hitting questions such as, "Don't you believe in the separation of church and state?" The correct answer was, "Nowhere in the Constitution of the United States does the phrase 'separation of church and state' exist. It is only in the U.S.S.R. constitution."[175]

Judge Hull's order set the stage for a second appeal to the Sixth Circuit Court of Appeals. Hull's decision divided those who had followed the case. The sympathetic reaction to CWA's case that Podesta had referred to extended even to fellow PAW lawyers. According to one source, Barbara Parker, head of PAW's National Schools and Libraries Project and coauthor of *Protecting the Freedom to Learn: A Citizen's Guide,* conceded privately that if the plaintiffs had been Old Order Amish instead of evangelical Protestants, "People for the American Way might have *defended* their right" to an alternative reader, instead of opposing them.[176] But PAW has long potrayed itself publicly in oppositional terms—today its Web site describes the organization as "fighting the

Right," especially the "Religious Right as they seek to impose their views on a diverse and democratic society."[177] The presence of CWA in a lawsuit meant that PAW was likely to be interested in taking the opposing position. Tony Podesta put it this way: "Michael Farris was not unknown to us. Where he popped up, we tended to pop over."[178]

The *Mozert* case caused consternation among other liberal groups, including Americans United for Separation of Church and State, the American Jewish Congress, and—perhaps most telling—the American Civil Liberties Union (ACLU). At a meeting hosted by PAW to plan the appeal, representatives of these groups were reported to have complained that Tony Podesta had incited press hysteria about the case. Several also pointed out that they thought Hull's decision was the right one: "Hey, what's wrong with letting them read that [alternative, state-approved] book and take a standardized test?"[179] The meeting became "very heated," according to Marc Stern of the American Jewish Congress, especially because Timothy Dyk argued that any accommodation would violate the establishment clause.[180] Lee Boothby of Americans United described Dyk and PAW as "antireligious" rather than just separationist: "They were kind of appalled that we thought those [fundamentalists] had any rights."[181]

Even the ACLU, which in CWA rhetoric represented an arm of Satan, thought that *Mozert* was worth taking seriously. Executive Director Ira Glasser acknowledged that he believed the case was colored by other attempts by conservative Christians "to impose their religious beliefs on the schools."[182] Glasser was referring to a case supported by the televangelist Pat Robertson in Alabama, *Smith v. Board of School Commissioners of Mobile County,* which was a by-product of the Alabama legislature's attempt to impose a moment of vocal or silent prayer at the start of the school day. Brevard Hand, the flamboyant federal judge for the Southern District of Alabama, sustained the prayer statute on the utterly indefensible theory that the establishment clause should not apply to the states.[183] Despite the clear command of the Supreme Court in the *Everson* case, decided decades earlier, Judge Hand rejected the long-standing legal rule.

Hand also suggested to the litigants that, should the appellate courts reverse his decision (a predictable result), he would reexamine the curriculum of the Mobile schools to determine whether or not they had been contaminated by "other religious teachings," such as secular humanism. As Hand put the question, "If the state cannot teach or advance Christianity, how can it teach or advance the Antichrist?" Propagating secular humanism, evolution, or communism, he said, would advance the religion of the Antichrist.[184] Pat Robertson's National Legal Foundation, established in 1985 and headed by attorney and fellow charismatic Christian Robert Skolrood, litigated the Mobile case, which resulted in the judge's conclusion that forty-four textbooks were laced with secular humanism. While the *Smith* opinion (and Judge Hand) were widely considered an embarrassment, the timing could not have been worse for CWA and Vicki Frost. The trial in the *Smith* case occurred just as *Mozert* was being appealed to the Sixth Circuit for the second time.[185]

Yet *Mozert* was not *Smith*—nor, for that matter, was it *Grove*. In both those cases, plaintiffs sought to remove humanist materials from the school curriculum; they were trying to "censor" the materials for all students. Vicki Frost wanted to excuse her children from a reading program that she believed was indelibly secular. This more modest strategy may not have been what irate Christian parents (or even CWA) would have preferred for the public schools, but they did not claim they had a right to remove the Holt, Rinehart readers from the schools entirely. Differentiating *Mozert* from other litigation in the field was exactly what Timothy Dyk and PAW wanted to avoid—they courted the media, effectively coloring Frost and her allies with censorship and bigotry. "Media wasn't just an auxiliary function," bragged Tony Podesta, "it was our purpose. . . . CWA didn't know what hit them."[186]

Farris sputtered in response, accusing PAW of "lying" about the case, and threatening that if the plaintiffs lost in the end, there would be a civil rights uprising the likes of which hadn't been seen since the Civil War.[187] Frost was hounded by the press, so much so that even her opponents came to feel for her. As Dorothy Massie of the NEA put it after attending the *Mozert* trial, PAW "made headlines and raised money on these poor benighted people in Tennessee. . . . They were using these people."[188]

Despite the overwhelmingly bad press, the *Mozert* case presented a dilemma when viewed in light of the *Smith* litigation. Could it be that a given believer might find parts of a secular curriculum objectionable for genuinely religious reasons? If such a thing were possible, could the free exercise clause protect the parents and children, even if the establishment clause did not prohibit the inclusion of the material?[189] One exasperated legal commentator argued that *Mozert* should more accurately be compared to the flag salute cases of the 1940s, rather than being mislabeled "Scopes II."[190]

Those who believed that the *Smith* decision was untenable but that *Mozert* was a credible reading of the requirements of the free exercise clause were forced into an awkward bind. They had to argue both that secular humanism was not a religion, for purposes of the establishment clause, and that it could interfere with freedom of belief in violation of the free exercise clause. This was the position defended by ACLU lawyer (and future ACLU president) and law professor Nadine Strossen. As Strossen saw it, the secular values of the Holt, Rinehart series, including "a tolerance for diverse nationalities, cultures and religions; a belief in equality of individual opportunity regardless of such uncontrollable factors as nationality, sex or creed," were so central to "our constitutional system," that their inculcation could not violate the establishment clause.[191] Yet when faced with a free exercise claim, Strossen argued, courts should "defer to the allegations of those who profess [a religious belief]."[192]

Making the distinction between what counts as religion for one constitutional purpose (disestablishment) and what counts for another (free exercise) would allow Vicki Frost to educate her children with an alternative, state-approved reading series. At the same time, the distinction would reject the claim that secular humanism was a religion from the perspective of the establishment clause. This proposed expansion of religion under the free exercise clause, combined with a careful circumscription of religion under the establishment clause, was a more plausible alternative to Judge Hand's contention that the establishment clause should not apply to the states. It appealed to those looking for a way to temper the winner-take-all strategy that was central to PAW, and that underscored claims among the conservative members of CWA that there was no place for Christians in the public schools. If this approach had won the day, compromise might have been possible between secular educators and believing parents such as Vicki Frost.

Yet just such a dual definition had been routed in Judge Adams's *Malnak* opinion. Laurence Tribe, whose advocacy in favor of such duality had generated such a powerful refutation, abandoned the effort.

In the next edition of his treatise on constitutional law, Tribe gracefully retracted the proposal, calling it "a dubious solution."[193]

Strossen did not persuade her colleagues at the ACLU that they should support the trial court opinion. According to reports of the organization's internal deliberations, Strossen stressed that the one-size-fits-all approach of many public schools "can be very threatening to civil liberties." In cases like Frost's, Strossen said, "we have to protect the right of the minority."[194] Yet a majority of the national ACLU board concluded that this was not really a free exercise case. Instead, the board decided that the lawsuit was actually an attempt to introduce religion into the public school curriculum.[195]

The most articulate support for the *Mozert* opinion came from the liberal Protestant organization, the National Council of Churches (NCC), represented by law professor Douglas Laycock. The NCC maintained that in allowing the plaintiffs to opt out of the reading program, the district court successfully reconciled the establishment clause's prohibition on teaching religion with the free exercise interests of "parents of all faiths [who wish] to send their children to public schools without encountering unnecessary burdens on their religious beliefs."[196] Like programs of "shared time" between public and private religious schools, or "dual enrollment," the home-schooling option provided by the district court, Laycock argued, protected "religious minorities without inserting religion into the public school curriculum."[197] Failure to acknowledge the plaintiffs' genuine dilemma, the NCC argued, would undermine religious freedom across the board.

This active support from the NCC and the significant debate within the ACLU belied LaHaye's charge that both organizations were indelibly secularist and anti-Christian. Instead, these groups recognized that *Mozert* was indeed a more sophisticated and subtle approach to the problem posed by secularism in public education. When liberal Protestants (and even influential members of the avowedly secular ACLU) conceded that an alternative reader was an appropriate resolution to the *Mozert* litigation, the value of secular humanism as a tool of legal analysis was demonstrated for a broad spectrum of interested actors.

The Sixth Circuit heard the appeal in July 1987. Everyone now understood that this case was *the* test for the claim that secular humanism was an anti-Christian religion, and that secular humanists had used the public schools as their proving ground.[198] Vicki Frost had been falsely arrested; she had coherent plans for educating her children without the Holt reading series; CWA had crafted a careful case. Twenty years later, *Mozert* is still excerpted in leading legal casebooks as the defining moment for secular humanism in the courts.[199]

The appellate court reversed Judge Hull a second time, however, stressing that coercion was absent, even though students were required to read and discuss the assigned materials. Despite the fact that Frost's and the other plaintiffs' children were young and impressionable, the court brushed aside the notion that they might feel pressured by their experience as students. The key point, the court held, was that no student was compelled to *agree* with the readings; instead, "the plaintiffs appeared to assume that materials clearly presented as poetry, fiction and even 'make-believe' in the Holt series were presented as facts which the students were required to believe. Nothing in the record supports this assumption."[200] Put this way, Frost's objections were reduced to claims that even the presence of objectionable ideas violated the free exercise clause. Unlike cases that involved a mandatory affirmation of belief (such as a compulsory flag salute), in *Mozert,* the Church Hill schools merely presenting divergent views through the Holt series. Rather than placing a burden on religion, the court stressed, the required reading mandated only "a civil tolerance. . . . It merely requires a recognition that in a pluralistic society we must 'live and let live.'"[201]

Judge Danny Boggs, a Reagan appointee new to the Sixth Circuit, concurred in the judgment. Boggs would have preferred to hold that the plaintiffs' beliefs dictated that studying the Holt series would require them to engage in religiously prohibited conduct, yet he also stressed that such a change in the law should come only from the Supreme Court. Boggs pointed to the rapid growth in private schools of many religious denominations. This development, he said, reflected the fact that "public schools offend some people deeply." He deplored the deterioration of the debate in Church Hill to a point where "children and parents [are] put to the hard choice posed by this case."[202] With such a clarion call for appeal, LaHaye had reason to hope that the Supreme Court would hear the case. The high court turned down the plaintiffs' petition, however, without a recorded dissent.[203] Thus were Vicki Frost's hopes dashed; the career of secular humanism as a religion sputtered. Since *Mozert,* arguments that secularism in public schools violates the free exercise rights of students and their parents have been rejected virtually across the board.[204]

The definition of religion for constitutional purposes remains a vexed and unresolved problem.[205] The fundamental question of what can be included as religion for constitutional purposes may not grab headlines today as it did in the late 1980s, but CWA's campaign against secular humanism sent shockwaves through the world of law. Experts in the field understand well the thorny and still controversial issues raised by LaHaye. Yet in law, as Douglas Laycock charged, it was now the de facto rule for public education that "schools could teach absolutely anything, however hostile or offensive to a student's religious beliefs, so long as they did not support or establish a religion."[206]

Beverly LaHaye and CWA gave constitutional heft to the widespread dismay among evangelicals, and provided a way for like-minded women to connect their concerns to positive legal action. She embodied a new activism among conservative women; President Ronald Reagan and a host of political leaders on the Right endorsed her combination of prayerful traditionalism and aggressive legal tactics. Indeed, Reagan appeared at the 1987 CWA annual convention and summed up his admiration for LaHaye and her organization: "It is as if the reinforcements have arrived," he declared to a sea of cheering women.[207] There was a moment when compromise in the public schools seemed possible. That moment passed after *Mozert.*

CWA's momentum gradually slowed over the course of the 1990s. Even though she remained at the helm of CWA until the mid-1990s, LaHaye curtailed her involvement, and largely withdrew from law and legal activism by 1990. She was not able to pass on the formula that made her such a star. Perhaps LaHaye's charisma was truly irreplaceable, with her capacity to reach her beloved churchwomen and also strategize with the best of them in Washington legal circles. Or it may be that LaHaye represented a generation whose commitment to fighting secularism was too highly charged to last. Or CWA's very traditional reliance on men may have undermined the women she claimed to represent, as some feminists have argued.[208] Tim LaHaye turned his energy from politics to fiction, growing rich as he and Beverly retired to a less confrontational life in upscale Rancho Mirage, California.[209]

Certainly CWA, instead of setting the agenda, has become just one of many groups litigating and praying in the Protestant Right. It may have been the first to apply conservative religious theory to popular constitutionalism, but CWA could not preserve the monopoly.[210] Leadership, especially, became a key issue. Beverly LaHaye formally resigned as president in 1998. Since then, CWA has had four presidents, and the post has stood vacant for two of the past ten years. The National Organization for Women has also declined—perhaps the heyday of women's organizations as powerful actors on the national stage has passed.[211] Yet it would be a mistake to dismiss CWA, or Beverly LaHaye, as mere has-beens. LaHaye taught herself and the country how effective women's faith, traditionalism, and the law could be when deployed together in popular constitutional theories and arguments.

Rediscovering the ways that religious commitments and constitutional law were mutually constitutive in CWA reveals how much we have overlooked in the basic story of recent legal and religious history. Conservative Protestant women and Beverly LaHaye conducted their own holy war in the 1980s. Their concern that the liberal women who opposed them were the most likely source of deterioration and corruption has been borne out by subsequent events. The lesbians and gay men LaHaye was convinced lurked behind women's rights activism have proved that removing traditional restrictions on women was indeed a precursor to same-sex activism. What LaHaye did not predict was that religious organizations would nurture and give voice to so much of the "homosexual agenda," calling committed same-sex relationships holy. Progressive women in the clergy, especially but not only in liberal Jewish movements, have led the charge.

CHAPTER 6

Covenants of Love

Progressive Judaism, Interfaith Activism, and Marriage, 1970–2007

"We become most fully human when we love another person," proclaimed the Declaration of Religious Support, the central organizing text of the Religious Coalition for the Freedom to Marry (RCFM). Founded in 1998, the group of ordained clergy and religious leaders in Massachusetts drew on a venerable tradition of progressive social critique and legal reform—a tradition every bit as much a part of American history and religious life as the Woman's Christian Temperance Union that Concerned Women for America claimed as its forebear. This self-consciously liberal strand of American religious life built on a legacy of activism, growing out of religious impulses but also invoking legal remedies. "From the shameful history of slavery in America," stated RCFM, "the injustice of forbidding people to marry is evident as a denial of basic human rights. . . . Denial of the status of marriage, to those who would freely accept its responsibilities, creates . . . injustice. We feel called to protest and oppose this type of injustice."[1]

The Religious Coalition invoked a tradition of protest for starkly different objectives than Beverly LaHaye's. It was organized fundamentally to oppose the vision of marriage—and the understanding of human sexuality—championed by LaHaye and her supporters. In RCFM's view, truly free marriage had to be open to same-sex couples as well as heterosexuals. Only then would Americans complete their halting progress toward religious and legal equality for all people in marriage. Like racial equality, RCFM said, marital equality was demanded by religious belief and the divine command for human flourishing. Rabbi Devon Lerner of Boston, RCFM's director, was ordained as a Reform rabbi in 1979. She was part of a new wave of women clergy in liberal denominations across the religious spectrum. Like others of her era, Lerner brought an inclusive ethic as well as spiritual longing to her seminary training and life in the rabbinate. Her feminism made her sensitive to exclusions of all sorts, especially those connected to gender and sexuality.

Beverly LaHaye recognized and condemned the connections between equality (especially for women) and same-sex marriage. In the 1970s, as the conservative campaign against the Equal Rights Amendment gathered steam, religious opponents accused its feminist proponents of lesbianism. As LaHaye put it, "[Lesbian] feminists and homosexual men hope to gain the legal right to live their perverted lifestyle protected by the laws of the land."[2] What LaHaye did not anticipate, and what surprised many onlookers, was the presence of religious groups at the forefront of activism in favor of what is often called "marriage equality" (a happy blend of equality and marriage theories).

In self-described "progressive" denominations, especially, debates over same-sex relationships led many congregations to embrace such unions for parishioners. These groups welcomed modernity in theological as well as social dimensions. Blessing the commitment of same-sex couples and "celebrating" their marriages, even when such marriages were not legally recognized, became an increasingly central element in modern approaches to even the most ancient religious traditions, such as Judaism, in the late twentieth century. Although most press coverage of debates over same-sex marriage has emphasized more orthodox condemnations like LaHaye's, progressive religious groups developed coherent and sustained counterarguments.

The commitment to marriage equality did not emerge full-blown in religious advocates' minds: instead, it developed over decades of thought, argument, division, and discord. There was (and is) deep disagreement about same-sex marriage; there is blood on the floor within liberal denominations as well as across American society. Yet the idea of marriage as a site of justice for all members of society has been prominent among a range of denominations and religious leaders. A dedicated cadre of religious progressives on the side of marriage equality emerged in the final decades of the twentieth century.

Debates over sexuality and same-sex marriage have roiled American religious life and legal standards. Of the many issues that divided believers in the late twentieth and early twenty-first centuries, questions of gender and sexuality (including the ordination of women, gay, lesbian, and transgendered clergy, and, finally, same-sex marriage) have been the most wrenching. The backlash in law, furthermore, arguably exceeds the gains in favor of same-sex marriage by so much that the price of the battle has been extraordinarily high. As of this writing, thirty states (including California, Florida, and Arizona in November 2008) have enacted constitutional provisions banning same-sex marriage.[3] The public disagreements and heartache that have characterized many denominational debates about sexuality have produced schism and lawsuits over church property in the Episcopal Church, church disciplinary trials for United Methodists, and separatist denominations within Catholicism.[4] These divisions are deep and painful.

In other religious communities, the challenge of welcoming human sexuality among same-sex as well as heterosexual couples has brought relative consensus. The Unitarian Universalists, Reform and Reconstructionist (and, most recently, Conservative) Jews, and others across the progressive spectrum adapted and rethought scriptural traditions in light of an inclusive mandate.[5] Within Judaism, in particular, the complex legal foundations of marriage, combined with a long-standing yet relatively simple interpretation of same-sex relations as contrary to the will of God (rather than as, say, "unnatural" because such unions do not of themselves include the transmission of life, as many Christians have argued), gave the debate a particularly law-bound flavor.[6]

The debate among Jewish movements was also more susceptible to resolution in favor of same-sex unions. Substantial work toward equality between men and women, especially the ordination of women rabbis, and a venerable tradition of rabbinical independence meant that same-sex marriage was not as great a leap for Jewish liberals. Many Christians, in contrast, had infused heterosexuality with natural law as well as scriptural command. In some senses, interfaith marriage was (and remains) a more difficult quandary for liberal Jewish movements. The executive director of Garden State Equality, New Jersey's leading marriage equality group, who is also a Reconstructionist rabbinical student, declared recently that he gladly performs same-sex weddings but not interfaith weddings.[7] Still, the decision to reinterpret scriptural injunctions against same-sex relationships that had long been the mainstay of Jewish law and culture was no small matter; angry reverberations echo even among progressive congregations.

Tracing the development of such changes within liberal Jewish communities, and connecting them to similar exercises among liberal Christians, shows how progressive believers gradually became engaged in shaping marriage in secular as well as religious life. The establishment of an interfaith group to advocate for same-sex marriage unified law and religion to reflect the ways that believers approached marriage equality. Religious leaders of progressive Jewish and Christian denominations, through the Religious Coalition for the Freedom to Marry, challenged government to validate their conviction that human flourishing—and thus human rights—demanded that same-sex marriage be available to all who are called to live out their deepest commitments in marriage and within religious communities. These progressives sought to upend the comfortable notion, as one put it, that "the Judeo-Christian tradition [is] chaplain to the status quo."[8] They fought not just to expand the category of the marriageable. Instead, RCFM focused on the convergence of state and religious practice in marriage. Their success paved the way for other groups, nurturing a revitalized "religious left." Currently, five states—Massachusetts, Connecticut, Iowa, Vermont, and New Hampshire—have legalized same-sex marriage; others have rejected suits for legalization, overturned judicial decisions by constitutional amendment, or withdrawn legislative authorization by popular referendum. In every major case since 2003, groups of liberal clergy have filed briefs to declare their support for same-sex marriage, following the lead of RCFM.[9]

Same-sex marriage was not a new topic in the late twentieth century— it had traveled along the edges of civil rights campaigns for decades. In some ways, the question of marriage equality played the same notes as earlier debates over marriage and race. In the late 1940s, the California Supreme Court held that antimiscegenation statutes (legislation prohibiting interracial marriage) violated the state's constitution.[10] Twenty years later, the United States Supreme Court followed suit in

Loving v. Virginia, holding that marriage is a fundamental right of a free people, and that racial classifications for marriage violate the rights of every citizen under the Fourteenth Amendment.[11] Marriage as an issue of civil rights, therefore, has a substantial pedigree in relatively recent law at the state and national levels.

Liberal reformers have lamented the failure of the fight against racially discriminatory marriage laws to do more than just equalize access to marriage without regard to race. Color blindness, they maintain, is not a truly transformative agenda: it did not change the underlying institution of marriage.[12] Conservatives have embraced color blindness as a means of opposing affirmative-action programs and even the keeping of racial statistics.[13] Marriage and freedom, liberals add, occupy very different places. For many women across American history, marriage wasn't a question of freedom but a complex potion of duty, sacrifice, and the acquisition of an identity as a wife.[14] The inequities of a relationship that both conditioned access to full citizenship and structured intimate life, argued the women's historian Nancy Cott, were obscured by a powerful reconfiguration of marriage as a badge of freedom in the late twentieth century. In reality, Cott said, marriage was shaped and controlled by government every bit as much as by spouses.[15]

American government rewarded marriage. In the middle decades of the twentieth century, the modern welfare state redistributed income from the unmarried to married couples, through taxation as well as benefits. Even after divorce became widely available, legislators increased the rewards for being married, especially for husbands, who reaped more than twice the benefits accorded to wives.[16] As the historian of sexuality Margot Canaday put it, "A homo/heterosexual binary [has been] inscribed in government policy."[17] The fight for same-sex marriage has reignited the recognition that marriage occupies public as well as private space.

Opponents and proponents of same-sex marriage both claim to be truer to the core goals and values of marriage than those on the other side. They disagree, of course, about what those goals and values are, but both sides maintain they are fighting for the same ultimate goal: the health of marriage, families, and, ultimately, society. In some ways it is surprising that there is such a fight—even twenty-five years ago marriage seemed on the verge of collapse. In the twentieth century, enormous changes in access to birth control, rates of divorce, cohabitation outside marriage, and even "pre-nups"—private contractual negotiations over the ongoing life of a marriage—led some commentators to predict that marriage would all but disappear.[18]

But the resilience of marriage was so remarkable that recent treatments focused instead on the constants, especially the ways that legitimacy and social standing were still confirmed through marriage.[19] Such a focus illuminates how and why prior battles over marriage, like this one, have drawn such passionate combatants. Social standing and legitimacy were powerful cultural and political factors in American life of course. But such a focus misses the ways that religion and religious practice were central elements in controversies over marriage, and in its resilience. Equally important, the religious emphasis on marriage as a blessed and affirmed relationship of love within communities of faith undergirds and underscores the ways that Americans, who have lived for the past generation in the midst of a great religious revival—an "awakening"—connected the blessings of spiritual unions with the law of marriage.[20]

In Americans' personal experience, the two are blurred. Across the twentieth century, for example, the proportion of weddings celebrated with religious ceremonies rose steadily. It is, of course, difficult (and perhaps unnecessary) to make any direct translation between increasing numbers of religious ceremonies and ongoing religious practice; more important are the many ways that a religious ceremony generated a marriage in the eyes of participants. Religious impulses created and sustained substantial pressures for reform.[21] Religious groups have been among the most ardent of those who challenged and reformed understandings of marriage, in society as well as among the faithful.

Even before the great twentieth-century debates over race and marriage, in the late nineteenth century a substantial and long-lasting conflict over Mormon polygamy presaged later battles. Like modern disputes over same-sex marriage, the polygamy conflict involved questions of local difference, religious freedom, and equality within marriage. After migrating westward in the late 1840s, members of the Church of Jesus Christ of Latter-day Saints (commonly known as Mormons) began openly to practice "plural marriage." In 1830 their founder and first prophet, Joseph Smith, told of translating the golden plates containing the *Book of Mormon* before they were taken up to heaven by an angel. Smith also promulgated a range of practices, beliefs, and rituals based on revelations given to him in those "latter days."[22] The 1843 Revelation on Celestial Marriage established the vital importance of marriage to faith and salvation, as well as a (re)commitment to the marriages of the biblical patriarchs—polygamous unions.[23]

The rest of the country was horrified; their reaction was conditioned by mid-nineteenth-century politics, law, and religion. Most important was slavery and the growing sectional conflict over the South's peculiar domestic institution. Especially among northern evangelicals, slavery occupied an ever greater and more troublesome space in religious thought and activism; most of them considered polygamy to be a new form of enslavement, this time explicitly for women. Worried that action against polygamy would be a forerunner to antislavery legislation, Southerners blocked all attempts to enact antipolygamy legislation in Congress before the Civil War. Only in the 1880s did widespread criminal prosecutions of polygamists, together with political and economic sanctions against the church and its members, finally bring Mormons to heel.[24] The church officially abandoned its support for polygamy in 1890.[25] In the nineteenth century, religious difference provided no refuge for the Saints, as they called themselves. Instead, monogamy and uniformity of marital practice triumphed.[26]

These conflicts over marriage blended law, race, religion, and protection for women, establishing powerful connections between faith and family in American history. The importance of marriage, in this sense, lay in its capacity to unite religious and legal meaning in the lives of individual men and women, as well as in the broader society.[27] This blended quality became a particularly contentious element in recent debates over same-sex marriage. Proponents of marriage equality vied with opponents who argued that religious tradition and social practice generated an unassailable moral world in which marriage was—by definition—the union of one woman and one man.[28] If the lesson of the polygamy controversy taught us anything, it was that tinkering with the definition of marriage can unleash enormous, even unstoppable opposition. Mormons internalized this truth: they became ardent defenders of "traditional marriage."[29]

The wagons circled around this core definition in the late twentieth century. Those who sought to expand the "couple" to include two women or two men were often portrayed as seeking to destroy what was left of marriage. All of society would suffer, said opponents, from the collateral damage to traditional marriage.[30] This argument relied on a predictable if powerful mix of rising divorce rates, abortion on demand, unwed mothers and deadbeat dads, abused children and rampant sexual promiscuity. The final straw, a "whole new stage of marital decline," as one writer put it, would be to take marriage as it had been known in America and substitute something quite different—same-sex couples.[31] According to opponents, it all started with those who claimed in the 1970s (especially feminists) that marriage was "stultifying and oppressive." Their ultimate ambition was nothing less than the destruction of the true nature of marriage—the vulnerable yet priceless union of religion and law in heterosexual intimacy.[32] The logical outcome of feminism, charged conservative commentator David Frum—the "latest round in an argument over marriage and the family that began some 35 years ago"—was same-sex marriage, which would "abolish marriage and put a new, flimsier institution in its place."[33] The "homosexual agenda," according to opponents, would tear marriage from its religious roots, "trample religious freedom and leave a trail of broken bodies in the dust."[34]

This potential downhill slide into marital chaos horrified Beverly LaHaye and those who shared her traditional understanding of the sanctity of marriage and its role in American life and law. Yet LaHaye's own investigation of sexuality drew on a reevaluation of human flourishing in the mid-twentieth century that occurred across a broad spectrum of religious groups. From a similar starting point, progressive religious communities followed different paths, and reached different conclusions than fundamentalists. They generally agreed that the late twentieth century was a time of upheaval, reexamination, and redefinition. Frequently, the upheavals in progressive communities produced new assumptions about how to live lives of inclusion and outreach, how to navigate tradition in a changed world. Exploring the ways that progressive religious groups revised their own understanding of human sexuality reveals how the relationship between religion and sexuality was reconfigured—often in unexpected ways. Especially important, law and legal change became central to debates within religious communities about love, marriage, morality, and justice.

There are many ways to begin the story, perhaps with the influential work of Sigmund Freud in the late nineteenth and early twentieth centuries, or with the "sexologist" Alfred Kinsey, whose mid-twentieth-century studies of American sexual behavior dominated discussions of the breadth and variety of sexual experience in America, for women as well as men.[35] Significant new attention to sexuality, and often meaningful change, characterized several religious groups well before 1970.[36] Yet the late 1960s and early 1970s were a distinct era in liberal denominations' approach to same-sex relationships. By late 1967, both Episcopalian and United Church of Christ leaders endorsed organizations that worked toward the understanding and support of homosexuals.[37] The Unitarian Universalist Association (commonly known as the Unitarians) first ordained an openly gay minister in late 1969.[38] The Metropolitan Community Church (MCC), founded in late 1968 as "a Christian church for all people with an outreach to the gay community," opened its first church building in 1971; by 1972 there were twelve churches and twelve missions, including a new Metropolitan Community Temple in Los Angeles (which later became Beth Chayim Chadashim and is now part of Reform Judaism). Today the MCC denomination includes more than 300 churches and claims 43,000 members.[39] In 1973, the first independent gay synagogue, Congregation Beth Simchat Torah, was initiated in New York; it currently includes more than 800 households.[40] Pastoral counselors and chaplains had embraced the insights of researchers such as Kinsey for many years, and they began to argue openly that loving relationships between persons of the same sex "should be judged by the same criteria as a heterosexual marriage—that is, valued and affirmed if intended to foster a permanent relationship of love."[41] Also in 1973, the American Psychiatric Association officially dropped homosexuality from its list of mental disorders.[42]

These developments in religious life and in medicine were matched in law. In June 1969, resistance to legal discrimination against gay men catapulted onto the stage with the now-famous Stonewall riot in Greenwich Village after police conducted a routine raid at a gay bar. Instead of retreating, patrons of the Stonewall Inn fought back, drawing crowds of supporters to demonstrations that continued for days.[43] Those demonstrations were followed in the 1970s by the repeal of sodomy laws in more than half the states, the passage of antidiscrimination statutes by more than thirty municipalities, and the endorsement of gay rights by politicians and in the Democratic Party platform of 1980, and the lifting of the ban on employment of lesbians and gays by the Civil Service Commission.[44]

Although none of these early advances explicitly called for recognition of same-sex marriage, several equated love between people of the same sex, in both moral and religious value, with that between husband and wife in a heterosexual marriage. Among gay rights activists outside religious communities, however, marriage was decidedly not a central goal. Many lesbian feminists argued that marriage was indelibly a patriarchal institution based on the oppression of women.[45] As lawyer Paula Ettelbrick saw it, "Marriage runs contrary to two of the primary goals of the lesbian and gay movement: the affirmation of gay identity and culture and the validation of many forms of relationships."[46] Marriage for lesbians and gay men might "dilute" the patriarchal dynamic, Ettelbrick argued, but it would "not transform society."[47] Others were even more forthright. Legal scholars Nancy Polikoff and Martha Fineman argued that marriage was positively harmful, whether for heterosexuals or same-sex couples. Polikoff advocated doing away with using marriage "as the bright dividing line between relationships that count and those that don't," arguing that marriage discriminated against anyone who didn't fit the one-size-fits-all marriage model.[48] Fineman called marriage an "overrated idea" that "impede[d] the development of effective social policies."[49]

But marriage still promised to transform individual lives; and even though leaders of the movement were after other, less traditional goals, same-sex couples wanted to experience that transformation. As one exasperated observer reflected, "No one was more surprised by the rise of the gay marriage issue than many veterans of early forms of gay activism. . . . [Even worse,] the campaign for marriage . . . depend[ed] for its success on the courts."[50] Despite the discouragement of movement leaders, however, the issue of marriage remained alive in religious communities, where many couples found welcome and encouragement. They sought a different measure of success, a union that described and validated love and daily life through religious and social meaning. This kind of experience is central to what scholars now commonly call "lived religion."[51] Religious practice, as one commentator put it, "comes into being in an ongoing, dynamic relationship with the realities of everyday life."[52] In the language of lived religion, through the intersections between belief, sexuality, commitment, community, and more, the everyday lives of married persons are structured by the private and public identity of spouses. Knitting together such threads of meaning and aspiration is a quintessentially religious undertaking.[53] So many same-sex couples wanted this complex and experiential validation that an official of the Metropolitan Community Church, which has been performing same-sex weddings since its founding in 1968, estimated that by 2004 it had performed 85,000 separate marriage ceremonies, and that its membership hovered around 23,000.[54] The desire of ordinary people to live in a religiously sanctified relationship of mutual trust and physical intimacy outpaced the more radical spirit of most of the gay-rights movement's leaders. Like many aspects of a tradition of lived religion, the movement bubbled up from below.

The vast majority of couples sought only religious ceremonies in the heady years of the early 1970s. A few—maybe as many as two dozen—pushed for formal legal recognition as well, by walking boldly into county clerks' offices and applying for marriage licenses. First were James Michael McConnell, a librarian, and his partner, Richard John (Jack) Baker, a law student, both from Minneapolis. On May 18, 1970, the two "donned their best suits and ties," called a press conference, "went on local TV and told thousands of viewers of their intention," and then went to the Hennepin County clerk's office to apply for a marriage license.[55] They claimed that because Minnesota's statute authorizing marriage did not specify that applicants must be male and female, they qualified for a license. Technically, they were right; the statute did not require that applicants be heterosexual couples—it just assumed that that was who would apply.[56] The bemused clerk forwarded the application straight to the county attorney, who instructed the clerk to reject it.

McConnell and Baker welcomed the flood of publicity that predictably followed. *Look* magazine ran a three-page photo spread on the couple in its "American Family" issue of January 26, 1971.[57] Baker built on the press attention in a successful run for president of the University of Minnesota Student Association, with a poster that featured him dressed in tight jeans and wearing high heels, and the slogan "Put Yourself in Jack Baker's Shoes."[58] Baker's victory was such news that the iconic TV news anchor Walter Cronkite announced on *CBS Evening News* that "an admitted homosexual" had been elected head of the university's student body.[59]

McConnell and Baker sued the county clerk, arguing that they had a statutory and constitutional right to marry. The trial court upheld the refusal, and the Minnesota Supreme Court affirmed, after listening to Baker's argument in "stony silence."[60] One justice even turned his back during the argument for Baker and McConnell, physically showing his disdain for their claim.[61] In an opinion that presaged later decisions in other states, the court held that any "sensible" reading of Minnesota's marriage statute made it clear that the "common usage" was what was intended, "meaning the state of union between persons of the opposite sex."[62] McConnell and Baker had based their constitutional claim on the Fourteenth Amendment to the Constitution, which they said (citing *Loving*, the interracial marriage case) prohibited irrationality and discrimination in eligibility for marriage under state statutes. The court rejected this argument, holding that the "historic institution [of marriage] is as old as the book of Genesis . . . [and] more deeply founded" than the purely "contemporary" interests that Baker and McConnell claimed made them eligible for marriage.[63] As the court put it, "in commonsense and in a constitutional sense, there is a clear distinction between a marital restriction based merely upon race and one based upon the fundamental difference in sex."[64]

Baker and McConnell were already "married" by the time the Minnesota Supreme Court ruled on their case, however. Using the name "Pat Lyn McConnell," Michael McConnell had applied with Jack Baker for a marriage license in another Minnesota county. The ruse worked (temporarily), and the two were married "with license in hand" by the Reverend Roger W. Lynn of the United Methodist Church, who declared them "joined in marriage, in the name of the Father, the Son and the Holy Spirit, Amen."[65]

A second suit, this time brought in Kentucky by Marjorie Jones and Tracy Knight, added religious freedom to the mix of legal claims. Jones and Knight argued that their faith was fully consistent with their union—indeed, it demanded that they be allowed to marry. The Kentucky Supreme Court dismissed the argument that religion could affect the law of marriage, even though it stressed that marriage had been "a custom long before the state commenced to issue licenses for that purpose," a reference to the traditional authority of religious courts over marriage in pre-Reformation Europe.[66] In the United States, however, the court stressed, the polygamy cases of the nineteenth century had established that religious interests "cannot be extended to make the professed doctrines [of any faith] superior to the law of the land and in effect permit every citizen to become a law unto himself."[67]

A third case expanded the distance between claims for same-sex marriage and even the most liberal mainstream legal standards in the 1970s. In late 1971, John Singer (a typist) and Paul Barwick (the manager of the Gay Community Center in Seattle) applied to the King County clerk for a marriage license. They had staged a press event, like Baker and McConnell's, but this time coverage was limited to local papers and the gay press. The sensation had diminished as plaintiffs' legal arguments seemed less likely to succeed, and as courts grew more adept at addressing the antidiscrimination arguments of same-sex couples. After their application was refused, Singer and Barwick brought suit. As their case wended its way through the courts, Washington State enacted a new constitutional provision, an equal rights amendment that prohibited sex discrimination. This created opportunities (or dangers, according to one's perspective): perhaps the new rights for women could be extended to uphold rights for lesbians and gay men. Thanks to the amendment, the case attracted far more attention when it reached the Washington Court of Appeals in 1974 than it would otherwise have received.

Singer and Barwick invoked the new state constitutional provision, and drew on the work of two young law students, Sam Perkins and Arthur Silverstein. Their jointly authored student commentary, "The Legality of Homosexual Marriage," was published in the *Yale Law Journal* in 1973. Perkins and Silverstein argued that because the federal Equal Rights Amendment (ERA) would prohibit sex discrimination in the same way that the Fourteenth Amendment prohibits racial discrimination, same-sex marriage would become a constitutional right. The *Loving* case, they said, "raise[s] a strong presumption that homosexual couples could not be uniformly denied marriage licenses after ratification of the [Equal Rights] Amendment."[68] An equal rights amendment, said other legal scholars, was even less flexible than the equal protection clause of the Fourteenth Amendment, on which the *Loving* court based its ruling.[69] Indeed, another controversial *Yale Law Journal* article, this one published in 1971 by feminist supporters of the ERA, argued that the effects of the amendment would fundamentally change women's lives, and thus all of society. This article generated considerable discussion in Congress and around the country as the proposed constitutional amendment was debated.[70] Concern about a radically new social order began to undermine ERA support.

This new work in law reviews caused deep concern among feminists, who were scrambling to respond to ERA critics. It also provided a complementary sense of opportunity for Singer and Barwick. Their lawyer deployed the argument suggested by the two Yale law students, invoking Washington State's amendment (which tracked the language of the proposed federal amendment precisely—saying that "equal rights and responsibility . . . shall not be denied or abridged on account of sex"). This language meant that the heterosexual definition of marriage created "an unconstitutional classification 'on account of sex,'" they said.[71] This argument and the lawsuit that raised it created potentially devastating issues for supporters of the ERA, which had been sent to the states with overwhelming support from Congress, and had been ratified by thirty of the required thirty-eight states by the end of 1973. *Singer v. Hara* arose just as supporters of the amendment were put on the defensive by claims that the ERA would sanction "unisex toilets, the drafting of women [into the armed forces], and homosexual marriage."[72]

Feminist leaders found themselves backing away from the implications of the amendment, distancing the pro-ERA movement from same-sex marriage, an issue that for many of them was really beside the point. Some (like Paula Ettelbrick) hoped to leave gay marriage out of discussions of sex discrimination altogether. Others were willing to sacrifice lesbian and gay issues for equal rights for women.[73] Whatever the motivation, they succeeded: the Washington Court of Appeals rejected the notion that women's rights and gay and lesbian rights were analogous. "Equal pay for equal work," said Chief Judge Herbert Swanson, did not create new rights, it only equalized those that already exist. The right to marry was based on the fundamental capacity to procreate within the marital union (even if no such duty existed once a couple was married), and on the fact that same-sex marriage was equally unavailable to men and women, Swanson maintained. The court held that the limitation of the right of marriage to heterosexual couples was both nondiscriminatory and socially beneficial.[74] Leading pro-ERA feminist scholars hoped that this opinion would stem the flood of criticism from the right. In 1977, citing *Singer v. Hara* as their sole source, feminists stated unequivocally that "the equal rights amendment does not preclude the states from refusing to recognize [a same-sex] relationship as marriage."[75]

As the next decade and more demonstrated, suits for same-sex marriage were virtually foreclosed after *Singer.* State equal rights amendments, especially but not only in the eyes of those who supported them, turned out to be an unproductive angle—at least for the time being. Still, the question of same-sex relationships, and especially marriage, dogged feminists and the ERA. In Florida, the home state of antigay activist Anita Bryant, the legislature not only refused to ratify the ERA in 1977 but also enacted a statute declaring that "a marriage license shall not be issued unless one party is a male and the other party is a female."[76] Other states also modified their marriage statutes in the 1970s to ensure that only opposite-sex couples could be married within their boundaries.[77] The flood of legislation against same-sex marriage was aimed at entrenching "the notion that marriages *must* be opposite sex so firmly in law that it could never again be questioned."[78] The lesson was a harsh one: raising the marriage question carried toxic consequences. Activists moved on to other fields, campaigning for the repeal of criminal sodomy statutes, rights of association and privacy, domestic partnership laws, antidiscrimination policies at colleges and universities, and so on.[79] Marriage, it seemed, was off the table.

Or was it? Among religious communities, the question stayed alive. They emphasized the importance of transformative ritual, stressing the value of membership in a community knit together by attention to "ultimate questions." For them, marriage was not primarily a legal or political event but a religious one. Recall the Reverend Roger Lynn, the United Methodist minister who married Jack Baker and Michael McConnell in 1971. In 2004 he reflected on the ways that their wedding ceremony had changed his own life. "It's been one of my successful marriages, but more than that, it has been a defining moment in my life. From that moment on it was clear who I was in regard to the [issues] of gay marriage . . . and being willing to take a public stand on social justice issues."[80] The transformation occurred not just for those who were married, that is, but also for the celebrant. The marriage ceremony was a "defining moment" on multiple levels, especially as a spiritual matter, for the officiant of the ceremony.

Frequently, media coverage of same-sex marriage placed religion on the other side of the question. The surge in organizational and political engagement among more conservative religious groups dominated public awareness of religion for the past generation. Although almost all religious groups claimed that they were routinely ignored or derided by the mainstream media, those on the left were especially dismayed by what they saw as the presumption that they virtually no longer existed.[81] As research showed, however, "The religious left [was] just about the same size as the religious right" in the early twenty-first century.[82] Many religious liberals took stands on important issues that they believed deserve recognition and respect.[83]

Key among those areas of concern were the rights and interests of gay and lesbian people. Religious organizations and clergy provided vital support and affirmation for rethinking the place of same-sex relationships in civil rights as well as in religious life. Beginning in the 1960s, religious groups supported and helped define gay activism, goals, strategies, and ideas. Religion and religious actors were central to the development of new approaches to human sexuality in practice as well as theory. Pastoral counselors, for example, stressed the need for mutuality, respect, and commitment in sexual intimacy—ethical requirements that many considered as likely to be satisfied in same-sex encounters as in heterosexual ones.[84]

Same-sex marriage became a central issue for many in the religious left in the 1970s and beyond, along with other questions of social justice in America and around the world.[85] The debate over marriage, however, had unique importance not only for the broader society outside the bounds of liberal congregations but also for congregants within them. Marriage equality brought progressive religious leaders into a debate that had the potential to revive and extend the public's sense of their relevance and their power to lead through example and advocacy.[86] Whether or not they would have selected this as their entry into the spotlight, same-sex marriage provided the space for progressive denominations to demonstrate the vitality and the ethical health of liberal religion.[87]

The central question for many progressive clergy was the public and also personal nature of a committed relationship lived out within a religious community. As Roger Lynn put it, "The basic issue is . . . the social benefits—familial and communal—that come to a married couple. Marriage is a public statement, before God and the couple's supportive community, friends and family. It states that they are a unit needing the community's blessing and support. . . . These blessings, supports, and expectations contribute to the success and the quality of the relationship. To deny that to gay and lesbian members of our community is a grave injustice and diminishes our whole community."[88] Others, it turned out, thought the same way. Through the 1970s and beyond, progressive religious communities responded to the call for inclusion.[89] Their sympathies were excited by the evident needs of congregants and potential congregants.

The process, frequently, was halting, complicated, and filled with recrimination. Within the Episcopal Church (the American church affiliated with the Anglican Communion, a worldwide organization with the Church of England at its hub), Bishop James Spong, a liberal, described his surprise at learning that many gay men in the 1970s opposed the elevation of women to positions of power within the church. Closeted gay priests, he said, especially in faiths where celibacy is required (such as Roman Catholicism) or highly valued (the Catholic wing of the Anglican Church), could live out respected lives in a homophobic society.[90] The Episcopal Church first officially ordained women in 1976. Also in 1976, the church affirmed that "homosexuals are children of God" and called for the equal protection of gay and lesbian people under secular law.[91] The connection between the two developments, and especially the hostility flowing from priests toward women aspiring to ordination within the church, led Bishop Spong to look more closely at the discrimination practiced in his own Christian community. These issues have divided Episcopalians in subsequent decades, and, as Beverly LaHaye feared, the relationship between women's equality and same-sex marriage deepened and spread.[92]

Ordained women, especially, became vocal proponents of reevaluating what counts as blessed sexuality to include same-sex relationships. God's law of love, they said, meant that even ancient barriers must be reexamined.[93] "Two, four, six, eight, God does not discriminate!" chanted MCC pastor Carolyn Mobley with the crowd gathered for the first Boise, Idaho, gay pride parade, in 1990.[94] Mobley said God had guided her understanding of her own sexuality. The ethic of inclusion envisioned in the New Testament, Mobley explained, meant that her capacity for love, which mirrored the love of God, was intact and vital, despite what any cultural or ritual "rules" might dictate. "God didn't deliver me from my sexuality. God delivered me from guilt and shame and gave me a sense of pride and wholeness that I really needed. My sexuality was a gift from God, and so is everyone's sexuality, no matter how it's oriented. It's a gift to be able to love."[95] The ethic of love, in Mobley's view, meant that she was a creature of God every bit as much as anyone else.

Mobley appropriated and reconfigured her place within a new, inclusive religious view of sexuality that defied the cultural rejection of same-sex relationships.[96] Others fashioned their own pastiches of innovation and tradition, dissent and accommodation. They became irrepressible, challenging their synagogues and churches to adapt to their perspective. They were also prompted by experiences of birth and death—events that, like marriage, are traditionally marked by liturgical rituals that help make sense of loss and celebrate new members of a community. In the 1980s and across the early 1990s, gay men, especially, found themselves trapped in the cruel and deadly AIDS epidemic. At the same time, the "lesbian baby boom" of the 1980s highlighted the needs of families for recognition, support, inclusion.[97] But the seeds of religious change had been planted well before new experiences of birth and death confronted religious liberals. Creating community, even (and perhaps especially) a community of two, had already become an individualized celebration of accomplishments and aspirations.

Americans of many different stripes expressed and underscored their religious creativity in marriage, particularly in the rituals that they designed to celebrate their weddings. "Marriage" may have had more or less defined meanings in law and religious authority, but in the lives of those entering into it, the experience was endlessly variable. A law student recently reported that his Catholic priest objected strenuously to the eclecticism of the wedding ceremonies he had been called upon to officiate. "These modifications have made weddings less spiritual," he reported the priest as saying.[98] Spirituality for the participants may not be the same as for the officiant, however. The layers of personal meaning that the participants (and perhaps the congregation) injected into what might otherwise be an undifferentiated ceremony were chosen precisely because those who were to be married conceived them as meaningful. One researcher reported that marriage, more than any other single ceremony, prompted participants to "become ritually active in designing, deciding, and choosing elements for the rite."[99]

These calculated alterations or additions conveyed ownership of the ritual, tailoring it to resonate in the lives and experiences of the couple. In the work of the influential anthropologist Victor Turner, creativity allows ritual to accomplish transformation: by definition, rituals inhabit the liminal space between culture and change, recreating rather than simply buttressing the status quo.[100] In this sense, the reinvention of the marriage celebration for each marriage transformed it from an empty "ceremony" into a transformative ritual. Critical scholars who lamented the failure of a new, color-blind regime to transform marriage into anything more than an illusory freedom overlooked the ways that religious weddings were remade to reflect the aspirations of the participants, as well as the tradition of the denomination.

There were limits, however. The "autonomy" that characterized such additions and subtractions became ubiquitous in the enormous wedding industry. The eclecticism that the priest bemoaned was so predictable that its absence may have been more remarkable than its presence. With distressing monotony, wedding planners claimed they were deeply invested in the mass production of such "meaningful" ceremonies.[101] Yet the freedom that couples felt in planning their wedding inverted the traditional authority over the celebration of a marriage, allowing them a sense of control over what previously had been a top-down exercise. Certainly, marriages that crossed boundaries—religious, racial, and social—that had once been considered inviolate increasingly became the norm.[102]

More structural challenges to religious authority in the late 1970s and throughout the 1980s were conditioned by concepts of social liberation and their relationship to communities of faith over time. Flowing first from Catholic priests in Latin America but spreading quickly among progressive Protestants and Jews, liberation theologians shifted their gaze away from abstraction and into engagement with those at the very bottom of the ladder, wherever they might be. Self-styled "Third World theologians" met in Tanzania in 1976, led by Gustavo Gutierrez, Roman Catholic bishop of Peru, who famously viewed the fundamental Christian mandate as service to "the poor and oppressed against all forms of injustice and domination." Looking at the "underside of history," Gutierrez argued, was key to the practice of theology, a means of escaping tired academic theorizing.[103]

Liberation theology, as this movement came to be called, spread across the progressive religious spectrum. By the late 1980s, one exasperated commentator (arguing for liberation for Native Americans, who seemed to have been left out of the galloping replication) listed separate liberationist theologies for "African Americans, Hispanic Americans, women, Asian Americans, even Jews."[104] Indeed, the work of liberation seemed to have no logical stopping point, as each new exposure of injustice led to the discovery of others. While some might argue that the adoption of liberationist ideas across the spectrum diluted the theory's essential message, others deployed the focus on the "underside" to flip tradition on its head.

Frequently, the role of history (especially the propriety of deciding that some biblical texts are the product of their time and place and do not apply to contemporary settings) has been crucial to the process of reinterpretation from a liberationist perspective. In progressive Christian treatments of sexuality, scholars deployed historical and contextual arguments for the recovery of long-buried egalitarian impulses.[105] The influential feminist Rosemary Radford Ruether, professor of theology at the Pacific School of Religion in Berkeley, California, exemplified the ways that liberal interpreters interrogated history to recover perspectives they claimed had been lost over time. According to Ruether, Christianity in its first hundred years or so spread through the marginalized people of the ancient world—that is, through women, children, and slaves. The new faith, therefore, was widely considered to be subversive, as first-century Christians comprised a "new kind of family, a voluntary community gathered by personal faith, which [stood] in tension with the natural family or kinship group."[106] Three centuries later, after the emperor Constantine embraced Christianity as a recognized faith of the Roman Empire, the radically egalitarian, voluntary family of the first century was compartmentalized within monastic communities.[107] Patriarchy was reinstated in later New Testament writings, argued Ruether, albeit with a new mandate for husbandly benevolence toward dependents. Ruether viewed "ancient Christianity" as embracing a "variety of forms" of the family; recovering this ancient perspective would give late twentieth-century Christians the chance to redefine family as "committed communities of mutual service" in an older, purer, more truly Christian mold.[108]

Within liberal Judaism, the process of rethinking women's roles in society and religion created the potential for reconsidering gay and lesbian rights, as well.[109] Reform and Reconstructionist Judaism have long understood their goal as the reinterpretation and invigoration of the tradition in light of Diaspora and change. Both movements share a commitment to interpreting the Torah and Jewish law as consistent with contemporary society and fundamental individual autonomy.[110] Reform began within cosmopolitan European Jewry, brought to American shores by Rabbi Isaac Mayer Wise, whose commitment to American democracy and opportunity in the late nineteenth century led him to equate the flourishing of Judaism with America, and vice versa.[111] Reconstructionism, which developed as a distinct movement in the middle decades of the twentieth century, partially out of Rabbi Mordecai Kaplan's sense that the Reform movement had abandoned too much of value in the ancient Jewish heritage, reinterpreted much of law and scripture in light of traditional folkways and history, rather than as binding in the contemporary world.[112] In this sense, both movements are distinctively American forms of Judaism, committed to the relevance of Jewish life and practice through creative adaptation to modern culture and values, especially (but not only) equality.[113] As Kaplan put it, "We look to the past for a vote, but do not empower it to give us a veto."[114]

The commitment to ongoing interpretation and creative tension with past traditions were tested by the process that led to the ordination of women as rabbis and their acceptance as cantors. American Reform, for example, included "the absolute equality of men and women in religious obligations" as one of its founding principles in the mid-nineteenth century, but only in the late twentieth century were women ordained.[115] Many different aspects of the movement were destabilized by the change. The political and interpretive dilemmas posed by the movement to embrace equality for women, "smashing our notions of God and gender," as one commentator noted, "[meant that] the atmosphere was ripe for other innovations as well."[116]

In the late 1960s, religion writer for the *New York Times* Edward Fiske argued that debates over sexuality were conducted according to fundamentally different premises depending on the faith tradition. The issue in Judaism was far less contentious than among Christians, Fiske said, because the prohibitions in the Torah meant that homosexual acts violated God's law tout court. Christians had more leeway to interpret the divine commands of the Old Testament in light of the New Testament.[117] Subsequent events revealed there were no easy answers, whether in Judaism or Christianity. Reform Jews have traveled far from the blanket rejection of homosexuality that Fiske claimed was obvious to all Jews. Rabbi David Saperstein, long-time director of the Religion Action Center for Reform Judaism, boasted recently: "Culturally, there's no group more progressive on the social issues—whether you're talking about separation of church and state . . . equal rights for gays and lesbians—that more strongly embraces those ideas than the Jewish community does."[118]

This issue of homosexuality proved difficult, Saperstein notwithstanding, especially because of the direct toraitic command: "Do not lie with a male as one lies with a woman, it is *to'evah*" (commonly translated as "an abomination"), part of the Holiness Code in the book of Leviticus.[119] Two chapters later, the text adds that the penalty for such transgression is death.[120] Jewish law was developed among a small and exclusively male group of elite leaders, retorted commentators from progressive Jewish movements.[121] Moreover, as some advocates interpreted the ethical focus on marginality, Jews' own historical oppression formed a parallel to the oppression of lesbians and gays.[122] A leading Reform rabbi argued in 1989, "We who were Marranos in Madrid, who clung to the closet of assimilation and conversion in order to live without molestation, we cannot deny the demand for gay and lesbian visibility!"[123] Jews should be especially attuned to the oppression of those in their midst, this argument went, interrogating their law in light of changing and expanding notions of tradition and ritual.

Yet the divisiveness of incorporating rights for lesbian and gay Jews into Jewish law, as one scholar noted, became "so explosive [that it threatened] to divide the entire Reform Jewish enterprise."[124] The question was laid to rest (sort of) by a resolution introduced by the Women's Rabbinic Network in 2000, allowing (but not requiring) Reform rabbis to officiate at lesbian and gay weddings. Rabbinical autonomy already meant that rabbis had the right to follow their conscience, and many had been officiating at same-sex weddings, but the debate over the resolution revealed how deeply the presence of women affected the pace and tenor of change. One outraged observer reported that the e-mail traffic in the months prior to the 2000 meeting included charges that the Women's Rabbinic Network was a nest of lesbians, and that they had formed a cabal to undermine the authority of the male rabbinate. Another charged that more conservative Reform rabbis "threaten[ed] to reduce Jewish law to irrelevancy."[125] The ordination of women, then, stirred up controversy and even resentment that exploded in response to women rabbis' advocacy of full equality for gay men and lesbians.

Traditional Jewish scholars' presumptions about sexuality and marriage were formed with their own power and desires foremost, claimed progressive critics. Traditional theories submerged and oppressed those (all women and gay men) whose interests and commitments were simply not considered relevant. Especially with regard to sexuality, says feminist theologian Judith Plaskow, ancient proscriptions could not capture multiple modern approaches to sexual life. Indeed, the obsession with sex, she argues, was itself misguided. "For many people, sex is not a central life issue," she maintains, even though the "ideologies" built around sexual behaviors assume that sex is the single most important element.[126] The direct biblical condemnation in Leviticus, said the new feminist scholars, was embedded in a culture of profound patriarchy, in which all relationships were structured by the power and dominance of men over women. A sexual act that would expose a man to a submissive role would endanger the essential dynamic of a patriarchal society.[127]

In modern America, by contrast, Jewish practice should be concerned with expressing sexuality through attention to the sacred, respect for all persons, and as generative of bonds between humans that represent the sanctified covenant between God and humanity.[128] The key, Jewish liberals stressed, must be the quality of social and interpersonal relationships; the ethics of sexual behavior depend not on "arbitrary" elements of gender but on the nature of what is achieved through loving intimacy. Through Jewish ritual, said progressives, committed relationships are invested with the central value of *kedushah* (holiness).[129] Much in the same way that many liberal Jews welcomed female rabbis and cantors, the expansion of marriage to include those whose committed loving relationships are with those of the same sex seemed logical, even predictable, according to proponents.[130]

While Christian conservatives like Beverly LaHaye were vitally important to the invigoration of antifeminist and antigay movements beginning in the 1970s, the role of religious progressives in leading the opposing forces has elided historians' gaze. To be sure, the lack of attention to the story told here is not surprising. LaHaye's Concerned Women for America captured headlines and political imagination. The election and reelection of President George W. Bush cemented the popular identification of "religious" voters with a conservative agenda.[131] Opponents, including the well-known authors Richard Dawkins and Christopher Hitchens, tended to equate all religion with visceral conservatism and self-delusion.[132]

Political consultant Robert Jones argues that religious progressives were drowned out by the religious right because they were significantly more diverse—both theologically and demographically. Equally important, liberal religious leaders often worked in organizations that had no explicit religious identity (think of the group Americans United for Separation of Church and State), but which nonetheless were motivated and sustained deeply, if quietly, by faith. Underlying and exacerbating all of these factors, the fundamentally right-wing inclinations of the mainstream press, Jones charged, mean that conservative religious leaders grabbed the headlines four times as frequently as liberals, even though the progressives grew in the last decade of the twentieth century to virtually the same size as the Right.[133]

Jones exaggerated, however. Media coverage was colored more by a failure to understand the complexities and extraordinary diversity of American religious life, said other observers, than by any desire to valorize the Christian right.[134] That there are relatively equal proportions of the population divided between religious conservatives and liberals is also consistent with survey reports for the past twenty-five years.[135] Regardless of the explanation, it was true that many progressive religious leaders were convinced that they had been silenced, ignored by the press and forgotten by the larger society. Many turned inward, focusing on the communities they served.[136]

Progressive Jewish leaders were drawn into debates about sexuality by their congregants, and often by the women they themselves had welcomed into the rabbinate and the ranks of cantors. As Devon Lerner described her own experience as a seminarian and then as the leader of a Reform congregation in the late 1970s and through the 1980s, she began to understand the devastating loneliness of the closet while training for the rabbinate at Hebrew Union College in Cincinnati. There, a gay man she knew could not disclose his true identity, for he would have been expelled from the seminary. Her sympathy for her colleague prompted her to question the rules that still excluded him, especially as the doors to training had been opened for her only a few years before. After graduation, she immersed herself in the lives of her congregants and the demands of her role. She became known for celebrating interfaith weddings, still a topic of great controversy within the community. Same-sex unions, if composed of two Jewish men or women, were in some senses less disruptive.[137]

Lerner and other progressive rabbis confronted these issues not only because their own religious leanings led them there but also because the demands of lesbian and gay Jews forced them to grapple with the idea of the intrinsic holiness of same-sex relationships and the love that flows through them. Same-sex couples' insistence that they should be included, in the fullest sense of the word, into Jewish ritual and cultural life made these topics compelling. The desire for a ritual life that was also affirming generated an urgency and a creativity among those whose religious lives were inseparable from their marital, familial, communal, sexual, personal selves. Describing her own experience, Lerner said, "[I] came out to myself," speaking of her move to Boston. She began to connect feminist theology with political activism as a means of unifying the social and religious commitments that animated her spirituality.[138]

The integration of religious and secular in the experience of same-sex Jewish couples who called on tradition to sustain and help define their lives together defied attempts to compartmentalize neatly what is "sacred" or "profane." Scholars of religion who have explored the myriad ways that religion functions in individual experience have probed the incoherence of such dualisms.[139] As they have documented, religious meaning and practice overflow with bottom-up creativity—as it is lived, religion is far too active, mobile, and unpredictable for comfortable categorizations. The boundaries that those outside imagine as impermeable—say, between secular and religious marriage, or even between same-sex and heterosexual marriage—may not exist within relationships.[140]

Marriage integrates social and legal as well as religious meaning in individual lives. Especially over the past generation, this integrative capacity became particularly vital. It imbued the decision to marry, and marriage ceremonies, with unexpected significance, surprising to those who predicted the "withering away" of marriage in the 1970s and 1980s.[141] Marriage rates belied assumptions that highly educated and professionally successful women would be less likely to marry, while less educated women would benefit more from marriage and thus would be more likely to "increase their utility by exchanging . . . [their] home work for men's labor market work."[142] Instead, studies of the late twentieth century established that marriage rates for poorer women were lower than predicted.[143] The explanation for the decline lay not in failure to maximize utility, but in poorer women's sense of the importance of marriage socially and spiritually. In one study conducted among poor women in Philadelphia, marriage symbolized and cemented an achievement, not just in economic terms (although those were crucial) but also in symbolic terms. Marriage, said experts, became a form of marking personal achievement and a statement about the maturity of a relationship, rather than a prepackaged social formula.[144] American rates of marriage remained noticeably higher than those in other developed nations, even as the average age at marriage rose steadily after 1970, confirming the sense that marriage by the early twenty-first century could accurately be described as a "capstone" rather than a beginning.[145]

The exceptionally high rate of marriage among Americans tracks rates of religious commitment and participation as well. More than 83 percent of Americans surveyed in mid-2007 reported a discernible religious self-identity and affiliation.[146] In addition, 80 percent of weddings are religious, according to recent studies, up from 68 percent in the period 1925 to 1944 and 74 percent in 1990.[147] As these figures illustrate, the determination to be married once a person has reached a recognizable maturity, and the growing desire to be married within a community of faith that affirms the couple's experience and hope for the future, are shared by a broad spectrum of Americans. It is also true, no doubt, that churches and synagogues lent gravitas to the ceremony, as well as providing a dramatic and beautiful space that is built to hold large numbers of people.[148] An aspirational combination of "spontaneity and solidity, freedom and intimacy" was the (often unarticulated) goal of the marriage for new spouses.[149] The extraordinary freight that couples placed on their relationship made marriage both vitally important and fragile; Americans married and divorced at higher rates than people in other countries—a pattern that students of marriage and the family have described as a high "marriage metabolism."[150]

Among marrying same-sex couples, the desire for spiritual commitment and communal ritual appeared as prominently as among heterosexual couples, often even more poignantly. Those whose identities were the subject of contest and even condemnation experienced the joy of mutual and community recognition in the ritual of marriage especially intensely. As a formerly secular lesbian ethnographer put it, her own wedding (celebrated by a Reform rabbi in the mid-1990s) changed her view "forever about the value of ritual." Through the process of discussing, creating, and then participating in a traditionally Jewish ceremony, she said she learned to see same-sex weddings as a valuable means of affirming the transcendence of the emotional bond between the couple, the authenticity of religious practice, and its meaning in society.[151]

This utterly quotidian yet profound sense of the place and meaning of marriage in religion and life, and couples' increasing sense of personal ownership of the ritual of marriage in the 1980s and '90s, ran headlong into the stark prohibition in law. Even after the uniformly negative results of the cases from the 1970s, however, progressive religious communities wrestled with same-sex marriage, many of them gradually but steadily embracing the concept as a fundamental issue of justice for those within the faith. In addition to explicitly inclusive new denominations formed in Jewish, Catholic, and Protestant traditions, such as Congregation Beth Simchat Torah, Dignity, the Church of the Beloved Disciple, and the Metropolitan Community Church, liberal denominations within Judaism and Protestantism increasingly focused on inclusion as their congregants insisted that their own sexual identities reflected God's love.[152]

Reconstructionists, who created the bat mitzvah, a coming-of-age ceremony for girls that parallels the bar mitzvah for boys, traveled a relatively smooth path to inclusion. The movement first admitted openly gay rabbinical students in 1984. They embraced the full equality of lesbian and gay Jews in 1992, supporting "Jewish ceremonies conducted to celebrate the loving commitment between same-gender couples," and at the same time condemning prejudice against gays and lesbians from the perspective "of a people who have been vilified" and who thus have a special concern with the equal treatment of all people.[153] In 2000, the Central Conference of American Rabbis (CCAR), the Reform rabbinate representing 1.5 million Jews, declared for the first time that it would support rabbis who celebrate same-sex unions, even if civil marriage was not available to the couple. Notwithstanding the internal controversy noted earlier, Reform Judaism was the first major religious group to say unequivocally that "it will support its rabbis if they participate in these ceremonies," boasted CCAR vice president Rabbi Paul Menitoff.[154] And although neither denomination requires its rabbis to officiate at same-sex ceremonies, the trend in favor of such celebrations has deepened and spread. In 2004, for example, Reform rabbi Sharon Gladstone of Los Angeles said, "I was ordained last year, and the first marriage I officiated at was a marriage of two women. I think that more and more rabbis are officiating, certainly in the Reform and Reconstructionist movements."[155] Across the country in Massachusetts, others had blazed the trail.

The Religious Coalition for the Freedom to Marry was born out of the conviction that marriage equality was particularly important among liberal clergy in and around Boston in 1998. The signers of the Declaration of Religious Support for the Freedom to Marry, a one-page document signed by "faith leaders," denounced a heterosexual marital regime that "favor[ed] the convictions of one religious group over another to deny individuals their fundamental right to marry."[156] Composed entirely of clergy from Massachusetts denominations across the liberal spectrum, RCFM leapt into the culture wars. Coalition members pledged themselves to "public action, visibility, education and mutual support" in advocating the right and freedom to marry.[157] The group initially included a half dozen rabbis and ministers, but its numbers grew to 1,000 in just nine years.[158] They argued that their own religious convictions impelled them to welcome same-sex couples to their houses of worship, to value the commitments of lesbians and gays, and—most important—to celebrate their marriages in religious ceremonies.

They also drew a straight line in the sand. In its early years, RCFM divorced religion from law, as it argued that diversity among religious beliefs should be contrasted with the uniformity demanded by law. There is a fundamental difference between marriage as a religious event blessed by a community of faith, they said, and marriage as a civil right conferring legal status and privileges. Traditionally, such severing of religious rules governing marriage from legal ones has been viewed by clergy as an antireligious effort by the state to reduce the power and range of religion in society.[159] Yet RCFM embraced and even exaggerated the vaunted distinction between the two concepts of marriage.

This approach was strategic: it allowed RCFM to describe religious marriage as varied and variable according to the underlying beliefs of differing groups. Law, on the other hand, it imagined as uniform and distinct from religion. Uniformity and equality in law, said RCFM leaders, meant that marriage could not be denied simply because the couple shared the same gender. Religion was another matter altogether. In this way, RCFM translated decades of theological, institutional, and liturgical innovation among progressive religious groups into an active plan of litigation and lobbying. In the process, it sought to disaggregate rather than integrate the public rule of law and religious lives. It didn't last—eventually, RCFM bridged the divide between religious and secular marriage. Early on, however, the notion that marriage had two distinct identities was a constant in RCFM rhetoric.

The group's Declaration of Religious Support explained that RCFM was "called to protest and oppose" the injustice of denying two people the right to form a family that would "let them be more fully loving, thus more fully human." The signers' faith traditions, they said, counseled them to celebrate such unions, even though they fully understood that other religious communities disagreed about the theological and liturgical justification for same-sex marriage. While they adamantly stated their aversion to forcing any clergy to celebrate or bless unions they could not in conscience support, RCFM also said that the denial of their own ability to ensure civil recognition of such marriages was a form of "dishonor" to their own religious convictions.[160]

Most of all, they were offended at "appeals to sacred texts and religious traditions" to bolster antimarriage rhetoric, which they credited with generating the "overwhelming source of opposition" to the marriage equality they sought to nurture. This, they said, was the fault of the new religious right, whose powerful voice shouted down more thoughtful interpretations of ancient traditions. "Fundamentalism," said RCFM, produced "virulent bigotry" instead of the affirmation of love and humanity so central to their own views of marriage.[161] Religious conservatives in Massachusetts, argued RCFM member the Reverend Judy Deutsch in *The Sudbury Town Crier*, failed to appreciate that "it is people, not God, who have created and developed the institution of marriage. . . . And it is people, not God, who have written about marriage, even in the Bible."[162]

This combination of historical analysis and opposition to biblical literalism was central to RCFM, as it was to other progressive supporters of same-sex marriage. Yet the coalition applied it to the more widespread conviction that social justice demanded they welcome and celebrate loving same-sex unions in religious ceremonies, challenging conservatives on their own ground. Key to this stance was a sense of strength in interfaith unity, and a commitment to building a coalition of liberals that could wield political and legal clout. By virtue of its membership, which included a broad spectrum of progressive religious groups from Jewish, Christian, and Buddhist traditions, as well as a variety of New Age groups, RCFM could argue that limiting civil marriage to heterosexual couples preferred some religious beliefs over others. As a result, the group maintained, the law was not religiously neutral.

The coalition adopted and adapted popular constitutional ideals about separation of church and state to progressive priorities and strategies. As RCFM put it, Americans were charged by the "founding fathers" with protecting "minority religious communities." Preventing progressive clergy from celebrating legally recognized same-sex marriages would elevate one set of religious beliefs—the majority's— "while denying those rights and protections to couples married according to our [beliefs]." In this way, argued RCFM, prohibitions of same-sex marriage ratified "sectarian beliefs" in violation of "religious freedom and the democratic society we all cherish."[163] Marriage equality and religious freedom traveled together in RCFM rhetoric, which combined progressive religious practice with constitutional theory. As Devon Lerner said of her experience, marriage equality was the logical next step for a feminist rabbi.[164] She integrated her long-standing commitment to feminism with the new insight that "Love is love. It is gender blind."[165]

Indeed, RCFM was dominated by women. Many of the signers of RCFM's Declaration of Religious Support were women. Among the 146 Unitarian Universalist ministers who signed, 87 were women. Among the 119 Episcopalians, 52 were women, in a denomination that had ordained women only since 1976. The Reform movement ordained its first woman rabbi in 1972; Conservatives in 1985.[166] Among Jewish signers, 34 of 85 were women. No surprise that all of the Wiccan signers were women, as were the vast majority of neo-pagans. Three of four RCFM presidents and both directors were women, including Lerner, long-time executive director and the group's only paid employee.

By 1999, when Lerner published a book on how to "create your Jewish/Christian [wedding] ceremony," she estimated that she had performed two hundred such marriages.[167] Almost half of Reform and Reconstructionist rabbis do officiate at such marriages, which are entirely rejected by Orthodox and Conservative Jews. Lerner defended her decision against the standard objection that an interfaith marriage is just a loss of another Jewish family to assimilation: "I've seen how interfaith marriages really bring a lot of important insights into the Jewish community and revitalize us," Lerner reported. "Jewish couples [often] say that the Christian partner has gotten them more involved in their Judaism, and made them think about their traditions in new and positive ways."[168]

Taking an inclusive view, Lerner said, meant that welcoming interfaith couples enriched marriage and Jewish identity; just as taking an inclusive view meant that same-sex couples also deserved the same respect for their love, even though it transgressed boundaries once considered sacrosanct. In an article titled "Why We Support Same-Sex Marriage," Lerner quoted a New Testament passage from the first letter of Paul to the Corinthians: "Love takes no pleasure in other people's sins, but delights in the truth. It is always ready to excuse, to trust, and to endure whatever comes. Love does not end."[169] This text, Lerner said, was "moving," although it came from outside her own tradition.[170] The rituals that celebrate love, she argued, should likewise recognize the injustice of imposing gender restrictions on loving relationships. The connection between marriage and justice drew Lerner into political action, joining her personal convictions for the first time to legal action. As she put it, the "religious voice" in advocacy for marriage equality had been a missing link.

With the founding of RCFM, a religious message on the side of same-sex marriage began to be articulated, even though the group was small and underfunded. Often, secular activists in the marriage equality movement discounted the importance and distinctiveness of an explicitly religious coalition, Lerner reported.[171] Because the "public face of the opposition" to same-sex marriage was identified with religion, many secular activists were "afraid of religious voices." RCFM proved its worth, however, by taking on the most powerful local opponent—namely, the Catholic Church in Massachusetts. As Lerner saw it, the "progressive religious voice *must* be up front and in the center, given equal time with secular equality movements."[172] Only then would the complexity and diversity of religious viewpoints be understood.

RCFM was effective not only because it deployed women like Lerner, who made religious arguments against narrow assumptions about the place of religion in political debate. Lerner and RCFM also demonstrated that varying concepts of marriage exist within religious communities. Instead of claiming that those who disagreed with them were "wrong" about the Bible or theology or even liturgy, RCFM claimed that separation between church and state mandated that no religious tradition could validly dictate the shape of marriage in the United States. RCFM submitted an amicus brief in the *Goodridge* case, the litigation that resulted in 2003 in a Massachusetts Supreme Judicial Court opinion holding that the equality provisions contained in the state constitution mandated that same-sex marriage be legalized statewide.[173]

The RCFM brief argued that the word "marriage" was popularly but mistakenly assumed to include two events that should be distinguished—a religious wedding, a ceremony performed by and within a religious community that conveyed a spiritual and social meaning within the community; and a civil marriage, a certification process that conferred a legal status "accompanied by a panoply of rights, protections and obligations."[174] Despite the overlap in popular culture, RCFM maintained, the sacred ceremony should not be in any way confused with the essentially separate interests and privileges conferred by the state. Religion, explained the brief, is riddled with difference, diversity, and, yes, disagreement. "Voices of faith," RCFM claimed, do not speak the same language as law. Theirs were rituals that implicated the sacred, the communal, the transcendent, but that did not—at least in RCFM's view—affect state interests in marriage. Religious limitations on marriage were often fundamentally at odds with state-sanctioned unions. Think, just to give two prominent examples, of the rejection of interfaith marriages in Conservative Judaism, or Roman Catholicism's refusal to allow remarriage after divorce.[175]

In contrast, the brief implied, the law of civil marriage rested on uniform treatment of all people. If the state determined that remarriage after divorce was valid within its borders, then "religiously-based interests are and have always been separate from and subordinate to the law with respect to civil marriage."[176] In other words, said RCFM, the mere fact that Roman Catholics who remarried after divorce are not considered married within the faith had no impact on the legality of their marriage for all state purposes. This claim about the law of marriage did not square perfectly with history or with early twentieth-century legal practice, however. In Massachusetts, as elsewhere, the civil and religious aspects of the law of marriage have long been particularly difficult to tease apart. It is fair to say that Protestants—including the Puritans, who RCFM's brief claimed were entirely opposed to religious celebrations of marriage—traditionally were willing to desacramentalize marriage. Yet they reacted to what they considered excessive Catholic ritual, rather than the belief that the relationship itself had no religious significance, it must be said.[177]

Marriage retained profound and in some senses even increased religious significance in modern America. Marriage was often credited with uniting faith and family in the fundamental building block of society and a stable political culture. It became a "fundamental right" guaranteed by the Constitution, an important individual and communal religious occasion, and a vector for privileges and obligations in society.[178] Marriage occupied a complex space that was at once personal and religiously derived, and (paradoxically) state-created and managed.[179] Across American history, the civil law of marriage was challenged repeatedly by those who argued that religion is the moral core of marriage: think antidivorce activism in the nineteenth and twentieth centuries, antipolygamy action, and so on.[180] These challenges were based on religious principles, which proponents argued were essential to the flourishing of marriage at every level, governmental as well as religious.

RCFM glossed over this complexity, implying that religion and law could both operate in separate and distinct spheres. For a group of clerics to say directly that their own religious interests in marriage were "subordinate" to government interests, however, was to embrace a remarkable and powerful devolution of power from religion to the state. This concession exceeded even that of those Protestant clergy in the nineteenth century who argued that Mormons should not be allowed to dominate politics and law in territorial Utah, knowing full well that separation of church and state in that situation would mean the eradication of polygamy in the territory.[181] In twenty-first-century Massachusetts, by contrast, RCFM argued that religious diversity and civil power combined to make religion irrelevant to state treatment of same-sex marriage. Equally important, RCFM rejected the idea that religious objections to marriage equality should receive any kind of deference. Individual religious organizations would have no viable cause to object to same-sex marriage, RCFM argued, because none would be "forced to perform any civil marriage."[182] This blithe assurance elided the many ways that the celebration of a marriage is just the beginning of religious as well as governmental interests in a marriage. Yet it fit in well with RCFM's central claim that law is uniform, while religion is inherently complex and divided.

RCFM also relied on its capacity to claim an interfaith coalition. A variety of religious organizations were represented in the group, including the American Friends Service Committee and other Quaker organizations and congregations, the Union of American Hebrew Congregations, the Central Conference of American Rabbis, the Unitarian Universalist Association, the United Church of Christ, a pagan coalition called the Church of the Sacred Earth, the Wiccan Covenant of the Goddess, the Universal Fellowship of Metropolitan Community Churches, and more.[183] The presence of these faiths and their support for same-sex marriage, the argument went, meant that appeals to the historic opposition of religious groups, and especially to present opponents among more conservative Protestants, Jews, Muslims, and Catholics, were themselves based on an incomplete and partial understanding of religious life in Massachusetts. The truth of the matter, they implied, was so complicated and contentious that no one religious position could be singled out as representative.[184] RCFM took out a newspaper advertisement in Catholic areas that was endorsed by liberal Catholics who favored same-sex marriage, highlighting the diversity on the issue even among Massachusetts Catholics.[185]

The success of the *Goodridge* plaintiffs in the Supreme Judicial Court did not rest on RCFM. Indeed the group itself wrote to assure the justices that religion should not be an issue, rather than the other way around. In that sense, the secular focus of the opinion was a victory. As the majority opinion concluded, "In Massachusetts, civil marriage is . . . a wholly secular institution."[186] By injecting its progressive religious perspective into the legal debate, RCFM effectively removed religion from the factors the court considered relevant. RCFM was widely perceived to be successful not only in the *Goodridge* litigation but also in the maneuvering that followed, especially in the state legislature through opposition to a proposed constitutional amendment.

Part of this success may stem from a shift in RCFM strategy after *Goodridge*. The furor that followed the decision of the Massachusetts court produced a long-standing (and eventually unsuccessful) campaign to amend the state constitution to overturn the case. The debate between RCFM and conservative opponents of same-sex marriage turned rancorous. As the state legislature began debating the proposed amendment in late 2003, the Catholic Church took the lead in the opposition. Archbishop (soon to be Cardinal) Sean O'Malley worked tirelessly, lobbying state legislators personally, issuing statements with his fellow bishops that were read from the pulpit and distributed at mass in Catholic churches across the state, and even joining a rally that featured right-wing evangelical Protestants, including representatives from Concerned Women for America and the Family Research Council.[187] In early 2004, the Reverend H. B. London of Colorado's conservative organization Focus on the Family addressed a crowd of pastors gathered in Boston: "You who lead the church in Massachusetts have a unique role in the history of America. The whole world will be looking at this state in a few weeks," he said.[188]

RCFM fought back. Rabbi Lerner organized prayer breakfasts, postcard mailings, telephone calls to legislators, and more. Most effective, however, was RCFM's constant and escalating argument that religious leaders did not all agree with Cardinal O'Malley. In an open letter to O'Malley and the bishops of Massachusetts, RCFM charged that their own traditions respected the "Roman Catholic magisterium," and asked only for the same respect in return. Instead, RCFM claimed, the church sent "a message that our faith communities are immoral. You are harming us and our families."[189] RCFM clergy, joined by two lay Catholic leaders, accused the church of "promoting prejudice" through its campaign against same-sex marriage, and claimed that "thousands of Roman Catholics have signed our statement in support of marriage equality."[190] Arline Isaacson, cochair of the Massachusetts Gay and Lesbian Political Caucus, credited RCFM with changing "the nature of the debate from religion versus gays to religion versus religion. So now we can forcefully assert," Isaacson added, "that denying us marriage rights is the equivalent of choosing one set of religious views over another."[191]

A half-page ad in the *Boston Globe* in early 2004 extended RCFM's earlier claims. The ad, which was signed by some ninety-five Reform rabbis, announced their support for the "freedom to marry," and urged interested people to contact RCFM for more information. Before *Goodridge*, the argument had been phrased in terms of the lack of religious interest in the civil law of marriage; by 2004 the claim had shifted. As the ad put it, "For us any Constitutional amendment that denied same-sex couples civil marriage rights would be a violation of our religious freedom."[192] Now the ability to celebrate legally recognized marriages, rather than the claim that religious and civil marriage were entirely separate undertakings, was the centerpiece. This mission creep should perhaps not be surprising—being a winner in the Massachusetts marriage wars drew RCFM clergy back into the embrace of law and legal thinking. And yet the group's initial stance had envisioned a more constrained position, one that relied on a bright-line distinction between spiritual and state "unions."

This more aggressive approach brought RCFM new members and attention. *In Newsweekly,* a New England magazine focusing on lesbian and gay issues, named RCFM its Organization of the Year in 2006, calling the group the "God Squad of Equality" and noting that it had become "the public voice of progressive religious communities" in Massachusetts.[193] Newspaper coverage of the campaigns promoting or opposing an amendment to the Massachusetts constitution routinely covered RCFM and included statements from Lerner and others in their stories.[194] In the press, as at the Supreme Judicial Court, the presence of RCFM demonstrated that the "religious voice" in America was divided. The group grew steadily through July 2007, when the final attempt to introduce an anti-gay-marriage amendment was defeated in the state legislature, 151 to 45, and hope of overturning *Goodridge* evaporated.

RCFM declared victory, and disbanded. Rabbi Lerner now officiates at same-sex as well as interfaith wedding services. Hillary and Julie Goodridge separated in 2006 and have filed for divorce.[195] RCFM's example has been followed in other jurisdictions; most recently in the amicus brief of California Faith for Equality, which listed 140 clergy from around the state, twelve California-based organizations, including both denominational (Pacific Southwest Council of the Union for Reform Judaism) and interfaith (California Council of Churches), and nine national groups, including Affirmation: Gay and Lesbian Mormons, and the Buddhist group Soka-Gakkai International-USA.[196] Religious coalitions have sprouted in other states as well—as of this writing, such organizations exist in thirty-two states, from Alabama to Washington.[197]

Equally important, the Religion and Faith Program of the nationwide Human Rights Campaign was launched in 2005, with a mission "to reclaim the faith-based debate over LGBT [lesbian, gay, bisexual, and transgender] issues from the radical right" and "to amplify the voices of faith leaders willing to speak out for justice for LGBT people."[198] Drawing especially on the model of RCFM, Harry Knox, director of the Religion and Faith Program, now emphasizes the interfaith and ecumenical yet undeniably spiritual voice of the resurgent progressive religious community.

The price of victory has been steep, however. Wrenching debates within as well as outside liberal traditions, constitutional amendments in thirty states, the federal and thirty-seven state Defense of Marriage Acts, all testify to the reaction against same-sex marriage. When asked about the ways that religious as well as secular arguments for marriage equality have redounded against same-sex unions, Rabbi Lerner replied that she had no doubt whatsoever that she and other members of RCFM had done the right thing. She felt truly safe in Massachusetts, she said: however painful the turbulent legal and political debates over same-sex marriage in other jurisdictions, marriage among same-sex couples in Massachusetts now seemed "normal."

The relative calm in Massachusetts sent another message as well, however. The seamless transition also made it clear that expanding marriage to include same-sex couples would not transform society. Instead, the adjustment had been more or less painless, as demonstrated in mid-2007 by the Massachusetts legislature's overwhelming refusal to forward a constitutional amendment banning same-sex unions.[199] If Lerner was right, then Paula Ettelbrick, Nancy Polikoff, and other feminist scholars who said marriage was an unlikely path to social transformation also were right all along.[200]

Devon Lerner claimed recently that "collectively, our banding together" across denominations "is unprecedented, as far as I am aware."[201] She was wrong, of course—the tradition of banding together across denominations and even outside faith traditions is one that has characterized American religious activism since the early twentieth century. Genuinely interdenominational and interfaith coalitions have become common since the middle decades of the twentieth century. The Federal Council of Churches and the National Conference of Christians and Jews, as well as Protestants and Other Americans United for Separation of Church and State (now known as Americans United), and groups such as Beverly LaHaye's Concerned Women for America, demonstrate that these coalitions have long made religious as well as legal history. They have also found themselves representing—or even been created to represent—divisions between believers; often they have been dominated by liberal or conservative outlooks politically as well as theologically. In the late twentieth century, such divisions have become ubiquitous.

In a Gallup survey in 1984, those who identified strongly with one or another side of this religious divide (there was no question in most people's minds about the existence of the divide) were split about equally between self-described liberals and conservatives.[202] In the intervening quarter century, there has been significant momentum on the right, with liberal denominations stagnating in membership, cultural and political appeal, and more. Same-sex marriage, which was debated and agonized over in progressive religious communities, helped to galvanize liberal clerics and their congregations. The strength of the progressive movement in favor of marriage equality has surprised secular activists and mobilized believers in jurisdictions across the country.

The mushrooming of such organizations nationwide in the wake of the success of RCFM bolstered the strength of a new religious left, which attracted comment in the press and attention from politicians and on prominent Web sites such as the Pew Forum on Religion and Public Life.[203] Some observers relished this as a *Return of the Jedi* moment; others, including some secular liberals, were appalled.[204] Rabbi Lerner would argue that she and other signatories of the Declaration of Religious Support were principled and courageous. They found a voice that carried in the debates over marriage equality. In this field, Lerner and 1,000 other Massachusetts clergy converged on the connections between marriage and law, forcing supporters as well as opponents to grapple with the notion that diversity in religious belief and practice means that the religious voice speaks in many different languages.

The legacy of women's rights and women's ordination in progressive religious traditions reverberated in this new campaign to reform marriage. Two out of three same-sex couples applying for marriage licenses in Massachusetts have been female.[205] As Beverly LaHaye predicted, "lesbian feminists" fought for legal recognition of their "perverted lifestyles."[206] What LaHaye did not anticipate, however, was that many of those feminists would be talking religion. Equally ironic, religion may be responsible for folding same-sex couples so seamlessly into society, as weddings are celebrated within progressive religious traditions, couples claim ownership of their ceremonies, and marriage equality becomes gender-blind in the twenty-first century, much as color blindness in the twentieth domesticated and normalized interracial marriage.

Epilogue: The Resilience of Religion

"Every time religion is denied in one place," said Jordan Lorence in 2009, "it squirts up in another."[1] Lorence, one of the litigators for Concerned Women for America in the 1980s, now works for the Alliance Defense Fund, an organization founded by some thirty Christian ministries in 1994 that shares many of the same commitments to litigation as CWA in its early years. Like Beverly LaHaye and the organization she led, the Alliance Defense Fund describes itself as defending "religious liberty, the sanctity of life, and family values."[2] A newcomer in the early 1980s, Lorence is now a seasoned veteran. When he spoke of the resilience of religion, he was referring to the ways that he and the Alliance Defense Fund have added other constitutional provisions to their religion clause claims in recent years. He pointed especially to freedom of speech as a supplement to the constitutional protections of religion.[3]

The defiant prediction that religious litigants will rise up in new places grows out of a sense of danger. The new constitutional world is precious to many, including those who are dismayed at one or another of its structures. Like Lorence, they are concerned that the constitutional world is vulnerable, perhaps disappearing.

The meeting point of popular and technical constitutionalism created a world that grew until it shrank, you could say. For one thing, a central player has tried to shut it down. Over the past twenty years, the Supreme Court justices have disagreed vehemently about the best way to proceed, as is their wont. This time, however, the end result may well be a sharp curtailment of religion clause litigation. According to a bare majority of the nine justices, the law of religion should be re-stricted in the interest of government flexibility and efficiency. The world that brought believers to law and law to believers is under siege.

Seventy years' duration means that this constitutional landscape is no longer truly new, even measured in terms of the remarkably long-lived American Constitution. This world has aged, showing gaps and vulnerabilities that have made judges wary. The volume of litigation has not generated reliable rules or elegant legal doctrines. Instead, the legal system has found religion hard to digest. Deciding where religion is (and isn't) has been grueling—from the perspective of lawyers and judges, the task has been daunting in part because religion is not like anything else. In many religious traditions, fidelity to a transcendent sovereign (or other religious mandate) takes a dizzying variety of forms depending on individual, denominational, and theological differences. Constant and unpredictable change in patterns and practices of faith have defied attempts to construct clear boundaries around religion in scholarly work as well as in judicial decisions.[4]

Law professor and advocate Douglas Laycock claimed that the very attempt to decide where religion ends or begins is a religious exercise, one that the courts must not undertake. As he put it, "The only way to avoid [discriminating among religions] is to recognize that for constitutional purposes, any answer to religious questions is religion."[5] Winnifred Fallers Sullivan, a religion and law scholar who has served as an expert witness in two recent constitutional cases, maintains that "'religion' can no longer be coherently defined for purposes of American law."[6] As Sullivan sees it, religion "may be necessary for human survival but [its] truth and goodness and definition . . . [are] not taken for granted, and therefore cannot claim special legal protection."[7] The naïveté of the religion clauses, composed in the late eighteenth century, simply cannot stand up to the massive changes that have ravaged the concepts of religious freedom embedded in the First Amendment, Sullivan argues. "I believe that 'religion' is not a useful term for U.S. law today, because there is no longer any generally accepted referent that is relevant for defensible political reasons."[8] The constitutional protection of religion, in this view, is hopelessly past its sell-by date.

These critics have a point. Instead of resolving and steadying the course of constitutional doctrine, ongoing litigation has become integral to the way Americans understand religious life and their own place in society. They are manipulated by law, and in their turn seek to manipulate it. The escalation of resentment and uncertainty has become predictable over the decades. So what's next? Will it just get worse? Or is it all over?

Pressure to define religion in law has eased somewhat over the past twenty years, not because there is agreement on what should be included in the category, but because the Supreme Court has pulled back sharply on both religion clauses. Beginning in 1990 with *Employment Division v. Smith,* the Supreme Court announced its intention to recover an older approach to the free exercise clause. Reaching back to 1879, the Court held that the rules of the premodern constitutional world should be revived. According to this standard, "neutral laws of general applicability" do not—even if they infringe sincerely held and clearly religious beliefs—give rise to a free exercise clause claim for exemption.[9] The Court even quoted Justice Frankfurter's 1940 opinion in *Gobitis,* the flag salute case that was overruled only three years later. Frankfurter had rejected the claims of Lillian and William Gobitas in language that the *Smith* case relied on fifty years later: "The mere possession of religious convictions which contradict the relevant concerns of a political society does not relieve the citizen from the discharge of political responsibilities."[10] The decision that had so disturbed Frankfurter's own friends and unleashed a wave of violence against Jehovah's Witnesses traveled back into case law.[11]

In 2000, the Court held in *Mitchell v. Helms* that federal loans of instructional materials (computers, projectors, software, and so on) to parochial as well as public schools did not promote religion in violation of the establishment clause, unraveling decades of school funding decisions.[12] Two years later, the Court upheld a school voucher program that assisted both public and private education; more than 95 percent of all funding that went to private schools supported religious education.[13] Finally, in *Hein v. Freedom from Religion Foundation,* the justices reined in the capacity of citizens to sue federal government programs for alleged establishment clause violations, holding that if Congress did not appropriate the funding in question (as opposed to a federal agency or the executive branch), then the establishment clause was not at issue.[14]

One scholar has speculated that "difficulties in defining religion as opposed to other conscientious belief systems" may be the real reason that the Supreme Court has eviscerated prior religion clause jurisprudence.[15] Others have argued in related fields that the justices' power to shape public life is undermined when the Court defies public opinion. This approach concludes that the long-standing unpopularity of decisions involving religion must generate extraordinary pressure on the justices. Eventually they would succumb to mainstream criticism of outlying positions.[16] If these scholars are right, closing down the religion clauses would be a predictable retreat in the face of public condemnation. Whatever the reason, defenders of the new constitutional world who follow the intricacies of Supreme Court doctrine are afraid.

There are technical as well as popular reasons to question whether the end result will be the radical reduction plan that some justices anticipated. For one thing, doing away with the unwieldy legal regime has been broadly unpopular. Remarkably enough, wide dissatisfaction with legal results has not morphed into a desire to trash the new constitutional world. Constitutionalism at ground level is a hardier specimen—no surprise to those who have read this far. Opposition to the *Smith* case was widespread and long lasting. Statutes reinstating more capacious standards for decision have emerged from both Congress and state legislatures.[17] And while the Supreme Court retorted that Congress has no power over the Court's relationship with states, the Court conceded that federal government actions are subject to congressionally inspired standards.[18] In other areas where the Court has pulled back on doctrine, its decisions have left substantial latitude for lower federal and state court action.[19]

Equally aggravating to those in search of a more elegant jurisprudence: on a single day in 2005 the Court itself held that two closely related establishment clause cases yielded opposite results.[20] Some constitutional scholars (as well as the swing justice in the two five-to-four decisions, Stephen Breyer) defended the results in both cases, which held that the Ten Commandments may validly be displayed on the grounds of the Texas state capitol, but not on the walls of a Kentucky courthouse.[21] The broader public was not satisfied.[22] Ironically, there may be some comfort for those who have invested in the new constitutional world: the Court's legendary inconsistency and internal divisions apparently survived the attempts to pave it over. Even in a more chastened, twenty-first-century setting, agreement and consistency elude the Supreme Court in religion clause cases. Technical constitutionalists at the highest level remain at loggerheads. The results so far are mixed, but it is clear that a concerted effort to dismantle the new world has met fierce resistance on and off the Court.

For another thing, the Supreme Court is not all powerful, despite what law professors (especially those who teach constitutional law) often tell their students. Forty-five years ago, the constitutional law scholar Mark DeWolfe Howe remarked on what he called the two "stupendous powers of the Supreme Court." The first, Howe said, was the power to interpret history as a means of guiding decisions. The second, related capacity was the power to make history through deciding cases.[23] Howe focused on legal history, but the new constitutional world was just as remarkable for the ways that law made religious history, and vice versa. From this vantage point, the Supreme Court was powerful, yes; stupendous, not so much. Frequently, the most interesting stuff happened outside the high court's direct line of vision. The state and lower federal courts that saw much of the religion clause traffic dealt with how to make the law work on the ground. They "made" religious history every bit as much as the Supreme Court did. The process has been a constant yet unremarked effect of the technical law of religion. It has been met and challenged by a broad array of popular constitutional claims.

In the claims and arguments of believers, popular constitutionalism is alive and well, vigorous despite the tremors caused by the Court's recent attack. These religiously motivated actors have always been more attuned to their own constitutional claims than to the niceties of legal doctrine. Lawyers and judges notwithstanding, the litigants studied here have proven highly resistant to doctrinal guidance from courts. After seventy years, the Religious Coalition for the Freedom to Marry was no more technically adept than the Jehovah's Witnesses. In that sense, popular constitutionalism among religious folk has been a resilient strain, vulnerable more to disappointment than to devastation.

Predictions fall outside the standard historian's portfolio. Nevertheless, the vigor of popular constitutional commitments among religious actors bodes well for their longevity. Despite the strictures imposed by the Supreme Court, the vitality of this lived constitutionalism outlasted earlier ice ages. Even if the (aging) new world implodes, they may well survive to fight another day.

Retrospection is far more comfortable. Was the creation of the new constitutional world worth the candle? Has the (often unhappy) marriage of technical and popular constitutionalism produced something worthwhile, or would divorce be best for both sides? Looking at the ways that two distinct and powerful constitutional cultures have converged on the same territory, turbulence is hardly surprising. Battles over dissent, sectarianism, peoplehood, secularism, and sexuality involved momentous issues. Their gravity and ubiquity in religious as well as legal life meant that upheaval was the constant. The value attached to stability and transparency in other areas of law eluded technical constitutionalists in this world where fresh developments in religious life were the norm. Despite repeated attempts by judges to guide religion clauses into reliable—or at least less stormy—channels, litigants pressed constantly on the weakest parts of judicially crafted doctrine. So the frustration has gone both ways.

And yet—the turn to law has also been enormously productive. It has highlighted and nurtured creativity and diversity in religious life. The proponents of "goodwill" in the 1930s and beyond, the opponents of sectarianism and secular humanism, the dissenting witnesses to government oppression in prisons, the clergy determined to celebrate the marriages of their parishioners—all these and more have imagined a constitutional landscape that is hospitable to the claims of faith and religious practice. Each and every one pushed and pulled a resistant legal system. They have generated a dazzling array of new insights. Since 1940, religious life in America has been revealed—often through litigation and judicial opinions—as vibrant, creative, and unexpectedly heterodox. This variety fascinates (and often horrifies) the judges who have been called upon to make difficult and predictably temporary decisions about the limits of government power. To some, appalled by the apparently limitless parade of new and divisive lawsuits, the only solution appears to be the bulldozer.

A flatter landscape would be more predictable—perhaps even elegant, from a lawyer's perspective. It would be drab and perhaps even deadly, however, for those whose popular constitutionalism would be divorced from its technical counterpart, flattened and smoothed over. This would not, as some commentators have imagined, be a return to the old constitutional world. Instead, it would be something new, just as the new landscape that was called into being in the 1940s was not the inevitable outcome of the Founders' vision. There is no single "au-

thentic" world of religion and law—popular and technical constitutionalists have constructed a landscape that cannot simply be written
out of existence. In this sense, excavation of an older legal ethic would
not replicate the old, pre-1940 world but would itself be a new terrain.

Some scholars think abandoning the current world would be less
problematic than continuing to live in it. They argue that courts have
been so intrusive and destructive of vulnerable religious communities
and expression that such a divorce would be a welcome relief.[24] Others
argue that courts have been too lenient, catering to religious claims
and systematically underrating the government's own interests.[25] Still
others maintain that courts have forced an unwarranted and drastic
secularism on the country, especially in the school funding cases that
preoccupied Protestants and Other Americans United for Separation
of Church and State, and the school prayer decisions that took POAU
by surprise. All in all, there is substantial support from judges and
scholars for pruning back the law sharply.

There is one angle that hasn't been extensively explored in legal
opinions, religious writing, or scholarship but is revealed in the history
of religious life and litigation in the decades since 1940. This line of vision looks beyond the case law, stepping back to think about lived
constitutionalism in America. There is a dose of American exceptionalism in a recent attempt to articulate how and why the constitutional
world has been a useful construct. In those much-maligned Ten Commandments cases, retiring justice Sandra Day O'Connor voted both
times with the group that found the displays violated the establishment
clause. In the final opinion of her Supreme Court career, O'Connor
wrote of her dismay at her fellow justices' attempts to dismantle the
new constitutional world. First, she argued, writing popular or even
doctrinally graceful opinions should not be the goal of the Supreme
Court. In language that is equally applicable to other controversial precedents, such as the school prayer decisions, O'Connor acknowledged
that many Americans "find the Commandments in accord with their
personal beliefs." But, she argued, "we do not count heads before en-
forcing [the religion clauses]."[26] The fact that the result in a given case
(or even many cases) drew widespread criticism of the Court could not
be a valid means of gauging the legitimacy of the law of religion.

More important still, O'Connor said, the system worked. The law of
religion functioned smoothly in the United States, she maintained, es-

pecially when compared with countries wracked by religious strife and violence. By keeping religion "a matter for the individual conscience, not for the prosecutor or the bureaucrat," Americans were spared the conflict that undermined security and prosperity abroad. Instead, O'Connor stressed, they combined religious commitment, at higher levels than the rest of the developed world, with tolerance and respect for the beliefs of others. "Those who would renegotiate the boundaries between church and state must therefore answer a difficult question: why would we trade a system that has served us so well for one that has served others so poorly?"[27]

O'Connor's rhetorical question raises another query: how could she describe the law of religion as a success? The Court's decisions were controversial, she acknowledged. Respect for the Supreme Court, evidently, cannot be the yardstick we use to measure the Court's achievements. The lack of clarity and consistency in the case law, as well as the widespread sense, just to cite one common complaint, that the federal courts imposed secularism on the country, meant that the high court was especially singled out for criticism. Within days of the birth of the new constitutional law of religion, the *Gobitis* case unleashed a horrific wave of violence against Jehovah's Witnesses. Only three years later, a second case overruled *Gobitis* but left the role of free exercise perilously unclear. Within a few more years, the *Everson* case horrified many Protestants; only a year later a second establishment clause case horrified Catholics—and the race was on. Over the decades of controversy and recrimination directed at the Court—complete with "Impeach Earl Warren" signs in the early 1960s after the school prayer case, *Engel v. Vitale*—the justices have searched in vain for tools to sculpt a more reliable jurisprudence. None has succeeded.

Perhaps this is the real lesson, and the real value of the new constitutional world. When Charles Evans Hughes, Louis Marshall, and other proponents of goodwill founded the National Conference of Christians and Jews in the 1920s, they were worried. Anti-Semitism was a growing phenomenon and interfaith enmity a harsh reality. Such prejudice was met by cogent defenses of diversity, to be sure, but the overall picture was a dark one. Religious identity and strife too often went hand in hand. In the first decade of the twenty-first century, there has been plenty of enmity and hate-filled rhetoric. Much of it, however, has been directed against the Supreme Court. Cooperation across faith traditions in attacks on one or another aspect of the law of religion is now so common that it is hardly noticed.[28]

It is, however, evidence of a set of constitutional practices that have acquired deep and persistent roots in American society. When Americans do religion in law, they construct alliances and have conversations across denominational, organizational, and ideological boundaries. They understand themselves to have sacred rights and generally recognize that others do, too.[29] They argue about these rights in explicitly constitutional terms. Recall Jordan Lorence, whose work for the Alliance Defense Fund opened this epilogue. He and several other lawyers for ADF argued in a recent friend-of-the-court brief to the Supreme Court that a high school student who challenged his ten-day suspension for holding a banner at a high school event that read "Bong Hits 4 Jesus" should be protected by the First Amendment.[30] Lorence and ADF understood that defending the student's right to speak would also extend to other, more respectful speech about Jesus. The student, who was represented by the American Civil Liberties Union (which supports much of what ADF opposes), lost at the high court.[31] But that is not the end of the story—in this world, there is always a new problem, and new claims, new hope. If Jordan Lorence is right about the unstoppable claims of religious folk, popular constitutionalism has the adaptive capacities and resilience that sustain practices of faith and law.

The constitutional practice that drew Jehovah's Witnesses, Protestants devoted to separation of church and state, the Nation of Islam, conservative evangelical women, and progressive clergy to law has become a staple of religious life over the past seven decades. The value of such practice is not readily quantifiable, but it has at long last—perhaps at the end of the world that made it possible—been noticed. If there was any merit to Justice O'Connor's claim that this constitutional world and the aspirations that sustain it are responsible for religious tolerance in America, then its value is immense, even if the uncertain constitutional boundaries between religion and government trouble us still.

Notes

1. The New Constitutional World

1. Interview with Rabbi Devon Lerner, Arlington, Mass., December 7, 2008 (notes in possession of the author).
2. Michael P. Young, "Confessional Protest: The Religious Birth of U.S. National Social Movements," *American Sociological Review* 67, no. 5 (October 2002): 660.
3. R. Laurence Moore, "The End of Religious Establishment and the Beginning of Religious Politics: The Parallel Rise of Churches and Political Parties," in *Selling God: American Religion in the Marketplace of Culture* (New York, 1994), 66–89.
4. Sarah Barringer Gordon, "Law and Religion, 1790–1920," in *The Cambridge History of Law in America,* ed. Michael Grossberg and Christopher Tomlins, 3 vols. (Cambridge, 2008), 2:417–448; Mark Douglas McGarvie, *One Nation under Law: America's Early National Struggles to Separate Church and State* (De Kalb, 2004); Anson Phelps Stokes, *Church and State in the United States: Historical Development and Contemporary Problems of Religious Freedom under the Constitution,* 3 vols. (New York, 1950), 1:358–446.
5. Letter to Major John Cartwright, dated June 5, 1824, in *The Writings of Thomas Jefferson,* ed. Andrew A. Lipscomb (Washington, D.C., 1904), 26:48. See also "Whether Christianity Is a Part of the Common Law?" Appendix, *Jefferson's Virginia Reports* 1 (Charlottesville, 1829), 137, 138, 142; Daniel Walker Howe, *What Hath God Wrought: The Transformation of America, 1815–1848* (New York, 2007); Bertram Wyatt-Brown, "Prelude to Abolitionism: Sabbatarian Politics and the Rise of the Second Party

System," *Journal of American History* 58, no. 2 (September 1971): 316–341; Richard R. John, "Taking Sabbatarianism Seriously: The Postal System, the Sabbath, and the Transformation of American Political Culture," *Journal of the Early Republic* 10 (Winter 1990): 517–567.

6. Joseph Story, *Commentaries on the Constitution*, 3 vols. (Boston, 1833), 3:723–724, 728, sections 1865–1871. On Story's concept of the proper relationship between Christianity and the governments of the United States (state and federal), see James McClellan, *Joseph Story and the American Constitution* (Norman, 1971), 118–159.

7. "General Christianity" was central to the decision of Chancellor James Kent in *People v. Ruggles*, 8 Johns. 290, 291, 293 (1811), a landmark early national blasphemy prosecution.

8. *Commonwealth v. Kneeland*, 20 Mass. 206 (1838); Sarah Barringer Gordon, "Blasphemy and the Law of Religious Liberty in Nineteenth-Century America," *American Quarterly* 52, no.4 (December 2000); Leonard Levy, ed., *Blasphemy in Massachusetts: Freedom of Conscience and the Abner Kneeland Case* (New York, 1973).

9. The New York Constitution of 1777, article 38, provided: "The free exercise and enjoyment of religious profession and worship, without discrimination or preference, shall forever hereafter be allowed, within this State, to all mankind: *Provided,* That the liberty of conscience, hereby granted, shall not be so construed as to excuse acts of licentiousness, or justify practices inconsistent with the peace or safety of this State"; www.stateconstitutions.umd.edu (accessed May 31, 2009).

10. On the "police power" (the power to regulate behavior in the interests of the health, safety, and welfare of society), see William J. Novak, "Governance, Police and the American Liberal Mythology," in *The People's Welfare: Law and Regulation in Nineteenth-Century America* (Chapel Hill, 1996), 1–18.

11. *Barron v. Mayor and City of Baltimore*, 7 Pet. 243 (1833); *Permoli v. First Municipality of New Orleans*, 44 U.S. (3 How.) 589 (1845).

12. Sarah Barringer Gordon, *The Mormon Question: Polygamy and Constitutional Conflict in Nineteenth-Century America* (Chapel Hill, 2002), 132–145, 208–219.

13. Recent work on popular constitutionalism has stressed elected (legislative) versus appointed (judicial) officials as the source of popular doctrine. Larry Kramer, *The People Themselves: Popular Constitutionalism and Judicial Review* (New York, 2004); Robert Post and Reva Siegel, "Popular Constitutionalism, Departmentalism, and Judicial Supremacy," *California Law Review* 92 (2004): 1027–1048.

14. Governor Lilburn W. Boggs to General John B. Clark, October 27, 1838, reprinted in *Among the Mormons: Historic Accounts by Contemporary*

Observers, ed. William Mulder and A. Russell Mortensen (New York, 1958), 102–103.

15. On Smith's crowning and the organization of the "political kingdom of God" within Mormonism, see D. Michael Quinn, *The Mormon Hierarchy: Origins of Power* (Salt Lake City, 1994), 109–141. On Smith's final months, the assassination, and its aftermath, see Richard Lyman Bushman, *Joseph Smith: Rough Stone Rolling* (New York, 2005), 526–550; Dallin H. Oaks and Marvin S. Hill, *Carthage Conspiracy: The Trial of the Accused Assassins of Joseph Smith* (Urbana, 1975), 6–29.

16. John M. Murrin, "A Roof without Walls: The Dilemma of American National Identity," in *Beyond Confederation: Origins of the Constitution and American National Identity,* ed. Richard Beeman, Stephen Botein, and Edward C. Carter II (Chapel Hill, 1987), 333–348.

17. Elizabeth B. Clark, "'The Sacred Rights of the Weak': Pain, Sympathy, and the Culture of Individual Rights in Antebellum America," *Journal of American History* 82, no. 2 (September 1995): 463, 464.

18. Hendrik Hartog, "The Constitution of Aspiration and 'The Rights That Belong to Us All,'" *Journal of American History* 74, no. 3 (December 1987): 1013–1034.

19. Susan G. Davis, *Parades and Power: Street Theatre in Nineteenth-Century Philadelphia* (Philadelphia, 1986); Glenn Altschuler and Stewart Blumin, *Rude Republic: Americans and Their Politics in the Nineteenth Century* (Princeton, 2000); Simon P. Newman, *Parades and the Politics of the Street: Festive Culture in the Early American Republic* (Philadelphia, 1997); Adam Winkler, "Law and Political Parties: Early Political Regulation in the State Courts, 1886–1915," *Columbia Law Review* 100 (2000): 873.

20. See the report of the incident in "Our Prison Columns!" *The War Cry,* June 6, 1885, 1. See generally Lillian Taiz, *Hallelujah Lads and Lasses: Remaking the Salvation Army in America, 1880–1930* (Chapel Hill, 2001), 141–164.

21. "Jail Bird Smith of Iowa," *The War Cry,* February 8, 1890; "Imprisoned for Jesus," ibid., December 21, 1889, 1.

22. Edward H. McKinley, *Marching to Glory: The History of the Salvation Army in the United States, 1880–1992,* 2nd ed. (Grand Rapids, Mich., 1995), 246.

23. On this point see Diane Winston, *Red-Hot and Righteous: The Urban Religion of the Salvation Army* (Cambridge, Mass., 1999), 13–18; Taiz, *Hallelujah Lads and Lasses,* 73–89; John W. Wertheimer, "Free-Speech Fights: The Roots of Modern Free-Expression Litigation in the United States," Ph.D. diss., Princeton University, 1992.

24. Sallie Chesham, *Born to Battle: The Salvation Army in America* (New York, 1965), 68–69.

25. Herbert A. Wisbey, Jr., *Soldiers without Swords: A History of the Salvation Army in the United States* (New York, 1955), 73.

26. "Order of Service at the Funeral of Staff-Captain Joseph Garabed," Joseph Garabed File, Salvation Army Archives and Research Center, quoted in Chesham, *Born to Battle*, 70.

27. Wisbey, *Soldiers without Swords*, 73.

28. "Behind Prison Bars," *The War Cry*, March 17, 1888, 15.

29. See, e.g., "Officers Arrested at Butte City," *The War Cry*, January 9, 1892.

30. *In re Garrabad*, 54 N.W. 1104 (Wisc., 1893); *People v. Garabed*, 20 N.Y. Misc. 127 (App. Div., 1897).

31. McKinley, *Marching to Glory*, 52.

32. *In re Frazee*, 63 Mich. 396, 399 (1886). Tabatha Abu El-Haj, "Changing the People: Transformations in American Democracy, 1880–1930," Ph.D. diss., New York University, 2008, 186–217.

33. "The First Feathers in Religious Freedom," *The War Cry*, July 3, 1897; "Religious Liberty," ibid., May 8, 1897, 4.

34. *The War Cry*, May 25, 1889, 14.

35. *In re Frazee*, 63 Mich. 396 (1886); *Anderson v. City of Wellington* 19 P. 719 (Kan., 1888); *In re Gribben*, 47 P. 1074 (Okla., 1897); *Chicago v. Trotter* 136 Ill. 430 (1891). Cf. C. Edwin Baker, *Human Liberty and Freedom of Speech* (New York, 1989), 139, arguing that parading was protected by every state but Massachusetts.

36. David Rabban, *Free Speech in Its Forgotten Years* (New York, 1997), 116. Often, the results of the conflict have been misunderstood. Rabban concludes that lower courts generally were hostile to the Army's claims, despite widespread success achieved by Salvationists before 1900.

37. Diana Eck, *A New Religious America: How a "Christian Country" Has Become the Most Religiously Diverse Nation* (San Francisco, 2002); Robert Wuthnow, *America and the Challenges of Religious Diversity* (Princeton, 2005).

2. The Worship of Idols

1. "God's in His Heaven," *Newsweek*, July 5, 1943, 81–82.

2. Although the group did not adopt the Jehovah's Witnesses name until the early 1930s, it is how they are commonly known; this chapter follows the common practice.

3. On the history of Jehovah's Witnesses and the flag salute controversy, see Shawn Francis Peters, *Judging Jehovah's Witnesses: Religious Persecution and the Dawn of the Rights Revolution* (Lawrence, Kans., 2000); David

Manwaring, *Render unto Caesar: The Flag Salute Controversy* (Chicago, 1962).

4. For a recent unfavorable treatment of the Witnesses, see Harold Bloom, *The American Religion: The Emergence of the Post-Christian Nation* (New York, 1992), 159–170; Chris Christensen, *A Pronouncement: Concerning Justice for Jehovah's People* (n.p., 1974). Cf. Peters, *Judging Jehovah's Witnesses.*

5. Edwin Scott Gaustad and Philip L. Barlow, *The New Historical Atlas of Religion in America* (Oxford, 2001), 164–173.

6. On Adventism generally, see Jonathan M. Butler, "Adventism and the American Experience," in *The Rise of Adventism: Religion and Society in Mid-Nineteenth Century America,* ed. Edwin S. Gaustad (New York, 1974), 173–206.

7. Jan Shipps, "From Peoplehood to Church Membership: Mormonism's Trajectory since World War II," *Church History* 76 (June 2007): 241–261.

8. Jerry Bergman, in "Dr. Jennifer Henderson Interview with Jerry Bergman on Watchtower Attorney Hayden Covington," May 18, 2002, 4; www.freeminds.org/history/covington2.htm (accessed October 8, 2007).

9. Seanna Shiffrin and Vincent Blasi, *Constitutional Law Stories,* ed. Michael Dorf (St. Paul, 2004); Charles Alan Wright, "My Favorite Opinion: The Second Flag-Salute Case," *Texas Law Review* 74 (May 1996): 1297–1300.

10. R. Laurence Moore, *Religious Outsiders and the Making of Americans* (New York, 1986), 144.

11. See the official Left Behind series site, www.leftbehind.com (accessed July 7, 2008); Amy Johnson Frykholm, *Rapture Culture:* Left Behind *in Evangelical America* (Oxford, 2004).

12. James F. Findlay, Jr., *Dwight L. Moody: American Evangelist, 1837–1899* (Chicago, 1969).

13. Sydney E Ahlstrom, *A Religious History of the American People,* 2nd ed. (New Haven, 2004), 806–807.

14. Martin E. Marty, *Modern American Religion,* 3 vols. (Chicago, 1986), 1:255–256.

15. Timothy P. Weber, *Living in the Shadow of the Second Coming: American Premillennialism, 1875–1925* (New York, 1979); Ronald L. Numbers and Jonathan M. Butler, eds., *The Disappointed: Millerism and Millenarianism in the Nineteenth Century* (Knoxville, 1993); Jerry Bergman, "The Adventists and Jehovah's Witness Branch of Protestantism," in *American's Alternative Religions,* ed. Timothy Miller (Albany, N.Y., 1995), 33–46.

16. Ruther Alden Doan, *The Miller Heresy, Millennialism, and American Cul-*

ture (Philadelphia, 1987). For a study of European premillennialists, whose sympathies were as likely to become revolutionary as reactionary, see Eric Hobsbawm, *Social Bandits and Primitive Rebels: Studies in Archaic Forms of Social Movements in the 19th and 20th Centuries* (Glencoe, Ill., 1959).

17. Ahlstrom, *A Religious History of the American People,* 806.
18. M. James Penton, *Apocalypse Delayed: The Story of Jehovah's Witnesses,* 2nd ed. (Toronto, 1985), 57.
19. Royston Pike, *Jehovah's Witnesses: Who They Are, What They Teach, What They Do* (New York, 1954), 14.
20. Penton, *Apocalypse Delayed,* 35, 36–37, 346n106.
21. Barbara Grizzuti Harrison, *Visions of Glory: A History and a Memory of Jehovah's Witnesses* (New York, 1978), 57; Peters, *Judging Jehovah's Witnesses,* 29.
22. There was the time, for example, when Russell and other "living saints" stood on a bridge in Pittsburgh, apparently waiting for their ascension to heaven. Although several newspapers reported the story, Russell—implausibly—denied having been there, feeding his reputation as a fraud. See, e.g, Peters, *Judging Jehovah's Witnesses,* 29.
23. Penton, *Apocalypse Delayed,* 42–44.
24. See, e.g, Stanley High, "Armageddon, Inc.," *Saturday Evening Post,* September 14, 1940, 19, 50; Harrison, *Visions of Glory,* 172; Penton, *Apocalypse Delayed,* 47.
25. Marley Cole, *Jehovah's Witnesses: The New World Society* (New York, 1955); Penton, *Apocalypse Delayed,* 47–76.
26. Paul Johnson, *Harvest Siftings Reviewed* (Brooklyn, 1917), 19.
27. Penton, *Apocalypse Delayed,* 74; Harrison, *Visions of Glory,* 138–139.
28. Quoted in George Marsden, *Fundamentalism and American Culture: The Shaping of Twentieth Century Evangelicalism, 1870–1925,* 2nd ed. (Oxford, 2006), 38.
29. Butler, "Adventism and the American Experience," 194.
30. Gaines M. Foster, *Moral Reconstruction: Christian Lobbyists and the Federal Legislation of Morality, 1865–1920* (Chapel Hill, 2002), 99, 108, 198.
31. Harrison, *Visions of Glory,* 173–176.
32. *Rutherford v. United States,* 258 F. 855 (2nd Cir. 1919); Joseph Rutherford quoted in "20-Year Sentences for Seven Followers of Pastor Russell," *New York Tribune,* June 22, 1918, 14.
33. *Watchtower,* 1917, cited in Harrison, *Visions of Glory,* 176.
34. Penton, *Apocalypse Delayed,* 66.
35. High, "Armageddon, Inc.," 18–19.
36. Richard Harris, "I'd Like to Talk to You for a Minute," *New Yorker,* June 16, 1956, 84.

37. A. H. Macmillan, *Faith on the March: My Life of Joyous Service with Jehovah's Witnesses* (Englewood Cliffs, N.J., 1957), 47, 52.

38. Jerry Bergman, *Jehovah's Witnesses and Kindred Groups: A Historical Compendium and Bibliography* (Westport, Conn., 1984), xxviii–xxx.

39. H. Rutledge Southworth, "Jehovah's 50,000 Witnesses," *Nation*, August 10, 1940, 110.

40. Joseph F. Rutherford, *Enemies* (Brooklyn, 1938), 282–283.

41. Bloom, *American Religion,* 162.

42. See Joseph F. Rutherford, *Religion: Origin, Influence upon Men, and the Result* (Brooklyn, 1940), 196–197.

43. Herbert Hewitt Stroup, *The Jehovah's Witnesses* (New York, 1945), 47–71; Penton, *Apocalypse Delayed,* 70–71.

44. Karl Evanzz, *The Messenger: The Rise and Fall of Elijah Muhammad* (New York, 2001), 118; Warith Deen Muhammad, *As the Light Shineth from the East* (Chicago, 1980), 19.

45. Diane Winston, *Red-Hot and Righteous: The Urban Religion of the Salvation Army* (Cambridge, Mass., 1999), 180–190.

46. Ronald Lawson, "Seventh-day Adventists and the U.S. Courts: Road Signs along the Route of a Denominationalizing Sect," *Journal of Church and State* 40 (Summer 1998): 553–588, 558.

47. Editorial, *Review and Herald,* July 24, 1941, 4.

48. On this accommodation with America among most premillennial groups, see R. Laurence Moore, "Premillennial Christian Views of God's Justice and American Injustice," in *Religious Outsiders and the Making of Americans,* 128–149.

49. Peters, *Judging Jehovah's Witnesses.*

50. Peter Irons and Lillian Gobitas, "Here Comes Jehovah!" in Peter H. Irons, *The Courage of Their Convictions* (New York, 1988); see also *Watchtower* magazine from 1935: "The more opposition and persecution from Satan's organization we endure, the nearer we know we are to his final destruction and to the vindication of Jehovah's name," quoted in Malcolm Logan, "Jehovah's Witnesses Glory in 'Martyrdom,'" *New York Post,* July 16, 1940.

51. Between May and October of 1940, the American Civil Liberties Union (ACLU) documented 1,488 cases of violence against Jehovah's Witnesses. See American Civil Liberties Union, *Liberty's National Emergency: The Story of Civil Liberty in the Crisis Year, 1940–1941* (New York, 1941), 27; American Civil Liberties Union, *Jehovah's Witnesses and the War* (New York, 1943).

52. See John Haynes Holmes, "The Case of Jehovah's Witnesses," *Christian Century,* July 17, 1940, 896.

53. Leonard Dinnerstein, *Anti-Semitism in America* (New York, 1994); Jona-

than Sarna, *American Judaism* (New Haven, 2004); Manwaring, *Render unto Caesar.*

54. Peters, *Judging Jehovah's Witnesses,* 25–28; Merlin Owen Newton, *Armed with the Constitution: Jehovah's Witnesses in Alabama and the U.S. Supreme Court, 1939–1946* (Tuscaloosa, 1994), 74–80; Harrison, *Visions of Glory,* 189–191.

55. Tilman Allert, *The Hitler Salute: On the Meaning of a Gesture* (New York, 2008), 30.

56. "I consider them quacks. . . . I dissolve the 'Earnest Bible Students' in Germany; their property I dedicate to the people's welfare; I will have all their literature confiscated." Pronouncement of Adolf Hitler, April 4, 1935, quoted without further attribution in *Minersville School District v. Gobitis,* 108 F.2d 683, 684n3 (3rd Cir. 1939).

57. "The Great Multitude (Part 1)," *Watchtower* (1935), 227, 235, quoted in Manwaring, *Render unto Caesar,* 31.

58. Peter H. Irons, *The Courage of Their Convictions* (New York, 1988), 17, quoting from a radio address.

59. Manwaring, *Render unto Caesar,* 31, quoting from the *Boston Post,* September 21, 1935.

60. A third student, Edward Wasliewski, also refused to salute and was subjected to similar treatment. Irons and Gobitas, "Here Comes Jehovah!" 27.

61. Irons and Gobitas, "Here Comes Jehovah!" 28.

62. See *Defending and Legally Establishing the Good News* (Brooklyn, 1950), a primer on the current state of the law that advised the faithful on how to continue witnessing to God's law while also complying, where possible, with the "law of man." See also Patrick J. Flynn, "'Writing Their Faith into the Laws of the Land': Jehovah's Witnesses and the Supreme Court's Battle for the Meaning of the Free Exercise Clause, 1939–1945," *Texas Journal on Civil Liberties and Civil Rights* 10 (Winter 2004); Jennifer Jacobs Henderson, "The Jehovah's Witnesses and Their Plan to Expand First Amendment Freedoms," *Journal of Church and State* 46 (Autumn 2004): 811–832.

63. Manwaring, *Render unto Caesar,* 11–14.

64. For a thoughtful discussion of Witness isolation and community identity, see Moore, *Religious Outsiders,* 137–139.

65. See, e.g., Penton, *Apocalypse Delayed,* 139.

66. See, e.g., Harrison, *Visions of Glory,* 146–148.

67. Penton, *Apocalypse Delayed,* 55, 59, 70–71; Newton, *Armed with the Constitution,* 3–8; Jennifer Jacobs Henderson, "Hayden Covington, the Jehovah's Witnesses and Their Plan to Expand First Amendment Freedoms," Ph.D. diss., University of Washington, 2002, 83–85.

68. Henderson, "Hayden Covington."

69. "Witness's Angle," *Newsweek*, March 22, 1943, 70.

70. Ibid., 68.

71. Henderson, "Hayden Covington"; ibid., 68; see also "Interview with Watch Tower Attorney Hayden Covington," November 19, 1978, www.free minds.org/history/covington (accessed June 13, 2007).

72. Henderson, "Hayden Covington."

73. *Nicholls v. Mayor and City of Lynn*, 7 N.E.2d 577, 580 (Mass. 1937).

74. *State ex rel. Bleich v. Board of Public Instruction*, 190 So. 815, 816–817 (Fla. 1939). See also Manwaring, *Render unto Caesar*, 72–73; Peters, *Judging Jehovah's Witnesses*, 162–177.

75. Mulford Q. Sibley and Philip E. Jacob, *Conscription of Conscience: The American State and the Conscientious Objector, 1940–1947* (Ithaca, N.Y., 1952), 498.

76. 21 F. Supp. 581, 587 (D.C. Pa. 1937). The plaintiffs' names was misspelled in both this case and the suit that eventually resulted in the overruling of *Gobitis, West Virginia Board of Education v. Barnette*. The correct spellings are "Gobitas" and "Barnett."

77. "Albert Branson Maris," in *West's Encyclopedia of American Law*, 2nd ed., ed. Jeffrey Lehman and Shirelle Phelps (Detroit, 2005), 429–430.

78. 24 F. Supp. 271, 274 (D.C. Pa. 1938).

79. Irons and Gobitas, "Here Comes Jehovah!" 30.

80. Testimony of Superintendent Charles Roudabush, *Gobitis v. Minersville School District*, 24 F. Supp. 271 (E.D. Pa. 1938) Record, at 93. For a fuller account of the trial, see Manwaring, *Render unto Caesar*, 82–106.

81. 24 F.Supp. at 274.

82. *Gobitis*, 108 F.2d at 686.

83. Respondents' Brief at 9–13, *Minersville School District v. Gobitis*.

84. Quoted in *"Dred Scott* and the Flag," *Consolation* 21 (July 1940): 24.

85. John Frank, "Review of *The Brandeis/Frankfurter Connection*," *Journal of Legal Education* (1981): 432, 442.

86. *Gabrielli v. Knickerbocker et al.*, 306 U.S. 621 (1939), affirming 12 Cal.2d 85, 82 P.2d 391 (Calif. 1938).

87. *Minersville School District v. Gobitis*, 310 U.S. 586, 591 (1940).

88. *Cantwell v. Connecticut*, 310 U.S. 296, 303 (1940).

89. See "High Court Voids Jehovah Sect Curb," *New York Times*, May 21, 1940, 23.

90. 310 U.S. at 591, 595, 599.

91. Ibid., 598, 600.

92. Felix Frankfurter to Harlan Fiske Stone, May 27, 1940, in Alpheus Mason, *Security through Freedom* (Ithaca, N.Y., 1955), 217–220; Alpheus Mason, *Harlan Fiske Stone: Pillar of the Law* (New York, 1956), 526–529.

93. Mason, *Harlan Fiske Stone*, 530–532.

94. 310 U.S. at 602, 606 (Stone, J., dissenting).

95. The day after the decision was handed down, for example, and well before the onslaught of violent retribution against the Witnesses, the *New York Times* ran an editorial that argued "reverence for the ideals for which the flag stands is more important than any gesture," *New York Times*, June 5, 1940, 24.

96. Katharine Graham, *Personal History* (New York, 1997), 122.

97. Richard Danzig, "Justice Frankfurter's Opinions in the Flag Salute Cases: Blending Logic and Psychologic in Constitutional Decision-making," *Stanford Law Review* 36 (1984): 675–724.

98. Christian Smith, "Correcting a Curious Neglect, or, Bringing Religion Back In," in *Disruptive Religion: The Force of Faith in Social Movement Activism*, ed. Christian Smith (New York, 1996), 2–5.

99. Kenneth J. Heinemann, *A Catholic New Deal: Religion and Reform in Depression Pittsburgh* (State College, Pa., 1999); Elizabeth Fones-Wolf and Ken Fones-Wolf, "Lending a Hand to Labor: James Myers and the Federal Council of Churches, 1926–1947," *Church History* 68 (March 1999): 62; Michael Janson, "A Christian Century: Liberal Protestantism, the New Deal, and the Origins of Post-War American Politics," Ph.D. diss., University of Pennsylvania, 2007. Cf. Richard Hofstadter, *The Age of Reform: From Bryan to F.D.R.* (New York, 1955); William Leuchtenberg, *Franklin D. Roosevelt and the New Deal, 1932–1940* (New York, 1964).

100. Ronald Isetti, "The Moneychangers of the Temple: FDR, American Civil Religion, and the New Deal," *Presidential Studies Quarterly* 26 (1996): 678–693, quotation on 686.

101. Radio Address, Brotherhood Day, February 23, 1933, in *The Public Papers and Addresses of Franklin D. Roosevelt* (New York, 1938), 5:85–87; Isetti, "Moneychangers of the Temple," 686.

102. Ibid.

103. Egal Feldman, "American Ecumenicism: Chicago's World's Parliament of Religions of 1893," *Journal of Church and State* 9 (1967): 180.

104. F. Max Mueller, "The Real Significance of the Parliament of Religions," *Arena* 51 (December 1894): 6.

105. Richard H. Seager, *The World's Parliament of Religions: The East/West Encounter, Chicago, 1893* (Bloomington, 1995), 58.

106. "Address of Chairman John Henry Barrows of the General Committee," in *The World's Parliament of Religions,* ed. John Henry Barrows (Chicago, 1983), 75–76. The inclusion of Buddhists among the list of theists caused consternation among Buddhist delegates. See Diana L. Eck, *A New Religious America: How a "Christian Country" Has Now Become*

the World's Most Religiously Diverse Nation (San Francisco, 2001), 152–153.

107. Martin E. Marty, *The One and the Many: America's Struggle for the Common Good* (Cambridge, Mass., 1997); Henry F. May, *Protestant Churches and Industrial America* (New York, 1949), 163–234; cf. Winthrop S. Hudson, *The Great Tradition of the American Churches* (New York, 1953), 226–242.

108. For recent treatments of debates about pluralism and diversity, see Robert Wuthnow, *America and the Challenges of Religious Diversity* (Princeton, 2005); William R. Hutchison, *Religious Pluralism in America: The Contentious History of a Founding Ideal* (New Haven, 2003).

109. Robert A. Schneider, "Voice of Many Waters: Church Federation in the Twentieth Century," in *Between the Times: The Travail of the Protestant Establishment in America, 1900–1960,* ed. William R. Hutchison (Cambridge, 1989), 95–121, 98–101.

110. Elias B. Sanford, *Origin and History of the Federal Council of Churches of Christ in America* (Hartford, 1916), 225–272; Elias B. Sanford, *Federal Council of the Churches of Christ in America: Report of the First Meeting of the Federal Council, Philadelphia, 1908* (New York, 1908), 18.

111. W. T. Stead, *Chicago To-Day: The Labour War in America* (London, 1894); Louis Menand, *The Metaphysical Club* (New York, 2001), 292.

112. Charles M. Sheldon, *In His Steps* (1896; Uhrichsville, Ohio, 2005); Henry F. May, *Protestant Churches and Industrial America* (New York, 1963), 210–211.

113. For this point, see Paul S. Boyer, "*In His Steps:* A Reappraisal," *American Quarterly* 23 (1971): 60–78.

114. Gaines M. Foster, *Moral Reconstruction: Christian Lobbyists and the Federal Legislation of Morality, 1865–1920* (Chapel Hill, 2002).

115. See Federal Council of Churches, "Social Creed of the Churches," 1912; Ferenc Szasz, *The Divided Mind of Protestant America: 1880–1930* (Tuscaloosa, 1982); Martin Marty, *Modern American Religion,* 3 vols. (Chicago, 1986), 1:150–190.

116. Paul Fussell, *The Great War and Modern Memory* (New York, 1975).

117. Benny Kraut, "A Wary Collaboration: Jews, Catholics, and the Protestant Goodwill Movement," in *Between the Times: The Travail of the Protestant Establishment in America, 1900–1960,* ed. William R. Hutchison (Cambridge, 1989), 193–230, 198.

118. "Denies Reflection on Jews: Dr. Burgess Explains Scope of Episcopal Church Program," *New York Times,* September 26, 1919, 10.

119. "Sees Foreign Born as Church Problem: Bishop Burch Declares Christian Element Must Assume the Burden of Training," *New York Times,* September 24, 1919, 14, quoting the Rev. John L. Zacher.

120. "Memorandum of Conference between Representatives of the Prot-

estant Episcopal Church and the Central Conference of American Rabbis" (CCAR Papers, Box 11, Folder 21, American Jewish Archives, Cincinnati, October 13, 1919), quoted in Benny Kraut, "Towards the Establishment of the National Conference of Christians and Jews: The Tenuous Road to Religious Goodwill in the 1920s," *American Jewish History* 77 (1988): 318–412, 392.

121. Ibid.

122. Victoria Saker Woeste, "Insecure Inequality: Louis Marshall, Henry Ford, and the Problem of Defamatory Antisemitism, 1920–1929," *Journal of American History* 91 (2004): 877–905.

123. See National Conference for Community and Justice, www.faith streams.com/topcs/members-and-partners/national-conference-for-com munity-and-justice (accessed September 16, 2008); "Aims to Harmonize National Groups," *New York Times,* December 11, 1927, 1.

124. "The Purpose and Program of the National Conference of Christians and Jews," *Journal of Educational Sociology* 16 (February 1943): 324–326, 324–325.

125. *Baptist* 13 (February 13, 1932): 205. Ibid., April 25, 1932, 531, quoted in Paul A. Carter, *The Decline and Revival of the Social Gospel, 1920–1940* (1956; Hamden, Conn., 1971), 148. Desmond S. King and Rogers M. Smith, "Racial Orders in American Political Development," *American Political Science Review* 99 (February 2005): 75–92.

126. *Christian Advocate* 57 (May 19, 1932): 527.

127. *Quadrennial Report of the Federal Council of the Churches of Christ in America, 1932* (New York, 1932), 57–74; Samuel McCrea Cavert, *The American Churches in the Ecumenical Movement, 1900–1968* (New York, 1968), 142–145.

128. Isetti, "The Moneychangers of the Temple," 678.

129. Quoted without further documentation in Cavert, *American Churches in the Ecumenical Movement,* 143.

130. James Farley, *Behind the Ballots: The Personal History of a Politician* (New York, 1938), 208, quoted in Isetti, "Moneychangers of the Temple," 687.

131. Franklin D. Roosevelt, "Radio Address on Brotherhood Day," February 23, 1936, www.presidency.ucsb.edu (accessed September 17, 2008).

132. Richard W. Steele, "The War on Intolerance: The Reformulation of American Nationalism, 1939–1941," *Journal of American Ethnic History* (Fall 1989): 9–35; Philip Gleason, *Speaking of Diversity: Language and Ethnicity in Twentieth-Century America* (Baltimore, 1992), 153–187.

133. Raymond Clapper, "What about Unity?" *Life,* November 18, 1940, 29.

134. Wendy L. Wall, "'Our Enemies Within': Nazism, National Unity, and

America's Wartime Discourse on Tolerance," in *Enemy Images in American History,* ed. Ragnhild Fiebig-von Hase and Ursula Lehmkuhl, (Providence, 1997), 209–229, 215.

135. "National Conference of Christians and Jews," *Bulletin,* July 1941 and March 1942; Office of War Information, Bureau of Motion Pictures, *U.S. War Information Films* (Washington, D.C., 1943); Wall, "Our Enemies Within," 220–221.

136. Wall, "Our Enemies Within," 220–221.

137. On this point, see "Hughes in a Clash on Religious Right," *New York Times,* March 30, 1940, 12; Alpheus Thomas Mason, *Harlan Fiske Stone, Pillar of the Law* (New York, 1956), 525–526 and 853n48, comments during oral argument in *Cantwell v. Connecticut,* decided shortly before *Gobitis.* Chief Justice Hughes joined the unanimous opinion in *Cantwell.* Note also that Hughes was responsible for the first paragraph of Stone's *Carolene Products* footnote, and arguably the resulting "preferred position" that became so clearly identified with Stone. Footnote four of the *Carolene Products* opinion is widely viewed among legal scholars as a precursor to later decisions protecting rights of conscience, speech, and assembly. Louis Lusky, "Footnote Redux: A *Carolene Products* Reminiscence," *Columbia Law Review* 82 (October 1982): 1093–1105, 1098–1102.

138. Merlo Pusey, *Charles Evans Hughes* (New York, 1951), 2:728–729.

139. Bloom, *American Religion,* 167.

140. "The Flag Salute Case," *Christian Century,* June 19, 1940, 791.

141. Francis Biddle, "Address to the Pennsylvania Bar Ass'n," June 19, 1940; Francis Biddle, *In Brief Authority* (Garden City, N.Y., 1962).

142. On the push to eliminate avowed Communists from control of the ACLU in the late 1930s, and for the substitution of socialists, see Judy Kutulas, *The American Civil Liberties Union and the Making of Modern Liberalism, 1930–1960* (Chapel Hill, 2006), 33–39.

143. John Haynes Holmes, *I Speak for Myself: The Autobiography of John Haynes Holmes* (New York, 1959). On Holmes's ecumenicism, see Carl Hermann Voss, *Rabbi and Minister: The Friendship of Stephen S. Wise and John Haynes Holmes* (Cleveland, 1964).

144. On anti-Witness violence, see American Civil Liberties Union, *Jehovah's Witnesses and the War* (New York, 1943); Peters, *Judging Jehovah's Witnesses,* 72–177.

145. Holmes, "The Case of Jehovah's Witnesses," 898.

146. Ibid.

147. "Starvation into Patriotism," *Christian Century,* October 30, 1940, 1334.

148. On this point, see Robert H. Jackson, *The Struggle for Judicial Supremacy*

(New York, 1941), 284; Mark Graber, "Counter-Stories: Maintaining and Expanding Civil Liberties in Wartime," in *The Constitution in Wartime: Beyond Alarmism and Complacency* (Durham, N.C., 2005), 104; John M. Ferren, *Salt of the Earth, Conscience of the Court: The Story of Justice Wiley Rutledge*, ed. Mark Tushnet (Chapel Hill, 2004), 187–188.

149. *Jones v. Opelika*, 316 U.S. 584, 623 (Douglas and Black, JJ., dissenting).

150. Franklin D. Roosevelt, "Annual Message to Congress," January 3, 1936. Elizabeth Borgwardt, *A New Deal for the World: America's Vision for Human Rights* (Cambridge, Mass., 2005); Robert L. Tsai, *Eloquence and Reason* (New Haven, 2008).

151. Roosevelt, "Annual Message to Congress," January 3, 1936.

152. On this point, see Robert L. Tsai, "Reconsidering *Gobitis:* An Exercise in Presidential Leadership," *Washington University Law Review* 86 (2008): 363, 386–391.

153. *Barnette v. West Virginia Board of Education,* 47 F.Supp. 251, 253 (S.D.W. Va., 1942).

154. *Douglas v. Jeannette,* 319 U.S. 157, 166–182 (1943) (Jackson, J., concurring).

155. *West Virginia Board of Education v. Barnette,* 319 U.S. 625, 634 (1943).

156. 310 U.S. at 598.

157. 319 U.S. at 640.

158. Ibid., 642.

159. Ibid., 641.

160. Vincent Blasi and Seana Shiffrin, "The Story of *West Virginia Board of Education v. Barnette:* The Pledge of Allegiance and the Freedom of Thought," in *Constitutional Law Stories,* ed. Michael C. Dorf (New York, 2004), 433–475, 434.

161. 319 U.S. at 643 (Black and Douglas, JJ., concurring).

162. 319 U.S. at 646 (Murphy, J., concurring).

163. H. N. Hirsch, *The Enigma of Felix Frankfurter* (New York, 1981), 176; James F. Simon, *Antagonists: Hugo Black, Felix Frankfurter and Civil Liberties in Modern America* (New York, 1990), 118–119. At the time, his colleagues urged Frankfurter to tone down the language of the dissent, but he refused. See Joseph Lash, ed., *From the Diaries of Felix Frankfurter* (New York, 1975), 253–254.

164. 319 U.S. at 654 (Frankfurter, J., dissenting).

165. Ibid., 658.

166. Ibid., 658–660.

167. "Court Upholds Freedom of Conscience," *Christian Century,* June 23, 1943, 731.

168. Penton, *Apocalypse Delayed,* 84–87; Harrison, *Visions of Glory,* 150–157; Peters, *Judging Jehovah's Witnesses,* 295–298.

169. Today the Witnesses come to court primarily to contest blood transfusions, and they lose those battles routinely. See *Klassy v. Physicians Plus Ins. Co.*, 371 F.3d 952 (7th Cir. 2004); *Novak v. Cobb County Kennestone Hospital Authority*, 74 F.3d 1173 (11th Cir. 1996); *Application of President and Directors of Georgetown College, Inc.*, 118 U.S.App. D.C. 80, 331 F.2d 1000 (D.C.Cir.), *cert. den.*, 377 U.S. 978 (1964).

170. See Steven V. Roberts, "Bush Intensifies Debate on Pledge, Asking Why It So Upsets Dukakis," *New York Times*, August 25, 1988, 1.

171. Public Law No. 396 (1954), codified at 4 U.S.C. sec. 4.

172. *Newdow v. U.S. Congress*, 292 F.3d 597 (9th Cir. 2002), modified, 328 F.3d 466 (en banc).

173. Howard Fineman, "One Nation, Under . . . Who?" *Newsweek*, July 8, 2002, 20; Lee Canipe, "Under God and Anti-Communist: How the Pledge of Allegiance Got Religion in Cold War America," *Journal of Church and State* 45 (2003): 305; John E. Thompson, "What's the Big Deal? The Unconstitutionality of God in the Pledge of Allegiance," *Harvard Civil Rights–Civil Liberties Law Review* 38 (2003): 563.

174. *Elk Grove Unified School District v. Newdow*, 542 U.S. 1 (2004).

175. See, e.g., Canipe, "Under God and Anti-Communist," 305–323.

176. On the widespread (and problematic) use of the term after World War II, see Mark Silk, *Spiritual Politics: Religion and America since World War II* (New York, 1988), 40–53.

177. Harry S. Truman, "St. Patrick's Day Address" (New York City, March 17, 1948), in *Public Papers of the Presidents of the United States, Harry S. Truman* (Washington, D.C., 1966), 189.

178. Martin E. Marty, *Modern American Religion: Under God, Indivisible, 1941–1960* (Chicago, 1996), 3:272.

179. Dwight D. Eisenhower, June 14, 1954, *Public Papers of the Presidents of the United States, Dwight D. Eisenhower* (Washington, D.C., 1958), 563.

180. On Eisenhower's discussions about his religious beliefs with evangelist Billy Graham before being elected, see Billy Graham, *Just As I Am: The Autobiography of Billy Graham* (New York, 1997), 189–192. Graham reportedly urged Eisenhower to join a church, and advised Eisenhower that the Presbyterians were "fairly close" to the River Brethren sect of Mennonites to which Eisenhower's family had originally belonged. Marshall Frady, *Billy Graham: A Parable of American Righteousness* (Boston, 1979), 256–258. Mamie Eisenhower was a Presbyterian, which offers an alternative explanation for his choice. John Pollock, *Billy Graham: Evangelist to the World* (San Francisco, 1979), 165–166; Robert D. Linder and Richard Pierard, *Twilight of the Saints: Biblical Christianity and Civil Religion in America* (Downers Grove, Ill., 1978), 93–99.

181. Jerry Bergman, "Why President Eisenhower Hid his Jehovah's Witness

Upbringing," *Jehovah's Witness Research Journal* 6 (July–December 1999), posted at www.seanet.com (accessed October 6, 2008); Marley Cole, *Jehovah's Witnesses* (New York, 1955), 189–192

182. Merlin Gustafson, "The Religion of a President," *Christian Century,* April 30, 1969, 613.

183. See, e.g., Dwight D. Eisenhower, *At Ease: Stories I Tell to Friends* (Garden City, N.J., 1967), 305.

184. Paul Hutchinson, "The President's Religious Faith," *Christian Century,* March 24, 1954, 362–369, quotation on 365.

185. "Dwight Eisenhower, Inauguration, 1957," www.eisenhower.archives.gov (accessed October 6, 2008).

186. The change was noticed and criticized at the time by Witness leaders. See N. H. Knorr, "Conspiracy against Jehovah's Name," *Watchtower* 78 (June 1, 1957): 323–324.

187. Quoted without further attribution in Gustafson, "The Religion of a President," 611.

188. "Text of Eisenhower Speech," *New York Times,* December 23, 1952, 16.

189. Ezra Taft Benson, *Cross Fire: The Eight Years with Eisenhower* (Garden City, N.Y., 1962). For the quotation, see Gustafson, "The Religion of a President," 612.

190. According to one source, half of all young adults raised "in the truth" later abandon the Witnesses. Bergman, "Why President Eisenhower Hid His Jehovah's Witness Upbringing," 18.

191. Quoted in Hutchinson, "The President's Religious Faith," 362 (without further attribution).

192. Ibid., 369.

193. William Lee Miller, "Perils of Freedom," *Time,* August 4, 1958, www.time.com (accessed October 7, 2008); see also Miller Center of Public Affairs, University of Virginia, "About Us: William Lee Miller," http://millercenter.org (accessed October 7, 2008).

194. Hutchinson, "The President's Religious Faith," 364.

195. The survey of 1,602 people was conducted in the spring of 1953. See *The Gallup Poll: Public Opinion, 1935–1971* (New York: 1972), 2:1140. The poll showed that 69 percent of the public favored the idea, 21 percent opposed it, and 10 percent had no opinion.

196. See Mark Silk, "Under Whatever," *Religion in the News* 6 (Fall 2003), www.trincoll.edu (accessed October 7, 2008).

197. Christopher J. Kauffman, *Faith and Fraternalism: A History of the Knights of Columbus, 1882–1982* (New York, 1982), 385, 394.

198. Richard J. Ellis, *To the Flag: The Unlikely History of the Pledge of Allegiance* (Lawrence, Kan., 2005), 130.

199. Congressman Rabault of Michigan introducing H.J. Res. 243 To

Amend the Pledge of Allegiance, 83rd Cong., 1st sess., *Congressional Record* 99, no. 10 (April 21, 1953): appendix A2063.

200. The original copy of the sermon with Docherty's notes is posted on the New York Avenue Presbyterian Church Web site, www.nyapc.org/congregation/Sermon_Archives/text/1954/under-god-sermon.pdf (accessed April 9, 2009). See also George M. Docherty, *I've Seen the Day* (Grand Rapids, Mich., 1984), 158–160; Craig Howie, "One Nation, under God: How a Scotsman Re-wrote America's Pledge," September 27, 2005, http://heritage.scotsman.com/heritage/One-nation-under-God-How .2664830.jp (accessed October 4, 2009).

201. Ellis, *To the Flag*, 133.

202. Congressman Barratt O'Hara, quoted in the *Congressional Record*, June 7, 1954, 7761; cited in Ellis, *To the Flag*, 258n41.

203. Docherty, *I've Seen the Day*, 160.

204. *Dennis v. United States*, 341 U.S. 494, 561 (1951) (Jackson, J., concurring).

205. Edward A. Purcell, *The Crisis of Democratic Theory: Scientific Naturalism and the Problem of Value* (Lexington, Ky., 1973); Richard A. Primus, *The American Language of Rights* (Cambridge, 2004), 177–233, also makes the point that American constitutional law since World War II is shot through with anxiety to provide an adequate defense against totalitarianism.

206. Charles Oakman, R-Mich., *Congressional Record* 100, Part 2 (February 12, 1954): 1697.

207. Will Herberg, *Protestant, Catholic, Jew: An Essay in American Religious Sociology* (Garden City, N.Y., 1955).

208. Eisenhower spoke of his "joyous, generous and confident dedication [to] the idea of human freedom—that glorious gift of our Judeo-Christian tradition." Richard H. Parke, "Memorial Diners Hear Eisenhower," *New York Times*, October 16, 1952, 19.

209. *Minersville School District v. Gobitis*, 310 U.S. at 598.

3. The Almighty and the Dollar

1. Mark Silk, *Spiritual Politics: Religion and America since World War I* (New York, 1988).

2. Frank I. Kluckhohn, "N.E.A. Is Assailed before Catholics," *New York Times*, April 11, 1947, 18; Frank I. Kluckhohn, "Cushing Stresses Parents' Rights," *New York Times*, April 10, 1947, 18.

3. Gladwin Hill, "Methodist Bishops Attack Catholics," *New York Times*, May 8, 1947, 26, quoting statement issued by the Council of Bishops of the Methodist Church, "the largest Protestant sect in the country."

4. Kluckhorn, "N.E.A. Is Assailed before Catholics," 18.
5. See Catholic-Public School, Letter from Msgr. Howard J. Carroll of the National Catholic Welfare Conference to American Archbishops and Bishops, September 2, 1948, marked "confidential" and enclosing a memorandum discussing cooperation between Catholic and public educators based on a survey of 75 percent of Catholic dioceses, and reporting 1,218 religious—up from 632 in 1937—currently teaching in approximately 340 schools (on file with author). In 1959, Protestants and Other Americans United for Separation of Church and State conducted a survey of its own, finding 2,055 religious teachers and administrators in public schools in twenty-two states. C. Stanley Lowell, *Embattled Wall: Americans United: An Idea and a Man* (Washington, D.C., 1966), 96–97. For a discussion of *Zellers* and the history of Catholic–public school cooperation in New Mexico, see Katherine Holscher, "Habits in the Classroom: A Court Case regarding Catholic Sisters in New Mexico," Ph.D. diss., Princeton University, 2008.
6. E-mail from Professor Roger Groot, Washington and Lee Law School, to Sarah Barringer Gordon, University of Pennsylvania Law School, February 24, 2004 (on file with author): "I promised to email you about the school I attended in TX. It was 'St. Elmo's School' or 'The St. Elmo School' in Travis County (Austin) TX, right around 1950. It was a public school, but it did have either crosses or crucifixes in the halls. If any of the teachers were nuns, they were not in habit. At least some of the teachers were married."
7. See, e.g., Patrick W. Carey, *Catholics in America: A History* (Westport, Conn., 2004), 27–46; John T. McGreevy, *Catholicism and American Freedom* (New York, 2003), 19–42.
8. Scholars have treated these developments indirectly. See, e.g., Robert Wuthnow, *The Restructuring of American Religion: Society and Faith since World War II* (Princeton, 1988); James D. Beumler, "America Emerges as a World Power: Religion, Politics, and Nationhood, 1940–1960," in *Church and State in America: A Bibliographical Guide*, ed. John F. Wilson, vol. 2: *The Civil War to the Present Day* (New York, 1987), 225.
9. 330 U.S. 1 (1947).
10. For brief discussions of the *Everson* case, see Philip Hamburger, *Separation of Church and State* (Cambridge, Mass., 2002), 454–463, and John Jeffries and James E. Ryan, "A Political History of the Establishment Clause," *Michigan Law Review* 100 (2001): 284–287.
11. See Daryl R. Fair, "The *Everson* Case in the Context of New Jersey Politics," in *Everson Revisited: Religion, Education, and Law at the Crossroads*, ed. Jo Renée Formicola and Hubert Morken (Lanham, Md., 1997), 1;

Daryl R. Fair, "*Everson v. Board of Education:* A Case Study of the Judicial Process" (1975), unpublished manuscript, on file with New Jersey State Library.

12. Bob Leach, *The Frank Hague Picture Book* (Jersey City, 1998).

13. Dayton David McKean, *The Boss: The Hague Machine in Action* (Boston, 1940); Alfred Steinberg, *The Bosses* (New York, 1972), 10–71.

14. McKean, *The Boss,* 224.

15. Steinberg, *The Bosses,* 46.

16. In 1944, for example, Hague opposed the draft New Jersey constitution. He framed it "as a drive against the Catholic Church and the parochial school system" and "then his Irish machine put on quite a show." Richard J. Connors, *A Cycle of Power: The Career of Jersey City Mayor Frank Hague* (Metuchen, 1971), 158; Mark S. Foster, *The Early Career of Mayor Frank Hague* (1967); www.cityofjerseycity.org/hague/earlycareer (accessed October 23, 2009).

17. Christopher J. Kauffman, *Faith and Fraternalism: The History of the Knights of Columbus* (New York, 1992), 385–386. For background on Monsignor Glover's involvement, see Fair, "*Everson v. Board of Education:* A Case Study," 6n24, citing an article from the *Newark Evening News* dated June 4, 1941. Fair speculates that "other elements of the [Roman Catholic] hierarchy were probably more involved than the public record indicates" (30n24).

18. *Everson v. Board of Education,* 39 A.2d 75, 75–76 (N.J. Super. Ct. 1944): "Including the transportation of school children to and from school other than a public school, except such school as is operated for profit" (quoting N.J. Stat. Ann. sec. 18:14–18 [West 1941]). Given that the legislative history reveals no concern among legislators over "for-profit" schools, it is not clear what this restriction was designed to accomplish.

19. The JOUAM was founded in Philadelphia in 1885, the junior branch of United American Mechanics. Membership was limited to "white males, between the ages of 16 and 50, of good moral character, believers in the existence of a Supreme Being, in favor of separation of church and state, and supporters of free education through the Public School System." Records of the Junior Order United American Mechanics Harmony Council, No. 23 Cheswold, Delaware, www .lib.udel.edu/ud/spec/findaids/jouma.htm (accessed June 8, 2007). The organization, which has fallen on hard times and may no longer be extant, changed significantly in the twentieth century. It became primarily a social and life-insurance organization, and openly welcomed Jews, African Americans, Roman Catholics, and women as

members. The organization had endorsed and supported the Atlanta KKK periodical *The Searchlight* in the 1920s; Hamburger, *Separation of Church and State*, 455–456. On the Patriotic Order, see Shawn Francis Peters, *Judging Jehovah's Witnesses: Religious Persecution and the Dawn of the Rights Revolution* (Lawrence, Kans., 2000), 42.

20. As one commentator put it, "Hague doesn't need a Democratic legislature; the Republicans will always lend him theirs!" Letter from Richard Connors to Daryl R. Fair, January 6, 1975, quoted in Fair, "The *Everson* Case," 6.

21. The states were Connecticut, Illinois, Indiana, Kansas, Louisiana, Maryland, Massachusetts, New York, New Hampshire, Oklahoma, Vermont, West Virginia, and Wisconsin. Leslie W. Kindred, Jr., "Public Funds for Private and Parochial Schools: A Legal Study," Ph.D. diss., University of Michigan, 1938, 66–67.

22. The constitutions of thirty-seven states contain mini-Blaine Amendments, responding to the proposed (but never ratified) national constitutional amendment introduced in 1875 by Senator James G. Blaine. The provisions of state constitutions vary significantly; for a collection of state constitutions, see New York Constitutional Convention Committee, *Constitutions of the States and United States* (New York, 1938). The constitutionality of such amendments against a free-exercise challenge was upheld in *Locke v. Davey*, 540 U.S. 712 (2004).

23. Note, "Catholic Schools and Public Money," *Yale Law Journal* 50 (1941): 917, 926.

24. See, e.g., *State ex rel. Traub v. Brown*, 172 A. 835 (Del. 1934); *State ex rel. Johnson v. Boyd*, 28 N.E.2d 256 (Ind. 1940); *Sherrard v. Jefferson County Board of Education*, 171 S.W.2d 963 (Ky. 1943); *Borden v. Louisiana State Board of Education*, 123 So. 655 (La. 1929); *Board of Education v. Wheat*, 199 A. 628 (Md. 1938); *Chance v. Mississippi State Textbook Rating & Purchasing Board*, 200 So. 706 (Miss. 1941); *Judd v. Board of Education of Union Free School District No. 2*, 15 N.E.2d 576 (N.Y. 1938); *Gurney v. Ferguson*, 122 P.2d 1002 (Okla. 1941); *Mitchell v. Consolidated School District No. 201*, 135 P.2d 79 (Wash. 1943); *State ex rel. Van Straten v. Milquet*, 192 N.W. 392 (Wis. 1923).

25. See *Cochran v. Louisiana State Board of Education*, 281 U.S. 370 (1930), sustaining the state provision of textbooks to parochial school pupils against a due process clause challenge; *Reuben Quick Bear v. Leupp*, 210 U.S. 50 (1908), holding that federal funding for schools on Indian reservations, 96 percent of which were Catholic, did not violate the Fifth Amendment.

26. *Cochran*, 281 U.S. 370.

27. Ibid., 375.
28. Robert J. Franciosi, *The Rise and Fall of American Public Schools: The Political Economy of Public Education in the Twentieth Century* (Westport, Conn., 2004).
29. The schools in question were St. Mary's Cathedral High School, St. Hedwig's Parochial School, St. Francis School, and Trenton Catholic Boys High School. The cost of such transportation for the 1942–43 school year was $859.80. Ewing Township students who attended public schools went to Trenton Junior High School, Trenton Senior High School, and Pennington High School. *Everson v. Board of Education*, 330 U.S. 1, 30n7 (1947) (Rutledge, J., dissenting); New Jersey Court of Errors and Appeals, vol. 1786 (1945).
30. The Patriotic Order was very active in anti-Jehovah's Witness activity and legal tactics. See Peters, *Judging Jehovah's Witnesses,* 42.
31. Fair, "The *Everson* Case," 7 and n42; see also Richard C. Cortner, *The Supreme Court and the Second Bill of Rights: The Fourteenth Amendment and the Nationalization of Civil Liberties* (Madison, 1981), 110.
32. Hamburger, *Separation of Church and State,* 457n157, citing Christine L. Compston, "The Serpentine Wall: Judicial Decision Making in Supreme Court Cases Involving Aid to Sectarian Schools," Ph.D. diss., University of New Hampshire, 1986, 113.
33. *Everson v. Board of Education,* 39 A.2d 75, 76 (N.J. Super. Ct. 1944).
34. Ibid. (emphasis added), citing *Trustees of Rutgers College v. Morgan,* 57 A. 250, 255 (N.J. 1904); *In re Voorhees' Estate,* 196 A. 365 (N.J. 1938).
35. *Everson,* 39 A.2d at 77 (Helier, J., dissenting); *Cochran v. Louisiana State Board of Education,* 281 U.S. 370, 374–375 (1930).
36. Fair, "The *Everson* Case," 10.
37. *Everson v. Board Of Education,* 44 A.2d 333, 336–337 (N.J. 1945). The majority was composed of Chancellor Luther Campbell, Justices Thomas Brogan, Joseph Bodine, and Ralph Donges, and Judges William Dill and John Rafferty.
38. Ibid. at 339 (Case, J., dissenting).
39. Ibid., 340.
40. Black's law clerk in *Everson* was Louis Oberdorfer. Daniel J. Meador, "Justice Black and His Law Clerks," *Louisiana Law Review* 15 (1962): 57, 63.
41. *Everson v. Board of Education,* 330 U.S. 1, 7 (1947), citing *Cochran v. Louisiana State Board of Education,* 281 U.S. 370 (1930).
42. Ibid., quotations on 16.
43. See *West Virginia State Board of Education v. Barnette,* 319 U.S. 624 (1943).

44. Brief Amici Curiae of National Council of Catholic Men and National Council of Catholic Women, *Everson*, 330 U.S. 1 (No. 52), 21; "The presence or absence of religious instruction in non-profit private schools could well appear in the eyes of the State as an immaterial element in relation to the State's [secular educational] aim" (ibid., 13).

45. Ibid., 36. On this and other briefs submitted by the church, see Jo Renée Formicola, "Catholic Jurisprudence on Education," in *Everson Revisited*, 83, 84–87.

46. *Everson*, 330 U.S. at 15.

47. Ibid., 18.

48. Justice Black followed what was by then a tradition in constitutional law. The meaning of the religion clauses, the Supreme Court first held in 1879, could be discerned by understanding what had motivated the "Father of Democracy" a century earlier. *Reynolds v. United States*, 98 U.S. 145, 162–164 (1878).

49. Sarah Barringer Gordon, *The Mormon Question: Polygamy and Constitutional and Conflict in Nineteenth Century America* (Chapel Hill, 2002), 6–8, 132–135.

50. McGreevy, *Catholicism and American Freedom*, 176; Merrill D. Peterson, *The Jefferson Image in the American Mind* (New York, 1960), 355–362.

51. *Everson*, 330 U.S. at 9.

52. Thomas C. Berg, "Anti-Catholicism and Modern Church-State Relations," *Loyola University Chicago Law Journal* 33 (2001): 121, 127–128; Roger K. Newman, *Hugo Black: A Biography* (New York, 1994), 363–364.

53. Berg, "Anti-Catholicism and Modern Church-State Relations," 127; Hamburger, *Separation of Church and State*, 461–462; McGreevy, *Catholicism and American Freedom*, 183–184.

54. Brief of American Civil Liberties Union as Amicus Curiae, *Everson*, 330 U.S. 1 (No. 52) at 19.

55. *Everson*, 330 U.S. at 24 (Jackson, J., dissenting).

56. Ibid., 29 (Rutledge, J., dissenting).

57. Ibid., 39.

58. Ibid., 40.

59. See, e.g., Lewis Wood, "High Court Backs State Right to Run Parochial Buses," *New York Times*, February 11, 1947, 1.

60. Benjamin Fine, "Religious Attack Stirs Educators," *New York Times*, March 6, 1947, 27.

61. Note, "Public Funds for Sectarian Schools," *Harvard Law Review* 60 (1947): 793, 799; Note, "Establishment of Religion Clause Applied to the States," *Cornell Law Quarterly* 33 (1947): 122, 128.

62. See Hamburger, *Separation of Church and State,* 465–468.

63. Risa L. Goluboff, *The Lost Promise of Civil Rights* (Cambridge, Mass., 2007).

64. Anson Phelps Stokes and Leo Pfeffer, *Church and State in the United States,* rev. ed. (New York, 1964), 327–328.

65. See, e.g., "U.S. Envoy to Pope Called Temporary," *New York Times,* June 12, 1946, 11, reporting on Bishop G. Bromley Oxnam, president of the Federal Council of Churches, who called on President Harry Truman to clarify the role of Roosevelt's representative Myron Taylor after Roosevelt's death. Oxnam also argued that the presence of a representative was a violation of the separation of church and state.

66. See Alessandra Stanley, "Pope Beatifies Croat Prelate, Fanning Ire Among Serbs," *New York Times,* October 4, 1998, 13.

67. Richard E. Morgan, "Backs to the Wall: A Study in the Contemporary Politics of Church and State," Ph.D. diss., Columbia University, 1967, 22–23. There are conflicting assessments of Catholic anticommunism and the relationship of anticommunism to fascist tendencies in the United States. See Fred J. Cook, *The Nightmare Decade: The Life and Times of Senator Joe McCarthy* (New York, 1971), 289 (Spellman and "a large and powerful segment" of the church vigorously supported McCarthy); Donald F. Crosby, *God, Church, and Flag: Senator Joseph R. McCarthy and the Catholic Church, 1950–1957* (Chapel Hill, 1978), 228–251 (Catholics deeply divided on McCarthy); Mark S. Massa, *Catholics and American Culture: Fulton Sheen, Dorothy Day, and the Notre Dame Football Team* (New York, 1999), 57–81 (Catholics were both the strongest supporters and most trenchant critics of McCarthy); Leo Pfeffer, *Creeds in Competition: A Creative Force in American Culture* (New York, 1958), 13 (Catholics maintained "almost monolithic uniformity" in support of McCarthy).

68. On January 31, 1947, Republican senator Robert Taft of Ohio proposed a bill that would return a portion of federal income tax revenues to states for education, and would charge states with distribution of the funds according to state constitutional provisions. Because most states had explicit provisions banning public support for sectarian institutions, many of them explicitly targeting religious schools, such legislation had consistently and effectively been opposed by the National Catholic Welfare Conference. See Note, "Catholic Schools and Public Money."

69. Benjamin Fine, "Education in Review," *New York Times,* April 20, 1952, E11.

70. Fine, "Religious Attack Stirs Educators."

71. Ibid.

72. Frank L. Kluckhohn, "Cushing Stresses Parents' Rights," *New York Times,* April 10, 1947, 18.

73. Frank L. Kluckhohn, "N.E.A. Is Assailed before Catholics," *New York Times,* April 11, 1947, 18.

74. "Spellman Charges Protestant Bias," *New York Times,* June 12, 1947, citing Cardinal Spellman, Commencement Address at Fordham University, June 11, 1947.

75. John D. Childs et al., Letter to the Editor, "Sectarian Education," *New York Times,* October 1, 1947, 28.

76. Gordon, *The Mormon Question,* 78–79; Sarah Barringer Gordon, "Blasphemy and the Law of Religious Liberty in Nineteenth Century America," *American Quarterly* 52 (2000): 682.

77. Jesse T. Peck, *The History of the Great Republic, Considered From a Christian Stand-Point* (New York, 1868), 205–206.

78. Perry Miller, "Mr. Blanshard's New Book: The Vatican, the Kremlin, and Democracy," *New York Herald Tribune,* June 10, 1951, 5 (book review), arguing that the Catholic church, like the Soviet government of Josef Stalin, was fundamentally opposed to both democracy and liberty; see also Hamburger, *Separation of Church and State,* 449–454; McGreevy, *Catholicism and American Freedom,* 175–188.

79. Ellis H. Dana, *Protestant Strategy in the Making* (Boston, 1948).

80. Protestants and Other Americans United for Separation of Church and State, "Separation of Church and State: A Manifesto," *Christian Century,* January 21, 1948, 79, (hereinafter, "Manifesto").

81. *Church and State,* May 15, 1948, 1.

82. Luke Eugene Ebersole, *Church Lobbying in the Nation's Capital* (New York, 1951), 72.

83. *Church and State,* July 10, 1948, 5.

84. POAU, "Manifesto," 79; "New Body Demands Church Separation," *New York Times,* January 12, 1948, 1.

85. POAU, "Manifesto," 80.

86. Ibid.

87. Ibid., 81.

88. Ibid. The Manifesto called for "a reconsideration of the two decisions of the Supreme Court upholding the use of tax funds (a) for providing the pupils of parochial schools with free text-books, and (b) for the transportation of pupils to parochial schools."

89. "Criticizes Separation Drive," *New York Times,* January 13, 1948, 1, reporting on Knights of Columbus.

90. Ibid.

91. "Denies Catholics Oppose Separation," *New York Times,* January 26, 1948, 17, quoting John T. McNicholas, archbishop of Cincinnati and chairman of the National Catholic Welfare Conference; "Oxnam Says Cushing Attempted 'Smear,'" *New York Times,* February 16, 1948, 5, quoting Archbishop Cushing.

92. John C. Bennett, "Editorial Notes," *Christianity and Crisis,* February 2, 1948, 2.

93. Morgan, "Backs to the Wall," 49, quoting Oxnam.

94. Harold E. Fey, *With Sovereign Reverence: The First Twenty-Five Years of Americans United* (Rockville, 1974), 12. See also Ebersole, *Church Lobbying in the Nation's Capital,* 105, quoting a speech by Archer calling for more space in the "religious press," as secular newspapers might be "throttled by fear of boycotts and reprisals."

95. *Illinois ex rel. McCollum v. Board of Education of School District No. 71,* 333 U.S. 203 (1948).

96. Ibid. at 212.

97. Glenn L. Archer and Albert J. Menendez, *The Dream Lives On: The Story of Glenn L. Archer and Americans United* (Washington, D.C., 1982), 53–55.

98. Ibid., 55.

99. Ibid., 65, 67; quotation on 67.

100. Reports to the Board by the Executive Director (1950–1951), Americans United for Separation of Church and State, Box 2, Princeton University Archives.

101. *American Freedom and Catholic Power* expanded several articles that Blanshard had written a year earlier in *The Nation.* See Paul Blanshard, *American Freedom and Catholic Power,* 2nd ed. (Boston, 1949). Both the magazine and the book were banned from New York City public school libraries by the Board of Education. The book (and the ban) caused an explosive controversy in New York. As the *New York Times* reported in a retrospective article twenty-five years later, "In the ensuing furor a committee to defend freedom of information fought the ban, and Cardinal Spellman picked a quarrel with Eleanor Roosevelt." Israel Shenker, "At 80, Blanshard Twins Still Back the Unpopular," *New York Times,* August 28, 1972, 31; "School Ban on *The Nation* Stays, Reversal by Court to Be Sought," *New York Times,* June 24, 1949, 25.

102. Blanshard authored many books, all of them argumentative. See, e.g., Paul Blanshard, *Freedom and Catholic Power in Spain and Portugal: An American Interpretation* (Boston, 1962); *God and Man in Washington* (Boston, 1960); *The Irish and Catholic Power: An American Interpretation* (Boston, 1953); *Paul Blanshard on Vatican II* (Boston, 1966); *Personal*

and Controversial: An Autobiography (Boston, 1973); *Religion and the Schools: The Great Controversy* (Boston, 1963); *The Right to Read: The Battle against Censorship* (Boston, 1955). At the age of eighty, Blanshard embraced atheism. Steven R. Weisman, "Paul Blanshard, Writer and Critic of Catholic Church, Is Dead at 87," *New York Times,* January 30, 1980, B4.

103. For scholarly treatments of Blanshard's anti-Catholic writings, see Philip Gleason, *Speaking of Diversity: Language and Ethnicity in Twentieth-Century America* (Baltimore, 1992), 213; John T. McGreevy, "Thinking on One's Own: Catholicism in the American Intellectual Imagination, 1928–1960," *Journal of American History* 84 (1997): 97, 97–98; and Philip Gleason, "American Catholics and Liberalism, 1789–1960," in *Catholicism and Liberalism: Contributions to American Public Philosophy* ed. R. Bruce Douglass and David Hollenbach (Cambridge, 1994), 45.

104. Paul Blanshard, *Communism, Democracy, and Catholic Power* (Boston, 1951).

105. Miller, "Mr. Blanshard's New Book."

106. See, e.g., George H. Dunne, "Mr. Blanshard and the Catholic Church" (Parts 1–7), *America,* June 4, 1949, 309; June 11, 1949, 339; June 18, 1949, 359; June 25, 1949, 379; July 16, 1949, 438; July 23, 1949, 459; July 30, 1949, 477. J. M. O'Neill, "Mr. Blanshard's New Book: The Vatican, the Kremlin, and Democracy," *New York Herald Tribune,* June 10, 1951, 5 (book review).

107. "Indecent Controversy," *Christian Century,* February 18, 1948, 198, 199.

108. Ibid.

109. "Protestants United Issue Manifesto," *Christian Century,* January 21, 1948, 68.

110. "Joseph Martin Dawson," *Religion and Politics: A Reference Handbook,* ed. John Woodrow Storey and Glenn H. Utter (Santa Barbara, 2002), 71–72.

111. "Denies Catholics Oppose Separation," quoting Archbishop John McNicholas.

112. Frank J. Sorauf, *The Wall of Separation: The Constitutional Politics of Church and State* (Princeton, 1976), 54.

113. "1948 Report of the Executive Director," Americans United for Separation of Church and State, Box 2, Princeton University Archives. C. Stanley Lowell reported that the Masons supplied the funds to purchase POAU's first office building on Massachusetts Avenue in Washington, D.C.—part of a "fine relationship" that was maintained at least until Lowell wrote in 1966. Lowell, *Embattled Wall,* 140; see also Sorauf,

Wall of Separation, 223, noting the ongoing relationship between "Masonry, especially Scottish Rite Masonry," and POAU.

114. Sorauf, *Wall of Separation,* 54.

115. David B. Tyack, "The Perils of Pluralism: The Background of the *Pierce Case,*" *American Historical Review* 74 (1968): 77.

116. *Pierce v. Society of Sisters,* 268 U.S. 510 (1925), quotation at 535.

117. Tyack, "Perils of Pluralism," 85, quoting an advertisement in the *Silverton Appeal* from October 13, 1922.

118. See the discussion earlier in the chapter about JOUAM and its relationship to the Ku Klux Klan.

119. Morgan, "Backs to the Wall," 178, interview with Director John C. Mayne, August 1962.

120. For example, Archer reported with pride to the POAU Board of Trustees in 1951 that the Council of Bishops of the Methodist Church, Archer's own denomination, "endorsed POAU's principles and called on Methodists to support our work." "Report of the Executive Director," October 17, 1951, Americans United for Separation of Church and State, Box 2, Princeton University Archives.

121. Morgan, "Backs to the Wall," 84, interview with Glenn Archer (May 22, 1962). The NCCJ was established in 1928 as an antidote to the influence of the Klan.

122. See McGreevy, "Thinking on One's Own," 128.

123. Will Herberg, *Protestant-Catholic-Jew: An Essay in American Religious Sociology* (Garden City, N.Y., 1955), 258.

124. Ibid., quotations on 254, 256, 257.

125. Herberg, who was Jewish by birth but became a Marxist in his youth, encountered Niebuhr's work as he began to reject his prior leftist commitments. According to reports, Herberg sought out Niebuhr in New York. After several discussions with him, Herberg announced his intention to become a Christian. Niebuhr advised Herberg instead to search his own faith, and directed him to the Jewish Theological Seminary. Herberg's explorations there resulted in his first major work, *Judaism and Modern Man* (New York, 1951). In the same period he began a voyage from political liberalism to conservatism. By the late 1950s he had joined other ex-Communists at William F. Buckley, Jr.'s *National Review.* See David G. Dalin, "Will Herberg in Retrospect," *Commentary* (July 1988), reprinted in *From Marxism to Judaism: The Collected Essays of Will Herberg,* ed. David G. Dalin (New York, 1989); Harry J. Ausmus, *Will Herberg: From Right to Right* (Chapel Hill, 1987) and *Will Herberg: A Bio-Bibliography* (Westport, Conn., 1986), 34n13; June Bingham, *Courage to*

Change: An Introduction to the Life and Thought of Reinhold Niebuhr (Lanham, 1993), 188–190.

126. Morgan, "Backs to the Wall," 318.

127. "Report of the Executive Director," January 31, 1950, Americans United for Separation of Church and State, Box 2, Princeton University Archives.

128. Ibid., October 17, 1951.

129. See, e.g., Harold E. Fey, "Preview of a Divided America," *Christian Century*, May 28, 1947, 682; Frank S. Mead, "Shadows over Our Schools," *Christian Herald* 71 (February 1948): 1.

130. E-mail from Roger Groot: "[They were] told we had to have a public school that was not Catholic." February 24, 2004 (on file with author).

131. See Sorauf, *Wall of Separation*, 123; C. Wayne Zunkel, "The Pennsylvania School Bus Fight," *Christian Century*, August 25, 1965, 1036–1037.

132. See, e.g., Fey, *With Sovereign Reverence*, 25; Lowell, *Embattled Wall*, 68–69.

133. According to one scholar, POAU lawyers were "never . . . very careful about the technical development of [their] cases; one has the sense that [POAU] cares more about having cases on particular issues in particular places than about quality and craftsmanship or even chances of success." Morgan, "Backs to the Wall," 264; Sorauf, *Wall of Separation*, 94.

134. *Church and State*, May 15, 1948, 2.

135. Lowell, *Embattled Wall*, 95.

136. Stanislaus Woywod, "Catholic Schools," *The New Canon Law: A Commentary on and Summary of the New Code of Canon Law*, 7th ed. (New York, 1940), 283–284: sec. 1.215 (Canon 1372), sec. 1216 (Canon 1373), sec. 1217 (Canon 1374), sec. 1224 (Canon 1381).

137. See Sorauf, *Wall of Separation*, 33–34.

138. *Zellers v. Huff*, 236 P.2d 949, 951 (N.M. 1951).

139. Mead, "Shadows over Our Schools," 2.

140. Ibid.

141. Blanshard, *Religion and the Schools*, 162–167.

142. Letter from Leo Pfeffer to Harry L. Bigbee, September 15, 1950, in Fey, *With Sovereign Reverence*, 16.

143. *Zellers*, 236 P.2d, 961 (N.M. 1951).

144. Brief of Amicus Curiae American Civil Liberties Union, *Zellers*, 236 P.2d 949 (No. 5332). Missouri was the sole exception; see *Harfst v. Hoegen*, 163 S.W.2d 609 (Mo. 1942).

145. Morgan, "Backs to the Wall," 208.

146. See, e.g., "Taos Grade School," *Daily Capital News*, (Jefferson City, Mo.), January 31, 1951, 3.

147. Richard Morgan reports one ripple of objection to Archer's program in the early 1960s, based on an interview conducted with a former POAU employee in the New York chapter. Morgan, "Backs to the Wall," 202, interview with Paul Duling (March 8, 1962). POAU's materials downplay such dissension.

148. Blanshard, *American Freedom and Catholic Power,* 108–111.

149. Lowell, *Embattled Wall,* 102, 104; quotation on 104.

150. *Berghorn v. Reorganized School District No. 8,* 260 S.W.2d 573 (Mo. 1953).

151. Lowell, *Embattled Wall,* 102.

152. Ibid., 105 ("Cases like those of Garden Plain, Kansas, and Bremond, Texas, were declared moot on the eve of trial because the defendants knew they were beaten and hastily corrected the sectarian abuses in the schools"); see, e.g., *Wooley v. Spalding,* 293 S.W.2d 563 (Ky. 1956); *Rawlings v. Butler,* 290 S.W.2d 801 (Ky. 1956); *Swart v. S. Burlington Town School District,* 167 A.2d 514 (Vt. 1961).

153. Lowell, *Embattled Wall,* 95–96.

154. Sorauf, *Wall of Separation,* 31, noting the "centralized, even autocratic style" of POAU.

155. Other groups, such as the National Council of Churches and the National Conference of Christians and Jews, shared their discomfort. Richard E. Morgan, *The Politics of Religious Conflict: Church and State in America* (New York, 1968), 52–54.

156. Sorauf, *Wall of Separation,* 81.

157. Ibid. Although at the end of the period studied here, Sorauf reported on the Legal Conference on the Establishment Clause, which included POAU in its councils for the first time in 1965 (83). According to Sorauf, POAU's involvement was tolerated only as a means to limit its "recklessness." The organization "became a vehicle for Leo Pfeffer's judgments and preferences" (86).

158. Ibid., 95.

159. Ibid., 126, Table 5-3. AJC had the highest success rate at approximately 65 percent. The ACLU was next at 52 percent, and the POAU was lowest at 44 percent.

160. Mary Fowler Beasley, "Pressure Group Persuasion: Protestants and Other Americans United for Separation of Church and State, 1947–1968," Ph.D. diss., Purdue University, 1970 (on file with author), 192, interview with Leo Pfeffer (May 28, 1969).

161. See Morgan, *Politics of Religious Conflict,* 52–53.

162. Pfeffer wanted to make sure that school prayer litigation did not lend itself to claims that Jews were opposed to God in schools, and over the course of the 1950s Jewish organizations debated whether to bring a

case. See Gregg Ivers, *To Build a Wall: American Jews and the Separation of Church and State* (Charlottesville, 1995), 113–145.

163. See Ebersole, *Church Lobbying in the Nation's Capital.*

164. Will Maslow, "The Legal Defense of Religious Liberty: The Strategy and Tactics of the American Jewish Congress," paper presented at the annual meeting of the American Political Science Association, St. Louis, September 6, 1961, cited in Sorauf, *Wall of Separation,* 47.

165. See, e.g., Beasley, "Pressure Group Persuasion," 185–217, providing comments of ACLU, AJC, and NCCJ leaders, political scientists, and interest-group strategists.

166. Lowell, *Embattled Wall,* 142; Letter from Glenn Archer to POAU Board, August 29, 1959, Americans United for Separation of Church and State, Box 2, Princeton University Archives.

167. After summarizing the pamphlet and claiming that more than 2,000 priests and nuns were on the public payroll, Lowell offered this explanation: "A captive school is a public school that has been taken over by a sectarian group and operated for its sectarian purposes. . . . Chief, and virtually sole offender, was the Roman Catholic Church. . . . [The] school would characteristically have two listings—one in the Roman Catholic School Directory . . . and another in the public school directory of the state." Lowell, *Embattled Wall,* 96.

168. *Captured* (Worldwide Pictures Ltd., 1959).

169. Lowell, *Embattled Wall,* 97: "The film was carefully prepared and its documentation was impeccable. The fact is that we eliminated some of the more objectionable items from the film even though they were strictly factual in order that no sensibilities would be offended. The film was violently attacked by the Catholics, nevertheless, and some Protestants wrote us that we ought to be ashamed of ourselves for such a bigoted attack on the Catholic Church!"

170. Holscher, "Captured!" 35–38.

171. *Engel v. Vitale,* 370 U.S. 421 (1962).

172. 374 U.S. 203 (1963).

173. Linda Przybyszewski, *Who Won the Bible War?* (Chapel Hill, forthcoming); R. Laurence Moore, "Bible Reading and Nonsectarian Schooling: The Failure of Religious Instruction in Nineteenth-Century Public Education," *Journal of American History* 86, no. 1 (March 2000): 1581–1599.

174. The New York Board of Rabbis opposed the Regents Prayer, arguing shortly after it was adopted in 1951 that it "will give rise to sectarian practices in the public schools," and claiming that separation of church

and state was "the foundation stone of American democracy and religious liberty." Quoted in "Regents Prayer Opposed by Rabbis," *New York Times,* January 4, 1952, 12. See also Ivers, *To Build a Wall,* 100–145.

175. See Rob Boston, "One Nation Indivisible?" *Church and State* (December 2003): 6, 9, charging that the "Religious Right" is "always eager to exploit emotional 'culture war' issues for political gain," and quoting current AU executive director Barry Lynn: "It's clear to me that the First Amendment stands for the proposition that government may not endorse religion—either in a specific sense or a generic one."

176. Beasley, "Pressure Group Persuasion," 223, citing interview with David Kucharsky, associate editor of *Christianity Today,* February 28, 1969.

177. *Rawlings v. Butler,* 290 S.W.2d 801 (Ky. 1956).

178. Quoting State Regent John F. Bosnan, addressing the Society of the Friendly Sons of St. Patrick in early 1952. *New York Times,* March 18, 1952, 20.

179. "The Supreme Court received a record 5,000 letters . . . in the first month" after *Engel* was announced, and "13,500 copies of the decision were sold by early 1964." Bruce J. Dierenfield, "*Engel v. Vitale,*" in *The Public Debate over Controversial Supreme Court Decisions,* ed. Melvin I. Urofsky (Washington, D.C., 2006), 215, 220; Louis H. Pollak, "Foreword: Public Prayers in Public Schools," *Harvard Law Review* 77 (1963): 62.

180. "Daily Prayer in All Schools Is Urged by State's Regents," *New York Times,* December 1, 1951, 1.

181. Ibid., 6.

182. Quoted in Bruce J. Dierenfield, *The Battle over School Prayer: How Engel v. Vitale Changed America* (Lawrence, Kans., 2007), 94.

183. Jeffries and Ryan, "A Political History of the Establishment Clause," 324n248; Alexander Burnham, "Court's Decision Stirs Conflicts," *New York Times,* June 27, 1962, 1; "The Court Decision—And the School Prayer Furor," *Newsweek,* July 9, 1962, 43.

184. Charles Wesley Lowry, *To Pray or Not to Pray! A Handbook for Study of Recent Supreme Court Decisions and American Church-State Doctrine* (Washington, D.C., 1963); see also Charles E. Rice, *The Supreme Court and Public Prayer: The Need for Restraint* (Bronx, 1964); Elliot H. Kraut, "An Analysis of the School Prayer Controversy since 1962 and Its Effect on the Balance between Church and State," Ph.D. diss., University of Connecticut, 1995 (on file with author).

185. "Spellman Renews Attack on Court's Decision," *New York Times,* June 28, 1962, 17.

186. Anthony Lewis, "Supreme Court Outlaws Official School Prayers in Regents Case Decision; Ruling is 6 to 1" *New York Times,* June 26, 1962, 16, quoting George Andrews of Alabama.

187. Charles Mohr, "Goldwater Hits U.S. Moral 'Rot,'" *New York Times,* October 11, 1964, 76.

188. Bruce J. Dierenfield, "Secular Schools? Religious Practices in New York and Virginia Public Schools since World War II," *Journal of Policy History* 4 (1992): 361; H. Frank Way, Jr., "Survey Research on Judicial Decisions: The Prayer and Bible Reading Cases," *Western Political Quarterly* 21 (1968): 189.

189. Congressman John Bell Williams, Democrat of Mississippi, quoted in Dierenfield, *Battle over School Prayer,* 149; Billy Graham quoted in ibid., 155. William M. Beaney and Edward N. Beiser, "Prayer and Politics: The Impact of *Engel* and *Schempp* on the Political Process," *Journal of Public Law* 13 (1964): 475.

190. See, e.g., House Committee on the Judiciary, *Hearings on Proposed Amendments to the Constitution Relating to Prayers and Bible Reading in the Public Schools,* 88th Cong., 2nd sess., 1964; "Amendment Sought on School Prayers," *New York Times,* September 11, 1963, 26.

191. See, e.g., Kenneth Dolbeare and Phillip Hammond, *The School Prayer Decisions: From Court Policy to Local Practice* (Chicago, 1971); Robert D. Smith, "Religion and the Schools: The Influence of State Attorneys General on the Implementation of *Engel* and *Schempp,*" *Southern Quarterly* 8 (1970): 221.

192. George Marsden, "The Sword of the Lord: How 'Otherworldly' Fundamentalism Became a Political Power," *Books and Culture* 12 (2006): 16.

193. Lisa McGirr, *Suburban Warriors: The Origins of the New American Right* (Princeton, 2001), 149–163, 225–237; Kraut, "An Analysis of the School Prayer Controversy."

194. Paul Hofmann, "Vatican Regrets Ruling on Prayer," *New York Times,* July 22, 1962, 36.

195. Lewis, "Supreme Court Outlaws Official School Prayers"; "Spellman Renews Attack on Court's Decision."

196. "Black Monday," *Binghamton Press,* July 22, 1962, 6, quoted in Dierenfield, "Secular Schools?" 369.

197. Ivers, *To Build a Wall,* 152, 176–179.

198. Leo Pfeffer, *Church, State, and Freedom,* rev. ed. (Boston, 1967), 235.

199. Robert H. Lord et al., *History of the Archdiocese of Boston: In the Various Stages of Its Development, 1604–1943* (New York, 1944), 585–602; Michael Grossberg, "Teaching the Republican Child: Three Antebellum

Stories about Law, Schooling, and the Construction of American Families," *Utah Law Review* (1996): 429, 454–455.

200. In 1953, Catholic and Jewish parents jointly challenged distribution of the Protestant Gideon's Bible in public schools, but Catholic parents withdrew from the case "after consultation with their priest . . . manifesting the change of position on the part of the Church." Leo Pfeffer, "Amici in Church-State Litigation," *Law and Contemporary Problems* 44 (Spring 1981): 83, 96, referring to *Tudor v. Board of Education,* 100 A.2d 857 (1953).

201. Compare, e.g., Philip B. Kurland, "Foreword: Equal in Origin and Equal in Title to the Legislative and Executive Branches of the Government," *Harvard Law Review* 78 (1964): 143, 176, and Mark Dewolfe Howe, *The Garden and the Wilderness: Religion and Government in American Constitutional History* (Chicago, 1965), 142–143, 146–147. See also Jeffries and Ryan, "A Political History of the Establishment Clause," 325–326.

202. Lewis, "Supreme Court Outlaws Official School Prayers"; Helen Dewar, "Theologian Sees Public Revolt over School Prayer Ban," *Washington Post,* July 4, 1962, A20, quoting sociologist Will Herberg.

203. "Billy Graham Voices Shock over Decision" *New York Times,* June 18, 1963, 27; C. P. Trussell, "Clergymen Split over Prayer Ban," *New York Times,* May 2, 1964, 25; Wallace Turner, "Pike Sees U.S. Deconsecrated by Decision on School Prayer," *New York Times,* July 14, 1962, 9.

204. Most historians of American religious conservatism, whose work has given us a rich picture of spiritual and social development, have only superficially treated the essential legal dimension of the battle against secularism and the political mobilization that accompanied it. See, e.g., Robert William Fogel, *The Fourth Great Awakening and the Future of Egalitarianism* (Chicago, 2000); George M. Marsden, *Fundamentalism and American Culture,* 2nd ed. (New York, 2006); Christian Smith, with Michael Emerson et al., *American Evangelicalism: Embattled and Thriving* (Chicago, 1998).

205. See generally Nancy Tatom Ammerman, *Baptist Battles: Social Change and Religious Conflict in the Southern Baptist Convention* (New Brunswick, N.J., 1990), 57–59; Randall Balmer, *Mine Eyes Have Seen the Glory: A Journey into the Evangelical Subculture in America,* 3rd ed. (New York, 2000); William Martin, *With God on Our Side: The Rise of the Religious Right in America* (New York, 1996); Marsden, "The Sword of the Lord," 16–17.

206. Morgan, *Politics of Religious Conflict,* 130.

207. See, e.g., Ronnie Prevost, "SBC Resolutions regarding Religious Lib-

erty and the Separation of Church and State (1940–1997): A Fundamental Shift," *Baptist History and Heritage* 34 (1999): 73.

208. Charles McDaniel, "The Decline of the Separation Principle in the Baptist Tradition of Religious Liberty," *Journal of Church and State* 50, no. 3 (Summer 2008), 413–430.

209. This campaign is addressed in Chapter 5.

210. David T. Morgan, *The New Crusades, the New Holy Land: Conflict in the Southern Baptist Convention, 1969–1991* (Tuscaloosa, 1996), 46; Carl L. Kell and L. Rayond Camp, *In the Name of the Father: The Rhetoric of the New Southern Baptist Convention* (Carbondale, Ill., 1999), 50–62.

211. Ammerman, *Baptist Battles*, 72–125; see also Barry Hankins, *Uneasy in Babylon: Southern Baptist Conservatives and American Culture* (Tuscaloosa, 2002), 139–164; Charles Austin, "Baptist Meeting Backs School Prayer Amendment," *New York Times,* June 18, 1982, B8.

212. Austin, "Baptist Meeting Backs School Prayer Amendment," quoting the Reverend Morris Chapman of Wichita Falls, Tex., and Charles Stanley of Atlanta.

213. Ibid. Sorauf, *Wall of Separation,* 294–295; Ellis Katz, "Patterns of Compliance with the *Schempp* Decision," *Journal of Public Law* 14 (1965): 396, 398.

214. See Jeffries and Ryan, "A Political History of the Establishment Clause," 327–328.

215. See Ronald James Boggs, "Culture of Liberty: History of Americans United for Separation of Church and State, 1947–1973," Ph.D. diss., Ohio State University, 1978, 697–727 (on file with author).

216. McGreevy, *Catholicism and American Freedom,* 236–257; John T. McGreevy, *Parish Boundaries: The Catholic Encounter with Race in the Twentieth-Century Urban North* (1996), 236–238; Sorauf, *Wall of Separation,* 320–333; cf. Fey, *With Sovereign Reverence,* 28–50.

217. "POAU in Crisis," *Newsweek,* October 5, 1964, quotations on 102, 103.

218. See, e.g., Albert J. Menendez, ed., *The Best of Church and State 1948–1975* (Silver Spring, 1975), 62–69.

219. In 2000, the Supreme Court held that the "sectarian" label had lost whatever constitutional meaning it had once possessed, rejecting a claim that a parochial school should not receive state aid because it was "pervasively sectarian." *Mitchell v. Helms,* 530 U.S. 793 (2000).

220. Archer and Menendez, *The Dream Lives On,* 242–248. For contemporary perspectives on AU and the religious right, see the Americans United Web site, www.au.org/resources/religious-right-research (accessed October 14, 2009). Archer retired in 1976 and died in No-

vember 2002. Obituary, "Glenn Archer," *Christian Century,* December 18, 2002, 17. Current AU membership is estimated at 75,000.

221. *Zelman v. Simmons-Harris,* 536 U.S. 639 (2002).

222. Austin C. Wehrwein, "Aid for Parents of Pupils Sought," *New York Times,* April 8, 1962, 67.

223. William H. Slavick, Letter to the Editor, "Private School Aid Wanted," *New York Times,* July 15, 1961, 18.

224. "Citizens for Educational Freedom, America's Voice for School Choice since 1959" (copy on file with author); www.educational-freedom.org.

225. Rob Boston, "Supreme Mistake," *Church and State,* July-August 2002, 4.

226. Herberg, *Protestant-Catholic-Jew,* 42n11.

227. For a thoughtful new treatment, see Barbara Dianne Savage, *Your Spirits Walk Beside Us: The Politics of Black Religion* (Cambridge, Mass., 2008).

4. Faith as Liberation

1. See Chapter 2.

2. C. Eric Lincoln, *The Black Muslims in America,* 3rd ed. (1961; Grand Rapids, Mich., 1994), 16.

3. Will Herberg, *Protestant-Catholic-Jew: An Essay in American Religious Sociology* (1955; Chicago, 1983).

4. See, for example, Karl Evanzz, *The Messenger: The Rise and Fall of Elijah Muhammad* (New York, 1999), 398–417; Edward E. Curtis IV, *Islam in Black America* (Albany, N.Y., 2002), 69; Claude Andrew Clegg III, *An Original Man: The Life and Times of Elijah Muhammad* (New York, 1997), 20–21.

5. Erdmann D. Beynon, "The Voodoo Cult among Negro Migrants in Detroit," *American Journal of Sociology* 43 (March 1938): 894–907, 896, quoting Sister Carrie Mohammad.

6. In 1916, for example, the Ford Motor Company sociological department listed 555 "Arab men" as factory workers. Curtis, *Islam in Black America,* 70.

7. Beynon, "Voodoo Cult," 895, quoting Sister Denke Majied.

8. Ibid., 897.

9. Thomas J. Sugrue, *Sweet Land of Liberty: The Forgotten Struggle for Civil Rights in the North* (New York, 2008), 32–44.

10. Fard, quoted without further citation in Lincoln, *Black Muslims in America,* 16.

11. The broad concept of "preparation," as the term is used among religious historians and religious studies scholars, blends intense focus on

past actions with the study of innovation; see, for example, Jonathan Z. Smith, "A Twice-Told Tale: The History of the History of Religions' History," *Numan* 28 (2001): 131–146; William Sims Bainbridge, *The Sociology of Religious Movements* (New York, 1997), 395–422. This focus shares much in common with social movement literature, especially the construction of identity within groups, mobilization, and the framing of issues; see Rebecca E. Klatch, "The Development of Individual Identity and Consciousness among Movements of the Right and Left," in *Social Movements: Identity, Culture, and the State*, ed. David S. Meyer, Nancy Whittier, and Belinda Robnett (New York, 2002), 185–201; Robert Wuthnow, *Communities of Discourse: Ideology and Social Structure in the Reformation, the Enlightenment, and European Socialism* (Cambridge, Mass., 1988). See also, e.g., John L. Brooke, "A Prepared People," in *The Refiner's Fire: The Making of Mormon Cosmology* (Cambridge, 1994), 3–88, tracing the lineage of the Latter-day Saints to the Radical Reformation of the early modern period, incorporating fundamental strains of folk practice as well as occult piety, including faith healing and other forms of primal folk religion.

12. The class aspirations of the early Nation are delineated in E. U. Essien-Udom, *Black Nationalism: A Search for an Identity in America* (Chicago, 1962), 104–105, and Michael A. Gomez, *Black Crescent: The Experience and Legacy of African Muslims in the Americas* (New York, 2005), 281.

13. Arthur Huff Fauset, *Black Gods of the Metropolis: Negro Religious Cults of the Urban North* (1944; Philadelphia, 2001), 46–47, and "Moorish Science Temple of America," in *Religion, Society, and the Individual*, ed. J. Milton Yinger (New York, 1957), 498–507.

14. Fauset, *Black Gods of the Metropolis*, 42.

15. Arna Bontemps and Jack Conroy, *They Seek a City* (Garden City, N.J., 1945), 175. Several Internet versions of Ali's text now exist. See, e.g., Drew Ali, "The Holy Koran of the Moorish Science Temple of America," www.hermetic.com/bey/7koran.html (accessed October 10, 2009). The Black Nationalist Marcus Garvey developed an analogous set of distinctly racialized Christian doctrines in his African Orthodox Church that commanded followers to "erase the white gods from your hearts." Edmund Cronon, *Black Moses* (Madison, 1948), 179. On the influence of both Ali and Garvey on early Black Muslims, see Lincoln, *Black Muslims in America*, 62–63; Essien-Udom, *Black Nationalism*, 63.

16. Fauset, *Black Gods of the Metropolis*, 43, quoted without further citation.

17. Ibid., 43n3.

18. Essien-Udom, *Black Nationalism*, 35.

19. Bontemps and Conroy, *They Seek a City*, 177. But see Essien-Udom,

Black Nationalism, 35–36, pointing out that leaders of the Nation of Islam disputed any connection between themselves and the Moors by the early 1960s.

20. The brief and dramatic history of the Abyssinian movement in Chicago, for example, includes a riot following a parade in 1920 that culminated in the burning of two United States flags. Grover C. Redding, the apparent leader of the movement, described the flag burning as the fulfillment of a biblical prophecy, marking the end of three hundred years of servitude and the beginning of a movement to "lead the Ethiopian back to Africa. . . . The burning of the flag . . . was a symbol that Abyssinians are not wanted in this country. That was the sign the Bible spoke of"; quoted in Bontemps and Conroy, *They Seek a City,* 174.

21. Fard's teachings were transmitted and are remembered orally. The account was drawn primarily from the work of sociologist Erdmann Beynon, "Voodoo Cult," 900–901.

22. Joseph R. Washington, Jr., *Black Religion: The Negro and Christianity in the United States* (Lanham, 1984); M. Karenga, "Black Religion," in *African American Religious Studies,* ed. Gayraud S. Wilmore (Durham, 1995), 271–300.

23. Beynon, "Voodoo Cult," 902.

24. Sherman A. Jackson, *Islam and the Blackamerican: Looking Toward the Third Resurrection* (New York, 2005), 20.

25. Curtis, *Islam in Black America,* 64–67.

26. Ibid.; Gomez, *Black Crescent,* 282.

27. Beynon, "Voodoo Cult," 900. Jehovah's Witnesses of African American descent were present in significant numbers by the 1930s. For example, the plaintiff in the Supreme Court case *Jones v. City of Opelika* was black. 316 U.S. 584 (1942). Since the 1950s the percentage of American Witnesses who are black has been increasing. See "Jehovah's Witnesses: U.S.-Born Religious Society Attracts Increasing Number of Negro Converts," *Ebony* 6 (October 1951): 98. In 1993, 52 percent of Witnesses in the United States made the group the only larger American denomination that had a "minority majority," including significant African American and Hispanic membership. Barry A. Kosmin and Seymour Lachman, *One Nation under God: Religion in Contemporary American Society* (New York, 1993), 35. By 2001, a similar survey placed the number at 37 percent African American. Barry A. Kosmin and Egon Mayer, *American Religions Identification Survey* (New York, 2001), 35. See also Jerry Bergman, "Jehovah's Witnesses, Blacks and Discrimination," http://seanet.com/~raines/discrimination.html; Firpo W. Carr, *A His-*

tory of Jehovah Witnesses: From a Black American Perspective (Hawthorne, Calif., 1993); Morley Cole, "Jehovah's Witnesses: Religion and Racial Integration," *The Crisis,* April 1953, 205–211.

28. Joseph F. Rutherford, *Riches* (Brooklyn, 1936), 294; Elijah Muhammad, *Message to the Blackman in America* (Chicago, 1965), 82–83, 247.

29. See, e.g., Joseph F. Rutherford, *Jehovah* (Brooklyn, 1934), 12; Muhammad, *Message to the Blackman,* 32, 210–211; William A. Maesen, "Watchtower Influences on Black Muslim Eschatology: An Exploratory Story," *Journal of the Scientific Study of Religion* 9 (Winter 1970): 321–325, 322; Bloom, *The American Religion,* 165–170 (on Witness eschatology).

30. Joseph F. Rutherford, *The Harp of God* (Brooklyn, 1921), 239; Muhammad, *Message to the Blackman,* 46.

31. Joseph F. Rutherford, *Deliverance* (Brooklyn, 1926), 271; Muhammad, *Message to the Blackman,* 45.

32. Clegg, *An Original Man,* 72–73.

33. These two estimates are drawn, respectively, from the Detroit Police Department and the Nation of Islam. See Beynon, "Voodoo Cult," 897 and n. 10.

34. Evanzz, *The Messenger,* 404–406.

35. Ibid., 84–91.

36. Clegg, *An Original Man;* Curtis, *Islam in Black America.*

37. Muhammad, *Message to the Blackman,* 241.

38. Curtis, *Islam in Black America,* 72.

39. *Black's Law Dictionary,* 6th ed. (St. Paul, 1991), 945.

40. See Ernest Allen, Jr., "When Japan Was 'Champion of the Darker Races'": Satokota Takahashi and the Flowering of Black Messianic Nationalism," *Black Scholar* 24 (Winter 1994): 23–46, 38–39.

41. Federal Bureau of Investigation, "Survey of Racial Conditions in the United States" (Washington, D.C., 1943), quoted in Allen, "When Japan Was 'Champion of the Darker Races,'" 37.

42. "Cultists 'Guilty'; 32 Given Jail Sentences," *Chicago Defender,* October 10, 1942, 1, 5, quoted in Clegg, *An Original Man,* 92 and 307n11.

43. "Sedition: Race Hate Used by Tokio [*sic*] to Lure 85 Nabbed by FBI," *Chicago Defender,* September 26, 1942, 4; "12 Negro Chiefs Seized by FBI in Sedition Raids," *Chicago Tribune,* September 22, 1942, 9; "Five Who Urged Revolt in Harlem and Aid to Japan Are Indicted," *New York Times,* September 15, 1942, 1.

44. Sultan Muhammad to Elijah Muhammad, December 9, 1941, quoted in Evanzz, *The Messenger,* 134 (citation to FBI file on Elijah Muhammad, section 2, 40–41).

45. Clegg, *An Original Man,* 91.

46. Gunnar Myrdal, *An American Dilemma* (New York, 1944), 1133.

47. Essien-Udom, *Black Nationalism,* 68. For a similar sense about those who had served prison time among Jehovah's Witnesses, see Barbara G. Harrison, *Visions of Glory: A History and Memory of Jehovah's Witnesses* (New York, 1978), 198: "When they returned, it was as if bas-reliefs representing virtue, allegiance, and integrity had sprung to life and moved. Having been in prison lent them an aura of moral authority. We expected that their deprivations had increased their wisdom and spirituality; their suffering had made them glamorous. And sexy."

48. Essien-Udom, *Black Nationalism,* 68; Clegg, *An Original Man,* 98; Curtis, *Islam in Black America,* 72–73.

49. J. B. Tietz, "Jehovah's Witnesses: Conscientious Objectors," *Southern California Law Review* 28 (February 1955): 123–138, 123n2; *Federal Prisons* (Washington, D.C., 1946).

50. Mulford Q. Sibley and Philip E. Jacob, *Conscription of Conscience: The American State and the Conscientious Objector, 1940–1947* (Ithaca, N.Y., 1952), 401–409.

51. On the Witnesses and conscientious objection, see J. B. Tietz, "Jehovah's Witnesses: Conscientious Objectors," *Southern California Law Review* 28 (February 1955): 123–137; Nathan Eliff, "Jehovah's Witnesses and the Selective Service," *Virginia Law Review* 31 (1945): 811–834.

52. Clegg, *An Original Man,* 72–73; Harrison, *Visions of Glory,* 173–178.

53. Mulford Sibley and Ada Wardlaw, *Conscientious Objectors in Prison, 1940–1945* (Philadelphia, 1945), 25–26.

54. James B. Jacobs, "Stratification and Conflict among Prison Inmates," *Journal of Criminal Law and Criminology* 66 (December 1975): 476–482, 478; Sibley and Jacob, *Conscription of Conscience,* 357.

55. *Kelly v. Dowd,* 140 F.2d 81, 82 (7th Cir. 1944).

56. Evanzz, *The Messenger,* 117–118; W. D. Muhammad, *As the Light Shineth from the East* (Chicago, 1980), 19.

57. Evanzz, *The Messenger,* 118.

58. Clegg, *An Original Man,* 304n57; Elijah Muhammad, *The Fall of America* (1937; Phoenix, 1997), 57, 165; Muhammad, *Message to the Blackman,* 323.

59. See Maesen, "Watchtower Influences," 321: "An informant told me that many Black Muslims are aware of the resemblances between the two, since the influences are often topics in the question-answer sessions of at least one Black Muslim Mosque of Islam. Furthermore the fact that Black Muslims explicitly and vehemently deny any causal relationship implies at least their recognition of the possibility of such influence."

60. Firpo W. Carr, *Jehovah's Witnesses: The African American Enigma* (Kearney, Neb., 2002), 81–84. Such a rekindled alliance seems unlikely, as Muslims have long been critical of Witness beliefs and practices adopted after Rutherford's death in 1942, such as the prohibition of blood transfusions, which developed during the late 1940s. See, e.g., "Noted Black Surgeon Charges Unscientific Christian Creeds Doom Millions to Needless Death," *Muhammad Speaks,* September 2, 1966, 7–8. See also Maesen, "Watchtower Influences," 323–324.

61. Maesen, "Watchtower Influences," 321.

62. On Muslim separatism, see *Pierce v. LaVallee,* 212 F.Supp. 865, 866 (N.D.N.Y. 1962).

63. See., e.g., Clegg, *An Original Man,* 96.

64. Sibley and Wardlaw, *Conscientious Objectors in Prison,* 12.

65. Lincoln, *Black Muslims in America.*

66. Harrison, *Visions of Glory,* 206, quoted without further attribution.

67. Ibid.

68. Malcolm X with Alex Haley, *The Autobiography of Malcolm X* (New York, 1965), 174.

69. Ibid., 187.

70. Ibid., 195, 199, 211.

71. Ibid., 191, 193.

72. Muhammad, *Message to the Blackman,* 111–117.

73. Elijah Muhammad, *Theology of Time,* Book 3 (1972; Charlotte, 1992), 191, 209; Muhammad, *Message to the Blackman,* 269; Gomez, *Black Crescent,* 312–313.

74. Muhammad, *Message to the Blackman,* 19–20.

75. Alex Hayley, *The Playboy Interviews* (New York, 1993), 33–34.

76. Elijah Muhammad himself had a mixed racial ancestry, and was light skinned and almond eyed. Essien-Udom, *Black Nationalism,* 75. On racial mixing and the Nation, see Gomez, *Black Crescent,* 314–315.

77. See, e.g., "Muslims Win Far-Reaching Court Verdict on Religious Freedom," *Muhammad Speaks* 1, no. 2 (December 1961): 3; "Monroe Case Nov. & Dec.," *Muhammad Speaks* 1, no. 1 (October-November 1961): 12; "Jail Official Admits Islam Benefits Prisoners," *Muhammad Speaks* 2, no. 4 (November 15, 1962): 3; "Blame N.Y. State for Leg Irons, Chains, Handcuffs on Muslims at Buffalo Trial," *Muhammad Speaks* 2, no. 8 (January 15, 1963): 18; "Goes to Jail But Comes Out—Fighting!" *Muhammad Speaks* 3, no. 14 (April 10, 1964): 18; "Muhammad's People Belong in Paradise, Not Prisons," *Muhammad Speaks* 4, no. 22 (April 23, 1965): 9.

78. Con. Lincoln, *Black Muslims in America,* e.g., who saw the Nation primarily as a political group. But see Jacobs, "Stratification and Conflict";

Curtis, *Black Muslim Religion;* Clegg, *An Original Man,* all of whom argue that the religious motives were central and defining.

79. See, e.g., Harrison, *Visions of Glory,* 198–201, noting Jehovah's Witnesses' aloofness, sense of superiority, and self-isolation, from an interview with Jim Peck and Ralph diGia, pacifists on the staff of the War Resisters League, who were imprisoned at the Danbury, Connecticut, federal prison. Witnesses made up almost 50 percent of the draft violators in the Danbury prison.

80. Ronald Berkman, *Opening the Gates: The Rise of the Prisoners' Movement* (Lexington, Mass., 1979), 53.

81. *Estep v. United States,* 326 U.S. 114 (1946); *Dickinson v. United States,* 346 U.S. 389 (1951); *Hull v. Stalter,* 151 F.2d 633 (9th Cir., 1945).

82. See Curtis, *Black Muslim Religion.*

83. "Prisoner Group Held Anti-White," *New York Times,* October 31, 1959, 48.

84. Lawrence O'Kane, "Muslim Negroes Suing the State," *New York Times,* March 18, 1961, 1.

85. *Ruffin v. Commonwealth,* 62 Va. 790, 793 (1871).

86. Berkman, *Opening the Gates,* 39, 72n16; John Irwin, *The Felon* (Englewood Cliffs, 1970).

87. Berkman, *Opening the Gates,* 38.

88. Gresham M. Sykes, *Society of Captives: A Study of a Maximum Security Prison* (Princeton, 1958), 63–83.

89. Donald R. Cressey, "Foreword," in *The Prison Community,* ed. Donald Clemmer (New York, 1958), 59.

90. Ibid.; Jacobs, "Stratification and Conflict," 476–482, 478.

91. Eugen Kogon, *The Theory and Practice of Hell: The German Concentration Camps and the System behind Them,* trans. Heinz Norden (New York, 1950), 43.

92. See, e.g., Marie Gottschalk, *The Prison and the Gallows: The Politics of Mass Incarceration in America* (New York, 2006), 176.

93. Eric Cummins, *The Rise and Fall of California's Radical Prison Movement* (Stanford, 1994), 65. Within prison populations, the increase in recruitment by the Nation of Islam increased racial polarization. At the same time, the Muslim prisoners, who distinguished sharply between political and spiritual worlds as well as between races, did not generally become politically active. Instead, they confined their activism to protecting their religious practice, especially through litigation. Such internal discipline had unlooked-for benefits from the perspective of prison administrators. Berkman, *Opening the Gates,* 52–55; Andrea D. Sullivan, "The Effect of the Nation of Islam upon the Prison Inmate Culture," Ph.D. diss., University of Pennsylvania, 1976.

94. John Pallas and Robert Barber, "From Riot to Revolution," in *The Politics of Punishment: A Critical Analysis of Prisons in America,* ed. Erik Olin Wright (New York, 1973), 243–247; Gottschalk, *The Prison and the Gallows,* 174.

95. *Brown v. Board of Education,* 347 U.S. 483 (1954).

96. See, e.g., Malcolm Feeley and Edward Rubin, *Judicial Policy Making and the Modern State* (Cambridge, 1998), 37.

97. Essien-Udom, *Black Nationalism,* 383, quoting *Jet,* November 5, 1959, 6.

98. Ibid., 306, quoting "Mr. Muhammad Speaks," *Los Angeles Herald-Dispatch,* November 21, 1959, 2.

99. See, e.g., *In re Ferguson,* 361 P.2 417 (Calif. 1961); *Sewell v. Pegelow,* 291 F.2d 196 (4th Cir. 1961); *Roberts v. Pegelow,* 313 F.2d 487 (4th Cir. 1963); *Coleman v. District of Columbia Commissioners,* 234 F. Supp. 408 (E.D. Va. 1964); *Banks v. Havener,* 234 F.Supp. 27 (E.D. Va. 1964); *Cooper v. Pate,* 324 F.2d 165 (7th Cir. 1963), *rev'd,* 378 U.S. 546 (1964); *Knuckles v. Prasse,* 302 F.Supp. 1036 (E.D. Pa. 1969).

100. *Pierce v. LaVallee,* 293 F.2d 233 (2d Cir., 1961).

101. Ibid., 235.

102. *Kelly v. Dowd,* 140 F.2d 81, 82 (7th Cir., 1944).

103. *Pierce v. LaVallee,* 293 F.2d, 235.

104. *Cooper v. Pate,* 324 F.2d 165 (7th Cir., 1963), *rev'd* 378 U.S. 546 (1964), citing *Pierce v. LaVallee.*

105. *Brown v. McGinnis,* 10 N.Y.2d 531, 180 N.E.2d 791 (1962).

106. 180 N.E.2d, 791.

107. Ibid., 792.

108. Ibid., 793.

109. Ibid., 794, (dissent of Justices Dye, Van Voorhis, and Burke, saying only that a prison "warden is not required to supply clergymen of every conceivable denomination or sect under all circumstances").

110. *Pierce v. LaVallee,* 212 F.Supp. 865, 866 (N.D.N.Y. 1962).

111. Ibid., 870–872.

112. For a secular counterpart to this religiously motivated constitution, see Bruce H. Mann, *Republic of Debtors: Bankruptcy in the Age of American Independence* (Cambridge, Mass., 2002), 147–165.

113. The phrase is drawn from John Phillip Reid's work on "law-mindedness," which he says traveled west with the wagon trains on the Overland Trail in the late 1840s and early 1850s. See Reid, *Law for the Elephant: Property and Social Behavior on the Overland Trail* (San Marino, Calif., 1980).

114. See Hendrik Hartog, "The Constitution of Aspiration and 'The Rights That Belong to Us All,'" *Journal of American History* 74 (December 1987): 1013–1034, 1016–1020.

115. Eric Foner, "Rights and the Constitution in Black Life during the Civil

War and Reconstruction," *Journal of American History* 74 (December 1987), 863–883.

116. See Jackson, *Islam and the Blackamerican*, 4, 17–18, 91–92.

117. Jan Shipps, "Remembering, Recovering, and Investing What Being a People of God Means: Reflections on Method in the Scholarly Writing of Religious History," in *Sojourner in the Promised Land: Forty Years Among the Mormons* (Urbana, 2000), 174–175.

118. R. Laurence Moore, "Insiders and Outsiders in American Historical Narrative and American History," *American Historical Review* 87 (April 1982): 397.

119. The Nation shared this commitment also with Christian Fundamentalists of the same era, who embraced the Book of Revelation's prophecy that a "small remnant" of true believers would preserve the faith in the last days. George Marsden, *Fundamentalism and American Culture*, 2nd ed. (New York, 2006), 43–48, discussing the "paradox" of a revivalist fundamentalism dedicated to outsider status.

120. For an argument that black Christianity is superficially Christian but more importantly "Blackamerican," see Jackson, *Islam and the Blackamerican*, 35–37. For anti–Martin Luther King rhetoric, see, e.g., Muhammad, *Message to the Blackman*, 240–242.

121. Lincoln, *Black Muslims*, 147.

122. *Pierce v. LaVallee*, 212 F.Supp., 869.

123. Ibid., 868n1.

124. Ibid., 868n2.

125. "Judge Paul R. Hays Is Dead at 76; Joined in Pentagon Papers Ruling," *New York Times*, February 15, 1980, D17.

126. *Sostre v. McGinnis*, 334 F.2d 906, 908 (2d Cir., 1964).

127. "Right to Practice Black Muslim Tenets in State Prisons," *Harvard Law Review* 75 (February 1962): 837–840; "Black Muslims in Prison: Of Muslim Rites and Constitutional Rights," *Columbia Law Review* 62 (December 1962): 1488–1504; "Discretion of Director of Corrections Not Abused in Refusing to Grant Black Muslim Prisoners Rights Afforded Other Religious Groups," *UCLA Law Review* 9 (March 1962): 501–509. Lincoln, *Black Muslims in America;* Essien-Udom, *Black Nationalism;* Louis E. Lomax, *When the Word Is Given: A Report on Elijah Muhammad, Malcolm X, and the Black Muslim World* (New York, 1963).

128. *In re Ferguson*, 301 P.2d 417, 422 (Cal. 1961). See also *In re Jones*, 372 P.2d 478 (Cal. 1962)

129. "Black Muslims in Prison," *Columbia Law Review*, 1503–1504.

130. *Sostre v. McGinnis*, 334 F.2d, 910.

131. Ibid., 909–911.

132. Ibid., 911–912. *Brown v. McGinnis*, 180 N.E.2d, 793 (1962), ordered the

Commission of Corrections to draft such "reasonable rules and regulations . . . as are 'consistent with the proper discipline and management of the institution'" under Section 610 of the Correction Law for the State of New York.

133. *Bryant v. Wilkins,* 45 Misc. 923, 258 N.Y.S.2d 455 (Sup. 1965), *rev'd* 24 A.D.2d 1077, 265 N.Y.S.2d 995 (4th Div., 1965).

134. 265 N.Y.S.2d, 996.

135. *SaMarion v. McGinnis,* 253 F. Supp. 738 (W.D.N.Y. 1966).

136. *In the Matter of the Applications of Freddie X. Youngblood, et al.,* Civ. 9395, Slip op., 3 (W.D.N.Y. September 20, 1966); *In the Matter of the Application of Jimmy X. Scott,* Civ. 9395, Slip op., 2–3 (W.D.N.Y. October 19, 1966).

137. *SaMarion v. McGinnis,* 35 A.D.2d 684, 314 N.Y.S.2d 715 (4th Div., 1970).

138. *Bryant v. McGinnis,* 364 F. Supp. 373, 387–88 (W.D.N.Y. 1978). The rollback in prisoners' rights that began in the 1980s featured Muslims prominently. See, e.g., *O'Lone v. Estate of Shabazz,* 482 U.S. 342 (1987), reversing Third Circuit opinion that held prison officials must establish that no reasonable method of accommodating Islamic rituals exists to sustain infringement.

139. See, e.g., Curtis, *Islam in Black America,* 94–95.

140. Karl Evanzz, *The Judas Factor: The Plot to Kill Malcolm X* (New York, 1992).

141. "Ex-Sweetheart of Malcolm X Accuses Elijah," *Amsterdam News,* July 11, 1964, 1.

142. Malcolm X, *Autobiography of Malcolm X,* 357.

143. Clegg, *An Original Man,* 222–224; Curtis, *Islam in Black America,* 109–113.

144. Curtis, *Islam in Black America,* 113–117.

145. Warrith Muhammad (formerly Wallace) and Louis Farrakhan embraced at the 2000 Savior's Day event, signaling a reconciliation between the two major branches of the Nation of Islam legacy. Southern Poverty Law Center, as of 2009, still maintained the Nation of Islam on its list of active hate groups in the U.S.; www.splcenter.org (accessed November 4, 2009).

146. James B. Jacobs, "The Prisoners' Rights Movement and Its Impacts, 1960–80," *Crime and Justice* 2 (1980): 429–470, 429–440; Gottschalk, *The Prison and the Gallows,* 175–176.

147. David Vidal, "The Prison Attorney: Martin Sostre," *New York Times,* December 25, 1975, 18. *U.S. ex rel. Sostre v. Festa,* 513 F.2d 1313 (2d Cir. 1975).

148. *Sostre v. Rockefeller,* 312 F. Supp. 863, 866 (S.D.N.Y. 1969).

149. Ibid., 868.

150. Ibid., 884–887.

151. Craig B. Whitney, "U.S. Writ Blamed in Prison Unrest," *New York Times*, June 13, 1970, 33.

152. *Sostre v. McGinnis*, 442 F.2d 178 (2d Cir. 1971), *cert. denied* 92 S. Ct. 719 (1971), reversing in part *Sostre v. Rockefeller*, 312 F. Supp. 863 (S.D.N.Y. 1970).

153. Quoted in *Sostre v. McGinnis*, 189.

154. Ibid., 181. For a review of the case, see Herman Schwartz, "A Comment on *Sostre v. McGinnis*," *Buffalo Law Review* 21 (Spring 1971–72): 775–798.

155. Vincent Copeland, *The Crime of Martin Sostre* (New York, 1970). *Frame Up! The Imprisonment of Martin Sostre*, Pacific Street Films (1974).

156. Vidal, "The Prison Attorney," 18.

157. "Free at Last," *New York Times*, December 28, 1975, personal ad.

Sostre was hired as an aide by Manhattan Democratic councilwoman Marie Runyon. He has faded from view but was the subject of a criminal prosecution in 1987. He was acquitted of attempted murder when the friend of a recently evicted tenant in the apartment building where Sostre worked broke into the building and, Sostre claimed, threatened him with a gun. The two struggled for the gun, he said, which went off accidentally. "Civil Rights Leader Is Acquitted," *New York Times*, June 18, 1987, B2.

158. See, e.g., Clegg, *An Original Man*, 210–212.

159. Evanzz, *The Messenger*, 286–287; Thomas Hauser, *Muhammad Ali: His Life and Times* (New York, 1991).

160. Clegg, *An Original Man*, 353.

161. Bob Woodward and Carl Bernstein, *The Brethren: Inside the Supreme Court* (New York, 1979), 137.

162. *Clay v. United States*, 397 F.2d 901, 918 (5th Cir. 1968).

163. Ibid.

164. Jennifer Jacobs Henderson, "Hayden Covington, the Jehovah's Witnesses and Their Plan to Expand First Amendment Freedoms," Ph.D. diss., University of Washington, 2002, 80.

165. Michael Meltsner, "Me and Muhammad," *Marquette Sports Law Review* 12 (Spring 2002): 583–592, 585–586.

166. "Clay Hires Expert Draft Lawyer," *New York Times*, August 9, 1966, 40; Henderson, "Hayden Covington," 80.

167. Quoted without further attribution in David Remnick, *King of the World: Muhammad Ali and the Rise of an American Hero* (New York, 1998), 289.

168. Quoted without further attribution in ibid., 291.

169. See, e.g., the collection of comments in Thomas Hauser, *Muhammad Ali: His Life and Times* (New York, 1991), 170ff.

170. Martin Waldron, "Clay Is Convicted on Draft Charge," *New York Times,* June 21, 1967, 1.

171. Ibid.

172. Henderson, "Hayden Covington," 80, citing an unpublished interview between Henderson and Witness author Jerry Bergman, May 18, 2002, Montpelier, Ohio; Don Atyeo and Felix Dennia, *The Holy Warrior: Muhammad Ali* (New York, 1975), 73: "Covington filed a $250,000 suit for unpaid salary." Ali's acknowledgment of Covington quoted from Muhammad Ali, *The Greatest: My Own Story* (New York, 1975), 174–175.

173. See Meltsner, "Me and Muhammad," 589–591; "Clay's Plea Gets A.C.L.U.'s Backing," *New York Times,* December 26, 1967, 42.

174. Gerald Early, *Culture of Bruising: Essays on Prizefighting, Literature and American Culture* (Hopewell, N.J., 1994); Remnick, *King of the World,* 291.

175. *Clay v. United States,* 403 U.S. 698, 702–703 (1971).

176. Ibid., 702, quoting from the Department of Justice letter.

177. Ibid., 704.

178. See the various versions of the story in Woodward and Bernstein, *The Brethren,* 162–165; Hauser, *Muhammad Ali,* 238–240.

179. For a detailed account of the riot and its bloody suppression, see Tom Wicker, *A Time to Die* (New York, 1975).

180. George Jackson, *Blood in My Eye* (London, 1972), 119.

181. New York State Special Commission on Attica, *Attica: The Official Report* (New York, 1972), 130–149.

182. Richard X. Clark, *The Brothers of Attica* (New York, 1973), 34, 73–74.

183. Ibid.

184. Bert Useen and Peter A. Kimball, "A Theory of Prison Riots," *Theory and Society* 16 (January 1987): 97.

185. Recent cases in federal courts, for example, have established that prisoner-run religious groups may include atheists, Wiccans, and Satanists, among others. *Cutter v. Wilkinson,* 544 U.S. 709 (2005) (Satanist, Wiccan, Asatru, and Church of Jesus Christ Christian); *Kaufman v. McCaughtry,* 419 F.3d 678 (7th Cir. 2005) (atheist).

186. An astute scholar of religion observed recently that "Americans are unusual . . . in the extent to which they profess attachment to religious beliefs and in the high rate at which they incarcerate their fellows." Winnifred Fallers Sullivan, *Prison Religion: Faith-Based Reform and the Constitution* (Princeton, 2009), 2.

187. Charles W. Colson, *Born Again* (Grand Rapids, Mich., 1976).

188. Gottschalk, *The Prison and the Gallows,* 41–76; David Garland, ed., *Mass Imprisonment: Social Causes and Consequences* (London, 2001).

189. Colson, *Born Again,* 326.
190. Ibid., 324–329.
191. For a detailed exploration of Colson's theory of just punishment, see Sullivan, *Prison Religion,* 101–111.
192. According to the Evangelical Council for Financial Accountability, Prison Fellowship Ministries has an annual operating budget of approximately $50 million and an organization of 40,000 volunteers. Evangelical Counsel for Financial Accountability, "Prison Fellowship Ministries," www.ecfa.org (accessed August 6, 2008).
193. See "About Chuck Colson," www.pfm.org (accessed August 5, 2008). On the role of Colson's Prison Fellowship Ministry (PFM) in recent "faith-based initiative" work by government, see *Americans United for Separation of Church and State v. InnerChange Freedom Initiative,* 432 F. Supp. 2d 863 (S.D. Iowa 2006), *aff'd in part, rev'd in part,* 509 F.3d 406 (8th Cir. 2007), *on remand,* 555 F. Supp. 2d 988 (S.D. Iowa 2008).
194. Colson, *Born Again,* 342–343. Control of prisoners' access to religious materials remains a goal of many prison officials. See, e.g., Laurie Goodstein, "Prisons Purging Books on Faith from Libraries," *New York Times,* September 10, 2007, www.nytimes.com/2007/09/10/us/prison .html (accessed October 9, 2009). Protests from religious groups, including Colson's PFM, forced the federal Bureau of Prisons to restore books removed from prison libraries under the bureau's nationwide Chapel Library Project.
195. Clifton E. Marsh, *From Black Muslims to Muslims: The Transition from Separatism to Islam, 1930–1980* (Metuchen, 1984); Jackson, *Islam and the Blackamerican,* 47–57, 132–152.
196. For a (PFM-funded) report that concludes that Colson's program is effective in helping inmates and newly released prisoners, see Byron R. Johnson and David B. Larson, *The InnerChange Freedom Initiative: A Preliminary Evaluation of a Faith-Based Prison Program* (Philadelphia, 2003); Tony Carnes, "Study Lauds Prison Program," *Christianity Today,* June 1, 2003, www.christianitytoday.com/ct/2003/juneweb-only/6–16 –43.0.html (accessed October 6, 2009).

5. Holy War

1. Beverly LaHaye, *Who But a Woman?* (Nashville, 1984), 133.
2. Ibid., 13.
3. LaHaye and other conservative theorists used the terms "secularism," "humanism," and eventually "secular humanism" interchangeably.
4. Concerned Women for America, *How to Lobby from Your Kitchen Ta-*

ble (pamphlet, n.d.); www.cwfa.org/brochures/index.asp (accessed August 9, 2008). LaHaye, *Who But a Woman?* 124–126.

5. Randall W. Balmer, *Mine Eyes Have Seen the Glory: A Journey into the Evangelical Subculture in America,* 3rd ed. (Oxford, 1989), 158, quoting Maxine Sieleman, CWA Iowa chapter leader.

6. See LaHaye, *Who But a Woman?* 29–30.

7. "Communications Department: Keeping CWA in the News," *Concerned Women for America News* 11, no. 7 (July 1989): 15, citing a membership of 600,000, up from 500,000 in 1986). In the 1980s, estimates placed the Eagle Forum at approximately 60,000. Donald T. Critchlow, *Phyllis Schlafly and Grassroots Conservatism: A Woman's Crusade* (Princeton, 2005), 221.

8. CWA claimed to receive most of its financial support from individuals but acknowledged funding from Pepsico, Levi Strauss and Company, Avon, American Express, Subaru, and Sun Company. *Concerned Women for America News* 11, no. 7 (July 1989): 15. Sara Diamond, *Spiritual Warfare: The Politics of the Christian Right* (Boston, 1989), 107.

9. Quoted in Susan Faludi, *Backlash: The Undeclared War against American Women* (New York, 1991), 253.

10. Three excellent studies have begun to piece together the conservative legal and religious worlds that are studied from a different angle here. See Steven M. Teles, *The Rise of the Conservative Legal Movement: The Battle for the Control of the Law* (Princeton, 2008); R. Jonathan Moore, *Suing for America's Soul: John Whitehead, the Rutherford Institute and Conservative Christians in the Courts* (Grand Rapids, Mich., 2007); Steven Brown, *Trumping Religion: The Christian Right, the Free Speech Clause and the Courts* (Tuscaloosa, 2004). The legal work of CWA, and CWA itself for that matter, have flown under scholars' radar. LaHaye's organization was unique in its dedication to litigation of conservative evangelical women's issues.

11. Lisa McGirr, *Suburban Warriors: The Origins of the New American Right* (Princeton, 2001); George Marsden, "The Sword of the Lord," *Books and Culture* (March/April 2006): 10–45.

12. Tim and Beverly LaHaye, *The Act of Marriage* (Grand Rapids, Mich., 1976).

13. Alex Comfort, *The Joy of Sex: A Gourmet Guide* (New York, 1972).

14. Leo Ribuffo, "Why Is There So Much Conservatism in the United States and Why Do So Few Historians Know Anything about It?" *American Historical Review* 99 (April 1994): 409–429; John A. Andrew III, *The Other Side of the Sixties: Young Americans for Freedom and the Rise of Conservative Politics* (New Brunswick, N.J., 1997); Rebecca Klatch, *A Generation*

Divided: The New Left, the New Right and the 1960s (Berkeley, 1999); Robert S. Ellwood, *The Sixties Spiritual Awakening: American Religion Moving from Modern to Postmodern* (New Brunswick, N.J., 1994), 6–36, 326–336; Ronald B. Flowers, *Religion in Strange Times: The 1960s and 1970s* (Macon, 1984), 31–60, 199–230.

15. Beverly LaHaye, *The Spirit-Controlled Woman* (Irvine, 1976), 73.

16. Faludi, *Backlash*, 250.

17. Paul Boyer, "The Evangelical Resurgence in 1970s American Protestantism," in *Rightward Bound: Making America Conservative in the 1970s*, ed. Bruce J. Schulman and Julian E. Zelizer (Cambridge, Mass., 2008), 29–51; Sara Diamond, *Roads to Dominion: Right-Wing Movements and Political Power in the United States* (New York, 1995), 5–6; Jerome L. Himmelstein, *To the Right: The Transformation of American Conservatism* (Berkeley, 1990), 97–99; McGirr, *Suburban Warriors*, 273.

18. Beverly LaHaye did not advocate a rigid pronatalism. Instead, she argued that "baby hunger" was natural and that enjoyment of sex was also natural. In *The Act of Marriage* (199–203), the LaHayes endorsed the use of (nonabortifacient) birth control, including "the Pill" and condoms. CWA's anti-abortion stance has been a hallmark of the organization: see www.cwfa.org/coreissues.asp, "sanctity of life" (accessed September 9, 2009); Teresa Mishler Kelly, "Questioning the Space between Feminists and Antifeminists: A Narrative Analysis of Two Social Movement Newsletters," Ph.D. diss., Wayne State University, 2001, 60–65. Cf. Shirley Rogers Radl, *The Invisible Woman: Targets of the New Religious Right* (New York, 1983), 168.

19. See generally Brenda E. Brasher, *Godly Women: Fundamentalism and Female Power* (New Brunswick, N.J., 1998).

20. For scholarly treatments of religion and conservative politics in the late twentieth century, see William Martin, *With God on Our Side: The Rise of the Religious Right in America* (New York, 1996); Diamond, *Roads to Dominion;* Ann Braude, "A Religious Feminist, Who Can Find Her? Historiographical Challenges from the National Organization for Women," *Journal of Religion* 84, no. 4 (October 2004): 555; James Davison Hunter, *Culture Wars: The Struggle to Define America* (New York, 1991); Christian Smith, *American Evangelicalism: Embattled and Thriving* (Chicago, 1998); Robert Wuthnow, *The Struggle for America's Soul: Evangelicals, Liberals, and Secularism* (Grand Rapids, Mich., 1989); Brasher, *Godly Women.*

21. LaHaye, *Who But a Woman?* 9, 23.

22. Ibid., 15, 116–117.

23. Ibid., 25. See also Beverly LaHaye, *I Am a Woman by God's Design* (Old

Tappan, N.J., 1980), www.cwfa.org/history.asp (accessed January 30, 2007); Balmer, *Mine Eyes Have Seen the Glory,* 156–175.

24. Balmer, *Mine Eyes Have Seen the Glory,* 158, quoting Maxine Sieleman.

25. Ibid., 157.

26. See Diane Winston, *Red-Hot and Righteous: The Urban Religion of the Salvation Army* (Cambridge, Mass., 1999), 82–85.

27. Sacvan Bercovitch, *The American Jeremiad* (Madison, 1978).

28. See Chapter 2. For other examples of spiritual warfare in the 1980s, see David Snowball, *Continuity and Change in the Rhetoric of the Moral Majority* (New York, 1991), 123–149, and Quin Sherrer and Ruthanne Garlock, *A Woman's Guide to Spiritual Warfare: A Woman's Guide for Battle* (Ann Arbor, 1991).

29. McGirr, *Suburban Warriors,* 217–273; George M. Marsden, *Fundamentalism and American Culture,* new ed. (Oxford, 2006), 236–243; James D. Hunter, *American Evangelicalism: Conservative Religion and the Quandary of Modernism* (New Brunswick, N.J., 1988); Clyde Wilcox, *God's Warriors: The Christian Right in Twentieth-Century America* (Baltimore, 1992).

30. Paul Harvey, *Freedom's Coming: Religion, Culture and the Shaping of the South from the Civil War through the Civil Rights Era* (Chapel Hill, 2005), 218–250.

31. Sarah Barringer Gordon, *The Mormon Question: Polygamy and Constitutional Conflict* (Chapel Hill, 2002), 233–234.

32. Laura Kalman, *Right Star Rising: A New Politics, 1974–1980* (New York, 2010), 271; Nancy F. Cott, *Public Vows: A History of Marriage and the Nation* (Cambridge, Mass., 2000), 213–221; Alan Crawford, *Thunder on the Right: The "New Right" and the Politics of Resentment* (New York, 1980), 146–159; Janna Hansen, "'The Role for Which God Created Them': Women in the United States Religious Right," senior thesis, Radcliffe College, 1997, 87–119.

33. Scholars and even some activists have begun to study conservative legal activism in the late twentieth century, and to connect this activism to religion. See, e.g., Steven M. Teles, *The Rise of the Conservative Legal Movement: The Battle for Control of the Law* (Princeton, 2008); Moore, *Suing for America's Soul;* Brown, *Trumping Religion;* Barry W. Lynn, *Piety and Politics: The Right-Wing Assault on Religious Freedom* (New York, 2006). The conservative legal work of women in general, and CWA in particular, has not been widely studied.

34. Joel Carpenter, *Revive Us Again: The Reawakening of American Fundamentalism* (Oxford, 1997), 234–235.

35. In a 1993 survey of CWA members, 65 percent of respondents identified themselves as Protestants, 23 percent as "other"; 10 percent identi-

fied themselves as Catholic. A 1996 survey found that 93 percent of all members were "Caucasian." Hansen, "The Role for Which God Created Them," 137. Scholarship on conservatism in the late twentieth century has begun to tease apart movements that had race and racial subordination at their core from those that focused more on opposing big government. Compare, for example, Joseph Crespino, *In Search of Another Country: Mississippi and the Conservative Counterrevolution* (Princeton, 2007), with Kim Phillips-Fein, *Invisible Hands: The Making of the Conservative Movement from the New Deal to Reagan* (New York, 2009). Recent analysis of conservative religion has tended to fall into the latter camp. See McGirr, *Suburban Warriors;* Marsden, "The Sword of the Lord," Neither LaHaye nor CWA was blatantly racist, nor was LaHaye openly anti-Semitic or even anti-Catholic. Yet the white and Protestant membership of CWA testifies to its appeal.

36. Betty Cuniverti, "Other Voices Crying Out against the Feminists," *Los Angeles Times,* October 2, 1985, D1. Nadine Brozan, "Politics and Prayer: Women on a Crusade," *New York Times,* June 15, 1987, C18; Critchlow, *Phyllis Schlafly,* 289–290.

37. Faludi, *Backlash,* 252–256; Hansen, "The Role for Which God Created Them," 38–70, www.cwfa.org/history (accessed January 30, 2007).

38. Cuniverti, "Other Voices," D8.

39. Hansen, "The Role for Which God Created Them," 89–90.

40. LaHaye, *Who But a Woman?* 60–61, 70. See also Michael Farris, "ERA: Only Three More States," *Concerned Women for America* [newsletter] 3 no. 6 (December 1981): 4.

41. LaHaye, *Who But a Woman?* 71.

42. Ibid., 77. Farris has been a prolific author as well as a litigator. See, e.g., Michael Farris, *Constitutional Law for Enlightened Citizens* (Purcellville, Va., 2006). Farris and Beverly LaHaye published a collection of prayers by congressional chaplains, titled *On This Day* (n.d.). He has also written pamphlets and monographs on home schooling and the law, tax-exempt organizations, and politics, and the mission statement of Patrick Henry University, which he founded: *Joshua Generation: Restoring the Heritage of Christian Leadership* (Nashville, 2005).

43. *Witters v. Commission for the Blind,* 102 Wash.2d 624, 689 P.2d 53 (1984).

44. *Witters v. Washington Dept of Services for the Blind,* 474 U.S. 481 (1986).

45. *Gregoire v. Centennial School District,* 907 F.2d 1366 (3d Cir. 1990); *Lamb's Chapel v. Center Moriches Union Free School District,* 508 U.S. 384 (1993).

46. Christian Smith, *Evangelical America? What Evangelicals Really Want* (Berkeley, 2000), 61–91.

47. Smith, *Evangelical America?* 55, 70. Most of those who agreed with the

statement, however, reported that they had not personally experienced such hostility.

48. On opposition to sex education, and the role of conservative women in opposing it, see Kristen Luker, *When Sex Goes to School: Warring Views on Sex—and Sex Education—Since the Sixties* (New York, 2006); McGirr, *Suburban Warriors,* 227–231.

49. LaHaye, *Who But a Woman?* 100.

50. Francis A. Schaeffer, *How Shall We Then Live?* (Old Tappan, N.J., 1976).

51. Ibid., 51–55, 121–124.

52. Francis A. Schaeffer and C. Everett Koop, *Whatever Happened to the Human Race?* (Old Tappan, N.J., 1979).

53. *Engel v. Vitale,* 370 U.S. 421 (1962); *Abington School District v. Schempp,* 374 U.S. 203 (1963).

54. Balmer, *Mine Eyes Have Seen the Glory,* 157, quoting Maxine Sieleman.

55. Tim LaHaye, *The Battle for the Mind* (Old Tappan, N.J., 1980). On the conservative takeover of the Southern Baptist Convention, see Barry Hankins, *Uneasy in Babylon: Southern Baptist Conservatives and American Culture* (Tuscaloosa, 2002); David Stricklin, *A Genealogy of Dissent: Southern Baptist Protest in the Twentieth Century* (Lexington, Ky., 1999), 149–57. On the Moral Majority and political activism among conservative Christians in the 1980s, see Susan Friend Harding, *The Book of Jerry Falwall: Fundamentalist Language and Politics* (Princeton, 2000).

56. Sectarianism, or the preference of one denomination over others, was the central target of POAU, studied extensively in Chapter 3. In many cases involving aid to religious schools, for example, courts inquired into whether the benefited institution was "pervasively sectarian." See, e.g., *Everson v. Board of Education,* 330 U.S. 1 (1947) (Jackson, J., dissenting): aid to Catholic school is "indistinguishable" from aid to the Church itself; *Roemer v. Board of Public Works of Maryland,* 426 U.S. 736 (1976): colleges with substantial institutional autonomy are not "pervasively sectarian."

57. T. Minnery, review of *The Battle for the Mind,* in *Christianity Today* 26 (May 7, 1982): 60–61; David Garrison, "Tim and Beverly LaHaye," in *Twentieth-Century Shapers of American Popular Religion,* ed. Charles Lippy (New York, 1989), 235.

58. LaHaye, *The Battle for the Mind,* 57–83 (chap. 4, "Humanism: The Wisdom of Man").

59. See www.americanhumanist.org/about/manifesto1.html (accessed October 1, 2009). Edwin H. Wilson, *The Genesis of a Humanist Manifesto* (Washington, D.C., 1995). A second Manifesto (1973) and a third (2003) have followed the first. In the late twentieth century the Ameri-

can Humanist Association claimed approximately 1,400 members. Edwin Scott Gaustad and Philip L. Barlow, *New Historical Atlas of Religion in America* (Oxford, 2001), 351. See also the Council for Secular Humanism, founded in 1980 by Paul Kurtz in Amherst, N.Y., www.secularhumanism.org (accessed October 1, 2009).

60. LaHaye, *The Battle for the Mind,* 92–93.

61. Ibid., 130, 138, 142.

62. Ibid., 137, 147; Schaeffer, *How Shall We Then Live?* 225.

63. Cf. Silk, *Spiritual Politics,* 171–172, arguing that secular humanism was a substitute for rather than a later manifestation of the anticommunist tradition in American religious thought.

64. LaHaye, *Who But a Woman?* 13.

65. Walter Johnson, ed., *The Papers of Adlai E. Stevenson* (Boston, 1974), 4:128, quoted in Silk, *Spiritual Politics,* 87.

66. Mildred Strunk, ed., "The Quarter's Polls," *Public Opinion Quarterly* 13 (1949–1950): 712. Seventy-seven percent of respondents did not agree that "a man can be a good Christian and at the same time be a member of the Communist Party."

67. John Foster Dulles, *War or Peace* (New York, 1950), 255–256.

68. William Hordern, *Christianity, Communism and History* (New York, 1954), 54–55. See also Walter Freitag, *Festschrift: a Tribute to Dr. William Hordern* (Saskatoon, 1985); Alexander Miller, *The Christian Significance of Karl Marx* (London, 1946).

69. Richard Crossman, ed., *The God That Failed: Six Famous Men Tell How They Changed Their Minds about Communism* (New York, 1949).

70. Hiss maintained his innocence until his death in 1996. See Alger Hiss, *In the Court of Public Opinion* (New York, 1957) and *Recollections of a Life* (London, 1988).

71. Allen Weinstein, *Perjury: The Hiss-Chambers Case* (New York, 1978).

72. Garry Wills, "The Honor of Alger Hiss," *New York Review of Books,* April, 20 1978, 25.

73. George Will, *Newsweek,* March 20, 1978, 96.

74. Quoted in Steven Haywood, *The Age of Reagan: The Fall of the Old Liberal Order, 1964–1980* (New York, 2001), 427; Kalman, *Right Star Rising,* 202. Melvyn P. Leffler, *For the Soul of Mankind: The United States, the Soviet Union and the Cold War* (New York, 2007), 259–288.

75. Kenneth E. Morris, *Jimmy Carter, American Moralist* (Athens, Ga., 1997), 266–267; Kalman, *Right Star Rising,* 264–285.

76. See Tim LaHaye, *The Battle for the Family: Humanism's Threat to Our Children* (Old Tappan, N.J., 1983).

77. Beverly LaHaye, *The Spirit-Controlled Woman* (Irvine, 1976). See also Ma-

rie Griffith, *God's Daughters: Evangelical Women and the Power of Submission* (Berkeley, 1997), 169–186.

78. LaHaye, *The Spirit-Controlled Woman,* 71–72, 72–73. See also Brenda E. Brasher, *Godly Women,* 148–152.

79. Leffler, *For the Soul of Mankind,* 281, quoting American foreign policy advisor Zbigniew Brzezinski.

80. LaHaye, *The Spirit-Controlled Woman,* 62.

81. See Hansen, "The Role for Which God Created Them," 48.

82. Margot Canaday, "Heterosexuality as a Legal Regime," in *Cambridge History of Law in America,* ed. Michael Grossberg and Christopher Tomlins, 3 vols. (Cambridge, 2008), 3:442–472.

83. LaHaye, *The Battle for the Mind,* 136, quoting James M. Parsons, *The Assault on the Family* (Melbourne, Fla., 1978), 10.

84. Balmer, *Mine Eyes Have Seen the Glory,* 158. Rhonda Dawn Schreiber, "'But Perhaps We Speak for You': Antifeminist Women's Organizations and the Representation of Political Interests," Ph.D. diss., Rutgers University, 2000, 110–115.

85. LaHaye, *The Battle for the Mind,* 217.

86. See Gayle White, "Evangelical Power Couple: Tim and Beverly LaHaye," *Atlanta Journal-Constitution,* July 7, 2001, B1.

87. Garrison, "Tim and Beverly LaHaye," 236. On Moon's courting of American religious leaders, especially conservative Christians, see Don Lattin, "The Moonies," *San Francisco Chronicle,* February 11, 2001, A1. See also Carlton Sherwood, *Inquisition: The Persecution and Prosecution of the Reverend Sun Myung Moon* (Washington, D.C., 1991).

88. R. Laurence Moore, *Selling God: American Religion in the Marketplace of Culture* (New York, 1994), 239–55; Razelle Frankl, *Televangelism: The Marketing of Popular Religion* (Carbondale, Ill., 1987); Steve Bruce, *Pray TV: Televangelism in America* (London, 1990).

89. Smith, *Evangelical America?* 15.

90. See, e.g., Silk, *Spiritual Politics,* 178–179.

91. See www.leftbehind.com (accessed August 3, 2009).

92. For the claim that CWA had broad appeal and religiously diverse membership that included a broad spectrum of Protestants and some Catholics, see Clyde Wilcox and Carin Larson, *Onward Christian Soldiers? The Religious Right in American Politics,* 3rd ed. (Boulder, 2006), 73–74. Cf. Hansen, "The Role for Which God Created Them," 135–138.

93. Faludi, *Backlash,* 252–253.

94. Garrison, "Tim and Beverly LaHaye," 237.

95. In two well-known conscientious-objector cases, for example, the Su-

preme Court held that idiosyncratic beliefs that did not include traditional elements of religion (such as a god or gods) qualified as religious for purposes of exemption from military service. *United States v. Seeger*, 380 U.S. 163 (1965); *Welsh v. United States*, 398 U.S. 333 (1970).

96. Note, "Toward a Constitutional Definition of Religion," *Harvard Law Review* 91 (March 1978): 1076, 1085.

97. See, e.g., *Sherbert v. Verner*, 374 U.S. 398, 414 (1963) (Stewart, J., concurring).

98. Ibid., 413.

99. See, e.g., Marc Galanter, "Religious Freedoms in the United States: A Turning Point?" *Wisconsin Law Review* 1966: 217, 265–268; Paul Freund, "Public Aid to Parochial Schools," *Harvard Law Review* 82 (1969): 1680, 1686–1687, n. 14; Note, "Toward a Constitutional Definition," 1085–1089.

100. Laurence H. Tribe, *American Constitutional Law* (Mineola, N.Y., 1978), section 14–16, 826–829.

101. *Malnak v. Yogi*, 592 F.2d 197, 212, 213 (3rd Cir. 1979) (Adams, J., concurring). See also *Everson v. Board of Education*, 330 U.S. 1, 32 (1947) (Rutledge, J., dissenting).

102. *Malnak v. Yogi; Africa v. Pennsylvania*, 662 F.2d 1025 (3rd Cir. 1981).

103. For a review of this pressure and the failure to resolve the definitional question, see Sarah Barringer Gordon, "The New Age and the New Law: *Malnak v. Yogi* and the Definition of Religion," in *Law and Religion: Cases in Context*, ed. Leslie Griffin (New York, 2010).

104. Tim LaHaye even wrote a follow-up to *The Battle for the Mind* directed explicitly to schools; see LaHaye, "The Religion of Secular Humanism," in *Public Schools and the First Amendment*, ed. Stanley M. Elam (Bloomington, 1983). See also Tim LaHaye, *The Battle for the Public Schools* (Old Tappan, N.J., 1983).

105. *Torcaso v. Watkins*, 367 U.S. 488, 495n11 (1961).

106. *Fellowship of Humanity v. Alameda County*, 153 Cal. App. 2d 673, 315 P.2d 394, 405–406, 409–410 (Cal. App., 1957); *Washington Ethical Society v. District of Columbia*, 249 F.2d 127, 128–129 (D.C. Cir. 1957). For more recent answers to the question see, e.g., the American Ethical Union Web site, aeu.org (accessed October 3, 2009).

107. On the Rutherford Institute, see www.rutherford.org/About/AboutUs.asp (accessed September 20, 2009); see also Moore, *Suing for America's Soul*, 37–68. On John Conlan, see bioguide.congress.gov/scripts/biodisplay (accessed September 20, 2009). John W. Whitehead and John Conlan, "The Establishment of the Religion of Secular Humanism and Its First

Amendment Implications," *Texas Tech Law Review* 10 (1979): 1, 61. See also Onalee McGraw, *Secular Humanism and the Schools: The Issue Whose Time Has Come* (Washington, D.C., 1976); Wendell Bird, Note, "Freedom of Religion and Science Instruction in Public Schools," *Yale Law Journal* 87 (1978): 515; Anand Agneshwar, "Rediscovering God in the Constitution," *New York University Law Review* 67 (1992): 205.

108. Whitehead and Conlan, "The Establishment of the Religion of Secular Humanism," 14–15.

109. Ibid., 34–36; Bird, "Freedom of Religion and Science Instruction," 524–525.

110. Whitehead and Conlan, "The Establishment of the Religion of Secular Humanism," 31.

111. Ibid., 55–56.

112. Ibid., 62–65.

113. LaHaye, *The Battle for the Mind*, 128–129; Francis Schaeffer, *A Christian Manifesto* (Westchester, Ill., 1981), 10–11, 36, 109–112.

114. LaHaye, *Who But a Woman?* 65, 79.

115. Ibid., 80.

116. Jack Nelson and Gene Roberts, Jr., *The Censors and the Schools* (Boston, 1973), 49.

117. National Education Association, *Inquiry Report, Kanawha County, West Virginia: A Textbook Study in Cultural Conflict* (Washington, D.C., 1975), 63–64; Kalman, *Right Star Rising*, 250–251.

118. See LaHaye, *The Battle for the Mind*, 141, listing ACLU, NEA, American Humanist Association, Ethical Culture Society, Sexuality Information and Education Council of the United States (SIECUS), National Organization for Women (NOW), and "unions" as indelibly humanist.

119. LaHaye, *Who But a Woman?* 82, 83.

120. Ibid., 85.

121. Ibid., 87.

122. Grove had apparently read a review by evangelical school and textbook critics Mel and Norma Gabler, who monitored materials for evidence of "humanism in textbooks"; see www.textbookreviews.org/index.html ?content=about.htm (accessed October 3, 2009); LaHaye, *Who But a Woman?* 91. See also Joan Delfattore, *What Johnny Shouldn't Read: Textbook Censorship in America* (New Haven, 1992), 138–166.

123. Ibid., 90.

124. *Grove v. Mead School District No. 354*, 753 F.2d 1528 (9th Cir. 1985).

125. Appellants' Brief, 49, quoted in *Grove*, 753 F.2d 1535.

126. *Grove*, 753 F.2d 1536.

127. Ibid., 1537.

128. Ibid., 1538, quoting Appellants' Brief, 44.

129. Ibid., 1539–1540.

130. The classic treatment is Richard Hofstadter, "The Paranoid Style in American Politics," *Harper's Magazine,* November 1964, 77–86.

131. Michael Schwalbe and Douglas Mason-Schrock, "Identity Work as Group Process," *Advances in Group Processes* 13 (1996): 113–147; Smith, *Evangelical America?* 56–57.

132. Smith, *Evangelical America?* 37–60; Alan Wolfe, *One Nation, After All* (New York, 1999), 39–87.

133. See, e.g., Bruce Dierenfield, *The Battle over School Prayer: How* Engel v. Vitale *Changed America* (Lawrence, Kans., 2007), 187–212; Rob Boston, "Forever and Ever Amen: The 30 Years' War over Prayer and Bible Reading in the Public School," *Church and State* 46 (June 1993): 7–10; Kenneth Dolbeare and Phillip Hammond, *The School Prayer Decisions: From Court Policy to Local Practice* (Chicago, 1971).

134. ABC News, "Public Schools in Conflict: A Question of Values" (1985). For a review and reprise of the special broadcast, see John Corry, "When TV Looks at Schools, the Lessons Can Be Murky," *New York Times,* November 10, 1985, H27. See also McGirr, *Suburban Warriors,* 227–231; Luker, *When Sex Goes to School.*

135. Crespino, *In Search of Another Country,* 248–256.

136. See, e.g., David Nevin and Robert E. Bills, *The Schools That Fear Built: Segregationist Academies in the South* (Washington, D.C., 1976); Joseph Crespino, "Civil Rights and the Religious Right," in *Rightward Bound: Making America Conservative in the 1970s,* ed. Bruce J. Schulman and Julian E. Zelizer (Cambridge, Mass., 2008), 90, 96–98.

137. Peter Kerry, "Christian Schools versus the IRS," *Public Interest* 61 (Fall 1980): 30–31; Martin, *With God on Our Side,* 173.

138. For an excellent discussion, see Crespino, "Civil Rights and the Religious Right," 102.

139. For a similar use of language of discrimination, see Sophia Z. Lee, "Whose Rights? Litigating the Right to Work," in *The American Right and U.S. Labor: Politics, Ideology, and Imagination,* ed. Nelson Lichtenstein (Philadelphia, forthcoming).

140. This suit was the latest in a long line of skirmishes between Bob Jones and tax officials. See *Bob Jones University v. Schultz,* (4th Cir. 1973); *Bob Jones University v. Simon,* 416 U.S. 725 (1974).

141. *New York Times,* January 31, 1980, B8. Aaron Haberman, "Into the Wilderness: Ronald Reagan, Bob Jones University, and the Political Education of the Christian Right," *The Historian* 67 (2005): 234, 244–245.

142. LaHaye, *The Battle for the Mind,* 10. As the *Bob Jones* litigation demon-

strated, "liberal" government was equated in much of conservative religious thought with both secularism and anti-religious discrimination by the late 1970s. The politics of race provided the subtext of such thought, even though many conservative religious leaders sought to distance themselves from the implications of their position.

143. 461 U.S. 574 (1983).

144. Ibid., 604. Even the lone dissenter, Associate Justice William Rehnquist, who maintained that only congressional legislation could validly change the definition of tax-exempt organizations to exclude Bob Jones and related institutions, agreed that such legislation would trump the religious interest, given the long-standing policy of the national government in favor of eradicating racial discrimination in all areas. Ibid., 622n3 (Rehnquist, J., dissenting).

145. Robert Dreyfuss, "Reverend Doomsday," *Rolling Stone,* February 19, 2004, 46–50; "Evangelicals in America," *Time,* January 30, 2005. Bob Jones repealed its interracial dating policy in 2000; www.bju.edu/welcome/who-we-are/race-statement.php (accessed October 4, 2009).

146. LaHaye, *Who But a Woman?* 110. LaHaye captured the distress of many observers outside the conservative ranks, as well. For a liberal law professor's interpretation of the ruling that shares much of LaHaye's dismay, see Robert M. Cover, "Foreword: Nomos and Narrative," *Harvard Law Review* 97 no. 1 (1983): 4, 60–68.

147. Dudley Clendinen, "Conservative Christians Again Take Issue of Religion in Schools to Courts," *New York Times,* February 28, 1986, A14.

148. LaHaye, *Who But a Woman?* 95–96.

149. Ibid., 93.

150. Clendinen, "Conservative Christians."

151. Stephen Bates, *Battleground: One Mother's Crusade, the Religious Right, and the Struggle for Our Schools* (New York, 1993), 66–67. See also Delfattore, *What Johnny Shouldn't Read,* 13–60.

152. *Grove v. Mead School District No. 354,* 753 F.2d 1528, 1533 (9th Cir. 1985); ibid., 1543 (Canby, J., concurring).

153. *Mozert v. Hawkins County Public Schools,* 647 F.Supp. 1194, 1196 (E.D. Tenn., 1986).

154. Delfattore, *What Johnny Shouldn't Read,* 29–30; Bates, *Battleground,* 124.

155. Quoted without further attribution in Bates, *Battleground,* 160.

156. *Mozert v. Hawkins County Public Schools,* 582 F.Supp. 201 (E.D. Tenn., 1984).

157. *Mozert v. Hawkins County Public Schools,* 765 F.2d 75 (6th Cir. 1985).

158. See, e.g., Alain L. Sanders, "Tilting at 'Secular Humanism': In Tennes-

see, a Modern Replay of the Celebrated 'Monkey Trial,'" *Time,* July 28, 1986, 68.

159. Dudley Clendinen, "Fundamentalists Win a Federal Suit over Schoolbooks," *New York Times,* October 25, 1986, 8, quoting Frost's testimony.

160. *Time,* July 28, 1986, 68, quoting N. R. Coleman, Jr.

161. Quoted in Connie Paige, "Watch on the Right: The Amazing Rise of Beverly LaHaye," *Ms.,* February 1987, 28.

162. Last two quotes come from the twenty-minute PAW documentary *Censorship in Our Schools* (1988).

163. Timothy Dyk is now a judge on the Federal Circuit Court of Appeals, having been nominated in 2000 by President Clinton, www.cafc.uscourts.gov/judgbios.html (accessed July 10, 2009).

164. Brozan, "Politics and Prayer," C18, quoting Podesta.

165. Ted Gest, "Media Bias, Sloppiness Mark 'Scopes II' Coverage," *St. Louis Journalism Review,* February 1987.

166. Betty Cuniberti, "Other Voices."

167. *Mozert,* 647 F.Supp. 1200.

168. Ibid., 1201.

169. Ibid., 1203.

170. "Fundamentalists Win Textbook Case in Tenn," *Atlanta Journal-Constitution,* October 25, 1986.

171. Editorial, "'Cinderella' in the Classroom," *Boston Globe,* October 28, 1986, 18; editorial, "Those Tennessee Books," *Baltimore Sun,* October 29, 1986, 10A.

172. C. Glennon Rowell, "Allowing Parents to 'Screen' Textbooks Would Lead to Anarchy in the Schools," *Chronicle of Higher Education,* November 26, 1986, 4.

173. Brozan, "Politics and Prayer," C18.

174. Ibid.

175. Cuniberti, "Other Voices," D8.

176. Parker quoted in Bates, *Battleground,* 149. Barbara Parker and Stephanie Weiss, *Protecting the Freedom to Learn: A Citizen's Guide* (Washington, D.C., 1983).

177. See site.pfaw.org/site/PageServer?pagename=issues_right_landing (accessed November 3, 2009).

178. Bates, *Battleground,* 149.

179. Oliver S. Thomas of the Baptist Joint Committee, quoted without further attribution in Bates, *Battleground,* 282.

180. Quoted in Bates, *Battleground,* 282.

181. Ibid., 283.

182. Ibid., 284.

183. *Jaffree v. Board of School Commissioners*, 554 F.Supp. 1104, 1118–1128 (S.D. Ala. 1983), *aff'd in part, rev'd in part and remanded with directions sub nom. Jaffree v. Wallace*, 705 F.2d 1526 (11th Cir. 1983), *aff'd*, 466 U.S. 924 (1984), *aff'd on other grounds sub nom. Wallace v. Jaffree*, 105 S.Ct. 2479 (1985).

184. *Jaffree v. James*, 544 F.Supp. 727, 732 (S.D. Ala. 1982).

185. *Smith v. Board of School Commissioners*, 827 F.2d 684 (11th Cir. 1987), reversing the district court and remanding "for the sole purpose of entry by the district court of an order dissolving the injunction and terminating this litigation."

186. Gest, "Media Bias," 10–11; Bates, *Battleground*, 249, quoting Podesta.

187. Quoted in PAW's film *Censorship in Our Schools*.

188. Quoted in Bates, *Battleground*, 265.

189. For a thoughtful treatment of just this dilemma in the *Mozert* case, see Nomi Maya Stolzenberg, "'He Drew a Circle That Shut Me Out': Assimilation, Indoctrination and the Paradox of a Liberal Education," *Harvard Law Review* 106 (January 1993): 581.

190. John G. West, Jr., "The Changing Battle over Religion in the Public Schools," *Wake Forest Law Review* 26 (1991): 361, 390.

191. Nadine Strossen, "'Secular Humanism' and 'Scientific Creationism': Proposed Standards for Reviewing Curricular Decisions Affecting Students' Religious Freedom," *Ohio State Law Journal* 47 (1986): 333, 398.

192. Ibid., 400.

193. Laurence H. Tribe, *American Constitutional Law*, 2nd ed. (Mineola, N.Y., 1988), 1186.

194. Quoted in meeting minutes of the ACLU National Board, January 1987, Princeton University.

195. Interview with Nadine Strossen, July 22, 2008 (notes in possession of the author).

196. Brief of National Council of Churches of Christ in the USA as Amicus Curiae Supporting Respondent, *Mozert v. Hawkins County Board of Education*, 827 F.2d 1058 (6th Cir. 1987) (No. 86-6144/87-5024).

197. Ibid.

198. See, e.g., Ronald B. Flowers, "They Got Our Attention, Didn't They? The Tennessee and Alabama Schoolbook Cases," *Religion and Public Education* 15, no. 3 (Summer 1988): 262–285.

199. See, e.g., Steven G. Gey, *Religion and the State*, 2nd ed. (Newark, 2006), 202–218.

200. *Mozert v. Hawkins County Board of Education*, 827 F.2d 937, 1064 (6th Cir. 1987).

201. Ibid., 1069.

202. Ibid., 1081 (Boggs, J., concurring).

203. *Cert. denied*, 484 U.S. 1066 (1988).

204. See, e.g., *Kalka v. Hawk*, 215 F.3d 90 (D.C. Cir. 2000). See also *Brown v. Hot, Sexy and Safer Productions, Inc.*, 68 F.3d 525 (1st Cir. 1995).

205. See Gordon, "The New Age and the New Law."

206. Douglas Laycock, with students at the University of Texas Law School, commentary on the "de facto" rule for American public schools (following Brief of National Council of Churches of Christ in the U.S.A., in *Mozert v. Hawkins County Public Schools*, 827 F.2d 1058 [6th Cir. 1987]), 14 (copy in possession of the author).

207. Quoted in "Powerhouse of the Religious Right? Beverly LaHaye's Concerned Women for America Succeeds at Mobilizing Grassroots Activists," *Christianity Today* 6 (November 1987): 34; Connie Page, "Watch on the Right: The Amazing Rise of Beverly LaHaye," *Ms.*, February 1987, 24–28; Alain L. Sanders, "Law: Tilting at Secular Humanism," *Time*, July 28, 1986, 67–68. See also Susan Faludi, *Backlash*, 252–254.

208. Cleo Kocol, "Feminist Update: The Women of the CWA," *Humanist* 49 (March/April 1989): 33.

209. See generally John Cloud and Andrea Sachs, "Meet the Prophet," *Time*, July 1, 2004, for a report on the success of the Left Behind series and its creator.

210. The field became far more populated in the 1990s. Jordan Lorence described his work on religious-freedom cases as shifting slightly when he left CWA to join the American Center for Law and Justice (founded in 1990), and then the Alliance Defense Fund (1994); interview with Jordan Lorence, April 25, 2007. Other groups, including the Becket Fund for Religious Liberty (1994) and Liberty Counsel (1989), were also active by the mid-1990s. The Rutherford Institute (TRI), which filed dozens of friend-of-the-court briefs after its founding in 1982 and claimed to have handled the vast majority of religious liberty litigation in the 1990s, was something of an outlier in its positions and leadership. Moore, *Suing for America's Soul*, 133–170.

211. According to some observers, LaHaye tried to direct CWA from afar by imposing her will on successors, who have eventually refused to be controlled and then been forced out. "20-Year-Old CWA Struggles to Find, Retain New Leader," *Washington Times*, September 12, 1999, C1 (interview with recently resigned CWA president Carmen Pate); "Sandy Rios Named CWA's New President," *Washington Times*, September 26, 2001, A6 (new president appointed more than two years after resignation of Pate). CWA's current president, Wendy Wright, was appointed in 2006.

6. Covenants of Love

1. "Declaration of Religious Support," www.rcfm.org.
2. Beverly LaHaye, *Who But a Woman?* (Nashville, 1984), 45.
3. See the Pew Forum on Religion and Public Life, http://pewforum .org/docs/?DocID=370 (accessed November 18, 2008).
4. On the Episcopal Church, see, e.g., *Episcopal Church Cases,* 45 Cal.4th 467, 87 Cal. Rptr.3d 275, 198 P.3d 66 (2009); *Episcopal Diocese of Rochester v. Harnish,* 11 N.Y.3d 340, 70 N.Y.S.2d 814, 899 N.E.2d 902 (2008); *Daniel v. Wray,* 158 N.C.App. 161, 580 S.E.2d 711 (2003); *All Saints Parish Waccamaw v. Protestant Episcopal Church,* 2009 S.C. Lexis 462 (S. Carolina Supreme Ct., September 18, 2009). In Virginia, the Supreme Court agreed in late 2009 to hear an appeal based on a Civil War–era statute that imposes majority rule on religious organizations in church property disputes. Michelle Boorstein, "Va. Episcopal Church Dispute Headed Back to Court," *Washington Post,* October 14, 2009. According to a Colorado diocesan report, the Episcopal Church spent $2.9 million in legal fees in a single lawsuit over a church in Colorado Springs. Edward E. Plowman, "Day in Court," *World Magazine,* October 24, 2009, www.worldmag.com (accessed November 8, 2009). Mark Strasser, "When Churches Divide: On Neutrality, Deference, and Unpredictability," *Hamline Law Review* 32 (2009): 427–475.

On the Methodist Church, see Neela Banerjee, "Methodist Court Removes Openly Lesbian Minister," *New York Times,* November 1, 2005, 1. On Catholic groups, see www.dignityusa.org (accessed November 7, 2009); "Catholics for Marriage Equality," queersunited.blogspot.com (accessed November 6, 2009); Seth Hemmelgorn, "Gay Catholics Discuss Marriage Equality," *Bay Area Reporter,* July 9, 2009, www.ebar.com (accessed August 12, 2009).
5. See, e.g., "Religious Groups' Official Positions on Same Sex Marriage," pewforum.org/docs/?DocID=291 (accessed November 18, 2008).
6. Edward J. Fiske, "Religion: Views on Homosexuals," *New York Times,* December 3, 1967, 263.
7. Steven Goldstein, founder and CEO of Garden State Equality, remarks made during visit to University of Pennsylvania, April 20, 2009; www.gardenstateequality.org.
8. William Countryman, "The Bible, Heterosexism, and Sexual Orientation," in *God Forbid: Religion and Sex in American Public Life,* ed. Kathleen M. Sands (New York, 2000), 170.
9. See, e.g., Brief of Amicus Curiae Iowa and National Faith Leaders

and Scholars; Connecticut Clergy for Marriage Equality, http://lmafoc
.convio.net/site/PageServer?pagename=ccmedeclaration (accessed November 29, 2008).

10. *Perez v. Sharp*, 32 Cal.2d 711, 198 P.2d 17 (1948).

11. *Loving v. Virginia*, 388 U.S. 1 (1967).

12. See, e.g., Peggy Pascoe, *What Comes Naturally: Miscegenation Law and the Making of Race in America* (New York, 2009), 288–306; Reva Siegel, "Equality Talk: Anti-subordination and Anti-classification Values in Constitutional Struggles over *Brown*," *Harvard Law Review* 117 (2004): 1470–1547.

13. Pascoe, *What Comes Naturally*, 287–296, 301–304.

14. Marie Griffith, personal communication, February 5, 2009; Hendrik Hartog, *Man and Wife in America: A History* (Cambridge, Mass., 2000), 93–135.

15. Nancy Cott, *Public Vows: A History of Marriage and the Nation* (Cambridge, Mass., 2000), 200–227.

16. Alice Kessler-Harris, *In Pursuit of Equity: Women, Men, and the Quest for Economic Citizenship in 20th-Century America* (New York, 2001).

17. Margot Canaday, "Heterosexuality as a Legal Regime," in *The Cambridge History of Law in America*, 3 vols., ed. Michael Grossberg and Christopher Tomlins (Cambridge, 2008), 3:455. See also Stephen Robertson, "What's Law Got to Do With It? Legal Records and Sexual Histories," *Journal of the History of Sexuality* 14 (2005): 161.

18. Mary Ann Glendon, "Marriage and the State: The Withering Away of Marriage," *University of Virginia Law Review* 62 (1976): 663–720.

19. George Chauncey, *Why Marriage? The History Shaping Today's Debate over Gay Equality* (New York, 2004); Mathew D. Staver, *Same-Sex Marriage: Putting Every Household at Risk* (Nashville, 2004); Ellen Lewin, "Does Marriage Have a Future?" *Journal of Marriage and Family* 66 (November 2004): 1000–1006; Andrew J. Cherlin, "American Marriage in the Early Twenty-First Century," *Future of Children* 15, no. 2 (Fall 2005): 33–34.

20. The religious historian William McLoughlin argued that awakenings in American life, and the religious revivals that are part of them, occur in periods of stress and dislocation. In their wake, awakenings create powerful movements for reform. William G. McLoughlin, *Revivals, Awakenings, and Reform: An Essay on Religion and Social Change in America, 1607–1977* (Chicago, 1978).

21. Michael P. Young, "Confessional Protest: The Religious Birth of U.S. National Social Movements," *American Sociological Review* 67, no. 5 (October 2002): 660, 684.

22. Jan Shipps, *Mormonism: The Story of a New Religious Tradition* (Urbana, 1985); Richard Lyman Bushman, *Joseph Smith: Rough Stone Rolling* (New York, 2005).

23. The Doctrine and Covenants of the Church of Jesus Christ of Latter-day Saints, Section 132, http://scriptures.lds.org/en/dc/132 (accessed November 6, 2009).

24. Sarah Barringer Gordon and Kathryn M. Daynes, *Convictions: Mormon Polygamy and Criminal Law Enforcement in Nineteenth-Century Utah* (Urbana, forthcoming).

25. Sarah Barringer Gordon, *The Mormon Question: Polygamy and Constitutional Conflict in Nineteenth-Century America* (Chapel Hill, 2002). The Mormon Church's official position coexisted with informal and unofficial continuation of the practice well into the twentieth century. B. Carmon Hardy, *Solemn Covenant: The Mormon Polygamous Passage* (Urbana, 1992), 336–362; Kathryn M. Dayner, *More Wives Than One: Transformation of the Mormon Marriage System* (Urbana, 2001), 173–187.

26. Sarah Barringer Gordon, "Chapel and State," *Legal Affairs* (January 2003).

27. Karen Lystra, *Searching the Heart: Women, Men, and Romantic Love in Nineteenth-Century America* (New York, 1989), 192–226.

28. See www.domawatch.org/index.php (accessed November 6, 2009).

29. For a recent example, see the joint amicus curiae brief of the Church of Jesus Christ of Latter-day Saints, California Catholic Conference, National Association of Evangelicals, and Union of Orthodox Jewish Congregations of America, http://newsroom.lds.org/Static%20Files/Newsroom/News%20Releases%202007/DOCS-1002214-v1-California_SGM_Brief—Supreme_Court.PDF.

30. Staver, *Same-Sex Marriage*, 1–22.

31. Stanley Kurtz, "The Marriage Mentality: A Reply to My Critics," *National Review Online*, February 2, 2004, www.nationalreview.com/kurtz/kurtz200405040841.asp (accessed November 7, 2008).

32. Ibid.

33. David Frum, "The Fall of France: What Gay Marriage Does to Marriage," *National Review*, November 8, 1999, 28.

34. Alan Sears and Craig Osten, *The Homosexual Agenda: Exposing the Principal Threat to Religious Freedom Today* (Nashville, 2003), 2–3.

35. Nathan Hale, *Freud and the Americans: The Beginnings of Psychoanalysis in the United States, 1876–1917* (New York, 1971); Raymond E. Fancher, "Snapshots of Freud in America, 1899–1999," *American Psychologist* 55, no. 9 (September 2000), 1025–1028; R. Marie Griffith, "The Religious

Encounters of Alfred C. Kinsey," *Journal of American History* 95 (September 2008): 349.

36. See, e.g., Heather Rachelle White, "Homosexuality, Gay Communities, and American Churches: A History of a Changing Religious Ethic, 1946–1977," Ph.D. diss., Princeton University, 2007; Harvey Cox, "Evangelical Ethics and the Ideal of Chastity," *Christianity and Crisis,* April 27, 1964, 75–80.

37. Edward B. Fiske, "Religion: Views on Homosexuals," *New York Times,* December 3, 1967, 263.

38. The Reverend James Stoll was ordained on September 5, 1969. See, generally, Mark Oppenheimer, "'The Inherent Worth and Dignity': Gay Unitarians and the Birth of Sexual Tolerance in Liberal Religion," *Journal of the History of Sexuality* 77, no. 1 (July 1996): 73–101.

39. See www.mcchurch.org (accessed October 30, 2009).

40. See Congregation Beth Simchat Torah, http://cbst.org/about_index .shtml (accessed November 6, 2008); www.lgbtran.org/Exhibits/CBST /index.aspx (accessed November 8, 2008).

41. Fiske, "Religion," 263; W. Norman Pittenger, *Making Sexuality Human* (Philadelphia, 1970).

42. See Ronald Bayer, *Homosexuality and American Psychiatry: The Politics of Diagnosis* (Princeton, 1987), 3–4.

43. D'Emilio, *Sexual Politics, Sexual Communities,* 231–239.

44. See ibid., 238.

45. See, e.g., Shulamith Firestone, *The Dialectic of Sex: The Case for Feminist Revolution* (New York, 1970), 227–242; Jill Johnston, *Lesbian Nation: The Feminist Solution* (New York, 1973).

46. Paula L. Ettelbrick, "Since When Is Marriage a Path to Liberation?" *Out/Look National Gay and Lesbian Quarterly* 6, no. 4 (Fall 1989), 258. Ettelbrick is currently executive director of the International Gay and Lesbian Human Rights Commission; see www.iglhrc.org (accessed November 9, 2008).

47. Ibid., 261.

48. Nancy Polikoff, *Beyond (Straight and Gay) Marriage: Valuing All Families under the Law* (Boston, 2008).

49. Law professor Martha Fineman called marriage "overrated" in 2002, arguing that marriage should not be "privileged" over other ties, such as caretaking or affection. Emily Eakin and Felicia R. Lee, "On Target and Off in 2002," *New York Times,* December 28, 2002, B7.

50. Michael Warner, *The Trouble with Normal: Sex, Politics, and the Ethics of Queer Life* (New York, 1999), 84–85.

51. For exploratory essays in the (relatively) new concept of lived religion as it is used in this chapter, see David D. Hall, ed., *Lived Religion in America: Toward a History of Practice* (Princeton, 1997); see also Robert A. Orsi, *Thank You, St. Jude: Women's Devotion to the Patron Saint of Hopeless Causes* (New Haven, 1996).

52. Robert A. Orsi, "Everyday Miracles: The Study of Lived Religion," in *Lived Religion in America,* 7.

53. Interview with Reconstructionist rabbi and professor of religion Rebecca Alpert, October 28, 2008. Emile Durkheim, *The Elementary Forms of Religious Life,* trans. Carol Cosman (Oxford, 2001), 25–46.

54. Jim Birkitt, MCC Communications Department, June 2004, cited in Chauncey, *Why Marriage?* 92, 182n4.

55. Kay Tobin and Randy Wicke, *The Gay Crusaders: In-Depth Interviews with 15 Homosexuals—Men and Women Who Are Shaping America's Newest Sexual Revolution* (New York, 1972), 145.

56. Minnesota Statutes, §517 (1971).

57. Jack Star, "The Homosexual Couple," *Look,* January 26, 1971, 69–71.

58. "Jack Baker (activist)," Wikipedia (accessed November 10, 2008).

59. Tobin and Wicke, *Gay Crusaders,* 135.

60. "License Fight Reaches Minnesota High Court," *Advocate* 13 (October 1971): 2, 32, cited in Peggy Pascoe, "Sex, Gender, and Same Sex Marriage," in *Is Academic Feminism Dead?* ed. Social Justice Group at the Center for Advanced Feminist Studies, University of Minnesota (New York, 2000), 115 n29.

61. Ken Bronson, "A Quest for Full Equality," 2004, www.may-18-1970.org /Quest.pdf (accessed November 6, 2008), 26; William N. Eskridge, Jr., and Darren R. Spedale, *Gay Marriage: For Better or for Worse? What We've Learned from the Evidence* (Oxford, 2006).

62. *Baker v. Nelson,* 291 Minn. 310, 191 N.W.2d 185, 185–186 (1971).

63. Ibid., 186.

64. Ibid., 187.

65. Bronson, "A Quest for Full Equality."

66. *Jones v. Hallahan,* 501 S.W.2d 588, 589 (Kentucky, 1973).

67. Ibid., 590 (citing *Reynolds*).

68. Note, "The Legality of Homosexual Marriage," *Yale Law Journal* 82 (1973): 573, 585.

69. See, e.g., Thomas Emerson, "In Support of the Equal Rights Amendment," *Harvard Civil Rights–Civil Liberties Law Review* 6 (1971): 225, 231.

70. Barbara A. Brown et al., "The Equal Rights Amendment: A Constitutional Basis for Equal Rights for Women," *Yale Law Journal* 80 (April

1971): 871–985, reprinted in U.S. Congress (Senate, 92nd Cong., 1st sess.), *Congressional Record* 27 (October 5, 1971), 35012–35041. On congressional debates about the article and the sweep of the ERA, see Donald G. Mathews and Jane Sherron De Hart, *Sex, Gender, and the Politics of ERA: A State and the Nation* (New York, 1990), 44–50.

71. *Singer v. Hara,* 11 Wash. App. 247, 250, 522 P.2d 1187, 1190 (Wash. App. 1974).

72. The quoted language is from the *Phyllis Schlafly Report* (1972); on Schlafly's use of same-sex marriage in the fight against ERA, see "Gays on the March," *Time,* September 8, 1975, 33–43, and Phyllis Schlafly, *Power of the Positive Woman* (New Rochelle, N.Y., 1977), 12. See also Donald T. Critchlow, *Phyllis Schlafly and Grassroots Conservatism: A Woman's Crusade* (Princeton, 2005), 212–227; Marjorie Spruill, "Gender and America's Right Turn," in *Rightward Bound: Making America Conservative in the 1970s,* ed. Bruce J. Schulman and Julian E. Zelizer (Cambridge, Mass., 2008), 71–89.

73. On feminists distancing themselves from same-sex marriage more generally, see Pascoe, "Sex, Gender, and Same-Sex Marriage," quotation on 98.

74. *Singer v. Hara,* 11 Wash. App., 259–260, 522 P.2d, 1195.

75. Barbara A. Brown et al., *Women's Rights and the Law: The Impact of the ERA on State Laws* (New York, 1977), 30.

76. Anita Bryant, *The Anita Bryant Story: The Survival of Our Nation's Families and the Threat of Militant Homosexuality* (Tappan, N.J., 1977); 1977 Florida Laws, ch. 77–139.

77. Colorado (1973), Maryland (1973), Texas (1973), Louisiana (1975), Montana (1975), Nevada (1975), North Dakota (1975), Oklahoma (1975), Virginia (1975), California (1977), Florida (1977), Illinois (1977), Minnesota (1977), Utah (1977), and Wyoming (1977).

78. Pascoe, "Sex, Gender, and Same-Sex Marriage," 102.

79. William N. Eskridge, Jr., *Gaylaw: Challenging the Apartheid of the Closet* (Cambridge, Mass., 1999), 98–148.

80. Bronson, "A Quest for Full Equality," 67.

81. For liberals' complaints, see Kathleen M. Sands, "Introduction," in *God Forbid: Religion and Sex in American Public Life,* ed. Kathleen M. Sands (New York, 2000), 5. For conservative complaints about being ignored by the press, see Mark Silk, *Unsecular Media: Making News of Religion in America* (Urbana, 1995), 33–46; Stephen Carter, *The Culture of Disbelief: How American Law and Politics Trivialize Religion* (New York, 1993), 59–60.

82. Steven Waldman and John Green, "The Twelve Tribes of American

Politics," www.beliefnet.com/news/politics/2005 (accessed November 6, 2009).

83. See the statements collected in Rebecca T. Alpert, ed., *Voices of the Religious Left: A Contemporary Sourcebook* (Philadelphia, 2000); Steven H. Shiffrin, *The Religious Left and Church-State Relations* (Princeton, 2009); Robert Wuthnow and John H. Evans, ed., *The Quiet Hand of God: Faith-Based Activism and the Public Role of Mainline Protestantism*, ed. Robert Wuthnow and John Hyde Evans (Berkeley, 2002).

84. Brian J. Distelberg, "'Organized Gay People': Hartford Conn.'s Kalos Society–Gay Liberation Front, 1968–75," paper presented at the annual meeting of the American Society for Church History, New York, January 2009 (copy in possession of the author); Wendy Cadge, "Vital Conflicts: The Mainline Denominations Debate Homosexuality," in *The Quiet Hand of God*, 265–286; Griffith, "The Religious Encounters of Alfred C. Kinsey," 354–360.

85. Gustavo Gutierrez, "Reflections from a Latin American Theologian," in *Voices of the Religious Left;* Christian Smith, *The Emergence of Liberation Theology: Radical Religion and Social Movement Theory* (Chicago, 1991).

86. The Unitarian Univeralist Association, for example, "stak[ed] its national reputation and future growth on wholeheartedly welcoming gay couples in Massachusetts." Alan Cooperman, "Massachusetts Clergy Are Divided on Eve of Historic Same-Sex Unions," *Washington Post,* May 16, 2004, A1.

87. Judith Plaskow, "Decentering Sex: Rethinking Jewish Sexual Ethics," in Sands, *God Forbid.*

88. Bronson, "A Quest for Full Equality," 68.

89. White, "Homosexuality, Gay Communities, and American Churches," 152–177.

90. Eric Marcus, *Making History: The Struggle for Gay and Lesbian Equal Rights, 1945–1990: An Oral History* (New York, 1992), 493.

91. "Resolution 1976–A071, Support the Right of Homosexuals to Equal Protection of the Law," Sixty-fifth Episcopal General Convention, 1976.

92. On the widening debate over both issues within the Episcopal Church and other Christian denominations, see "Global Schism: Is the Anglican Communion Rift the First Stage in a Wider Christian Split?" Faith Angle Conference, May 14, 2007, Pew Forum on Religion and Public Life, www.pewforum.org/events/?EventID=145 (accessed June 25, 2008).

93. See Ralph Blumenthal, "A Rabbi Whose God Is a Loving and Suffering Mother," *New York Times,* September 1, 2009, on Rabbi Margaret Moers Wenig, who first submitted the petition to ordain gay men and lesbians

to the (Reform) Central Conference of American Rabbis. Rabbi Wenig listed the resolution, approved in 1990, as her proudest accomplishment; www.newyorktimes.com (accessed September 1, 2009).

94. Quoted in Marcus, *Making History,* 331.

95. Ibid., 324.

96. Orsi, "Everyday Miracles," 14.

97. On the impact of AIDS and the baby boom, see generally Chauncey, *Why Marriage?* 96–111.

98. Timothy Soldani, University of Pennsylvania Law School, November 13, 2008.

99. Ronald L. Grimes, *Deeply into the Bone: Reinventing Rites of Passage* (Berkeley, 2000), 213.

100. Victor L. Turner, *The Ritual Process: Structure and Anti-Structure* (1969; New York, 1995).

101. See Ariel Meadow Stallings, *Off-Beat Bride: Taffeta-Free Alternatives for Independent Brides* (Emeryville, 2007); Jane Ross-Macdonald, *Alternative Weddings: An Essential Guide for Creating Your Own Ceremony* (London, 1997).

102. Herbert Anderson and Edward Foley, *Mighty Stories, Dangerous Rituals: Weaving the Human and Divine* (San Francisco, 1997).

103. Gutierrez, "Reflections from a Latin American Theologian," quotations on 45, 46; Gustavo Gutierrez, *A Theology of Liberation* (Maryknoll, N.Y., 1973); Smith, *The Emergence of Liberation Theology.*

104. Robert Allan Warrior, "Canaanites, Cowboys, and Indians: Deliverance, Conquest, and Liberation Theology Today," *Christianity and Crisis,* September 11, 1989, 261.

105. On liberal Christian theology in the late twentieth century, see Gary Dorrien, *The Making of American Liberal Theology: Crisis, Irony, and Postmodernity, 1950–2005* (Louisville, 2006).

106. Rosemary Radford Ruether, "Searching Scripture for a Model of the Family," *Conscience* 5, no. 2 (March/April 1984), 4.

107. On this point more broadly, see Peter Brown, *The Body and Society: Men, Women and Sexual Renunciation in Early Christianity* (New York, 1988).

108. Ruether, "Searching Scripture," 6.

109. This chapter focuses on Reform and Reconstructionist Judaism in particular. Other progressive movements, including Jewish Renewal (www.aleph.org, accessed November 14, 2008) and Secular Humanistic Judaism (www.ifshj.org, accessed November 14, 2008), much smaller than the two major progressive denominations, are also open to same-sex marriages.

110. Michael A. Meyer, *Response to Modernity: A History of the Reform Movement*

in Judaism (Detroit, 1988); Mordecai M. Kaplan, *Judaism as a Civilization: Toward a Reconstruction of American-Jewish Life* (1957; Philadelphia, 1994), and *The Meaning of God in Modern Jewish Religion* (1937; Detroit, 1994); Mitchell Silver, *A Plausible God: Secular Reflections on Liberal Jewish Theology* (New York, 2006).

111. Sefton D. Temkin, *Creating American Reform Judaism: The Life and Times of Isaac Mayer Wise* (Oxford, 1998), 235–244; Jonathan D. Sarna, *American Judaism: A History* (New Haven, 2004), 96–98.

112. Emanuel S. Goldsmith, Mel Scult, and Robert M. Selzer, *The American Judaism of Mordecai Kaplan* (New York, 1991); Rebecca T. Alpert and Jacob J. Staub, *Exploring Judaism: A Reconstructionist Approach* (New York, 1985).

113. Hasia R. Diner, *The Jews of the United States: 1654–2000* (Berkeley, 2004), 119–128, 249–251, 253–255.

114. Quoted in ibid., 254; Goldsmith, Scult, and Selzer, *The American Judaism of Mordecai Kaplan;* Hillel Cohn, "Why I Officiate at Mixed-Marriage Wedding Ceremonies," in *Contemporary Debates in American Reform Judaism: Conflicting Visions,* ed. Dana Evan Kaplan (New York, 2001), 160, 164.

115. Meyer, *Response to Modernity,* 379–380.

116. Denise L. Eger, "Embracing Lesbians and Gay Men: A Reform Jewish Innovation," in *Contemporary Debates in American Reform Judaism,* 180.

117. Fiske, "Views on Homosexuals," 263.

118. David Saperstein quoted in Robert P. Jones, *Progressive and Religious: How Christian, Jewish, Muslim, and Buddhist Leaders Are Moving beyond the Culture Wars and Transforming American Life* (Lanham, 2008), 26. See also www.rac.org (accessed January 30, 2009).

119. Leviticus 18:22. *To-evah* is commonly understood as an abomination, although among some scholars this word is considered unnecessarily inflammatory for a Hebrew term that also encompasses improper dress, carrying on Shabbat, or shady business practices. Joan Friedman, "Position Paper in Favor of Rabbinic Officiation at Same-Sex Ceremonies" (1998), www.davka.org/what/text/publishing/samesexceremonies.html (accessed November 14, 2008).

120. Leviticus 20:13.

121. Robert McAfee Brown, *Theology in a New Key: Responding to Liberation Theology* (Philadelphia, 1980), 60.

122. Yoel Kahn, "The Liturgy of Gay and Lesbian Jews," in *Twice Blessed: On Being Lesbian, Gay and Jewish,* ed. Christie Balka and Andy Rose (Boston, 1989), 186.

123. Rabbi Alexander Schindler, Presidential Address, Sixtieth General Assembly Union of American Hebrew Congregations, New Orleans, No-

vember 1989, 12, quoted in Eger, "Embracing Lesbians and Gay Men," 183.

124. Eger, "Embracing Lesbians and Gay Men," 186.

125. Ibid., 187; Bradley Shavit Artson, "Enfranchising the Monogamous Homosexual: A Legal Possibility, a Moral Imperative," *S'vara, A Journal of Philosophy Law and Judaism* 3, no. 1 (1993): 15.

126. Plaskow, "Decentering Sex," 36; Judith Plaskow, *The Coming of Lilith: Essays on Feminism, Judaism, and Sexual Ethics, 1972–2003* (Boston, 2005).

127. Friedman, "Position Paper in Favor of Rabbinic Officiation."

128. See, e.g., Rachel Adler, *Engendering Judaism: An Inclusive Theology and Ethics* (Philadelphia, 1998), 170; Friedman, "Position Paper in Favor of Rabbinic Officiation"; Rebecca T. Alpert, "Religious Liberty, Same-Sex Marriage, and the Case of Reconstructionist Judaism," in Sands, *God Forbid*, 126, 127–128.

129. Yoel Kahn, "The Kedusha of Homosexual Relationships," *Central Conference of American Rabbis (Reform) Yearbook* 99 (New York, 1989), 136.

130. On this point, see Shari Lash, "Struggling with Tradition: Making Room for Same-Sex Weddings in a Liberal Jewish Context," *Ethnologies* 28, no. 2 (2006): 133, 148–149.

131. Gary Langer and Jon Cohen, "Voters and Values in the 2004 Election," *Public Opinion Quarterly* 69, no. 5 (2005): 744–759.

132. Richard Dawkins, *The God Delusion* (Boston, 2006); Christopher Hitchens, *God Is Not Great: How Religion Poisons Everything* (New York, 2007).

133. Jones, *Progressive and Religious*, 10–13.

134. Silk, *Unsecular Media*, 49–56.

135. Robert Wuthnow, *The Restructuring of American Religion: Society and Faith since World War II* (Princeton, 1988), reporting on roughly equal numbers of religious liberals and conservatives in the 1984 Gallup survey; see esp. 132–134.

136. See, e.g., Wuthnow and Evans, *The Quiet Hand of God*.

137. Interview with Rabbi Devon Lerner, Arlington, Mass., December 7, 2008.

138. Ibid.

139. Orsi, "Everyday Miracles," 11.

140. See Daniele Hervieu-Leger, "'What Scripture Tells Me': Spontaneity and Regulation within Catholic Charismatic Renewal," in Hall, *Lived Religion in America*, 25–27.

141. See., e.g., Glendon, "Marriage and the State," 663; John R. Gillis, *For Better or for Worse* (New York, 1985); Pamela J. Smock, "The Wax and Wane of Marriage: Prospects for Marriage in the 21st Century," *Journal of Marriage and Family* 66 (1996): 968–971.

142. Gary S. Becker, *A Treatise on the Family* (Cambridge, Mass., 1981), 76.

143. Kathryn Edin and Maria Kefalas, *Promises I Can Keep: Why Poor Women Put Motherhood before Marriage* (Berkeley, 2007); M. M. Sweeney, "Two Decades of Family Change: The Shift in Economic Foundations of Marriage," *American Sociological Review* 67 (2002): 132.

144. Andrew J. Cherlin, "American Marriage in the Early Twenty-First Century," *The Future of Children* 15, no. 2 (Fall 2005): 33, 41.

145. For comparative data, see Alain Monnier and Catherine de Guilbert-Lantoine, "Demographics of Europe and Developed Countries Overseas," *Population,* 8 (1996), 235. For the average age at first marriage for American men (27.7 years), and women (26 years), see http://factfinder.census.gov (accessed November 21, 2008). Andrew J. Cherlin, "The Deinstitutionalization of American Marriage," *Journal of Marriage and Family* 66 (November 2004): 848, 855.

146. The Pew Forum on Religion and Public Life's Religious Landscape Survey found 83.1 percent; an additional 5.8 percent reported they were "religious" but not affiliated with any particular faith tradition. See http://religions.pewforum.org/reports (accessed November 22, 2008); see also Seymour Martin Lipset, "American Exceptionalism Reaffirmed," *Tocqueville Review* 19 (1990): 3.

147. For the earlier figures on weddings, see Martin K. Whyte, *Dating, Mating, and Marriage* (New York, 1990), 56; for the later figure, see "Marriage Ceremonies—Wedding Traditions," http://family.jrank.org/pages/1118/Marriage-Ceremonies.html (accessed November 21, 2008), citing David Knox and Caroline Schacht, *Choices in Relationships: An Introduction to Marriage and the Family* (Belmont, Calif., 2007).

148. On this point, see Grimes, *Deeply into the Bone,* 205.

149. Robert N. Bellah et al., *Habits of the Heart: Individualism and Commitment in American Life* (1985; Berkeley, 1996), 91.

150. Cherlin, "American Marriage," 45–46; Robert Schoen and Robin M. Weinick, "The Slowing Metabolism of Marriage: Figures from 1988 U.S. Marital Status Life Tables," *Demography* 39 (1993): 737.

151. Ellen Lewin, *Recognizing Ourselves: Ceremonies of Lesbian and Gay Commitment* (New York, 1998), xiii, and "Does Marriage Have a Future?" *Journal of Marriage and Family* 66 (November 2004), 1000, 1001. The officiant at Lewin's wedding, Rabbi Yoel Kahn, is the author of a guide for constructing Jewish celebrations of same-sex weddings. See Kahn, "The Liturgy of Gay and Lesbian Jews," 182.

152. On inclusive denominations, see also Leonard Norman Primiano, "The Gay God of the City: The Emergence of the Gay and Lesbian Ethnic Parish," in *Gay Religion,* ed. Scott Thumma and Edward R. Gray (Lanham, 2005), 7.

153. Report of the Reconstructionist Commission on Homosexuality, *Ho-

mosexuality and Judaism: The Reconstructionist Position (Wyncote, Penn., 1993), 30, 42; "Jewish Branch Adopts Liberal Rules for Gays," *Washington Post,* February 8, 1992, B7.

154. Quoted in Gustav Niebuhr, "Reform Rabbis Back Blessing of Gay Unions," *New York Times,* March 30, 2000.

155. Quoted in Laurie Goodstein, "Gay Couples Seek Unions in God's Eyes," *New York Times,* January 30, 2004, A1.

156. "Declaration of Religious Support: Massachusetts Declaration of Religious Support for the Freedom of Same-Gender Couples to Marry," www.fpuucanton.org/pdfs/declaration_equal_marriage.pdf (copy in possession of the author).

157. Ibid.

158. On July 17, 2007, one thousand clergy had signed the Declaration.

159. Lawrence Stone, *The Family, Sex and Marriage in England, 1500–1800* (New York, 1977) and *Road to Divorce: 1530–1987* (Oxford, 1990); Mary Ann Glendon, *The Transformation of Family Law: State, Law, and Family in the United States and Western Europe* (Chicago, 1989).

160. See "Declaration of Religious Support."

161. "Why Are We Doing This?" http://web.archive.org/web/200012041 803000/www.ftmmass.org/rcfm, accessed May 29, 2008. (Web site date: August 18, 2000; first record of Web site for RCFM.)

162. Judy Deutsch, "Marriage: Then and Now," *Sudbury Town Crier,* January 1, 2004.

163. Religious Coalition for the Freedom to Marry, Open Letter to Cardinal Sean P. O'Malley and the Roman Catholic Bishops of Massachusetts, June 27, 2006; www. pewroundtable.org/news/article.cfm?id= 4464 (accessed June 3, 2008; copy in possession of the author).

164. Interview with Rabbi Lerner, December 7, 2008.

165. Devon Lerner, "Why We Support Same-Sex Marriage: A Response from over 450 Clergy," *New England Law Review* 38, no. 3 (2003–2004): 527, 532.

166. Beth S. Wenger, "The Politics of Women's Ordination: Jewish Law, Institutional Power, and the Debate over Women in the Rabbinate," in *Tradition Renewed: A History of the Jewish Theological Seminary,* ed. Jack Wertheimer, 2 vols. (New York, 1997), 2:483.

167. Devon A. Lerner, *Celebrating Interfaith Marriages: Creating Your Jewish/ Christian Ceremony* (New York, 1999); Linda Matchan, "A Rabbi Honors Love beyond Faith," *Boston Globe,* November 22, 1999, D1.

168. Matchan, "Rabbi Honors Love"; Lerner, *Celebrating Interfaith Marriages,* xviii.

169. 1 Corinthians 13:5–8.

170. Lerner, "Why We Support Same-Sex Marriage," 532.

171. Interview with Rabbi Lerner, December 7, 2008.

172. Ibid.

173. *Goodridge v. Department of Health*, 440 Mass. 309, 798 N.E.2d 941 (2003).

174. Brief of Amici Curiae the Religious Coalition for the Freedom to Marry, and Others in Support of Plaintiff-Appellants, No. SJC-08860, *Goodridge v. Department of Health*, 3.

175. Leadership Council of Conservative Judaism, *Statement on Intermarriage* (March 7, 1995), www.rabassembly.org/info/intermar/ (accessed November 5, 2008); see also www.uscj.org/Jewish_ContinuityPre5916 .html (accessed June 7, 2008). Catechism of the Catholic Church: The Sacrament of Matrimony, #1665, www.vatican.va/archive /catechism /p2s2c3a7.htm (accessed November 5, 2008).

176. Brief of Amici Curiae the Religious Coalition for the Freedom to Marry, 10.

177. On this point, see Perry Dane, "A Holy Secular Institution," *Emory Law Journal* 58 (2009): 1147–1153, and "The Intersecting Worlds of Religious and Secular Marriage," in *Law and Religion: Current Legal Issues,* ed. Richard O'Dair and Andrew Lewis (London, 2001).

178. *Loving v. Virginia*, 388 U.S. 1 (1967), *Zablocki v. Redhail*, 434 U.S. 372 (1978); *Turner v. Safely*, 482 U.S. 78, 95 (1987).

179. Cass R. Sunstein, "The Right to Marry," *Cardozo Law Review* 26 (2005): 2081; Dane, "A Holy Secular Institution," 1151–1153; Note, "Same-Sex Marriage and the Right to Privacy," *Yale Law Journal* 103 (1994): 1495, 1496.

180. Gordon, *Mormon Question;* Lawrence Foster, *Religion and Sexuality: The Shakers, the Mormons, and the Oneida Community* (Urbana, 1984); Hartog, *Man and Wife in America,* 40–62.

181. Gordon, *Mormon Question,* 228–234.

182. Brief of Amici Curiae the Religious Coalition for the Freedom to Marry, 14.

183. Ibid., 18–21.

184. To be fair, the critique leveled by this claim against the appellate court in Massachusetts was misguided—the judge noted that Massachusetts inherited common law standards for marriage from England, which in turn were based (at some remove) on English ecclesiastical law. Statutes based on those standards should be interpreted consistent with them, held the lower court judge, including the restriction of marriage to one man and one woman.

185. Interview with Rabbi Lerner, December 7, 2008. The Mass Equality campaign director was furious when he learned about the ad, predict-

ing that it would backfire. Lerner recalled this as a successful tactic, based on principle, however, and very productive of coalition building in the Boston area among liberal Catholics. "A *great* ad," she said.

186. *Goodridge*, 798 N.E.2d, 954.

187. Kirsten Lombardi, "The Catholic War against Gay Marriage," *Boston Phoenix*, March 26–April 1, 2004, www.bostonphoenix.com/boston/news _features/top/features/documents/03702313.asp (accessed November 28, 2008).

188. Quoted in Jane Lampman, "Gay Marriage: Clergy Gear for Amendment Battle," *Christian Science Monitor*, January 9, 2004, 13.

189. Press release, "Massachusetts Clergy Challenge Roman Catholic Hierarchy to Stop Political Campaign against Same-Sex Marriage," June 27, 2006, www.pewroundtable.org/news/article_print.cfm?=4464 (accessed June 3, 2008).

190. Religious Coalition for the Freedom to Marry, Open Letter to Cardinal Sean P. O'Malley and the Roman Catholic Bishops of Massachusetts.

191. Brief of Amici Curiae the Religious Coalition for the Freedom to Marry, 21.

192. *Boston Globe*, February 11, 2004, B7.

193. Chuck Colbert, "Religious Coalition for the Freedom to Marry" *In Newsweekly*, December 28, 2006.

194. See, e.g., Eric Convey, "Same-Sex Coalition Crosses Religions," *Boston Herald*, March 3, 2004, 25.

195. "Julie, Hillary Goodridge to Divorce, Couple Led Gay Marriage Fight in Massachusetts," www.huffingtonpost.com, February 3, 2009 (accessed October 29, 2009).

196. See Brief of Amicus Curiae California Faith for Equality, *In re Marriage Cases*, No. S147999, www.cafaithforequality.org/news.html#amicus (accessed November 29, 2008). California Supreme Court—decision reported—43 Cal.4th 757, 76 Cal. Rptr.3d 683, 183 P.3d 384 (2008).

197. Following is a sampling of religious coalitions in various states. *Alabama:* Communities of Faith for Full Inclusion, http://coffialabama .org/index.htm. *Arizona:* No Longer Silent: Clergy for Justice, www.no longersilent.org. *California:* California Faith for Equality, www.cafaith forequality.org. *Colorado:* Colorado Clergy for Equality in Marriage, http://ccemco.blogspot.com; Interfaith Alliance of Colorado www.inter faithallianceco.org. *Delaware:* Toward Equality, www.towardequality.org. *Florida:* Florida Clergy for Fairness, http://flclergyforfairness.org. *Illinois:* Protestants for the Common Good, www.thecommongood.org; Chicago Coalition of Welcoming Churches, www.chicagowelcoming

churches.org. *Indiana:* Interfaith Coalition on Non-Discrimination, www.iconindiana.org. *Iowa:* Interfaith Alliance of Iowa, www.iowatia.org. *Michigan:* Faith Action Network, www.faithactionnetwork.org. *Minnesota:* Faith Family Fairness Alliance, www.faithfamilyfairness.org. *Missouri:* Faith Aloud, www.faithaloud.org; PROMO: Pro-Claim Faith Initiative, http://promoonline.org. *New Hampshire:* New Hampshire Freedom to Marry Coalition, www.nhftm.org. *New York:* Empire State Pride Agenda—Pride in the Pulpit, www.prideagenda.org. *North Carolina:* Religious Coalition for Marriage Equality, www.ncrc4me.org. *Ohio:* Equality Ohio—Faith and Religion, www.equalityohio.org. *Oregon:* Community of Welcoming Congregations, www.welcomingcongregations.org. *Rhode Island:* Religious Coalition for Same-Gender Marriage, http://marriageequalityri.wordpress.com. *Vermont:* Vermont Freedom to Marry, www.vtfreetomarry.org. *Virginia:* People of Faith for Equality in Virginia, www.faith4equalityva.org. *Washington:* Religious Coalition for Equality, www.equalrightswashington.org. (I wish to thank Jeremy Chase, J.D. University of Pennsylvania 2009, for assembling this information.)

198. Human Rights Campaign, "Who We Are: Our History," www.hrc.org/about_us/2514.htm (accessed January 31, 2009); www.hrc.org/about_us/2638.htm (accessed January 31, 2009).

199. Interview with Rabbi Lerner, December 7, 2008.

200. Ettelbrick, "Since When Is Marriage a Path to Liberation?"; Polikoff, *Beyond (Straight and Gay) Marriage;* Eakin and Lee, "On Target and Off in 2002."

201. Lerner quoted in Chuck Colbert, "The God Squad of Equality," *New England Blade,* December 28, 2006, www.innewsweekly.com (accessed June 3, 2008).

202. Wuthnow, *The Restructuring of American Religion,* 132–133.

203. See "Question and Answer: Assessing a More Prominent Religious Left," June 5, 2008, http://pewforum.org/events/?EventID=187 (accessed November 28, 2008).

204. See, e.g., Shiffrin, *The Religious Left and Church-State Relations;* E. J. Dionne, *Souled Out: Reclaiming Faith and Politics after the Religious Right* (Princeton, 2008); Timothy Egan, "Godless," June 11, 2008, http://egan.blogs.nytimes.com (accessed November 8, 2009).

205. Christopher Ramos, Naomi Goldberg, and M. V. Lee Badgett, "The Effects of Marriage Equality in Massachusetts: A Survey of the Experiences and Impact of Marriage on Same-Sex Couples," Williams Institute, May 2009, www.law.ucla.edu/williamsinstitute (accessed November 8, 2009).

206. LaHaye, *Who But a Woman?* 45.

Epilogue

1. Jordan Lorence, speaking at the University of Pennsylvania Law School, April 9, 2009 (notes in possession of the author).
2. See www.alliancedefensefund.org (accessed May 27, 2009).
3. See Steven P. Brown, *Trumping Religion: The New Christian Right, the Free Speech Clause, and the Courts* (Tuscaloosa, 2002).
4. Jonathan Z. Smith, "Religion, Religions, Religious," in *Critical Terms for Religious Studies*, ed. Mark C. Taylor (Chicago, 1998), 269–284; Walter H. Capps, *Religious Studies: The Making of a Discipline* (Minneapolis, 1995), 157–208; Talal Asad, *Formations of the Secular: Christianity, Islam, Modernity* (Stanford, 2003); Sarah Barringer Gordon, "The New Age and the New Law: *Malnak v. Yogi*, Transcendental Meditation, and the Definition of Religion," in *Law and Religion: Cases in Context*, ed. Leslie Griffin (New York, 2010).
5. Douglas Laycock, "Religious Liberty as Liberty," *Journal of Contemporary Legal Issues* 7 (1996): 313, 329.
6. Winnifred Fallers Sullivan, *The Impossibility of Religious Freedom* (Princeton, 2005), 150. See also Sullivan, *Prison Religion: Faith-Based Reform and the Constitution* (Princeton, 2009), 141–144.
7. Sullivan, *Impossibility*, 152.
8. Sullivan, *Prison Religion*, 18.
9. *Employment Division, Dept. of Human Services v. Smith*, 494 U.S. 872, 879, 882, 885 (1990).
10. *Minersville School District v. Gobitis*, 310 U.S., 586, 595 (1940), quoted in *Smith*, 494 U.S., 879.
11. Katherine Graham, *Personal History* (New York, 1998), 122; Shawn Francis Peters, *Judging Jehovah's Witnesses: Religious Persecution and the Dawn of the Rights Revolution* (Lawrence, 2000), 72–95.
12. *Mitchell v. Helms*, 530 U.S. 793 (2000).
13. *Zelman v. Simmons-Harris*, 536 U.S. 639 (2002).
14. *Hein v. Freedom from Religion Foundation*, 551 U.S. 587 (2007).
15. Thomas C. Berg, *The State and Religion* (St. Paul, 2004), 196.
16. Barry Friedman, *The Will of the People: How Public Opinion Has Influenced the Supreme Court and Shaped the Meaning of the Constitution* (New York, 2009).
17. The Religious Freedom Restoration Act of 1993, 42 U.S.C. Sections 2000bb et seq. (2000). Twelve states have enacted similar legislation that essentially tracks the language of the federal statute (Alabama, Arizona, Connecticut, Florida, Idaho, Illinois, New Mexico, Oklahoma, Pennsylvania, Rhode Island, South Carolina, and Texas). In addition,

Congress enacted a new statute, the Religious Land Use and Institutionalized Persons Act of 2000 (RLUIPA), reinstating the pre-*Smith* standard for free exercise cases in particular settings. 42 U.S.C. sections 2000cc et seq. (2000). The institutional portion of RLUIPA was upheld by the Supreme Court against a constitutional challenge: *Cutter v. Wilkinson*, 544 U.S. 709 (2005).

18. *Gonzales v. O Centro Espirita Beneficente Unaio Do Vegetal*, 546 U.S. 418 (2006).

19. The infamous *Lemon* test required that any government action have a secular purpose, a primary effect that did not advance or inhibit religion, or create excessive entanglement between religion and government. *Lemon v. Kurtzman*, 403 U.S. 602 (1971). The test was widely criticized by judges and commentators, including Justices Antonin Scalia, Clarence Thomas, Sandra Day O'Connor, Byron White, Anthony Kennedy, and former chief justice William Rehnquist. The result in *Lemon* was modified in *Agostini v. Felton*, 521 U.S. 203 (1997), and further curtailed in *Mitchell v. Helms* in 2000. Yet lower courts and the Supreme Court itself continue to apply the *Lemon* test. See, e.g., *Kitzmiller v. Dover School District*, 400 F.Supp. 2d 707 (M.D. Pa. 2007); *McCreary County v. American Civil Liberties Union*, 545 U.S. 844 (2005).

20. *Van Orden v. Perry*, 545 U.S. 677 (2005); *McCreary County*.

21. Christopher L. Eisgruber and Lawrence G. Sager, *Religious Freedom and the Constitution* (Cambridge, Mass., 2007), 140–147; 152–153.

22. Adelle M. Banks, "Supreme Court Rulings on Ten Commandments Leave Wake of Confusion," *Christianity Today*, June 29, 2005, www.christianitytoday.com/ct/2005/juneweb-only/32.0d.html (accessed May 30, 2009); Linda Greenhouse, "The Supreme Court: Justices Allow a Commandments Display, Bar Others," *New York Times*, June 28, 2005, 1.

23. Mark De Wolfe Howe, *The Garden and the Wilderness: Religion and Government in American Constitutional History* (Chicago, 1965), 3.

24. Winnifred Fallers Sullivan, "Religious Freedom and the Rule of Law: A Modernist Myth in a Post-Modern World," in *Religion in Cultural Discourse: Essays in Honor of Hans G. Kippenberg*, ed. Brigitte Luchen et al. (Berlin, 2004).

25. Marci A. Hamilton, *God vs. the Gavel: Religion and the Rule of Law* (Cambridge, 2005); William P. Marshall, "In Defense of *Smith* and Free Exercise Revisionism," *University of Chicago Law Review*, 58 (1991): 308.

26. *McCreary County v. American Civil Liberties Union*, 545 U.S., 884 (O'Connor, J., concurring).

27. Ibid., 882.

28. This is not evidence of a set of stable constitutional meanings, which a cogent critic once challenged me to describe. Hendrik Hartog, reader's report for Harvard University Press, January 2009.

29. A 2007 poll conducted by the Pew Forum on Religion and Public Life found that 70 percent of Americans affiliated with a religion (including majorities of evangelical Protestants and Catholics) agreed that other faiths can lead to eternal life, undercutting assumptions about religious commitment and intolerance; http://religions.pewforum.org (accessed May 30, 2009).

30. Brief of Amicus Curiae Alliance Defense Fund Supporting Respondent, *Morse v. Frederick* No. 06-268.

31. *Morse v. Frederick*, 551 U.S. 393 (2007).

Acknowledgments

In some ways, this is the best part. Now is the time to think back on a long project and to remember the many people, places, archives, and libraries that have been so instrumental in the joy and tribulations of research. There have been many over the past six years to whom I have been grateful. Indeed, the list is so long that I have had to truncate it just to fit within the bounds of reasonableness. Omissions, mistakes, and other faux pas are entirely my bad, of course.

Friends and colleagues (often, they are the same people) have been indispensable critics and editors. They include but are not limited to: Chris Beauchamp, Laurie Benton, Susan Branson, Ann Braude, Josh Dubler, Chris Eisgruber, Marie Griffith, Leah Grosghal, Steve Hahn, Janna Hansen, Dan Hulsebosch, Chip Lupu, Sophia Lee, Bruce Mann, Serena Mayeri, Laura Kalman, Stephanie McCurry, Ben Nathans, Bill Nelson, Bill Novak, John Reid, Dan Rodgers, Tanina Rostain, Chris Schmidt, Jan Shipps, Tom Sugrue, Winni Sullivan, Karen Tani, Beth Wenger, Vicky Woeste, Michael Zuckerman, and many more to whom I send my gratitude and apologize for lack of space to do you full honor.

Students also have provided wonderful research assistance, including Norah Bringer, Jeremy Chase, Melissa Rassas, Justin Simard, and Laura Weiss.

Dirk Hartog and Mark Silk read the entire draft manuscript, and pushed me to sharpen the focus and dig into the bigger narrative. Joyce Selzer at Harvard University Press, assisted by Jeannette Estruth, Julie Hagen, and Maria Ascher, guided the writing, helped me think about "audience," and caught mistakes. Geri Thoma took me on as a charity case, I am convinced, for which I will always be thankful.

Colleagues in the law school and history department at the University of

Pennsylvania have been wonderfully supportive, especially Dean Mike Fitts of the law school, whose own hard work and integrity provide a model for all who know him. In addition, the chance to present at the annual faculty retreat in 2008, as well as an informal ad hoc presentation over lunch, visits to classes and seminars, and more have enriched my approach. The Program in Law and Public Affairs at Princeton, then ably headed by Chris Eisgruber (now provost at Princeton), gave me a vital year of research and collegial interaction as well as the opportunity to present a draft chapter. Other presentations at the Annenberg Seminar in the Department of History at Penn, Boston University Law School, Brigham Young University, Cambridge University, Davidson College, DePaul Law School, George Washington Law School, Harvard Law School, King College, University College (London), University of Michigan Law School, NYU Legal History Colloquium, Radcliffe Institute, Princeton University, Vanderbilt Law School, Yale Law School, and the American Society for Legal History and American Historical Association annual meetings all provided the essential critique that makes scholarship such a pleasurable and cooperative venture.

Libraries and librarians have been so helpful and patient with endless requests that it is impossible to convey adequately my gratitude. Biddle Law Library at Penn has many dedicated reference librarians, but Ed Greenlee stands out even in a talented crowd. He has suffered through many late nights and difficult queries sent by e-mail before dawn. For his help as well as his friendship, I am particularly grateful. Also vital were Joe Parsio, Tom Laws, Ron Day, Ben Meltzer, Ann Davidson, Merle Slyhoff, and Rebecca Stanley. Thank you, one and all. Other libraries provided valuable manuscripts and other collections, including but not limited to Firestone and Mudd Libraries at Princeton University, Schlesinger Library at the Radcliffe Institute, Bobst Library at New York University, Widener Library at Harvard University, and the Presbyterian Historical Society, the Historical Society of Pennsylvania, and the Library of Congress.

Index

Abernathy, Ralph, 126

Abington School District v. Schempp, 85, 86, 91–92

Abyssinian movement (Chicago), 255n20

Act of Marriage, The (LaHaye and LaHaye), 135–136, 267n18

Adams, Arlin, 149–150, 164–165

Adventists, 16, 19–20, 22, 24–25, 61. *See also* Jehovah's Witnesses

Affirmation: Gay and Lesbian Mormons, 205

African Americans: *Bob Jones University* case, 155–156, 275n142; civil rights activism, 95; Fard and 1930s Detroit, 99–104; Jehovah's Witnesses, 108, 255n27; and popular constitutionalism, 119. *See also* Nation of Islam

Albee, Edward F., 39

Ali, Muhammad, 126–129

Ali, Noble Drew, 100–101

Alliance Defense Fund, 208, 216, 279n210

American Association of University Women, 61

American Center for Law and Justice, 279n210

American Civil Liberties Union (ACLU), 216; and captive-schools litigation, 80, 82–83; and CWA's *Mozert* case, 162–163, 164–166; *Everson* brief and child-benefit theory, 65–66; and Jehovah's Witnesses, 42, 47, 225n51;

and POAU, 69, 80, 82–83, 93; and school prayer rulings, 89

American Coalition for Traditional Values, 147

American Dilemma, An (Myrdal), 105

American Freedom and Catholic Power (Blanshard), 73, 81, 243n101

American Friends Service Committee, 106, 202

American Jewish Congress (AJC), 80, 82–83, 89, 162

American Psychiatric Association, 177

American Revolution, 5–6

Americans United for Separation of Church and State (AU), 93, 162

Amnesty International, 126

Anglican Communion, 185

Anti-Catholicism: and Jehovah's Witnesses, 24, 41, 103; and KKK, 73; and Nation of Islam, 103; and the POAU, 69–72, 73, 82–84, 92–93, 248n169

Anticommunism: and American Protestantism, 67, 144–147, 271n66; and battles over sectarianism, 59, 67, 71; and Catholic reactions to *Engel* ruling, 88; and fascism, 67, 241n67; and Hiss-Chambers case, 145; and Panama Canal Treaty, 145, 146; and secularism, 71, 87–88, 91, 138, 144–147

Antisectarianism. *See* Protestants and Other Americans United for Separation of Church and State (POAU);